RESISTING BRAZIL'S MILITARY REGIME

JOHN W. F. DULLES

Resisting Brazil's Military Regime

AN ACCOUNT
OF THE BATTLES
OF SOBRAL PINTO

UNIVERSITY OF TEXAS PRESS, AUSTIN

LIBRARY OF CONGRESS CATALOGING-IN-PUBLICATION DATA
Dulles, John W. F.
Resisting Brazil's military regime : an account of the battles
of Sobral Pinto / by John W. F. Dulles. — 1st ed.
     p.   cm.
Includes bibliographical references and index.
ISBN 978-0-292-71725-1 (cloth : alk. paper)
1. Pinto, Heráclito Sobral, 1893–1991.   2. Brazil—Politics and
government—20th century.   3. Lawyers—Brazil.   I. Title.
F2538.27.P565D85   2007
986.01092—dc22
[B]
2007010382

CONTENTS

Writers of the 1946 Constitution gather with lawyers Sobral Pinto (at left, facing camera) and Adauto Lúcio Cardoso (second from the right). (Arquivo Nacional)

Sobral Pinto and his wife, Maria José, observe their twenty-fifth wedding anniversary, 1947. (Courtesy of the Sobral Pinto family)

Luís Gallotti, newly appointed member of the Supreme Court, 1949. (Arquivo Nacional)

President Getúlio Vargas and Minas Gerais Governor Juscelino Kubitschek (at right), both elected in 1950. *(O Globo)*

Augusto Frederico Schmidt (in white suit) with Roberto Marinho. (Arquivo Nacional)

Senator Hamilton Nogueira, January 1952. (Arquivo Nacional)

Animated defense lawyer Evandro Lins e Silva arguing against Sobral Pinto (at right) and Tito Lívio Cavalcanti de Medeiros (behind Lins e Silva). (Courtesy of Tito Lívio)

Sobral Pinto in August 1955 organized the League to Defend Legality. (Arquivo Nacional/*Correio da Manhã*)

Juarez Távora embraces Eduardo Gomes. *(O Globo)*

President Kubitschek (1956–1961) with Cardinal Jaime de Barros Câmara. (Arquivo Nacional)

Kubitschek decorates Victor Nunes Leal. (Arquivo Nacional)

As urged by Sobral Pinto, Kubitschek calls on Affonso Penna Júnior. (Arquivo Nacional/*O Globo*)

Henrique Lott, Kubitschek's war minister, shown between Vice President João Goulart (at left) and Rio Grande do Sul Governor Leonel Brizola (in dark suit). (Arquivo Nacional)

Presidential candidate Jânio Quadros (at far left) campaigning in 1960. (Arquivo Nacional)

Alceu Amoroso Lima at left and Sobral Pinto at right, December 31, 1960.
(Courtesy of the Sobral Pinto family)

Completion of the metallic construction of Regine Feigl's Avenida Central
building, January 1960. (Arquivo Nacional)

Guanabara Governor Carlos Lacerda (in white suit) inaugurates the building, May 1961. Regine Feigl (wearing white hat) watches. (Arquivo Nacional)

A smiling Sobral Pinto sees Fritz Feigl receive a prize, presented by his wife Regine. *(O Globo)*

Following the resignation of President Quadros in August 1961, Minas Gerais Governor Magalhães Pinto (left) and São Paulo Governor Carvalho Pinto await his arrival in São Paulo. (Arquivo Nacional)

Dom Hélder Câmara, 1963. (Arquivo Nacional)

Congressman Adauto Lúcio Cardoso, 1963. (Arquivo Nacional/*O Globo*)

Catholic intellectual Gustavo Corção, 1963. (Arquivo Nacional; *JB ONLINE*/Evandro Teixeira)

Journalist Hélio Fernandes being arrested in July 1963 as ordered by President Goulart's war minister. (Arquivo Nacional)

Sobral Pinto between lawyer Dario de Almeida Magalhães (left) and businessman-diplomat Augusto Frederico Schmidt. *(O Globo)*

Sobral Pinto successfully defends Hélio Fernandes at the Supreme Court.
(Arquivo Nacional/*Correio da Manhã*)

Law Professor Sobral Pinto. (Archives of the state of São Paulo/*Última Hora*
and *O Estado de S. Paulo*)

Sobral Pinto (at left) addresses the Military Club in November 1963.
Listeners include Governor Carlos Lacerda (third from the right).
(Arquivo Nacional; *Correio da Manhã*/Gilmar)

Labor leader Oswaldo Pacheco. (*Jornal do Brasil*/Alberto Ferreira)

President Goulart (center) on March 24, 1964, with São Paulo Cardinal Carlos de Vasconcellos Mota and (at right) Dom Hélder Câmara. (Arquivo Nacional)

President Humberto Castello Branco (1964–1967), shown with Juracy Magalhães (at right), who became his justice minister in 1965. *(O Jornal* and *Jornal do Commercio)*

After Kubitschek's political rights were suspended on June 8, 1964, Sobral Pinto joined the former president (at left) and his wife Sarah (at right). (*O Cruzeiro*/Geraldo Simeão Viola)

Sobral Pinto and Kubitschek, following the latter's appearance at a Military Police Investigation (IPM) in October 1965. (Arquivo Nacional; *JB ONLINE*/Ronald Theobald)

Colonel Ferdinando de Carvalho, head of the IPM investigating Communism in Brazil. (*Tribuna da Imprensa*)

Colonel Osnelli Martinelli, head of an IPM, called himself "the toughest of the hard-liners." *(Jornal do Brasil)*

Colonel Gérson de Pina in July 1965 when he became head of an IPM. *(Tribuna da Imprensa)*

Colonel Gustavo Borges, security secretary of Guanabara state. *(Tribuna da Imprensa)*

Agents of the People's Republic of China, defended by Sobral Pinto after their arrest in Rio in April 1964. (Arquivo Nacional)

Miguel Arraes, former governor of Pernambuco, was imprisoned in April 1964. *(Manchete)*

Sobral Pinto, orating at the trial of his Chinese clients in December 1964. (*Última Hora* and courtesy of the Sobral Pinto family)

Miguel Arraes, with his lawyer Sobral Pinto, prepares to testify at an IPM in May 1965. (Arquivo Nacional)

Sobral's client, prisoner Francisco Julião, former leader of Peasant Leagues. (Manchete)

Another client was Mauro Borges, who was removed from the governorship of Goiás. (Tribuna da Imprensa)

Communist Gregório Bezerra, tortured and jailed in April 1964, realized his wish to be represented by Sobral. (Manchete)

Sobral Pinto at the Institute of Brazilian Lawyers (IAB) in October 1965. Because the Institute supported the government, he resigned as its president. (Archives of the state of São Paulo/Agência Jornal do Brasil)

In 1966 a photograph of Sobral Pinto is added to those of past IAB presidents. From left: Haroldo Valladão, José Ribeiro de Castro Filho (clapping), Sobral, and one of his granddaughters. (Courtesy of the Sobral Pinto family and Leandro Carvalho)

President Costa e Silva (1967–1969), at left, with Justice Minister Luís Antônio da Gama e Silva (facing camera). *(O Jornal* and *Jornal do Commercio)*

Peri Constant Bevilacqua, supporter of amnesty for people punished by the military regime, was removed in 1969 by Costa e Silva as a judge of the Superior Military Tribunal. *(Tribuna da Imprensa)*

President Emílio Garrastazu Médici (1969–1974). (Archives of the state of São Paulo/Agência Jornal do Brasil)

São Paulo Cardinal Paulo Evaristo Arns, active protector of victims of the government's repression. (*Jornal do Commercio*/Alibio Pereira)

Sobral Pinto with militant defense lawyer Heleno Fragoso. (Courtesy of Clemente Hungria)

Lawyer Dario de Almeida Magalhães. (Courtesy of Clemente Hungria and the Almeida Magalhães family)

Sobral and his daughter Ruth, seated, with office companions and some clients. Standing in middle row from left are Jessé Cláudio Fontes de Alencar, Jarbas Macedo de Camargo Penteado, and Benedita Novais (smiling). Tito Lívio Cavalcanti de Medeiros is at far right. (Courtesy of Jarbas Macedo de Camargo Penteado)

Sobral Pinto received the Ruy Barbosa Medal of the Order of Lawyers of Brazil (OAB) on his seventy-eighth birthday, November 5, 1971. He is between his wife (at right) and Victor Nunes Leal and with daughter Ruth (at left). (Courtesy of the Sobral Pinto family)

Sobral received the Teixeira de Freitas Medal of the IAB on his eightieth birthday. Among the speakers was José Ribeiro de Castro Filho (second from left). (Courtesy of the Sobral Pinto family)

Ernesto Geisel (second from right), president of Brazil, 1974–1979.
(Jornal do Commercio)

Sobral Pinto in April 1977. (Photograph by Iarli Goulart; courtesy of Maria Cecília Ribas Carneiro)

In his library, August 1978. (Agência O Globo)

The Sobral Pintos in 1978, bringing flowers to the graves of their children Maria do Carmo and José Luiz. (Agência Jornal do Brasil/ Almir Viega)

Petrônio Portella, Senate president, working late in Geisel's presidency for a transition to democracy. *(Jornal do Commercio/Correio Braziliense)*

Armando Falcão, Geisel's justice minister, shown with João Batista Figueiredo (at right). Upon succeeding Geisel, Figueiredo named Petrônio Portella justice minister. *(Jornal do Commercio)*

Sobral between Laércio da Costa Pellegrino (at left), head of the IAB, 1982–1984, and Bernardo Cabral, head of the OAB, 1981–1983. (Courtesy of the Sobral Pinto family)

Dom Hélder Câmara and Sobral
Pinto. (Courtesy of Tito Lívio
Cavalcanti de Medeiros)

Luiz Carlos Prestes and Sobral Pinto
in 1983. *(O Globo)*

Sobral Pinto (hand on face) at the rally in Rio, April 10, 1984, for a direct
presidential election. From right: Ulysses Guimarães and Tancredo Neves
(light suit). (Agência JB/Vidal Andrade)

Sobral Pinto with Tancredo Neves, 1984. (Courtesy of the Sobral Pinto family)

Sobral Pinto between President José Sarney (1985–1990) and Tito Lívio Cavalcanti de Medeiros (at right). (Courtesy of Tito Lívio Cavalcanti de Medeiros)

From left: Goiás Governor Iris Resende, Sobral Pinto, Federal District Governor José Aparecido de Oliveira (wearing glasses), and Chamber of Deputies President Ulysses Guimarães (at right). (Photograph by Olavo Rufino; courtesy of the Sobral Pinto family)

Sobral Pinto supports Congressman Álvaro Valle, candidate for mayor of Rio, 1985. (*Jornal do Brasil*/Luís Morier)

Labor leader Lula (Luís Inácio da Silva), candidate for president, 1989. (*Tribuna da Imprensa*/Jorge Reis)

Fernando Collor de Mello defeated Lula in the runoff for the presidency in December 1989. (*Tribuna da Imprensa*/Ailton Santos)

Sobral with past heads of the Order of Lawyers (OAB) José Ribeiro de Castro Filho (standing) and Haroldo Valladão. (Courtesy of Clemente Hungria)

Sobral Pinto and Rio de Janeiro Cardinal Eugênio de Araújo Sales. (*Tribuna da Imprensa*/F. Araújo)

RESISTING BRAZIL'S MILITARY REGIME

INTRODUCTION

After I spent a few years recording too many details of the career of lawyer Sobral Pinto between 1946 and the overthrow in 1964 of the government of President João Goulart, I was wisely informed by Sobral's grandson Roberto that what was most important in the career I was studying lay in the events that followed the coup against Goulart. And so my earlier effort was reduced to approximately one-third of its length, forming a Prologue that would allow that further research result in a full account of Sobral's reactions to the steps taken by the postcoup presidential administrations of a series of army generals and his reactions to the treatment, by the victors, of those who suffered after March 1964. About the politics and economics of those years I was much assisted by the works of Thomas E. Skidmore, Ronald M. Schneider, and Marshall C. Eakin.

Among Sobral's clients were former President Juscelino Kubitschek, whose life, Sobral pointed out, was turned into a "hell," and members of Goulart's administration, along with Governors Miguel Arraes and Mauro Borges. The list includes Francisco Julião, who had organized Peasant Leagues; Communists Carlos Marighella, Luiz Carlos Prestes, and Gregório Bezerra; and agents of the People's Republic of China who were in Brazil. Once-powerful labor leaders Clodsmith Riani and Oswaldo Pacheco turned for help to Sobral. So did the troubled bishop of Volta Redonda, foreign priests, "leftists" in the military, and militant journalists and students, in this period of about fifteen years, during much of which the torturing and killing of enemies of the military regime took place.

In a discussion about colonels who were threatening to imprison or otherwise punish Sobral in May 1965, Catholic writer Alceu Amoroso Lima asserted: "Sobral is the only person—I repeat the only person—who confronts them with his head held high and without mincing words."[1] But Sobral found himself deserted by friends, including lawyers, and in 1965 he resigned from the presidency of the Brazilian Institute of Lawyers because it objected to his aggressive denouncements of those in power. Dario de Almeida Magalhães, a prominent lawyer who knew Sobral well, called attention to the need for friendships of "this affectionate, sentimental person" and to his "true heroism," a never capitulating, fiery passion for justice that, Dario said, "strained" these friendships.[2] Sobral bewailed the loss of friends with some of his "cries of anguish."

To the generals who became presidents of Brazil, Sobral sent severe letters and telegrams. A letter sent to President Emílio Garrastazu Médici in 1971 brought a reply calling him "clearly afflicted by senility." Beyond Médici's office, however, the so-called senility came to be seen as heroism, and the lawyers' associations commenced to agree with its members who had been defying the military regime from the start and who declared, like Evaristo de Morais Filho and Heleno Cláudio Fragoso, that Sobral was their leader and inspiration.[3]

Former journalist José Aparecido de Oliveira, who occupied important government positions in the postmilitary regime, described Sobral as having been "the leader of the pro-civilian campaign and the vanguard of resistance in favor of human rights." "No one in contemporary life," historian José Honório Rodrigues told the Brazilian Academy of Letters, "has better represented the sacred spirit of humanism than Sobral Pinto, courageous and fearless defender of public liberties and individual guarantees."[4]

When many hundreds of thousands rallied enthusiastically in Rio de Janeiro on April 10, 1984, to demand a direct presidential election, the ovation for Sobral exceeded those given to well-known governors who were also opponents of undemocratic military rule, Leonel Brizola, Tancredo Neves, and Franco Montoro.

In that same year, the ninety-year-old Sobral became honorary president of the Movimento Nacional Tancredo Neves. After the indirect presidential election was won by Tancredo (whose death prevented his inauguration), Sobral immersed himself in generally unsuccessful election campaigns, local and national, of the conservative Partido Liberal.

Such was the reverence for Sobral, gained during the military regime, that honors were heaped upon him before he died at the age of ninety-eight. The feeling that he was a great figure remained strong even among many of those who disagreed with his positions. Famed architect Oscar Niemeyer, who could hardly agree with Sobral's criticism of Communism, saw in him "a person of greatest importance in the nation."[5]

Sobral displeased the advocates of legalized divorce and the adepts of Liberation Theology, and, in his last years, attacked politicians who had popular followings. This staunch Catholic who expressed admiration for the religious thinking of the seventeenth and eighteenth centuries continued to oppose the participation of women in professional and business activities in which men had predominated. The most important role of women, he argued, was the one they carried out in the family at home, preferably with "the spirit of renunciation" that he found in his wife, Maria José.

When I was in the late stages of gathering material for this biography, physical problems afflicted me and made it clear that this is my farewell to writing for publication. The problems prevented me from revisiting Brazil, and so it is with much gratitude that I acknowledge help in Brazil received from Roberto Sobral Pinto Ribeiro, Daphne F. Rodger, Francisco P. C. Teixeira, Clemente Hungria, Tito Lívio Cavalcanti de Medeiros, Valtair de Jesus Almeida, R. S. Rose (who devoted his outstanding research abilities to improving the photograph section), and my daughter Edith (a dear transporter of heavy piles of papers from Rio). In the United States I am deeply indebted to Flávia Leite, assistant in my office, and to Jan Rinaldi McCauley, producer of the manuscript. My largest debt of all is to those who, while helping me at home to tell this story, brought me happiness there with so much love, my wife CC and daughter Ellen.

J.W.F.D.

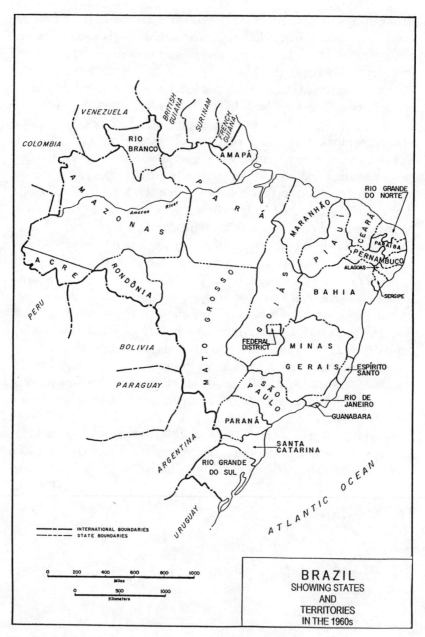

Brazil, showing states and territories in the 1960s.

PART I

Prologue (1946–1964)

1. Denouncing the Dutra Administration's Repression of Communism (1946–1948)

When democracy came to Brazil in 1945, following eight years of the Estado Novo dictatorship of Getúlio Vargas, Heráclito Fontoura Sobral Pinto was a fifty-two-year-old lawyer known for having defended victims of the police, the military, and politicians in power. His harsh attacks against the dictatorship and his declarations calling for democratic principles gave him a place in the political group that created the anti-Vargas party, the UDN (União Democrática Nacional), in 1945.

But Sobral, unlike the others, rejected any opportunities for receiving rewards or positions as a result of the birth of the new regime of popular elections. For him the fight for freedoms was a duty imposed by his understanding of the principles of Catholicism, which he never ceased to preach. In other ways, too, he was regarded as odd. He rejected legal fees from any defendants who, like his Communist clients, had been persecuted for their views, and in cases of a different sort he charged so little that he was continually in debt. He was famous also for his vast correspondence, which he filled with criticisms of friends as well as foes.

Sobral involved himself deeply in battling for his views and never hid the waves of personal feelings that seemed sometimes almost to overwhelm him. He had little time for diversions, such as the theater, but was forever crusading for his ideals—ideals for benefiting the downtrodden and for doing away with practices that he considered violations of his Catholic views of what was Christian and right. Letters of reproval came from Sobral to Catholic figures who acted on the assumption that achievements could best be won by good relations with men in power, and such letters came also to politicians in office who, in need of support for important projects, accepted deals that could be justified only for practical reasons.

If the UDN had won the presidential and congressional elections of December 1945, its men, after reaching power, would have received a stream of suggestions and no doubt also reproofs from Sobral. He regarded frank criticism as a form of friendship, and, while friendships were important to him, he was willing to suffer the heartbreak of lost friendships when he felt it necessary. The UDN, however, went down to defeat in the voting of December 1945. With the help of the PTB (Partido Trabalhista Brasileiro) of the deposed Vargas, the PSD (Partido Social Democrático) won the elections, bringing the presidency to General Eurico Gaspar Dutra, who had been Vargas's war minister.

Sobral was best known for his role, before and during the Estado Novo, as the lawyer of Communist leader Luiz Carlos Prestes. Prestes, after nine years in prison, was released in April 1945 and dedicated himself to running the PCB (Partido Comunista do Brasil) as its secretary general. He was elected a senator from the Federal District (mostly the city of Rio de Janeiro) on the ticket of the PCB after the party obtained legality in 1945.

Principles of Christianity and justice persuaded Sobral to continue to help Prestes and other Communists during the anti-Communist repression of the Dutra regime, but occasionally he declined to help because of two habits of the PCB: its attempt to use the name of Sobral to further its popularity and its description of itself as a moderate, democracy-loving political party.

At Sobral's large home in Rio's Laranjeiras district, acquired in 1935 thanks to a loan from his neighbor Affonso Penna Júnior, Sobral listened to Prestes ask for help to try to save the Union of Communist Youth, threatened by the Dutra administration. Writing to Prestes in April and May 1947, after their meeting, Sobral said he would favor the existence of the Union provided it would revise its statutes and make them honest, with a description of its true objective: to educate youth in the materialist philosophy, which opposed religion and called for the class struggle.[1]

By the time Sobral's letters reached Prestes, Dutra had suspended the activities of the Union of Communist Youth. Some of the congratulatory messages, flowing to Dutra, requested that the PCB itself be closed down. Sobral, on the other hand, favored a continuation of legality for the PCB, but he recommended that all parties and organizations be required to make known their true nature and objectives.[2]

The Tribunal Superior Eleitoral (Superior Electoral Tribunal) came to share Sobral's belief that the PCB's mild description of itself, presented when it sought legality in 1945, hid its true nature and support of Marxism, and, in May 1947, the Electoral Tribunal pleased the Dutra administration by canceling the registration of the PCB as a party. Luiz Carlos Prestes accused Dutra of outlawing the party "in obedience to the orders of President Truman." Sobral, as president of Resistência Democrática, a prodemocracy organization formed in 1945, issued a "Warning to the Nation" saying: "It is not the Communist Party that will be in danger of being forced to act illegally; it will be democracy itself."[3]

After Dutra's party, the PSD, worked in Congress for the passage of a law project, introduced by Senator Ivo d'Aquino, declaring all PCB mandates extinct, Sobral, at the request of Prestes, produced a study for protecting the mandates. Sobral's Catholic friend, Senator Hamilton Nogueira, tried to read the study aloud in the Senate but was constantly interrupted by supporters of the project, and the project was approved by a vote of 34 to 18 in the Senate late in October 1947.[4]

In the Chamber of Deputies, where the d'Aquino law project also needed approval, the lawmakers heard PCB Congressman José Maria Crispim read Sobral's study on November 1. There the Chamber's justice commission was beginning its work amidst a flurry of press comments that included Sobral's statements given in November in two installments to O Jornal's Samuel Wainer. Sobral told Wainer that "the closing of the Communist Party, the break in diplomatic relations with Soviet Russia, the raids—I should say official raids—on the Communist press, the intransigent prohibition of Communist rallies, and the forthcoming cancellation of the people's representatives on the PCB ticket are the result of the policy of force and violence that the government, with the approval of those who direct the nation, has been pursuing with an iron hand in defiance of the principle of liberty."[5]

The justice commission of the lower house ruled, on December 6, that the mandate cancellation was both constitutional and desirable, and on January 7, 1948, the Chamber of Deputies voted, 169 to 74, to cancel the mandates of PCB federal and local legislators. The Labor Ministry took over labor unions whose control was felt to be in the hands of Communists, and court orders called for the arrest of leading Communists.[6]

Prestes, in hiding on account of the court orders, issued a fighting manifesto late in January 1948. It described the Brazilian government as "a government of national treason, which, at the service of North American imperialism, starves our people," and he called on workers and peasants to organize themselves and "fight for the liberty, progress and independence of Brazil."[7]

2.   Sobral's Relations with Catholic Leaders (1947–1950)

The neuralgia that from time to time tormented Sobral on the right side of his face became so intense in January 1947 that he submitted himself to delicate, risky, and painful surgery for opening his skull and cutting nerves. Needing a rest after the ordeal, he went with his wife Maria José and their seven children to the Fazenda São Lourenço, a large isolated property in Rio de Janeiro state that belonged to an acquaintance. After returning to Rio at the end of March he informed a close friend, Catholic lay leader Alceu Amoroso Lima, that, while recuperating, he had meditated much about the "frequent failures of our campaign to restore the kingdom of Jesus Christ in society." He concluded that the Catholic archdiocese of Rio, in giving support to Dutra, was forgetting the workers.[1]

In June 1947 Sobral wrote the director of the *Correio da Noite*, organ of the Catholic hierarchy, to express the grief that filled him to read its article praising Dutra and the cancellation of the PCB's legality. The *Correio da Noite*, he wrote, was "prejudicial to the expansion of the Faith within the working class." "You," he wrote Padre José Távora in January 1948, "have been able to put the *Correio da Noite* on the side of Dutra, with the approval of the cardinal," and give support to "a policy of disobeying the constitution of Brazil and favoring brutal violence in order to crush the dignity and liberty of Brazilian citizens on account of their being Communists."[2]

In November 1947 Alceu Amoroso Lima and Sobral were reported to be among the directors of the anti-Dutra Movimento Renovador, formed by UDN politicians who opposed the alliance for governing Brazil that the top officers of the UDN had made with Dutra and the PSD. Therefore Padres José Távora and Hélder Câmara released a memorandum, approved by Rio's Cardinal Jaime de Barros Câmara, critical of Alceu and Sobral. In a letter to the cardinal, Sobral objected to the memorandum's assertion that the two lay Catholic leaders were displaying intellectual pride and seeking to place the ecclesiastic authority under the dominion of the laity.[3] Sobral wrote letters to the cardinal that were not answered and found it difficult to obtain audiences with him. Concluding that "the ecclesiastic authorities, for political reasons, unjustly suspect my religious orthodoxy," he resigned his directorship post in Ação Católica Brasileira, which had been founded in 1935 to give lay Catholics a role in the social program of the Church. He made his decision known to Alceu Amoroso Lima, the longtime president of Ação Católica, and to the cardinal, and also to Hélder Câmara, chosen by the cardinal to reorganize Ação Católica.[4]

To Catholic leaders in the United States who were working to hold the Third Inter-American Seminar of Catholic Social Action in Rio de Janeiro, Sobral wrote that the cardinal and José Távora were determined to please the nation's rulers and the rich. He was especially annoyed with Hélder Câmara, whom he accused of assuming "a superior silence" that indicated that he found Sobral's "wails" to be those of "an idiot," and he referred to Hélder's former participation in the fascist Integralista movement of the 1930s.[5]

Late in March 1948 the Church hierarchy withdrew a temporary ruling that had prevented Sobral from contributing articles to its *Correio da Noite,* and in April 1950 it demonstrated confidence in Sobral's professional work by asking him to be the legal representative of Jaime Câmara in an important lawsuit that began after the cardinal-archbishop tried to exert his authority over a group of Catholic worshipers, the Irmandade do Santíssimo Sacramento da Antiga Sé.[6] From the outset Sobral made known his "firm decision" to receive no fee for his work on this case, which was in the courts until 1959, when Sobral, with help from jurist José Sabóia Viriato de Medeiros, finally obtained a victory for Jaime Câmara.

3. Sobral's Relations with the UDN (1947–1950)

In the political field, Sobral worked closely with journalist Carlos Lacerda and lawyer Adauto Lúcio Cardoso, members of the UDN who had established the anti-Dutra Movimento Renovador. Both had been successful in the January 1947 elections to choose fifty members of the Municipal Council of the Federal District, with Lacerda winning far more votes than any other candidate. Both were at odds with the Federal District's mayor, General Ângelo Mendes de Morais, appointed by Dutra.

After Mendes de Morais opposed the Lacerda law project for requiring Rádio Roquete Pinto, the municipal government's radio station, to broadcast the Municipal Council proceedings, the Municipal Council, at the suggestion of Adauto Lúcio Cardoso, named Sobral its lawyer in the case.[1] A more serious struggle of the Municipal Council was against the clause in the Organic Law of the Federal District, passed by the Senate of the republic, giving itself, the Senate, and not the Municipal Council, the authority to rule on the mayor's vetoes of the Council's legislation. The Organic Law was passed by the lower house of Congress in December 1947, and, in response, Adauto and Lacerda lost no time in resigning from their seats. Sobral, criticizing Lacerda, told him that the Council would be left "impotent" without "its most prestigious voice for defending the common man."[2]

In March and April 1948, Lacerda's radio broadcasts and articles in the Correio da Manhã angered Mayor Mendes de Morais and the Rio police so much that Lacerda received, on April 17, a dreadful thrashing by five thugs in downtown Rio. Blows by pistol butts left serious wounds on his face, especially his left eye. No one was found guilty of the crime, whose intellectual author was widely believed to have been the mayor.[3]

Because Senators Hamilton Nogueira and José Américo de Almeida, the presidents, respectively, of the local and national UDN, had quarreled with Lacerda over his show of party "indiscipline," they did not add their voices to the many expressions of sympathy and support for the popular former councilman, and for their silence they were scolded by Sobral. At the same time, Sobral broke with a Catholic friend, Justice Minister Adroaldo Mesquita da Costa (PSD), declaring that he would never again set foot in Adroaldo's office unless he erected "an unbreakable barrier against this barbarous, bloodthirsty, and brutal policy being followed by the government of General Dutra."[4]

The Centro Dom Vital, a lay Catholic intellectual center founded in 1922 and headed by Alceu Amoroso Lima, was crowded in May 1949 when Lacerda, who had joined the Catholic Church a year earlier, was the speaker. In part the acclamation was a demonstration of support for his boldness in asserting his independence by bringing an end to his daily column in the *Correio do Manhã* after Paulo Bittencourt, owner of the newspaper, prevented him from writing what he wanted.[5]

In September 1949 Sobral became a member of the *conselho consultivo* (consultive council) of Lacerda's new daily, the *Tribuna da Imprensa*, which was yet to appear. The other members of this council, which had the task of making the newspaper a force for "the moralization of politics," were the ascetic Catholic Gustavo Corção and the less conservative Alceu Amoroso Lima (both responsible for bringing Lacerda into the Catholic Church), Adauto Lúcio Cardoso, and prominent anti-Getulista (Vargas opponent) Luiz Camillo de Oliveira Netto. When the first number of the *Tribuna* finally appeared on December 27, 1949, Sobral, hoping for "a truly Christian newspaper," was shocked by the large amount of space devoted to sports. "None of this," he wrote Lacerda, "is in harmony with the mission of our newspaper."[6]

Following further surgery for his facial neuralgia in October 1949, Sobral was again at the Fazenda São Lourenço with his family in January and February 1950. For years he had been professor of penal law at the Pontifícia Universidade Católica (PUC), and, in 1950 at the *fazenda*, he studied law books in preparation for becoming professor of criminology in the journalism department of the University of Brazil, an idea of a close friend, lawyer Dario de Almeida Magalhães, that had been approved by the university.[7]

Dario had helped raise money for the *Tribuna da Imprensa* and was a member of its three-man fiscal council. From the *fazenda*, Sobral wrote to ask him to persuade Lacerda to make the *Tribuna* the organ of Resistência Democrática. Sobral's grand scheme, which he revealed in letters also sent to Lacerda, Adauto Lúcio Cardoso, and José Fernando Carneiro, Catholic writer and physician, was to usher in a new era, favorable to "the real interests of the people," neglected, Sobral wrote, by the bosses of the principal parties, the PSD, UDN, and PTB. According to Sobral, Resistência Democrática would do the thinking, the *Tribuna da Imprensa* would provide the publicity, and the Movimento Renovador would carry out the action. "If," Sobral wrote Lacerda, "we are united, Brazil will be run, in ten years, by the younger members of our group, that is you, Dario, Carneiro, and Adauto." After Alceu Amoroso Lima returned in April 1950 from a trip to Europe, Sobral sent him copies of his letters. "My words," he wrote, "were met with total silence."[8]

By this time politicians of the PSD and UDN, partners in the Dutra administration, were seeking to agree on a candidate to succeed President Dutra in the election of October 3, 1950. To the delight of Sobral, Milton Campos, UDN governor of Minas Gerais, suggested the candidacy of Affonso Penna Júnior, who had been close to Sobral ever since the two had worked together in the 1920s, Penna as justice minister and Sobral as the government's top criminal prosecutor. Milton Campos argued that Penna, who was said to lack party affiliation, would be the ideal candidate "of political reconciliation." On the other hand, Senator Hamilton Nogueira, like many other *udenistas*, backed air force Brigadeiro Eduardo Gomes, the UDN's unsuccessful candidate in 1945; the senator was therefore reprimanded by Sobral for not favoring Penna.[9]

As Sobral feared, PSD stalwarts were uncomfortable with what they felt were the *udenista* inclinations of Penna. The UDN's leaders also turned from Penna after learning that his candidacy lacked the support of Brazil's third- and fourth-largest parties, the PTB (Labor Party) and the PSP (Partido Social Progressista). Again Eduardo Gomes became the UDN candidate.[10]

After the PTB and the PSP chose Getúlio Vargas as their candidate and the PSD named the relatively unknown Minas Congressman Cristiano Machado, the lively *Tribuna da Imprensa* and Lacerda tried to persuade the Tribunal Superior Eleitoral to declare the former dictator ineligible. Sobral, much as he disliked Vargas, described this effort as unconstitutional.[11]

The *Tribuna da Imprensa* undertook another unsuccessful campaign, again ignoring its *conselho consultivo*, when it called for a democratic coalition with the withdrawal of Eduardo Gomes or Cristiano Machado or both. Late in June the newspaper's *conselho consultivo*, by this time supportive of Brigadeiro Eduardo Gomes, held meetings that resulted in memorandums to Lacerda objecting to the *Tribuna*'s "radical changes of position" made without consulting it, and giving him Sobral's observation that the "disastrous" suggestion of withdrawal by Gomes was favorable only to the foes of the renowned *brigadeiro*.[12]

Lacerda disliked the staid campaigning of Gomes, "limited to the problem of liberty, abstractly considered," and forgetful of the working class, and he criticized the *brigadeiro* also for his election deal with Plínio Salgado, chief in the 1930s of the fascist Integralista movement. But on August 3 the *Tribuna* wrote: "In spite of everything, the candidacy of Eduardo Gomes is the only hope of Brazilian patriots." Sobral, in his correspondence, echoed this opinion and wrote that a return of Vargas would be a catastrophe. Alceu Amoroso Lima, campaigning for Gomes, declared that the defeat of the *brigadeiro* would cover Brazil with a black cloak of skepticism and melancholy and would mean the banishment of all ideals.[13]

Getúlio Vargas (PTB) easily defeated the *brigadeiro* on October 3, 1950. The PSD's Cristiano Machado did especially poorly because he was abandoned in favor of Vargas by many voters of the PSD who at the same time supported PSD candidates for local offices, such as Juscelino Kubitschek, winner of the Minas governorship. Vargas's running mate, João Café Filho (PSP), narrowly defeated the UDN's candidate for the vice presidency, although he had been called a "rancid red" by the Catholic Electoral League (LEC), which disliked his reputed socialism and agnosticism, and which also disapproved of his association with Ademar de Barros, leader of the PSP.[14]

In the Federal District, where the PTB was awarded twice as many votes for congressmen as the second-place UDN, Lutero Vargas (PTB), a son of Getúlio, was the major winner.

Sobral, in a letter to his office companion Wilson Salazar, wrote that with "the spectacular victory of Vargas . . . , the old social, political, and juridical structure of Brazil . . . is now going to crash to the ground. It is the barbarians who march to power and who will dominate the new generations. A new concept of life has just appeared, impetuous and brutal." Sharing Alceu's fear of a new dictatorship, Sobral told UDN Congressman Aliomar Baleeiro that a great danger was an alliance between the authoritarian mentality of Vargas and authoritarian mentality of the military chiefs.[15]

Writing to Gustavo Corção, Sobral agreed with the Catholic intellectual's recent article recommending patience and an effort to "reduce the distance that separates the best people from the common people who make up nine-tenths of Brazil's population." "Sometimes," Sobral told Corção, "I have the impression that the way we act in public life convinces people that we are crafty allies of those who enjoy riches that were acquired or maintained at the cost of the suffering of the workers."[16]

When the UDN argued that Vargas, having received 48.7 percent of the total, should not become president because he lacked an absolute majority, Sobral, like the Tribunal Superior Eleitoral, rejected the argument.[17]

4.   Sobral's Relations with Lacerda (1951–1954)

On February 28, 1951, Sobral sent Lacerda a telegram resigning from the *conselho consultivo* of the *Tribuna da Imprensa*. In addition to complaining later that the daily kept on showing his name in the list of *conselho* members, Sobral described himself as "truly fed up," not with Lacerda's friendship or person, but with the opinions and attacks in the *Tribuna* that he would have opposed if he had been consulted. He continued, nevertheless, to work on legal cases for Lacerda, such as the mayor's lawsuit to punish the *Tribuna* for what it wrote about "Mayor Mussolini de Morais" and his "hoodlums." The work of an attorney struggling for justice, he told Lacerda, had nothing to do with his client's political positions.[1]

In articles in the *Tribuna* in June and July 1951, Lacerda and Sobral stormed against each other with their opposing interpretations of revolutionary events in Brazil in 1922. After Sobral told Lacerda to get rid of his "haughtiness," Lacerda decided to stop publishing anything by Sobral, whereupon Sobral turned to the *Jornal do Commercio* to continue publishing his views.[2] He became angry again in January 1952 on account of the *Tribuna's* violent campaign against his friend Augusto Frederico Schmidt, a poet and businessman who had obtained for the Orquima Company a concession to produce Brazilian monazite, a source of thorium desired by nations building up nuclear fuel. "Why," Sobral asked Lacerda, "do you consider Orquima a den of thieves?"[3]

Alceu Amoroso Lima, who had gone to the United States to direct the Cultural Department of the Pan American Union, received Sobral's accounts, sent to him in February and March 1952, about the crisis of the *Tribuna's conselho consultivo* following what Sobral called "an incredible article by Carlos" in support of the desire of newspaper magnate Assis Chateaubriand to become senator from Paraíba. Adauto Lúcio Cardoso and Gustavo Corção maintained that, as *conselho* members, they should have been consulted, and therefore they resigned. At a heated *Tribuna* stockholders' meeting, Lacerda upheld his support of Chateaubriand. Sobral, with the backing of Dario de Almeida Magalhães, argued for a reorganized and "truly effective" *conselho*. Although Sobral's motion was adopted, nothing was done; and late in 1952, after Lacerda's attacks against Corção upset a new member of the *conselho*, Lacerda brought the *conselho* to an end.[4]

In December 1952, when Lacerda was arrested for slandering public authorities during his campaign against policemen who accepted bribes for overlooking prostitution, Adauto and Sobral presented a habeas corpus appeal on his behalf to the Supreme Court. While a wave of pro-Lacerda indignation filled Rio, Sobral gave the oral defense in the crowded courtroom. Following a unanimous court decision in Lacerda's favor, Sobral was surrounded by a throng expressing congratulations. The case helped persuade Congress to approve a new national security law. "Except for the jailing of Carlos," Sobral wrote Alceu, "we would not have the new law, much better than the old one but still defective."[5]

In December 1953, Lacerda called Sobral's friend Coriolano de Góes, of the Bank of Brazil, "a public thief." Refusing to publish Sobral's letter defending Coriolano, Lacerda telephoned Sobral on the 29th, using strong words to denounce him for seeking to "destroy the promorality campaign." Only the intervention of Dario de Almeida Magalhães prevented Sobral from suing Lacerda, but Sobral continued to demand an apology for the language used by Lacerda during the telephone call.[6] Making matters worse, Lacerda, in the *Tribuna*, assailed Alceu Amoroso Lima early in 1954 for accepting the Vargas government's invitation to be one of Brazil's representatives at the Tenth Inter-American Conference in Caracas, Venezuela. Sobral therefore advised Dario of his "irreparable" break with Lacerda and determination to represent him no longer as his lawyer, and he wrote to Alceu: "Leave it to me to deal with Carlos, who, like Getúlio, is the product of the moral putrefaction of the nation. He is nothing more than a swashbuckler."[7]

It was a great surprise for Sobral to receive at his home on April 13, 1954, a visit by Lacerda, and only a little later did he learn that it was brought about by Dario. Lacerda was accompanied by lawyer Fernando Velloso, who had helped Dario write the statutes of the *Tribuna*, and José Barreto Filho, a former congressman from Sergipe who had been close to Sobral since the 1920s. Most surprising of all was the humility shown by Lacerda, who apologized for his behavior during the telephone conversation of December 29. His complaints, which he admitted did not excuse his rudeness, had to do with the severity with which Sobral always treated him, never forgiving anything, and Sobral's failure to join his campaign against the pro-Vargas daily *Última Hora*, established in 1951 by Samuel Wainer with generous financial assistance from the Bank of Brazil. In support of Wainer's lawyer, Evandro Lins e Silva, Sobral had employed his severity in writing about Lacerda.[8]

Lacerda described himself as having more defects and fewer good qualities than Sobral. Calling Sobral a much better person than himself, Lacerda expressed the hope—he changed the word to certainty—that they would never have a really definite break.

"I can see now," Sobral wrote Dario, "that Carlos is much better than me. Angry, I spoke to mutual friends, calling him a rotten ingrate. He, however, although also angry, never spoke about me, not even to his friends to whom I spoke against him." Sobral added that Lacerda, while "covered with glory, popularity, and prestige," had been so kind as to look him up and had revealed "a humility that I, considered a Christian, fail to equal. And what touched me . . . was his bringing two friends, Barreto and Velloso, who heard everything and were witnesses." Sobral sent copies of this letter to Corção, Adauto, and José Fernando Carneiro.[9]

Lacerda, campaigning in mid-1954 for a seat in Congress, called his chief opponent, Vargas's son Lutero, a degenerate and a thief, and he said that Wainer's *Última Hora*, which depicted Lacerda as a raving black crow, had come into existence because Lutero, using his influence as the president's son, had made it possible for the newspaper to receive its large loan from the Bank of Brazil, thus opening the gates to a flood of corruption.[10] Lutero's lawyer, preparing to sue Lacerda for slander, said that Sobral, "a founder of the *Tribuna* who has left it," would be one of the witnesses to testify against Lacerda.[11]

Sobral wrote Lutero: "I regret that my position of lawyer of Lacerda prevents me from saying, as a witness, what I think of your participation in the scandalous financing of *Última Hora*," and he added that if any decency remained in Brazil, Lutero's testimony, given to the congressional commission that investigated the *Última Hora* affair, should have resulted in the downfall of Getúlio Vargas. Then Lutero and *Última Hora* gave sensational publicity to Sobral's adultery, which, in 1928, had led the husband of Sobral's partner in the adultery to try to whip Sobral in public in a Rio street.[12]

Amidst an outpouring of statements by prominent men supporting Sobral, Lacerda described the government as a gang of immoral monsters who could do nothing in the way of defense beyond insulting a man of the moral stature of Sobral. Sobral's reply to Lutero, published in *O Globo* and the *Tribuna* on July 13, called Lutero's discussion of Sobral's private life in his youth a dishonorable, cruel, and illicit act, and he promised never to touch on Lutero's private life.[13]

Sobral accompanied Lacerda when he appeared on July 26 at a district criminal court to testify in the case of slander brought against him by Lutero Vargas. The mob that was present to hear Lacerda filled the courtroom and some of the street outside and applauded Sobral as well as Lacerda. Sobral's twenty-eight-page preliminary brief *(defesa prévia)*, which was presented to the court by Sobral and by Adauto Lúcio Cardoso, a UDN candidate for a seat in Congress, maintained that the case was one for the press law and not the law being cited, and it added that all the remarks that Lutero Vargas considered defaming to his honor had been shown to be truthful.[14]

5. Legal Cases of Regine Feigl and Others (1951–1954)

Sobral held positions of importance in the Ordem dos Advogados do Brasil (OAB), established in 1930 for registering lawyers and protecting their interests, and in the much older, smaller Instituto dos Advogados Brasileiros (IAB), a lawyers' cultural association that studied juridical theses. Among his occasional quarrels with the directorships of these groups was one resulting from his attacks against President Dutra's police chief, made in 1946 when he ignored Affonso Penna Júnior's suggestion that he alter his combative ways. This quarrel brought an end to his membership in the top body of Brazilian lawyers, the OAB's national Conselho Federal, as a representative of the OAB's Conselho Seccional of the Federal District. However, he was returned quickly to the Conselho Federal because lawyers in Minas Gerais arranged for him to be a representative of their Conselho Seccional.[1]

A lengthy law case, handled by Sobral in the 1930s and 1940s, sought to win royalties owed to Julietta Naegel Beaufort by the gigantic Indústrias Reunidas F. Matarazzo. It was not won until 1951, by which time Julietta had died and her children had turned from Sobral to lawyer Jorge Dyott Fontenelle, opponent of Sobral in the controversy between the Irmandade do Santissimo Sacramento da Antiga Sé and Cardinal Jaime Câmara.

From his fee of several million cruzeiros, Fontenelle sent 500,000 cruzeiros ($27,000 U.S. currency) to Sobral. Thus Sobral was able to purchase, for 68,000 cruzeiros, a house so that Cecília Silva ("Cecy"), his faithful and efficient typist, would own a home. And it allowed Sobral to join his office companions Gabriel Costa Carvalho and Wilson Salazar in the purchase of a group of rooms for their law firm in a building on Debret Street in downtown Rio.[2]

Also in the latter part of 1951 Sobral received an unexpected check from Affonso Penna Júnior, which paid for the food for four hundred guests at the reception following the marriage of Maria do Carmo, the fourth daughter of the Sobrals and the first to marry. Penna explained that he was giving Sobral part of a legal fee from a case in which Sobral had helped him. Sobral, in a four-page letter of advice to the bride, urged her to confide fully in her husband and, if necessary, do what she could to have him limit his friendships to hardworking, honorable men of good habits. "Do not profane the sacrament of marriage by transforming the blessed conjugal bed into a mere instrument of pleasure that lacks the onus of begetting offspring, imposed by God on his creatures when he said to Adam and Eve 'procreate and multiply.'"[3]

Sobral, although suffering from his painful facial neuralgia in 1953, made an extended visit to Sergipe to prove the innocence of Senator Júlio César Leite, unfairly accused of the political shootings that had brought about several deaths.[4] For Cariocas (residents of Rio), an even more sensational case accepted in 1953 by Sobral was the defense of João de Alencar Athayde, who had been caught in a motel room with a married woman and who used his pistol there to defend himself, killing a police *delegado* (the aggrieved husband) and an assistant sheriff. Sobral was described by the *Diário de Notícias* as the representative of "vulgar assassins," but he won an acquittal. Rejecting a payment for legal services, he suggested that Athayde reward Adauto Lúcio Cardoso, who had assisted in the case, by paying for the printing of ballots that would be needed, in accordance with electoral practices, by Adauto, campaigning for a seat in Congress.[5]

The cases of Sobral that were of more importance and that for years caused the most political controversy concerned the real estate dealings of Regine Feigl with the Canadian-based Brazilian Traction, Light, and Power Company, known as the Light or Rio-Light. Regine and her husband, Fritz Israel Feigl, renowned chemist of the University of Vienna, were Jews who had fled from Europe with their son in 1939.

The Rio-Light was raising cash by selling real estate. One of its subsidiaries was a public utility with old concessions, exempt from property taxes, that were scheduled to revert to the municipality on December 31, 1960. Unlike these concessions, which were not to be sold, the company held other properties, among them the Avenida Hotel in downtown Rio, which Regine planned to buy and replace with Rio's tallest office building, and properties uptown, appropriate for the building of apartments.[6]

Sobral and his law associate Gabriel Costa Carvalho, in 1952 and later, obtained the many required approvals from authorities that Regine needed, but, as Sobral wrote, a campaign of adverse publicity was carried on "by the press and municipal councilmen, demagogic politicians, and *cabos eleitorais* [ward bosses]."[7] A leader of the campaign was Alexandre José Barbosa Lima Sobrinho, a former governor of Pernambuco who, as a Federal District *procurador*, accused the Rio-Light of remitting abroad large sums obtained from selling properties that would revert to the municipality. Regardless of official decisions that allowed Regine to proceed, local and federal legislators continued for a long time to accuse the Feigls of "shady deals" and "corruption."[8]

In March 1954, after the Federal District's Tribunal of Accounts rejected the accusations of Barbosa Lima Sobrinho, Sobral decided to leave his office for a month because of his neuralgia. Regine Feigl, in Switzerland to be at the side of her son during his treatment for cancer, had telephoned Sobral urging him to undergo surgery by Dr. John E. Scarff in New York at her expense.[9]

Sobral traveled alone, reaching New York by plane on April 25. He was joined by Regine, who explained her generosity. The Feigls, she told him, had been received with open arms by Brazil, and there, where they had become citizens, "her honest business negotiations, guided by Sobral's office," had provided her with a fortune. Seeing Sobral as "a person of rare vigor, able to struggle against the forces of evil that are active," she had decided to serve Brazil by freeing him from the pains that tortured him and prevented him from "giving our nation all that it has the right to expect" from him.[10]

During the surgery, performed by Dr. Scarff at New York's Presbyterian Hospital on May 3, 1954, the nerves on the right side of Sobral's head were severed, removing all feeling on that side of his face. For complete repose, ordered by the doctor, Sobral promised to find the necessary isolation in Brazil. He returned to Rio on May 15 and on the 17th went with his wife Maria to the *fazenda* of a friend in Poços de Caldas, Minas Gerais. Sobral wrote Cardinal Jaime Câmara to say that his operation in New York had been a complete success.[11]

At the *fazenda* on June 30 Sobral and Maria learned of the serious deterioration of the health of Hans, the Feigls' only child, in Switzerland. Therefore they went to Rio to be with Regine before her return to Switzerland. Early in October, a telephone call from Fritz Feigl in Switzerland informed the Sobrals that Hans was not expected to live, and in mid-October they learned of his death.[12]

6. Vargas's Suicide, Followed by Military Opposition to Kubitschek (1954–1955)

Revolver shots that were meant to kill Lacerda in front of his apartment, shortly after midnight on August 5, 1954, wounded him in an ankle. Other shots by the would-be assassin killed air force Major Rubens Vaz, who had accompanied the journalist from an election campaign rally.

Getúlio Vargas had nothing to do with this effort of a few Getulistas to eliminate his most forceful critic, but the ensuing storm of indignation against the president became intense after investigations disclosed that the shooting had been ordered by Gregório Fortunato, the poorly educated head of the president's personal guard. Soon it became evident that Gregório had become wealthy by using his influence to arrange Bank of Brazil loans and import licenses for people who paid him for these favors.

While Lacerda used radio and television to attack the Vargas administration with unprecedented effectiveness, air force *brigadeiros* and navy admirals issued manifestoes demanding that the president resign. Sobral, who continued to fear a democracy-ending coup by Vargas, wrote to War Minister Zenóbio da Costa calling on him to "render a service to our nation" by joining others in the military who favored the removal of the president.[1]

The culmination of the turbulent situation was the suicide of Vargas on August 24 and the prompt disclosure, in radio broadcasts, of his spirited farewell message, a declaration that told of his defense of the Brazilian people in the face of "constant pressure" and "slanders," unleashed during "the underground campaign by international groups" that had joined a similar campaign by "national groups." "If the birds of prey want someone's blood, if they want to go on draining the Brazilian people, I offer my life as a holocaust. I choose this means of being always with you. When they humiliate you, you will feel my soul suffering at your side."

Vargas in his final act assured a popular following for Getulismo. For the most part the people were sorrowful, but some disorderly demonstrations occurred, such as attempts to attack buildings of Standard Oil, the United States embassy, and the *Tribuna da Imprensa*. Mobs called for the "death" of Lacerda, Eduardo Gomes, and *O Globo*'s Roberto Marinho.

An article by Alceu Amoroso Lima attributed Vargas's suicide to "the unforgivable sin of despair," which "represents disbelief in the very essence of God: love, pardon, and mercy."[2] An article by Sobral expressed a somewhat similar religious view but conceded that Vargas, who had despaired on account of his own sins, might receive God's forgiveness because he had struggled, as no one else, for social justice, "that is, justice for the workers and the humble." Lacerda wrote that Vargas's many friends among the poor and the humble were putting the blame for his downfall on his bad friends and advisers.[3]

Vice President João Café Filho, on becoming president, named a cabinet that was anti-Getulista in part because many Getulistas, such as the pro-Vargas head of the PSD, refused to cooperate with him on account of opinions he had expressed during the crisis before Vargas's suicide.[4]

In the campaigning for the election of governors, senators, and congressmen, to be held on October 3, 1954, Getulistas made effective use of Vargas's sacrifice. The spectacular victory of Jânio Quadros, who won the governorship of São Paulo as candidate of some small parties, was said to have been assisted by his campaigning "at the side of the body of Vargas" and by the alleged role of the UDN in the suicide.[5] In Rio, Senator Hamilton Nogueira lost his reelection bid. But Carlos Lacerda topped the voting for congressmen from the Federal District, and Adauto Lúcio Cardoso, also a *udenista*, won a seat.

Getulistas in the PSD directorship agreed with Minas Governor Juscelino Kubitschek, contender for the PSD presidential candidacy in 1955, that the results of the 1954 contest had been encouraging.[6] But military men who had favored the removal of Vargas in August 1954 sent a memorandum to Café Filho late in December with the purpose of preventing the Kubitschek candidacy. Café Filho, showing the memorandum to Kubitschek in January 1955, tried without success to persuade him to withdraw.[7] Sobral, although no supporter of the PSD and Kubitschek, then sent nine pages to Café Filho, in which he called the president a mere spokesman of military men, and he wrote to Foreign Minister Raul Fernandes to say that although a Kubitschek administration would contribute to corruption, a much worse corruption would be the replacement of the voice of the people by the use of machine guns and tanks.[8]

In February 1955, when Kubitschek was nominated by the PSD, Congressmen Carlos Lacerda and Aliomar Baleeiro gave support to the idea of a military intervention because, they contended, Brazil's deplorably corrupt situation could not be corrected by holding elections on October 3. Sobral promised Adauto Lúcio Cardoso that he would "combat with a loud voice the regime of force that Carlos, Aliomar Baleeiro, Eduardo Gomes, and I do not know how many others wish to inaugurate." His "loud voice" was followed by an attack on him in Congress in March by the UDN leader there, Afonso Arinos de Melo Franco, who felt that a return of the Getulistas would be fatal to Brazil. In reply to the attack, Sobral wrote the congressman: "The great threat to the nation is the military coup being prepared stubbornly despite the firm opposition to it by War Minister Henrique Lott."[9]

On April 18 a PTB convention named João ("Jango") Goulart, Vargas's labor minister in 1953 and 1954, to be the running mate of Kubitschek, a development that added to the distaste for the Kubitschek candidacy felt by the military and conservatives. Sobral, although condemning Goulart as a "brazen-faced liar" in a letter that he published,[10] continued to defend the existence of candidacies he disliked. He came to feel in April that he was misunderstood by most of the members of the circle that dated from the Vargas era and for which the fight against Getulismo had been identified with patriotism. During a heated discussion with friends on the night of April 25 he became so wrought up that he followed it with letters to apologize to Dario de Almeida Magalhães and Adauto for his behavior and to say that he felt "isolated, dramatically isolated, terribly isolated." "Solitude will engulf me—a cold and frozen solitude in which my cries will die."[11]

In May 1955, when the campaigning for the presidential election was getting under way, São Paulo Governor Jânio Quadros convinced General Juarez Távora, who had headed Café Filho's *gabinete militar*, that the recent bitter quarrel between Távora and Café Filho would allow the general to seek the presidency with a clear conscience, that is, without Café Filho's support, and that if he did not do so, taking Paulista votes away from presidential candidate Ademar de Barros

(PSP), he would be responsible for a national disaster, the election of Ademar. Agreeing that Ademar was "even worse than Kubitschek," Távora resolved, without enthusiasm, to do his duty.[12] In May he accepted the candidacy of the PDC (Partido Democrata Cristão), and in June the UDN abandoned a candidate it had nominated in April in order to give its support to the well-known general.

Sobral, who was not keen on any military candidate, had serious reservations about Távora, author of the December 1954 anti-Kubitschek memorandum of the military leaders to Café Filho. When Resistência Democrática met in June, its president, Adauto Lúcio Cardoso, joined Gustavo Corção in placing the organization at the side of Távora by means of a motion in which Sobral was heavily outvoted.[13]

7. The Kubitschek Candidacy and Sobral's League to Defend Legality (1955)

The campaigning Távora called for sacrifices while the exuberant Kubitschek promised vast economic development. Lacerda attracted throngs to the galleries of Congress by speaking of the corruption that would characterize the election and of the need for a two-year dictatorship to clean up Brazil. He acclaimed the words of General Canrobert Pereira da Costa, head of the Military Club and chief of staff of the armed forces, who lamented "the democratic falsehood in which we insist on living."[1]

Afonso Arinos de Melo Franco and Aliomar Baleeiro, having become primarily interested in the election of Távora, condemned Lacerda and Canrobert for working for a coup. Sobral, also rebuking Lacerda for his position, turned to Congressman José Maria Alkmim, PSD floor leader, for political understandings to "fortify the representative regime," and he told him of his plan to form the Liga de Defesa da Legalidade for the "intransigent defense" of the democratic regime, "much threatened" by a *golpe* (coup).[2]

From the pro-Kubitschek *Diário Carioca*, enthusiastic about Sobral's endeavor, the public learned that the Liga de Defesa da Legalidade planned to broadcast each evening on TV Rio, and would be launched on the evening of August 23 at the União Metropolitana dos Estudantes (Union of University Students in Rio). When Sobral spoke at the inaugural event, in a speech broadcast by TV Rio, he announced that the new Liga would be active at the headquarters of the Catholics' Centro Dom Vital, where people could enroll in it.[3]

So many sought to enroll that the Liga moved its headquarters from the Centro Dom Vital to an office building. After Sobral visited Congress to enlist support, the PSB (Socialist Party) and the PTB named commissions to work with the Liga. The new movement attracted many university students in Rio, and, soon after, students elsewhere in Brazil organized local sections of the Liga. In São Paulo and Belo Horizonte, speeches on behalf of the Liga were given by Sobral, its president, and by Alceu Amoroso Lima (a Távora supporter), lawyer Evandro Lins e Silva, and Álvaro Lins of the *Correio da Manhã*.[4]

Anti-Communists such as Lacerda and Admiral Carlos Pena Boto, head of the Cruzada Brasileira Anticomunista, declared that the Liga was a front for the Communist Party (which was working for the Kubitschek-Goulart ticket) and "useful innocents" of Communism. In a series of TV Rio debates between Lacerda and Evandro Lins e Silva, which attracted much public attention, Lacerda sought to show that Sobral should "not remain in support of the Communists, the oligarchies, and the thieves who are in collusion with the Liga da Legalidade." Evandro retorted that the Liga was a result of "the regime of emergency that you want to install in Brazil." Lacerda, writing in the *Tribuna* about "a new category of useful innocents," described the Catholics' Centro Dom Vital as gaining unprecedented popularity among Communists.[5]

In a circular, Cardinal Jaime Câmara said that Sobral was guilty of issuing "political blasts" without having received prior advice. Nothing in the laws of the Church, Sobral wrote Dom Jaime on September 14, required a Catholic citizen to consult his bishop before defending the constitution, promulgated in the name of God and approved by the episcopate. He added that he wanted an early reply because he was being asked about his reaction to the circular. Receiving no reply, he issued a press release a week later in which he said he had spontaneously offered Dom Jaime explanations that "ought to remove completely from my name and from the Liga de Defesa da Legalidade any doubts arising from the circular."[6]

On election day, October 3, Sobral limited himself to voting for Milton Campos, vice presidential candidate of the UDN.[7] On the 8th, when it became clear that Kubitschek had defeated his three opponents (Távora, Ademar de Barros, and Plínio Salgado) and that Goulart had defeated his two opponents, War Minister Lott declared that the will of the people had been made known and should be respected. Sobral praised Lott's declaration, and, a little later, as president of the Liga de Defesa da Legalidade, he expressed "public applause" for Lott's dismissal of two generals from their posts for issuing statements disturbing the situation. Without success, Sobral called for punishment of the pro-Lacerda Clube da Lanterna for appealing to the nation to prevent the inaugurations of the election's victors.[8]

Attempts at a coup seemed unlikely because the UDN leaders and Távora rejected Lacerda's ideas and counseled against the use of violence, preferring, instead, to seek to have the election results overturned on account of fraudulent votes, particularly in Minas. Some, like Foreign Minister Raul Fernandes, argued that the illegal Communist Party had acted as a solid mass for Kubitschek and Goulart and the votes it had provided should be subtracted, giving the victory to Távora and his running mate, Milton Campos. Others, like Air Force Minister Eduardo Gomes, insisted that the Tribunal Superior Eleitoral had been in error in 1951 when it had declared that an absolute majority was unnecessary for election. Sobral, at a rally arranged by students fearful of a "new *golpista* campaign," devoted much of his speech to condemning the UDN for seeking to have the judiciary annul the election.[9]

In a letter sent late in October to UDN Congressman Rafael Corrêa de Oliveira, whose columns appeared in the anti-Kubitschek *Diário de Notícias, O Estado de S. Paulo,* and *Maquis* magazine, Sobral said he was beginning to regret having voted for Milton Campos, who, he said, was doing nothing to oppose the UDN's "incredible positions," inciting unrest. "You and your pro-*golpe* companions," Sobral wrote Rafael, "know full well that no really dangerous Communist infiltration exists . . . and that authentic Communists plus the leftists who sometimes accompany them do not represent even 3% of the electorate." "My companions," he also told the UDN congressman, "have turned their backs on constitutional legality because in successive elections they discovered that the people are not on their side."[10]

On November 1 the crisis was intensified during the funeral of General Canrobert Pereira da Costa, when Colonel Jurandir Mamede, speaking on behalf of the Military Club, said the recent election confirmed Canrobert's remarks about a "democratic falsehood." War Minister Lott, against the advice of Eduardo Gomes, decided to punish Mamede.[11] He sought the approval of Café Filho because Mamede's position was in the War College, which reported to a government organ commanded by the president and not by the army. But he found that the president was in a hospital, with a cardiovascular disturbance, and could not be consulted.

From "an honorable adversary," Sobral learned on the morning of November 7 that Café Filho, on account of his condition, would place the presidency temporarily in the hands of the next in line, Chamber of Deputies President Carlos Luz, a PSD dissident who opposed Kubitschek, and that Luz had a plan for removing Lott from his post. As Sobral explained later to Alceu Amoroso Lima, "I arranged at once to get this information to General Lott and to have the *Correio da Manhã* denounce the maneuver." The *Correio da Manhã*'s denouncement, in its leading front-page article on the 8th, told of intriguers working for "a *golpe*" to remove Lott, "the authentic guardian of Brazilian peace."[12]

Following the transfer of the presidency to Luz on the 8th, Lacerda wrote on the 9th in the *Tribuna da Imprensa:* "It is important that it be clearly—very clearly—understood that the president of the Chamber of Deputies did not take over the government in order to prepare the inaugurations of Juscelino Kubitschek and João Goulart. These men cannot take over, should not take over, and will not take over." Sobral, as president of the Liga de Defesa da Legalidade, issued, on the same day, a warning to Carlos Luz that appeared in the press: "It is inevitable that portentous voices have been announcing a plan for implanting a dictatorship. As an intermediary step, on the pretext of a cabinet reform or an incident of discipline, there will be the removal of the war minister, who dauntlessly embodies the principle of the stability of the institutions—a step for removal that has not yet been condemned by the commander-in-chief of the armed forces, the president of the republic."[13]

Luz, before Café Filho turned the presidency over to him, had been told by Lott that a decision against Mamede's punishment would result in his resignation as war minister. Also, before Luz advised Lott on November 10 that Mamede was not to be punished, an arrangement had been made to have the War Ministry taken over by Álvaro Fiuza de Castro, a violently anti-Kubitschek retired general. Luz, informing Lott of his decision, was acting in accordance with one of his favorite expressions: "I think they are bluffing and shall pay to see their cards."[14]

8. Lott's Coups against Luz and Café Filho (November 1955)

The prospect of command changes and other steps that Fiuza de Castro would be making, following the "fourth-class burial" of Lott, shocked army officers who had been appointed to troop command posts by Lott, and led to a plan for a coup against President Luz by General Odílio Denys, head of the army's Eastern Military Zone, with headquarters in Rio. Lott, after hesitating, accepted Denys's plan on the night of November 10, and so "Lott's coup" went into effect on the 11th, with Lott sending radio messages to army commanders about the need to "re-establish the application of disciplinary precepts."[1]

The coup dominated Rio on the 11th and Luz went to sea aboard the cruiser *Tamandaré*, accompanied by Admiral Pena Boto, Lacerda, Mamede, and important civilian members of his administration. Shots at the cruiser from Copacabana Fort, ordered by Lott, did not prevent it from leaving the Rio area and did not sink it.

On that afternoon the two houses of Congress voted that Luz, being *impedido* (in no condition to run the presidency), was to be replaced by the next-in-line, Senate Vice President Nereu Ramos, who favored the inaugurations of the election victors. The replacement of Luz was voted by a large margin because Kubitschek and PSD floor leader Alkmim had previously persuaded Ademar de Barros (PSP) and Plínio Salgado (Partido de Representação Popular) to join the PSD-PTB alliance.

Sobral, supporting Lott's coup, issued a statement on November 12 accusing Luz of having ignored the warning of the Liga de Defesa da Legalidade and of having, instead, "adhered to the conspiracy of the *golpistas*," thus betraying his duty. Alceu Amoroso Lima, however, reprimanded Sobral for his position, and the *udenistas* in Congress closed ranks behind the party leadership in opposing Lott.[2]

The *Tamandaré*, unable to land in São Paulo state because of army troops favorable to Lott, returned to Rio on November 13. Luz was permitted to go ashore only after he assured the coup's victors that he would not legally contest the vote of Congress against him, and he signed a resignation statement after reaching his apartment.

Lacerda, upon disembarking, was in danger of being put in a military prison. Sobral, who had already taken steps to end the occupation of the *Tribuna da Imprensa* by soldiers, sought to submit a habeas corpus petition to protect Lacerda, but Adauto Lúcio Cardoso informed him that the UDN was determined to reserve for itself this "privilege" and that Sobral's role should be limited to using his connections with the "victors of November 11" to prevent Lacerda's arrest. Sobral went to the home of pro-Kubitschek Augusto Frede-rico Schmidt, and there he learned that the Supreme Court's president had quickly approved a UDN petition for Lacerda, drawn up by Adauto and Congressman Gabriel Passos. While at Schmidt's home he also learned, in a message from Dario de Almeida Magalhães's son Raphael, that any pro-Lacerda habeas corpus petition by Sobral would be disavowed by Lacerda's friends and by Lacerda himself. "Never," Sobral wrote Raphael, "have I suffered so severe and unjust an affront."[3]

On November 21 Café Filho prepared to reassume the presidency and went to his residence, but troops made him a prisoner in his apartment and surrounded the presidential palace, and, before dawn on November 22, Congress voted that he was *impedido*, leaving Nereu Ramos in office. A state of siege, the first under the 1946 Constitution, was enacted by Congress on November 24 and was renewed every thirty days while Nereu Ramos was in the presidency, thus giving the Supreme Court a reason to decline to rule on the rights of Café Filho. Sobral, initially opposed to the state of siege, came around to finding it beneficial "when legal normality can be a hindrance to the defense of the constitution," especially when "the author of the disorder was the president of the republic, that is, Café Filho, in collusion with his successor Carlos Luz."[4]

Press reports in Brazil carried statements against Lott made by Lacerda in the United States, where he had exiled himself. Articles by others in the Brazilian press said that Sobral would become the government's chief prosecutor *(procurador geral da república)* in the forthcoming administration, which would commence with the in-augurations of Kubitschek and Goulart on January 31, 1956. Calling such stories insulting, Sobral informed *Manchete's* Otto Lara Re-sende: "I do not seek, nor wish, nor will accept anything from any government, present or future, and I have asserted, also in peremptory terms and with equally broad coverage, that I have been and am an intransigent adversary of the PSD and the candidacies of Juscelino Kubitschek and João Goulart. To attribute lowly personal ambitions to me is to deny the example set during my lifetime."[5]

On January 7 the Tribunal Superior Eleitoral confirmed the elections of Kubitschek and Goulart, but the pronouncement did nothing to diminish the passion-filled split in military ranks, where most of the air force officers supported Eduardo Gomes and remembered the murder of a companion of theirs at Lacerda's side in 1954, and where most of the navy officers remained angry about the shots at the *Tamandaré,* ordered by Lott. At an agitated meeting of the Instituto dos Advogados Brasileiros (IAB), Sobral was distressed to find the majority so opposed to "Lott's coup" that it called Brazil's interim president, Nereu Ramos, a "usurper." In some of his letters Sobral wrote: "My pastor broke with me," and "my closest friends desert me as though I were a traitor."[6]

On the night of January 30, Sobral spent three hours at the residence of Lott trying to persuade him to retire the next day. Retirement, Sobral insisted, would demonstrate that his motive in heading the movements against Luz and Café Filho had not been motivated by his wish to remain as head of the War Ministry. But Lott spoke of his determination to carry out his duty, as war minister, because, he told Sobral, "the forces of disorder continue brash, intact, and coordinated."[7]

During February 1956, after Kubitschek became president, Sobral acknowledged that he had given the wrong advice to Lott.[8] His change of mind was brought about by a rebellion by some anti-Kubitschek air force officers in the northern interior. After the rebellion was subdued by Lott's troops late in the month, its leaders, who had fled from Brazil, and their companions in Brazil were granted amnesty by Congress at the request of Kubitschek.

9. Sobral's Activities Following Kubitschek's Inauguration (1956–1958)

A devastating loss for Sobral was the death, from cancer, of his daughter Maria do Carmo, at the age of twenty-six, on August 9, 1956. Heaping praise on her life in his funeral oration, he recalled: "In our home and out of it, in your studies, in your affections, and, in the end, in your own home, you gave, to me and everyone, only charm and happiness."[1] Reflecting the sorrow that he said would "immerse him forever," Sobral resolved to wear in the future only suits that were black.

Already, in the first months of the Kubitschek administration, an unexpected return of Sobral's neuralgia occurred, this time on the side of his face that had not undergone surgery in New York. For this reason and on account of exhaustion, he went in March 1956 to rest for three weeks at the Fazenda Cruzeiro, belonging to a friend in São Paulo state.

Late in his stay at the *fazenda* he was brought a letter in which Kubitschek asked him to become a member of the Supreme Court. Declining the offer on April 2, Sobral wrote Kubitschek, whom he had never met: "The civic viewpoint that I assumed in defense of the democratic regime . . . which turned out to be helpful to your candidacy, opposed by me, prevents me, in good conscience, from accepting the high position, whereby you, laudably rejecting suggestions associated with sterile politics, propose to elevate my modest name."[2]

From the start of the new administration Sobral sought to be useful by advising Kubitschek about some appointments that he said should not be made or should not have been made because they would be "dangerous to the public interest," and he offered other names, as requested by Augusto Frederico Schmidt. It was heartening to learn of the president's acceptance of one of these names, Professor Victor Nunes Leal, to become *procurador geral* of the Federal District.[3] The appointment led to the promotion of Victor, late in 1956, to the headship of the presidential *gabinete civil*, a position of much influence. While Sobral was still at the *fazenda*, he suggested that Kubitschek fill the Supreme Court vacancy by naming Miguel Seabra Fagundes, Café Filho's first justice minister, and avoid playing politics by capitulating to the demand of São Paulo Governor Jânio Quadros that a Paulista be chosen.[4] Kubitschek, however, named a distinguished São Paulo law professor, Cândido Mota Filho.

Sobral communicated sometimes with Kubitschek, Lott, Denys, and the Rio police chief, General Augusto Magessi, about military and police actions that he said were illegal. His disgust for the views of the *Tribuna da Imprensa* and *Maquis* did not prevent him from accusing the authorities of breaking the law by invading their publication places and seizing editions that tried to give publicity to a manifesto of Lacerda, sent from Portugal, which called Kubitschek "a frenzied exhibitionist" and Goulart "a traitor." Sobral wrote Kubitschek that the steps against the *Tribuna* by the army police were contrary to the constitution under which he had assumed the presidency.[5]

Lacerda had already decided to have no more of his legal work handled by Sobral. Adauto Lúcio Cardoso, who had insisted with

Lacerda in the past, and without Sobral's knowledge, that Sobral work with him on Lacerda's cases, kept Lacerda's latest decision from Sobral in order first to consult Dario de Almeida Magalhães. But a letter from Lacerda to Sobral, written on August 9, 1956, and sent to Dario, made Lacerda's position clear and gave two reasons: (1) Lacerda's determination to bring a successful resolution to "the revolutionary crisis that consumes Brazil" and (2) the need to use the case against Gregório Fortunato, responsible for shootings near Lacerda's apartment in 1954, to give publicity to the political positions of Lacerda along with those of the murdered Major Vaz and his companions.[6]

Sobral, eager to denounce Gregório Fortunato and his partisans in the courtroom, was given Lacerda's letter on August 27. Replying quickly, he reviewed his past work for Lacerda, done without any fee, and he added that Lacerda's "dramatic blow" against Sobral's professional life had brought about "the darkest hour" of his career as a lawyer. Discussing Lacerda's two reasons, Sobral wrote that what Lacerda proposed would not end "the revolutionary crisis but, on the contrary, would exacerbate it catastrophically, gravely threatening the nation's Christian destination." "As to your second reason, I must warn you that the use of a judicial case as a means of political propaganda is one of the points of the Communist program." Lenin, he wrote, had recommended turning a courtroom into a stimulant of agitation.[7]

Lacerda returned to Brazil on October 11, 1956. He spoke to large, enthusiastic audiences and declared he could not recognize the legitimacy of the administration of Kubitschek, "a clown."

Accusations against Sobral's friends were made by Lacerda, the *Tribuna*, and *Maquis*, with Sobral issuing fierce replies. After Sobral lunched at the Mesbla Restaurant with Victor Nunes Leal and Minas politician Tancredo Neves, Lacerda published an article in which he wrote that a proposed press law was an imposition of Lott and his accomplices, such as "the sordid Victor Nunes Leal, who seeks to corrupt even his protectors, leading them to make a pact with Tancredo Neves and other reckless collaborators for transforming Brazil into a neototalitarian nation." Sobral, writing to Lacerda, denied any imposition by Lott and described Victor Nunes Leal as a man of valor and honesty who had not sought to corrupt anyone. "You know that I am not the protector of Victor."[8]

Many letters came to Sobral asking him for favors from Kubitschek. In reply to one of them, this one from lawyer Evandro Lins e Silva, he wrote in July 1956 that all these requests left him melancholy. "Everyone thinks I have left my friends . . . and become a member of the governing group."[9]

Sobral exchanged his first words with Kubitschek at a wedding in July 1956, and he met him later when the president paid a visit to the Federal Court of Appeals. Their third meeting, one that may have had important consequences, occurred on the night of November 23, 1956, during hours that Kubitschek later described as the most serious of his presidency. So alarming was the military and political turmoil that Kubitschek, recalling the suicide of Vargas, felt that "an August 24 was being prepared."[10]

The turmoil had begun on November 11 when Lott, observing the anniversary of his coup, had attended a rally at which thousands of workers cheered as Goulart presented him with a sword of gold. Oppositionists in Congress and elsewhere condemned the rally and its pro-Lott sponsor, the Frente de Novembro. During the following days, the military was busy handing out punishments to officers for making pronouncements about political matters. Juarez Távora, defying a ruling that extended such punishments to retired officers, sent a "declaration" to the press that denounced the president and war minister, and, on November 22, he gave a radio-television interview referring to political matters and his "declaration," already a press sensation.[11]

Kubitschek, on November 23, conferred at Catete Palace (the presidential office) with advisers. He forbade publication of a manifesto of Lott-hating navy officers, furious at the "brazenness" of the Frente de Novembro, and he agreed to the issuance of a decree that closed down both the Frente de Novembro and the pro-Lacerda Clube da Lanterna. Lott was ordered to place Távora under arrest for forty-eight hours, but he made it known that he had decided to leave the War Ministry on account of the decision to end the Frente de Novembro. Victor Nunes Leal, the new head of the *gabinete civil,* advised the Catete Palace group of Sobral's wish to speak with the president, news that at first disturbed Kubitschek. But what Sobral wanted was authorization to try to persuade Lott not to resign, and Kubitschek told Sobral to go ahead.[12]

At 5:00 A.M. Sobral succeeded in calling on Lott at his residence. Finding the general irate, Sobral observed that his reaction would have been justified if the Clube da Lanterna was not also being closed. And he argued that Lott's resignation might be interpreted as a step taken in support of Communists, who had been seeking to control the Frente de Novembro. Might such an interpretation and Lott's backing of the Frente renew the crisis in the navy? Lott yielded to Sobral's arguments. "You returned from Lott's home," Kubitschek wrote Sobral years later, "bringing the news that the general had decided not to follow his original idea of leaving the War Ministry."[13]

Alceu Amoroso Lima, writing in the *Diário de Notícias* in December 1956, denounced the "odious imprisonment" of Juarez Távora, "ordered by the war minister and authorized by the president." "You can imagine," Sobral wrote Alceu, "how sad your article has made me."[14]

An opportunity for the Kubitschek administration to convict Lacerda of endangering the national security arose when he revealed, in Congress in February 1957, the uncoded wording of a secret coded cable sent to the Foreign Ministry by its embassy in Argentina. Lacerda claimed that the information proved that Goulart was a traitor, but the Kubitschek administration used Lacerda's revelation to call on its majority in Congress to strip him of his congressional immunities so that he could be tried for making it possible for outsiders to decipher the code.

The sensational forty-five-day battle in Congress, a principal topic throughout Brazil during April and May 1957, finally resulted in the preservation of Lacerda's immunities, and, while the battle went on, Sobral wrote letters to Victor Nunes Leal in opposition to the government's position. He pointed out that the constitution gave "absolute impunity" to those who spoke in Congress in the course of carrying out their mandates. And he added: "Above all, the oppositionists are unfortunately being marvelously served by the Lacerda episode."[15] Sobral decided to say nothing publicly that might strengthen the "filthy" UDN campaign. His refusal to support Lacerda disappointed Adauto Lúcio Cardoso, Milton Campos, and others and caused the *Diário de Notícias* to publish an article, "Where Is Sobral Pinto?" Sobral explained to its publisher that the "*golpistas* and the Clube da Lanterna gang" would distort any comment he might make about the "inviolability" of congressmen.[16]

Maquis, directed by Fidélis Amaral Netto, who had headed the Clube da Lanterna, wrote in August 1957 that Victor Nunes Leal was one of the men responsible for "the plundering of the people's money" by the "bunch of criminals" at the Caixa Econômica of São Paulo. This led to the publication in *Maquis* of many articles and let-

Drawing by Adail José de Paula in *Marquis,* second half of October 1957

ters in which Amaral Netto and Sobral attacked each other. In September Amaral Netto called Sobral the "nursemaid" of Victor Nunes Leal, and in October *Maquis* published a cartoon showing "nursemaid" Sobral with "baby" Victor Nunes Leal on Sobral's desk wearing only a diaper.[17]

10.   Sobral Breaks with His Client, Jânio Quadros (1959)

Lawsuits against Assis Chateaubriand followed the failure of the media magnate to persuade industrialist José Ermírio de Morais and Governor Jânio Quadros to accept the favorable publicity he offered them in return for the money he needed to repay $653,000 to a New York bank, borrowed for the purchase of paintings for the São Paulo Museum of Art.[1]

Chateaubriand, carrying out what he called a "punitive expedition" against José Ermírio, used his newspapers and radio stations to describe the industrialist as a bastard, fathered by bandit Antônio Silvino, and "a degenerate" whose company, Votorantim, was in financial trouble. Dario de Almeida Magalhães asked Sobral to work with Adauto Lúcio Cardoso on the lawsuit in which José Ermírio and his two sons turned to the Supreme Court, accusing Chateaubriand of extortion and slander.[2]

Chateaubriand argued that he was protected by his immunities as a senator representing the state of Maranhão, whereas Sobral and Adauto asserted that although he continued to frequent the Senate, his acceptance of the ambassadorship to London had cost him his seat. Following a Supreme Court decision in Chateaubriand's favor in October 1957, Chateaubriand went to London. He was there in 1958 when Sobral and Adauto undertook to sue him a second time in the name of Ermírio, but their position was rejected by the *procurador geral da república* and by the Supreme Court's *relator* (the justice selected to give a preliminary opinion). They said that accusations of slanders in the media had to be submitted within one year and the charge of extortion had not been proved.[3]

Chateaubriand, before he went to London, obtained from the Caixa Econômica of São Paulo the money he had sought. Sobral maintained that so large a Caixa loan and the arrangement to convert it into dollars could not have been made without the approval of Finance Minister José Maria Alkmim. Writing Alkmim, he said: "You and Juscelino Kubitschek tremble before Chateaubriand . . . wanting the propaganda machine that he puts at your disposal for your political party."[4]

In July 1958 Sobral accepted the request of São Paulo Governor Jânio Quadros and the state's justice secretary, Oscar Pedroso Horta, that he represent the governor after Chateaubriand's *Diário de S. Paulo* called Quadros a "delirious imbecile," a "circus clown," a "fiendish demon," a "sick soul," and an "oaf."[5] Writing to Luís Gallotti and other Supreme Court justices, Sobral said that Chateaubriand's "cruel campaign" had been undertaken simply because the governor had refused to have his state pay millions of cruzeiros for a publicity contract. "The spectacular appearance of Amaral Netto, Carlos Lacerda, Samuel Wainer, Tenório Cavalcanti, and so many others who maintain a scandalous press that degrades the nation is the result of the total irresponsibility of people in the government, benefactors of men like Assis Chateaubriand."[6]

Sobral's brief, sent to Justice Minister Carlos Cirilo Júnior in the name of Quadros in August 1958, mentioned that Chateaubriand had declared publicly that he had tried and failed to obtain the money from Quadros. It quoted references to Quadros in Chateaubriand's articles, including recent ones calling Quadros a cheater, imposter, and liar, and "a man destitute of scruples . . . without moral or intellectual background." Cirilo Júnior quickly sent the document to the *procurador geral da república* with the recommendation that Chateaubriand be charged with violating the press law.[7]

In the October 1958 elections Quadros easily won a congressional seat from Paraná on the Labor Party (PTB) ticket and succeeded in getting Carlos Alberto Carvalho Pinto, his state finance secretary, elected governor of São Paulo. When Congress began its new session in 1959 Quadros visited Rio briefly to take his seat, and he returned to Rio a little later to embark by ship on a tour around the world. Sobral was disappointed that Quadros did not get in touch with him on either occasion. Nor was he given information about how to reach the world traveler.[8]

However, when Adauto Lúcio Cardoso spoke with Quadros in Paris early in August 1959, he suggested that Quadros not fail to participate in a correspondence that Sobral wished to have.[9] It was a pleasant surprise for Sobral to receive a letter from Quadros, sent from Paris on August 8, calling Sobral "the great lawyer and patriot." Quadros added: "As soon as I return I shall look you up and, with your permission, hear your views about the national situation. If you wish to distinguish me with some lines, send them to me in care of the embassy in Lisbon." As for the lawsuit, Quadros wrote that "the simple fact that we have replied in kind, as demanded by our honor, is satisfaction enough."[10]

For Sobral the words of Quadros were a welcome contrast to the attitudes that he felt had been assumed by Kubitschek and Lott, who, Sobral wrote Gabriel Costa Carvalho, "have no wish to heed my warnings and probably consider me impertinent." Kubitschek in April, needing support in Congress, had had to choose between the demands of congressional leaders and the pleas of Sobral about a judicial appointment, and he had infuriated Sobral with his decision. Sobral had told Victor Nunes Leal that he was ending his relations with the president. "Never again," he had written Kubitschek, "will you hear my voice."[11]

As for Lott, expected to be the presidential candidate of the PSD and PTB, Sobral had told him in June: "You cannot and must not agree to be a candidate," because to do so would represent the intervention of the military in party politics and would cause all the groups that opposed the Kubitschek administration to unite behind a movement demanding revenge for the outcome of the 1955 crises.[12]

To Quadros, who was likely to receive the UDN nomination for president with the strong support of Lacerda, Sobral wrote long letters in August, September, and October 1959 to tell him of his shortcomings. "In political life," Sobral wrote, "your acts are not inspired by solid convictions, reached after careful meditation." He told Quadros to abandon the "demagogic" practice of publishing his *bilhetes* (notes) with orders to subordinates that damaged the reputations of men, and he criticized Quadros for the informal attire he had sometimes worn in the course of governing.[13]

Quadros was told by Sobral that his waving of a broom for sweeping away crooks had a "revolutionary connotation" and should not be used against the honest Lott. The UDN, he wrote, was turning to Quadros, congressman of the PTB, simply because it believed that the wielder of the broom could defeat its opponents by describing them as thieves and traitors. "You can easily understand how a man of convictions is saddened and sometimes revolted to see public men moved primarily by inferior sentiments such as passion to rule and to take out revenge on the vanquished." Sobral, admirer of the majestic projects of Kubitschek, reminded Quadros of the creation of the new capital, Brasília, in the interior, the building of the Três Marias and Furnas hydroelectric plants, and the construction of far-reaching highways.[14]

Quadros was cordial in replying to Sobral's earliest letter and asked only to be allowed to disagree about the political situation, and he wrote him in October, after returning to Brazil, that his descriptions of the behavior of men in politics showed him to be afflicted by "deep pessimism." Later in October Sobral reprimanded Quadros for "raising the banner of revolution" in a "belligerent" political declaration that struck Sobral as "demagogic." "It is my duty," Sobral concluded, "to oppose your dreadful and depressing program."[15]

Early in November in Rio, where the UDN nominating convention was on the verge of choosing Quadros to be the party's presidential

candidate, Quadros joined Chateaubriand for a lunch of reconciliation that was given publicity in an article that Chateaubriand published in his newspapers on Sunday, November 29.[16]

Sobral, writing Dario de Almeida Magalhães of his shock, said:
"Quadros suddenly left me standing before the judges of the country's highest court, speaking in his defense, while he engaged in a
friendly, even affectionate conversation with precisely the person
whose attacks left him with wounds that remain without redress.
Regardless of my financial problems, I shall find a way to return the
100,000 cruzeiros that I received as a fee and thus be able to resign
the authorization that I received from him."[17]

On December 11 Quadros wrote Sobral about the deterioration of
relations between lawyer and client caused by the former's "impertinent" and "imprudent" remarks in his letters. Quadros also pointed
out that it was he, Quadros, who had to be the "exclusive judge" about
how he should "react to political contingencies." Sobral replied that
Quadros could not be the "exclusive judge" in the Chateaubriand
"episode." He sent Quadros a copy of a 100,000-cruzeiro check that
he deposited in Quadros's bank account, and he advised the Supreme
Court of his withdrawal from the case.[18]

Another client lost by Sobral was Cardinal Jaime Câmara. Sobral
was filled with "incredible joy" on July 24, 1959, when he won the
long controversy of the cardinal in the case of the Irmandade do Santissimo Sacramento da Antiga Sé, and he followed it up by undertaking in September 1960 to present to the cardinal a formula that
the defeated members of the Irmandade had drawn up and that included the withdrawal of their excommunications. It was Sobral's
belief that acceptance of the formula would reestablish peace in the
Irmandade and that the cardinal would welcome a return of the rebels
to his flock. The cardinal named a replacement for Sobral and wrote
him that he was relieving his "dear friend" of the bothersome work
that remained for implementing the court orders, not yet carried
out. In a reference to the Irmandade's lawyer, the cardinal wrote: "I
understand that your friendship for, and feeling of gratitude toward,
Jorge Dyott Fontenelle is impeding the conclusion of the case and is
making things difficult for you."[19]

Telling the cardinal of his "deeply wounded filial heart," Sobral
wrote that he was "crushed" to find himself called "a traitor" on account of his warm relations with Fontenelle.[20]

11. Elections and Controversies about Brasília and Rio's City Council (1960)

Udenistas, joyfully waving miniature brooms at their convention, nominated Quadros for president on November 8, 1959. Then a disagreement took place because the PDC (Partido Democrata Cristão), in nominating Quadros earlier, had given him a running mate different from the one chosen by the UDN. On November 25, during the bickering about which running mate should appear with the presidential candidate, Quadros "irrevocably" resigned his candidacy in a move that portrayed him as unwilling to have himself controlled by political leaders.

While a widespread movement was under way to persuade Quadros to save the nation by withdrawing his resignation, a few anti-Lott air force officers began a rebellion with a manifesto that said that the candidate's withdrawal had demonstrated the need for an armed revolution to free the country from corruption, subversion, and other ills. The uprising was subdued in two days, and Quadros returned to campaigning on December 6 with the understanding that the only running mate to appear at his side would be the *udenista.* Sobral told Dario that Quadros, "a politician without convictions," had returned after persuading Adauto Lúcio Cardoso and Lacerda that he could abandon principles held by the UDN.[1]

The arrangements whereby the PSD and PTB would unite behind Lott for president and Goulart for reelection to the vice presidency were concluded in February 1960 and were supported by the Communist Party of Brazil, which, like other backers of the PSD-PTB ticket, regretted the entry into the race of presidential candidate Ademar de Barros, likely to split the anti-Quadros ranks in São Paulo.

Lott, eager to avoid being considered pro-Communist, did not follow Quadros's example of pleasing the far Left, and he declined Fidel Castro's invitation to spend a week in Cuba. Quadros, on the other hand, accepted a similar invitation with words of praise for Castro, and he was congratulated by many *udenista* politicians and by the *Diário de Notícias,* which wrote that he was planning to introduce a foreign policy different from that of Kubitschek. Among the forty who accompanied Quadros on his trip to Cuba were Adauto Lúcio Cardoso, Afonso Arinos de Melo Franco, and João Ribeiro Dantas, who published the *Diário de Notícias,* and they and others received letters from Sobral with a warning that Castro, suppressor of press freedom, was determined to expand Marxism in the continent.[2] Quadros, upon returning from Cuba, declared that the Cuban revolutionary government practiced freedom of the press and showed "absolute respect for private property and juridical rules" and could not be called Communist. In order to speak about Cuban "reality," he said, one had to visit Cuba, as he had done.[3]

Many supporters of Quadros condemned the construction of Brasília, and they applauded the UDN candidate for calling the work on the Belém-Brasília highway a work for building a road to be used by jaguars. The struggle against the end of Rio's days as the nation's capital was felt by Sobral to be especially unfair and violent in articles appearing in the *Diário de Notícias, Correio da Manhã, Tribuna da Imprensa,* and *O Globo.* Agreeable again to have Kubitschek hear his voice, he wrote the president of the distress that filled him on finding himself "bitterly attacked by close friends and eminent Catholics." His letters replying to attacks on Brasília by Alceu Amoroso Lima, Adauto Lúcio Cardoso, former finance minister Eugênio Gudin, and Gustavo Corção, intellectual leader of the *anti-mudancistas* (opponents of the move to Brasília), were written after he spent two days in temporary wooden accommodations in the new city's bustling workers' area, admiring the "enthusiastic builders" and the massive edifices they were finishing. He could not agree with Gudin that this work had been caused by Kubitschek's "frivolity" or "morbid ambition to imitate the pharaohs." Alceu, Sobral felt, had become poisoned by the invective of Lacerda, who called Brasília "a cancer in the heart of Brazil."[4]

It was not certain that the Supreme Court would move to Brasília when the capital was to be transferred there on April 21, 1960, because half of its justices maintained that Brasília was not a fit place in which to live and work. A justice favorable to the move arranged for Sobral to write to Justice Hahnemann Guimarães, known to be an *anti-mudancista.* Sobral's letter to Hahnemann Guimarães reported on the excellent living conditions in the new capital and said that the lack of diversions there would have advantages. Above all, he wrote, the failure of Brazil's highest tribunal to adhere to the legislation about the move would be "a gigantic contribution to the spirit of rebellion that is active in powerful groups, ambitious and deranged." He sent a copy of the letter to Justice Luís Gallotti, "knowing that you are in agreement with Eugênio Gudin."[5]

The crowd that filled the chamber of the Supreme Court on April

13 to learn of its decision found that Hahnemann Guimarães and Cândido Mota Filho had left off being *anti-mudancistas*. Following the 7-4 vote for moving, Sobral wrote Gabriel Costa Carvalho: "My letter to Hahnemann not only brought him into the camp of the *mudancistas* but also had a decisive influence on Cândido Mota Filho, who became acquainted with it."[6] With the news of the court's decision, Congress proceeded to pass legislation for organizing the federal judiciary in Brasília and for the provisional organization of the new state of Guanabara, which would replace what had long been the Federal District.

The new building of the Supreme Court was inaugurated on April 15, and on June 15 the court began handling cases there. Sobral, whose wife objected to relocating the family in Brasília, obtained postponements of seventeen urgent Supreme Court cases until after his trip there on June 24. Because the Federal Court of Appeals also moved to Brasília, he spent in some months in the last half of 1960 almost half his time in the new capital. When he was not there, cases of his firm were handled in the two courts by Tito Lívio Cavalcanti de Medeiros, described by Sobral to Justice Nelson Hungria as his "brilliant office partner."[7]

In the first election for a governor of Guanabara, which would coincide with the presidential election on October 3, Carlos Lacerda, candidate of the UDN, PDC, and PR (Partido Republicano), faced three opponents, of whom Sérgio Magalhães (PTB-PSB) was the most formidable. Sobral could find no presidential candidate or gubernatorial candidate worthy of his vote and favored only Milton Campos, who had replaced the UDN's former candidate for the vice presidency. Sérgio Magalhães, Sobral believed, was "a Communist in disguise." An opinion about Lacerda's candidacy was given by Sobral when he learned that Alceu Amoroso Lima planned to vote for him: "You have no right to vote for . . . a vain, insolent, and ungracious man who has publicly sought to discredit us."[8]

On October 3 Quadros won easily, Goulart won a close contest, and Lacerda won also, thanks to the split in his opposition. Sobral, anticipating days that would be worse for him than under the Vargas dictatorship, explained to Adauto that his "personal incompatibility" with the new victors, "whose names I find it difficult even to mention," had not existed in the case of his "adversaries" during the Estado Novo.[9]

Lacerda became governor on December 5, prior to the inauguration of Quadros, and set to work to have the Guanabara state Constitutional Assembly, elected also on October 3, supplant the Municipal Council, the irresponsible "gilded cage" that had threatened to bankrupt the new state by authorizing large increases in the state's payroll. Municipal councilmen denounced the "Lacerda gang" and cited the congressional legislation of April 14, 1960, which ruled that they should continue to serve until January 1963, thus fulfilling mandates obtained in the elections of 1958.

On December 29 the Guanabara Constitutional Assembly voted what it called Constitutional Act Number One, giving itself, immediately, exclusive legislative power. Sobral, the lawyer representing the Municipal Council, went at once to the Tribunal de Justiça of Guanabara to obtain an injunction against the Constitutional Assembly and Lacerda, and early in January 1961 in Brasília he persuaded Cândido de Oliveira Neto, Kubitschek's *procurador geral da república*, to turn to the Supreme Court and argue that Guanabara's Constitutional Assembly and governor were in rebellion against the federal government. In discussions with Supreme Court members, Cândido and Sobral were opposed by Adauto, Dario, and Alcino Salazar, lawyers of the Constitutional Assembly.[10]

With the inauguration of Quadros on January 31, 1961, a new *procurador geral da república* announced that the federal government had no more interest in the case. Nevertheless Supreme Court Justice Ary Franco disappointed Lacerda and the lawyers of the Constitutional Assembly because he refused to withdraw a temporary injunction against Guanabara's Constitutional Act Number One. After Lacerda expressed his "vehement repugnance" for Ary Franco's decision, Sobral wrote to Raphael de Almeida Magalhães, the thirty-year-old chief of Governor Lacerda's office, to criticize him and "his allies" for taking "rebellious positions" and for "vilifying magistrates who dare to oppose your illegal pretensions." In May 1961 he told Regine Feigl that he could not attend the inauguration of her Edifício Avenida Central, Rio's tallest building, because Lacerda would lead the ceremony.[11]

The constitution writers of the new state, putting the finishing touches on their work in March 1961, resolved to abolish the Municipal Council and prohibit the incorporation of its fifty members into the state legislature, made up of the thirty constitution writers. For Sobral this setback was followed by his defeat in the crowded courtroom of the state Tribunal de Justiça on July 31, 1961, where the vote against him was 29 to 2. In January 1962 the Supreme Court denied Sobral's appeal by a 6 to 3 vote.[12]

12. The Imperiousness of President Quadros and His Resignation (1961)

President Jânio Quadros appeared to be determined to expose immoral acts of the past administration and to correct abuses. But by disregarding legal rights when he took steps detrimental to workers, business firms, and Kubitschek holdovers, he worried Sobral, who wrote Henrique José Hargreaves, a friend in Minas, that "dangerous days" lay ahead. Later Sobral complained to Adauto Lúcio Cardoso that Quadros was issuing regulations, some of them in his published *bilhetes* to cabinet ministers and others, that "allowed for no discussion and ignored laws and juridical order." When one of the *bilhetes* denounced a judge for finding a presidential decree unconstitutional, Sobral, in the *Jornal do Brasil,* said that the *bilhete* left citizens believing that, in Quadros's opinion, the most serious crimes in Brazil were those of obtaining court injunctions against his will.[1]

Sobral had his hands full with cases such as those emanating from what *O Globo* called the new administration's edict for the dismissal of "four thousand workers" in the federal government and in the companies managed by it. In one of his cases, Sobral represented 967 nurses, doctors, and others working in the field of medicine who sought an injunction against the elimination of the "extra pay for risk" clause in the statute covering civilian federal employees. After Quadros, seeking to "get rid of thousands of bad public servants," altered working hours to make it difficult to hold additional jobs, Sobral wrote the minister of industry and commerce that in the case of labor contracts covering workers in government-run companies, arrangements could not be changed by simple government decrees that violated labor laws and labor contracts.[2]

Among the investigations undertaken by the Quadros administration and disliked by Sobral was one that sought to show that Geraldo Carneiro, while serving as private secretary of President Kubitschek, had received "improper gratuities." When the government undertook to investigate a federal lottery concession, Sobral prepared a letter for the concession holder to send to Quadros. He limited his own correspondence with the president to a few formal lines about his continuing effort to return the fee received for representing Quadros against Chateaubriand.[3] After Hélio Fernandes, writing in the *Diário de Notícias*, demanded an investigation of the National Economic Development Bank (BNDE), Sobral addressed a petition to Justice Minister Oscar Pedroso Horta, accusing the journalist of slandering some of the important figures in the bank. Two of them, José Tocqueville de Carvalho Filho and his brother Gabriel Costa Carvalho, associated with Sobral's law firm, were dismissed from the BNDE, leading Sobral to sever his relations with the bank that he had represented in legal cases since 1955.[4]

Lacerda's manner of administrating also disturbed Sobral, but the personal enmity that he had felt was wiped out by the thoughtfulness of the governor following the suicide of Sobral's twenty-six-year-old son José Luiz on June 8, 1961. José Luiz, who had been receiving treatment for schizophrenia, plunged to his death from a window after breakfasting with Sobral and other family members. The sorrow that filled Sobral on account of the loss of this artistic son, who had shared Sobral's love of music and had hoped to become a professor of philosophy, was accompanied by an "indescribable remorse." The father felt that he had given insufficient attention to the young man's problems.[5]

Sobral was restrained by his daughters and Hélder Câmara from expressing, at the burial, the words of grief he had prepared. After the service, Carlos Lacerda, who was among the mourners, told his secretary to approach Sobral and say "the governor wants to take you to your home and pay you a brief visit there. Will you accept?" Sobral accepted.[6]

Several days later, Sobral called on Lacerda to thank him for his kindness. In a letter to Raphael de Almeida Magalhães about a state government matter, Sobral gave assurances of his friendship for Raphael "and for Carlos, despite our political differences."[7]

While Lacerda and much of the press criticized the Left-leaning "independent" foreign policy of Quadros, Alceu Amoroso Lima published columns filled with hearty approval of the independence shown by Quadros in national and international affairs. Sobral wrote Alceu that Brazil was marching in "accelerated steps" toward despotism, and on August 25 he wrote Adauto that the nation was "terror stricken," having witnessed for six months the "uninterrupted personal, despotic, aggressive, and illegal behavior of the president."[8]

On the night of August 24, before Sobral wrote these words to

Adauto, Carlos Lacerda gave a major TV-radio address to accuse Quadros of seeking to arrange a coup that would close Congress, allowing him to decree reforms without being blocked by it. Lacerda
had learned of the plan in a conversation in which Justice Minister
Pedroso Horta had sought his help in bringing it about.[9]

After Lacerda delivered his accusation, Quadros prepared to carry
out the coup. He resolved to resign the presidency, perhaps recalling the massive popular demand for his return after he had resigned
his candidacy. His military ministers, he knew, were determined
to act unconstitutionally, if necessary, to prevent the accession of
Vice President Goulart. He prepared a dramatic farewell message
such as Vargas, under attack by Lacerda in 1954, had written before
committing suicide. In it he paid high tribute to the armed forces
and denounced "the appetites and ambitions of individual groups,
including foreign ones," which, he wrote, shattered the tranquility
"indispensable for exercising" his authority.[10]

In Brasília on Friday morning, August 25, Quadros explained to
the military ministers that he could not govern "with this Congress,"
and he told them to "organize a junta" to run Brazil.[11] He instructed
his intimates to delay the release of his farewell message and resignation statement until 3:00 P.M., when most of the congressmen
would have left Brasília for the weekend. That he would head "the
junta" he had no doubt. "Brazil," he told government press secretary
Carlos Castello Branco, "needs three things: authority, capacity for
work, and courage and rapidity in making decisions. Outside of my-
self there is no one, no one, who combines these three requisites."
On his side also would be "the spontaneous clamor" of the people,
making his return, as he put it, "inevitable."[12]

Congressmen, preparing to leave Brasília for the weekend, were
summoned in mid-afternoon on August 25 by the PSD Senate vice
president to come from the airport to the Chamber of Deputies. Because Goulart was in Hong Kong, having completed a visit to Red
China, they put the interim presidency in the hands of Ranieri Mazzilli, head of the Chamber. Goulart's absence made it unnecessary
for the military ministers to act against the constitution to block the
vice president's right to the presidency.

Quadros, having flown to São Paulo, was shocked to learn of this
turn of events. It was evident also that the popular clamor was not on
behalf of a return of Quadros but was on behalf of Goulart's constitutional right. Quadros conceded that his "return" might take more

time than he had calculated,[13] and within a few days he left by ship for Europe while the forces favoring legality and Goulart stirred the country. Rio Grande do Sul's Governor Leonel Brizola was joined by the Third Army in the south in defying the military ministers' veto against Goulart, made known on August 28.

As early as August 26 Sobral drew up a "Pro-Legality" manifesto. Writing as the former president of the Liga de Defesa da Legalidade, he told "the nation and the armed forces" that "the president of the republic, by the will of the people and the determination of the constitution, is João Goulart." But the censorship in Rio, a result of the cooperation of Lacerda with the military ministers, prevented the publication of Sobral's manifesto.[14] Lott was imprisoned in Rio for pronouncing in favor of legality, and scores of military officers suffered the same fate for agreeing with him. The army and the Guanabara police moved to crush strikes threatened by labor unions and students who called for Goulart to become president.

The military ministers decided to accept having Goulart in a presidency shorn of its power by the adoption of a parliamentary form of government. This solution, or compromise for ending the crisis, was achieved by a constitutional amendment voted by Congress on September 2.

On September 5, before the inauguration of Goulart, the general in charge of the First Army ordered the arrest in Rio of far leftist Colonel Nelson Werneck Sodré and several other officers. Sobral came to their rescue with a habeas corpus petition to the Superior Military Tribunal that pointed out that no charges had been made against them.[15]

Goulart, flying from Rio Grande do Sul, took over the weakened presidency on September 7 and on the 8th his opponents who had headed the military ministries were replaced. To act as prime minister, Congress chose Tancredo Neves (PSD), a Mineiro who had served in the last Vargas cabinet and was favored by Goulart and Kubitschek and their political parties.

Sobral, in a letter to Francisco Negrão de Lima, Brazil's ambassador to Portugal, wrote: "Tancredo, as you know, has qualities that will allow him to lead us with skill, common sense, and dignity." He told Negrão that he had not been surprised by the crisis and added that "fortunately it was resolved without the destruction of public order." He described himself as hopeful that a period of political stability would follow.[16]

13. Activities of Sobral during Goulart's First Years (1961–1963)

Soon after the installation of the parliamentary regime, Sobral was writing letters to the new foreign minister, Francisco San Tiago Dantas, criticizing Brazil's pro–Soviet Union policy. He warned him, in November 1961, of the advance of Communism, under the guise of "nationalism," "populism," and other vague doctrines, and said that the idea of working with the Iron Curtain countries, "to pull the tail of Uncle Sam," was "crazy."[1]

San Tiago Dantas was nominated by Goulart to be prime minister late in June 1962, after Tancredo Neves resigned to run for reelection to the Chamber of Deputies. But Congress, with its PSD majority, rejected San Tiago Dantas, a member of Goulart's PTB. The rejection angered the powerful General Command of Strikes (CGG), which had been formed after President Goulart, late in 1961, had removed the Goulart haters from the control of the mammoth National Confederation of Workers in Industry (CNTI) and replaced them with his supporters, Communist labor leaders and their allies.

The CGG, formed by the CNTI and the Communist leaderships of the organizations of workers in banks, railroads, ports, shipping, and air travel, had brought workers to Brasília to exert pressure on Congress for votes for San Tiago Dantas in June, and on July 4 it ordered a general strike to force the acceptance of a prime minister it would accept. The general strike led to transportation tie-ups and scarcities of food, which, in turn, brought on riots in which over forty persons reportedly lost their lives in the state of Rio de Janeiro.[2] On July 10, Congress agreed to accept as prime minister Goulart's nomination of Francisco Brochado da Rocha, an "anti-imperialist" socialist belonging to the PSD who had assisted Rio Grande do Sul Governor Leonel Brizola in the expropriation of a property of the International Telephone and Telegraph Company.

In the press on July 15, 1962, Sobral published a letter to the presidents of the UDN and PSD deploring the "outlandish and intolerable strikes and the activities of labor unions that seek to tutor the Chamber of Deputies." Warning against a "vague and rattlebrained leftism," he said that if Congress agreed to Brochado da Rocha's "criminal" request to be granted vast powers to legislate undefined "basic reforms" it would mean the end of representative government.[3] Adding to the unrest that worried Sobral was a strike by university students to persuade Congress to require that one-third of the university councils consist of students, a view supported by Brochado da Rocha's education minister.[4] The directorships of student organizations, such as the National Union of University Students (UNE), were in the hands of leftists belonging to Ação Popular (Catholic Marxists) and the Brazilian Communist Party.

It upset Sobral to find Alceu attacking those who, like Sobral, blamed the crisis on "demagogues" and Communists, and to find cardinals and archbishops blaming the lamentable situation on members of the producing class who "exploited misery."[5] After the military ministers echoed a demand of Brochado da Rocha that a plebiscite about ending the parliamentary system be held on election day, October 7, 1962, Sobral wrote War Minister Nelson de Melo to express his sorrow to see the military seeking to "impose its will." Goulart, Sobral pointed out, had accepted the amendment that had created the parliamentary system and should not conspire against the legal order.[6] Lacerda, also attacking the campaign for an early plebiscite, was so disrespectful of Brochado da Rocha that the council of ministers gave wide publicity to an official note that called Guanabara's governor subversive. "I shall," Sobral wrote Lacerda, "be at your side to receive bullets that might be aimed at you."[7]

Brochado da Rocha, unable to persuade Congress to give him legislative powers or to hold a plebiscite on October 7, resigned on September 13. With a new strike being threatened by the General Labor Command (CGT), which was the CGG with another name, PSD congressional leaders consulted Kubitschek and Nelson de Melo and adopted formulas that allowed Goulart to name Professor Hermes Lima prime minister and resulted in an ordinary law that authorized a "popular referendum" to be held on January 6, 1963, to determine whether or not to continue with the parliamentary system. (Congress lacked enough votes for a constitutional amendment, required for an early plebiscite.)

The referendum, when it was held, showed vast dissatisfaction with the parliamentary system, and Congress found a way to return Brazil to the presidential system later in January 1963. By that time Ademar de Barros had defeated Quadros for the São Paulo governorship in the October 1962 elections. But the Left could take satisfaction in the setbacks for Lacerda in Guanabara, where Leonel Brizola was overwhelmingly elected to Congress, and in the election of Miguel Arraes de Alencar to the governorship of Pernambuco.

Miguel Arraes, while campaigning with the financial backing of industrialist José Ermírio de Morais and the political backing of the Brazilian Communist Party (PCB), had been so furiously attacked in the *Diário de Notícias* by Hélio Fernandes that he engaged the services of Sobral, who began a lawsuit against the journalist despite the failure of Arraes ever to look him up when he came to Rio.[8] After that, in July 1963, War Minister Jair Dantas Ribeiro imprisoned Hélio Fernandes for articles against Goulart and the war minister that were said to violate the national security law of 1953. Congress reacted by passing legislation granting amnesty to journalists, a step that ended the case of Arraes against Fernandes and allowed Sobral to reply affirmatively to the appeal for legal help made to him by Fernandes. Sobral's habeas corpus petition to the Supreme Court resulted in the freedom of the journalist on July 31, 1963.[9]

Goulart, upon obtaining full presidential powers, resolved to become a statesman, independent of the CGT. He placed the war ministry in the hands of anti-Communist General Amaury Kruel; and to be finance minister he appointed San Tiago Dantas, who upset the CGT by trying to carry out the anti-inflationary program of the Three Year Plan that Goulart had offered for the economic recovery of Brazil. The finance minister's austerity measures caused general discontent and, in particular, were loathed by the CGT, for they included a rigid wage policy, pledged by San Tiago Dantas in Washington. Goulart, undergoing severe attacks from labor organizations, met in May 1963 with CGT officers, among them Oswaldo Pacheco, a member of the Central Committee of the Brazilian Communist Party (PCB), and he promised them that he would abandon the rigid wage policy.[10] This blow to the Three Year Plan was followed by its burial in June when a reform of the entire cabinet made it clear that the CGT and Goulart would be working together again. The cabinet reform, hailed by Brizola, organized students, and the Nationalist Parliamentary Front, was described by Luiz Carlos Prestes as a result of the PCB's "alliance" with Goulart. Prestes foresaw the achievement of a socialist government without the need for a civil war.[11]

Evandro Lins e Silva, who had been head of the president's *gabinete civil*, became foreign minister in June 1963. At Evandro's home on July 7, the new *gabinete civil* head, Darcy Ribeiro, prepared a pronouncement to answer a particularly aggressive "Letter to the People" released by Lacerda. Darcy Ribeiro's pronouncement, calling Lacerda an obdurate conspirator, was broadcast by television and brought a reply from Sobral, published in the *Diário de Notícias*, that called Lacerda a victim of the federal government, which supported strikes that paralyzed public services in Rio while members of Goulart's inner circle sought to overthrow the governor. "What you seek, my dear Darcy, is to use the vast resources controlled by the president to get action by the masses against industrialists, bankers, and men of commerce for a reform of the constitution that will place the nation among the so-called popular democracies of the Iron Curtain."[12]

The PSD was proposing that bonds, issued to indemnify landowners for agrarian reform expropriations, have full monetary correction, with their values to be increased to reflect the total amount of inflation, thus providing complete protection. Goulart's rejection of the full-correction clause led the PSD to maintain that he was using the agrarian reform issue to create agitation, rather than fair legislation. Lacerda explained his misgivings about Goulart's ideas for agrarian reform in April 1963 at a UDN convention in Curitiba, where his victory over the reform-minded Minas governor, José de Magalhães Pinto, made it certain that he would become, later, the UDN presidential candidate. In a letter sent to Lacerda in July, Sobral suggested that their common views for improving Brazil should be established at a meeting, "since you do not appreciate the letters I send you."[13]

In August 1963 Goulart named Evandro Lins e Silva to the Supreme Court, an appointment that worried so many adversaries of the Left that Sobral, as he informed Evandro, made a point of assuring people that the new appointee would never waver from upholding constitutional order and the laws.[14]

Also in August Sobral became the lawyer in important cases. In the one that followed the death in Sweden of *Correio da Manhã* owner Paulo Bittencourt, Sobral represented Paulo's daughter Sybil against the heiress named in Paulo's will, Niomar Moniz Sodré, with whom Paulo had been living after separating from Sybil's mother. At Sobral's request, Dario de Almeida Magalhães assisted Sobral, who was spending much time in Brasília.[15] After many court hearings, an agreement was reached in 1968 that left Niomar in charge of the newspaper and Sybil the owner of the physical plant.

Another case that began in August 1963 followed the shootings in a public square in Itabaiana, Sergipe, that killed a Sergipe congressman and his son, a state legislator. In Brasília a Parliamentary

Investigation Commission (CPI) named Sobral to represent it and the family of the two victims. After Sobral and Tito Lívio Cavalcanti de Medeiros studied the situation in Sergipe, Sobral reported to the CPI that the governor, João de Seixas Dória, was a liar and "a prisoner" of the state's Military Police, whose members, responsible for the two "assassinations," remained unpunished.[16]

Some of the trips by Sobral to Brasília in December 1963 and the first part of 1964 were made because Senator Arnon de Mello, a friend from Alagoas, inadvertently killed Senator José Kairala with a revolver shot in the Senate on December 4. Sobral, who was asked by Arnon de Mello to join his defense lawyer, José Bonifácio Diniz de Andrada, argued in his briefs that Arnon had been threatened by his Alagoas rival, Senator Silvestre Péricles de Góes Monteiro, and that a shot made against an aggressor did not rule out the rights of defense just because it hit another senator. Sobral failed to convince the judges, but an appeal written by L. C. Miranda Filho and a closing oral argument by José Bonifácio Diniz de Andrada won the acquittal of Arnon.[17]

Late in August 1963, Sobral, at the urging of the outgoing president of the lawyers' Instituto dos Advogados Brasileiros (IAB), agreed to take over its presidency. When Sobral met with about fifty IAB members, who applauded his criticisms of the Goulart administration, a winning slate of officers was organized. At Sobral's request it included Gabriel Costa Carvalho as first secretary of the IAB.[18]

Sobral publicly rebuked the military ministers for their condemnation, late in September 1963, of Governors Lacerda and Ademar de Barros. He did not agree with the ministers' charge that Lacerda was using "conspiratorial techniques," and, in response to their charge that the economic difficulties were caused by the sensational attacks coming from the two governors, he attributed the difficulties to "uninterrupted political strikes, supported by the military ministers."[19]

Goulart, coming from Brasília to Rio in October, granted generous pay increases for bank workers, thus ending their strike, and he conferred with advisers who explained that only with a state of siege could legal steps be taken to depose the two governors for endangering the national security.[20] In requesting that Congress enact a state of siege, Goulart described it to the CGT as providing opportunities to carry out reforms and act against Lacerda and Ademar. But the statement of the military ministers in support of Goulart's request included a reference to the strikes, occurring constantly and serving as a pretext for rebelliousness by governors. The CGT found that union members feared that a state of siege might be used against the strikes, and it joined the general opposition to the measure, an opposition shared by the press, Luiz Carlos Prestes, and Brizola (whose support for the measure had been received earlier by Goulart).[21] The CGT, going further, threatened a general strike against a state of siege. Sobral and lawyers who had assembled with him to discuss his candidacy for the IAB presidency sent a telegram to Chamber of Deputies President Ranieri Mazzilli appealing for rejection of Goulart's request.[22] Rejection became unnecessary, however, because Goulart, finding Congress opposed, withdrew his request on October 7. The president felt bitter toward leftists who had opposed his request, and he broke with the CGT.

Goulart sought to build up, to replace the CGT, the União Sindical dos Trabalhadores (UST), reformist but not Communist. While he endured a barrage of attacks from the Frente de Mobilização Popular, made up of Brizola, the CGT, and other leftist organizations, he appealed to the PSD and other political groups to form a unified movement to enact reforms for saving Brazil from chaos.[23] But he was appealing to those who had become wary of the president. If one considers the anti-Goulart position of influential PSD Congressman Armando Falcão, the letter written to him by Sobral in October 1963 was probably unnecessary. Sobral told him that Goulart, "alleging he has broken with his friends of yesterday, urges the PSD to ally itself with important forces of the PTB and UDN to form a strongly united pro-Goulart bloc to obtain a constitutional reform for bringing about a dictatorship of the Left . . . and, after he obtains the reform . . . , he will resume his relations with the leftists."[24]

In observation of Sobral's seventieth birthday on November 5, Lacerda issued a decree naming a school after him, the Ginásio Estadual Sobral Pinto, an exceptional step because of the governor's practice of not giving schools the names of living Brazilians.

This birthday had a less auspicious result, however. According to the statutes of the Pontifícia Universidade Católica (PUC), attainment of the age of seventy required retirement from regular teaching. Learning in March 1963 of the requirement, Sobral, using strong words to protest this treatment by the university he had helped to establish, had resigned from the PUC.[25]

Sobral was still teaching criminology at the College of Philosophy (FNFi) of the University of Brazil. According to Arthur José Poerner's book, *O Poder Jovem,* "For the majority of young people at the FNFi in the last months of 1963, studies had become a 'small bourgeois deviation' . . . and the college represented a monument to *latifún-dio* [large land ownership]. It was necessary to overthrow everything and make the revolution, and only then recommence."[26] The student strike of September 1963, organized by the Diretório Acadêmico of the FNFi students, achieved its objective of obtaining the removal of FNFi Director Eremildo Luiz Vianna. But Sobral continued teaching 13 of his 15 journalism students, thus defying the order of Education Minister Paulo de Tarso Santos that all classes be suspended. The strike, Sobral maintained, was supported by a small minority: 280 "Communist" students who attended the assembly of the students' Diretório Acadêmico at a college with an enrollment of 1,900 students.[27]

In December, 13 of the 14 journalism students who were graduating from the FNFi decided to have, on December 30, a graduation ceremony separately from the other students of the college and to honor, at the event, Carlos Lacerda, Sobral Pinto, and Eremildo Vianna, who had been forced from the directorship in September. The students' Diretório Acadêmico called Sobral and Eremildo "violators of the law" and Lacerda "the Number One enemy of the students." Posters described them as a "triumvirate of gorillas." Sobral published a letter calling on his friends to be at the FNFi on December 30, and he told the press that he would know how to face agitators who planned to "prevent the ceremony with help from members of the Communist Party and the union of stevedores."[28]

Before the graduation ceremony was to start, about 100 anti-Lacerda students took over the FNFi building. Locking themselves inside, they bolted the main door and, according to the press, used the help of stevedores to set a heavy safe against the other door. While the honored guests mingled with the crowd outside the building, university President Pedro Calmon and FNFi Director José Faria Góis met with Education Minister Júlio Sambaqui and Justice Minister Abelardo Jurema and decided to ask War Minister Jair Dantas Ribeiro to send troops to preserve order.[29]

Troops of the army police surrounded the FNFi building. Sobral, believing their purpose was to guarantee the holding of the graduation ceremony, was bitterly disappointed because the soldiers made it clear that it would not take place. Occupiers of the building let out a cheer for the soldiers, and Lacerda, who had been waiting for four hours, was driven off in a car that was stoned. Shouts of "Victory" and "He did not enter" filled the square. A "hymn of triumph" was broadcast by Rádio Mayrink Veiga, the principal outlet of Congressman Brizola's propaganda in Rio.[30]

In the weeks that followed, the FNFi was reopened only briefly because students opposed to the separate graduation ceremony and possible presence of Lacerda reoccupied it. Sobral, in long letters that appeared in the press, accused prominent men, such as First Army Commander Armando Âncora, of having acted on December 30 to bring about the Bolshevik Revolution in Brazil. Commanders of the Second, Third, and Fourth Armies were warned by Sobral against the "Communist-inspired" plans of the government. Chiefly Sobral wrote to Abelardo Jurema because the justice minister told Goulart and the press that the disturbances of December 30 had been brought about exclusively by Lacerda, "seeking to gain headlines," and by Sobral Pinto, organizer of a group that would have caused a conflict, "with tragic consequences," had not the army intervened.[31]

14. Goulart Brings About a Military Denouement; "Inexplicably" It Disappoints Him (March 1964)

At the end of March 1964 Sobral declared that "the Bolshevik revolution began in Brazil" on December 30, when the army police "cooperated with the insubordination of Communist students."[1]

What Sobral feared might be said to have begun in January 1964 when the agitated contest for control of the CNTI (National Confederation of Workers in Industry) was settled. Gilberto Crockatt de Sá, Goulart's adviser on labor union matters, had followed Goulart's instructions to work for the UST, the non-Communist rival of the CGT. Calling the Communists "idiots" and offering favors to non-Communists, he had garnered the votes of twenty-two federations for the UST. Because the CGT could also count on twenty-two votes, and because ten federations remained on the fence, a decision by Goulart would break the tie, one way or the other.[2]

Goulart, being denounced as "the enemy of the workers" by Brazil's foremost labor leaders, and having received a negative response to his appeals to the PSD and other non-Communist political groups, was told by the heads of his *gabinete civil* and *gabinete militar* that the continued opposition of the CGT and far leftists, coupled with the increasing opposition of non-leftists, would leave him thwarted.

Goulart heeded these advisers. Victory in the CNTI election was therefore given to the CGT, which in short order expanded its domination over other labor confederations (including the new one for agricultural workers) and found itself in a strong position to have its wishes prevail in Brazil's executive branch. In return for the renewal of the CGT-Goulart alliance, Goulart could count on mass participation in rallies that were to be organized by the CGT to bring pressure on Congress and the people in favor of reforms, especially a radical agrarian reform, which needed a constitutional amendment.

In the months ahead, Communists who controlled the CGT and other organizations, often in collaboration with Catholic Marxists of Ação Popular, appeared to take every step imaginable to justify in the minds of many people the fears already expressed by Sobral. As for Goulart, he added to the unrest by making it seem doubtful that he wanted Brazil to have a presidential election in 1965. Disappointing friends of Kubitschek who sought the support of Goulart and the PTB for the reelection of the former president was Goulart's observation that the people had no interest in elections but only in reforms.[3] Goulart spoke with self-assurance following his realliance with the far Left, and he basked in the comforting words of *gabinete militar* head Argemiro Assis Brasil about a military backing that was invincible.

"What we are witnessing," Sobral told the commanders of the Second, Third, and Fourth Armies, "is not, as I once believed and as many believe, a work of disorder caused by capitulations of the president and his military ministers. It is a plan to replace the present constitutional regime" with a regime dominated by Goulart and the labor unions.[4] No longer did Sobral write that majorities of students and soldiers opposed the positions he disliked. He told Henrique Hargreaves in February that "the intellectuals, the Catholics, above all the young ones, . . . the students in their vast majority, many teachers, and a good part of the armed forces praise, stimulate, and defend this state socialism, in the belief that they are contributing to the progress of Brazil." "Never," he wrote Alceu Amoroso Lima, "have I accused you or Paulo de Tarso Santos, or Bishop Jorge Marcos de Oliveira, or São Paulo Cardinal Carlos de Vasconcellos Mota of being Communists. But I never cease to believe, with deep regret, that all of you are much closer to Luiz Carlos Prestes than to me."[5]

The rally of March 13 in Rio, organized by the CGT, was a stunning success. The multitude of about 150,000, some of the participants brought from adjoining states by the CGT, wildly acclaimed

"Jango" Goulart and shouted, "*Manda brasa,* Brizola!" (Heat up the fire, Brizola!). Cristiano Otoni Square was a sea of placards and banners. Signs called for the legalization of the Communist Party, the "Reelection of Jango," and "Gallows" for "the traitor Lacerda" and other "Gorillas." Prominent also were signs saying "Hail to the Glorious CGT" and "Out with the Yankees." A huge banner urged quick action: "We await your orders, Jango! Don't delay any more in freeing Brazil."[6]

Among the hard-hitting speakers were Governors Miguel Arraes and Seixas Dória, labor leaders, UNE President José Serra, and Guanabara Vice Governor Eloy Dutra. It had become impossible, Eloy Dutra declared, to defeat the organized masses. Brizola exhorted the president, whose name was always cheered, to "abandon the policy of conciliation," and he asserted that the "only peaceful solution" for the "impasse" was the termination of Congress and its replacement by a popular one "made up of laborers, peasants, sergeants, nationalist officers, and authentic men of the people." Goulart, with Communist Central Committee member Oswaldo Pacheco at his side, assailed "so-called democrats" for whom "democracy is a thing of privileges, intolerance, and hatred." He called the constitution antiquated and said it legalized "an extinct social-economic structure, unjust and inhuman." He announced that he had signed decrees expropriating privately owned petroleum refineries ("now they belong to the people!") and lands adjoining government highways, railroads, and dams, "with my thoughts turned to the tragedy of our Brazilian brother suffering in the interior." He promised to establish rent ceilings because rents were "exorbitant."[7]

The *Jornal do Brasil* wrote that Goulart had "chosen his option: he is going to try to remain in power" using demagogic words and "promiscuous relations with open enemies of Congress and the constitution." Lacerda said, "revolutionary war has been unleashed. Its ostensible chief is João Goulart until the Communists give it another chief." Even the usually silent former President Dutra had something to say: "Respect for the constitution is the word of order of patriots."[8]

Sobral complained that thousands of army soldiers and marines had guarded Cristiano Otoni Square when organized workers and students had arrived early for the rally, a "warlike demonstration" that had the protection of the military ministers. Publishing on March 19 a manifesto launching the Núcleos de Resistência Legal, he recognized that many millions of people rightfully wanted reforms, within the laws and constitution, for the elimination of misery, ignorance, and injustices, but he pointed out that fellow citizens throughout the country would have to form the Núcleos because "public peace, the existence of the regime, tranquility in our homes, the legitimate possession of property, the management of businesses, everything is in peril with the accelerated march in which the government conspiracy opposes a Christian and free Brazil. . . . Only the Núcleos de Resistência Legal can save Brazil."[9]

A more spectacular response to the rally of March 13 was the March of the Family with God for Liberty, the result of an idea of some conservative Catholic women in São Paulo. Held in São Paulo city on March 19, it far surpassed expectations. Two public squares and three kilometers of street between them were packed with several hundred thousand people. They shouted anti-Communist slogans along with refrains such as one demanding the "Jailing of Jango." Placards called the constitution "inviolable" and said, "Down with Red Imperialists," "Not here, Jango," "Resignation or Impeachment," and "Reforms yes, with Russians no." Organizers of the march called the "thrilling" outpouring of people a "miracle of faith" and attended a Mass held at the cathedral for the "salvation of democracy."[10]

On the other hand, Ação Católica Brasileira of São Paulo issued a manifesto expressing its "profound amazement at the exploitation of the faith and religious sentiment of the Brazilian people and the political use of religion." After a similar manifesto by Ação Católica in Belo Horizonte was issued to protest the march planned for that city on March 21, Sobral, irritated by it, wrote Alceu: "They tell me you had an important role in the decisions by Ação Católica in Belo Horizonte and São Paulo to publish their manifestoes against the popular demonstrations in those cities. It that true? Answer me."[11]

Carioca women belonging to CAMDE (Campanha da Mulher pela Democracia) returned to Rio from their exhilarating experience in the São Paulo march of the 19th and started to organize, with the support of Cardinal Jaime Câmara, a similar march for Rio to be held on April 2. Their opponents, members of the Movimento Nacionalista Feminino, decided to stage a mass meeting in Rio on April 3 to be addressed by Brizola's wife (sister of Goulart). Brizola, busy stirring things up, told the press that the nation had reached such a chaotic and explosive state of affairs that he did not believe a presidential election would occur in 1965.[12]

A March of the Family with God for Liberty took place in Santos, São Paulo, on March 25, and others were being organized elsewhere. Meanwhile the CGT scheduled rallies at which Goulart was to appear in five cities during April, to be followed by a gigantic May Day rally in São Paulo, where Goulart, the CGT hoped, would decree the expropriation of all nongovernment companies that were distributing gasoline in Brazil.[13]

On March 24 Goulart lunched at Laranjeiras Palace in Rio with São Paulo Cardinal Carlos de Vasconcellos Mota and Dom Hélder Câmara (whose altercations with Cardinal Jaime Câmara had brought him a transfer to Pernambuco to become the archbishop of Olinda and Recife). Together with pictures of the two prelates with Goulart, the lunch was given publicity in the press and on television. Because Dom Carlos and Dom Hélder were reported to favor Goulart's reform program and because they held the top posts of the CNBB (National Conference of Brazilian Bishops), many readers concluded that the CNBB supported Goulart.[14]

Sobral, writing to Dom Hélder, let out "a cry of anguish" against "this publicity move" made against Jaime Câmara, who, Sobral pointed out, was promoting Rio's forthcoming "March of the Family to Defend God and Liberty." He wrote Dom Carlos: "Your Eminence and Archbishop Hélder Câmara make a point of demonstrating the best of relations with the president, who participated in a rally of the Communist Party. . . . Both of you should look at Cuba, whose Episcopate supported Fidel Castro at the outset."[15]

On March 24 Navy Minister Sílvio Mota rejected Goulart's recommendation that he rescind ten-day prison sentences recently imposed by Sílvio Mota on leaders of the Sailors' Association for indiscipline. Calling the navy minister "infantile," some of the sailors refused to report for imprisonment and, instead, organized a mutiny with the help of the CGT. It took place at the Guanabara Metalworkers' Union building in Rio and began on March 25.[16]

Attended by about a thousand sailors, together with representatives of Brizola and the CGT, it became tumultuous. The speeches demanded a revision of the navy's disciplinary regulations and the removal of the "subversive" navy minister. Goulart, before going to Rio Grande do Sul to relax during the last days of Holy Week, told Justice Minister Jurema that the government did not want to lose the support of the "more than 20,000 sailors" who were "in revolution" against the decision of Navy Minister Sílvio Mota.[17]

On March 26 Sílvio Mota sent a detachment of forty marines to arrest the rebels, who were railing, in the building, against "perverted minds" controlled by the Pentagon in Washington. But after Marine Commander Cândido Aragão had a friendly chat with some of the rebels, his detachment joined the mutiny. The navy minister dismissed Cândido Aragão and ordered his arrest, and he persuaded a general to send army troops to the scene; but government officials decided that a "military intervention" in a labor union should not be carried out.[18]

Goulart and *gabinete militar* head Argemiro Assis Brasil returned from the south early on Good Friday, March 27, and they participated in discussions that resulted in the CGT's Oswaldo Pacheco and Dante Pelacani being sent to the union building to persuade the mutineers to leave it. The sailors and marines agreed to do so upon receiving assurances that they would be granted amnesty and that sixty-nine-year-old Paulo Mário da Cunha Rodrigues, their choice to be the new navy minister, would replace Sílvio Mota.[19]

The sailors celebrated that evening in downtown Rio with "people's admirals" Pedro Paulo Suzano and Cândido Aragão, the latter having been returned to the command of the marines, thanks to the new navy minister. Saturday morning newspapers carried front-page photographs of the victorious sailors singing and shouting and carrying Aragão and Suzano on their shoulders, a rowdy Good Friday display that, according to Justice Minister Jurema, had the "worst possible repercussions."[20]

Columnist Carlos Castello Branco believed that what sent the balance of opinion against Goulart was "the disastrous decision to support the revolt of sailors seduced by labor union agents. . . . This error broke the morale of the government's supporters and shifted the mass of undecided individuals from one camp to another." Goulart was shocked to find the *Correio da Manhã* deciding to join most of the Rio press in opposing him.[21]

Army Chief of Staff Humberto Castello Branco, coordinator of an alliance to prevent a coup by Goulart, found that the settlement of the navy revolt had upset so many officers that a movement against Goulart seemed probable.[22] But, according to *O Estado de S. Paulo*, such a movement seemed unlikely to occur in the air force or the navy. Reflecting on what air force officer Haroldo Veloso called the "extreme Communist infiltration" in the air force "and especially [among] its sergeants," the São Paulo daily wrote: "We have no air force worthy of being called such," and it added that "what remains of the navy truly does not deserve to be described as a military corporation." The CGT announced that sailors affiliated with it had immobilized most of the fleet, and that the cruiser *Barroso*, which could still function, was under the control of CGT-affiliated sailors.[23]

Sobral, asked years later whether he had participated in a movement to overthrow Goulart, replied: "I was approached . . . by a military officer who said the armed forces were preparing a movement to put a stop to João Goulart and were planning to set up a governing junta. The junta would consist of three military officers and a civilian. I was to be the civilian. I replied to the military officer, my friend, that I had never conspired and was not going to conspire."[24]

Sobral felt, late in March 1964, that "Jango" Goulart was in a strong position "to take the country to a military dictatorship." "The hour," he told the *Tribuna da Imprensa*, "is not one of jurists but belongs to the military," and therefore the *Tribuna*, instead of seeking opinions of jurists, should turn to military leaders and ask them to make known the effects, among their troops, of the "incredible acts of the president and his new navy minister, who have applauded the mutiny of marines and sailors and have ruled against the acts of Sílvio Mota, punished for defending discipline and the hierarchy in the military."[25]

On March 30, while Goulart and his cabinet prepared to attend that evening's meeting of the Military Police Sergeants' Benevolent Association, *gabinete militar* chief Assis Brasil reiterated that the government could count on invincible military power. Hoping to have twenty thousand sergeants and corporals acclaiming "Jango" at the meeting, the presidential office provided transportation and arranged to have the widest possible television coverage.[26]

If the president wanted to pay to see his opponents' cards he could not have done better. The show was one long taunt at his foes and featured thunderous applause for the Sailors' Association president, Cabo (Corporal) José Anselmo dos Santos, leader of the recent sailors' mutiny. Although only about two thousand sergeants and corporals gathered, they and the lustily cheered notables, such as Marine Commander Cândido Aragão and Justice Minister Jurema, made it clear that their tumultuous victory march could not be slowed down. In the words of one speaker, the successful struggle was against the "narrow-minded mentality of those who make of military discipline an accursed whip to enslave the Brazilian people."[27]

Throughout the nation television screens delivered such messages and showed the president being pushed this way and that by a sea of "anti-imperialists." Like Cabo Anselmo, he received frenzied acclaim. Jostlings sometimes made it difficult for the tired president to carry on with his improvised address. But his words were strong, those of the chief of invincible troops vigorously denouncing minority groups that opposed the enlargement of popular conquests. "Who," Goulart asked, "are the ones trying to stir up trouble for the president in the name of discipline? They are the same ones who in 1961, under the name of false discipline, arrested dozens of officers and Brazilian sergeants."[28]

When three-star General Olímpio Mourão Filho, in Juiz de Fora, Minas Gerais, viewed the broadcast, he decided that plotting and planning should be replaced by action to prevent Brazil's fall into Communist hands, and he found most of the men in his small force agreeable to undertaking at once the apparently dangerous march against Goulart and the military might in Rio. For a general who had, during several years, openly advocated the overthrow of Goulart, he was in the unusual situation of commanding troops, and he could count on support in Belo Horizonte, where for a few days Governor Magalhães Pinto and two-star General Carlos Luís Guedes, commander of the state troops, had been preparing to rebel.[29]

Mourão's two thousand men (including some from the state troops) reached the border of Rio de Janeiro state on the afternoon of March 31, whereupon Mourão, disdainful of a careful pronouncement by Magalhães Pinto about the need to have reforms and a restoration of constitutional order, issued his own aggressive manifesto that spoke of "spurious organizations of political syndicalism, manipulated by enemies of Brazil, confessedly Communist" and "particularly audacious" because of "the support and stimulation" provided by Goulart. The government, Mourão asserted, allowed these organizations to appoint and dismiss cabinet ministers, generals, and high officials in order to destroy democratic institutions.[30]

In Rio, General Humberto Castello Branco felt that his work to coordinate a force to oppose the plans of Goulart was incomplete. During a telephone call he told General Carlos Luís Guedes, "You are being precipitous," and then he put his own group on Mourão's side, fearful that an isolated movement might be crushed, with disastrous results.[31]

From São Paulo, General Amaury Kruel, head of the Second Army, answered urgent telephone calls from his friend Goulart. He told the president that he would back him if he would "leave the people" who "surrounded" him. The president, however, kept repeating that he could not carry on without their support. At length, late on March 31, Kruel issued a manifesto that described the Second Army as marching to Rio against "the circle of Communism which compromises the authority of the government."[32]

Sobral Pinto was among the volunteers who swarmed to Guanabara Palace to be with Governor Lacerda, busy preparing the defense of the palace against an attack that some Goulart supporters were planning to have made by the marines of Admiral Cândido Aragão. Writing to Henrique Hargreaves on April 2 about the anxiety at Guanabara Palace in the first hours of April 1, Sobral reported on a message received there from General Castello Branco, who, in opposing the defense of the palace, said that martyrs were not what the cause needed.[33]

The defense went ahead anyway. Arms were passed out to civilians. With reports of an impending attack, people lay on the floor, following instructions given on a megaphone. Outside, in a light rain, many stretched on the ground, weapons in hand. Sobral told Hargreaves, "Although the streets outside were protectively blocked by trucks" and the palace contained many machine guns and lots of munitions, "the atmosphere was one of great worry."[34] Indeed, the guns of Aragão would likely have prevailed.

Marines, eagerly awaiting an order to attack, were disappointed. Goulart forbade it. He added, however: "The beast, Lacerda, is cornered and will surrender before daybreak."[35]

As Goulart knew, the outcome of the struggle depended on significant developments in the army. And in rapid succession they occurred after Kruel's position became known. The First Army's Sampaio Regiment, with orders to crush Mourão, joined Mourão and his men after retired Marshal Odílio Denys asked its commander, his friend, "Are you going to fight for the Communists?"[36] In the northeast, the general in charge of the Fourth Army came out against Goulart at dawn.

Goulart admitted that the game was over. Before leaving Rio for Brasília at 1:00 P.M. on April 1, he said to Jurema: "Our military plan inexplicably failed. I can count only on the Third Army [in the far south] and that is not enough."[37] In Brasília he issued a manifesto denouncing the plundering of the people by reactionary forces, and then he flew to Rio Grande do Sul. From there on April 4 he went to

Uruguay, where he was joined, weeks later, by the more resistance-minded Brizola.

In Rio on March 31, the CGT called a "general strike," which briefly tied up the local transportation, and marines on April 1 invaded *O Globo*, but presently the anti-Goulart forces were in control and Oswaldo Pacheco and Cândido Aragão were among those arrested. Mobs, incited by Rádio Nacional's last pro-Goulart words, invaded the Military Club on April 1 but were defeated in an action that killed two of the invaders.[38] Soon it was the anti-Communists who were doing the invading. *Última Hora* and the UNE headquarters suffered. Opponents of the coup filled up the embassy of Uruguay.

While people at Guanabara Palace were celebrating on the afternoon of April 1, Sobral spoke to Lacerda to ask of him, following the victory, "a noble attitude of generosity and moderation." Lacerda replied: "Please pray for me."[39]

In May 1964, after the victors had spent a month proclaiming the virtues of the coup, a poll was taken to find out reasons for Goulart's overthrow. Thirty-four percent of the respondents said he was giving Brazil to the Communists, 21 percent said he was going to close Congress and become a dictator, and 17 percent said he had undertaken popular measures that provoked foreign and national economic powers.[40] It may be that he was poorly advised on how greatly the fear of the "Red Peril" affected the army and the public. In any event, he had, in late March 1964, nowhere to turn in politics unless he were to retreat from his latest alliance with the CGT, plead with men he had denounced as reactionaries, desert and infuriate organized labor, and present what his political mentor, Vargas, might have called "a demonstration of pusillanimity."[41] He was in no mood for "a demonstration of pusillanimity" when, against the advice of Tancredo Neves and others, he threw down the gauntlet at the Sergeants' Association meeting of March 30.

Sobral, in his letter of April 2 to Hargreaves, wrote: "Once more we must say, with pious pride and with no less gratitude, that God is Brazilian. As in 1945 and 1955, now in 1964 an extremely serious political crisis was resolved with a minimum of bloodshed, of economic setbacks, or of harm to the legality that governs the juridical structure of the nation." After mentioning "the anxieties experienced here in Rio, so much greater than those experienced by you in Juiz de Fora," Sobral concluded: "Please accept this cry of jubilation. Minas Gerais shone brilliantly and saved the country!"[42]

PART II

Defending Men Punished by the New Regime (1964–1965)

1. Sobral Opposes the Institutional Act and Castello Branco's Election (April 1964)

Artur da Costa e Silva, an anti-Goulart general who had been holding a desk job, declared himself Chief of the Revolution because he headed the army hierarchy, having been the longest in active service, with four stars. Early in April 1964 he started a campaign to eradicate corruption and subversion from Brazil by means of arrests, and he gave orders to the interim president of Brazil, Chamber of Deputies head Ranieri Mazzilli, about the cabinet, whose new military ministers (including Costa e Silva) made up the "Revolutionary Command."

Sobral Pinto and Dario de Almeida Magalhães explained in the press that the constitution required Congress to select a new president and vice president within thirty days of the vacancy caused by Goulart's departure.[1] Among army officers and Rio anti-Goulart civilian groups the overwhelming favorite for president was studious General Humberto Castello Branco, a lifetime supporter of legality whose rigorous training of army officers, during his career, had brought him respect. Governor Lacerda, calling Costa e Silva a dictatorial usurper, helped promote the pro–Castello Branco movement.

However, Sobral Pinto, in a telephone call to Dario, pointed out that the constitution forbade the election of Castello Branco because he had been in active service, as army chief of staff, within three months of the coming election. Dario replied that on account of "the revolution of March 31" the constitutional clause need not prevail, and he ended the conversation abruptly after Sobral objected to his view.[2] Dario found support among jurists, such as former Justice Minister Vicente Ráo, who interpreted the constitution's ineligibility regulation as applicable only to popular elections.

At the request of Costa e Silva, constitutional lawyers Carlos Medeiros Silva and Francisco Campos joined a group that included Justice Minister Luís Antônio da Gama e Silva, a friend of Costa e Silva, in drawing up an Institutional Act that proclaimed the right of the revolutionary victors, who had "saved Brazil from Bolshevism," to modify the constitution.[3] According to the modifications in the Institutional Act, which the military ministers promulgated on April 9, no one was ineligible in the presidential election by Congress to be held on April 11. Persons who had made the revolution necessary were to have their political rights suspended for ten years in accordance with decrees to be issued within sixty days of the Institutional Act by the Revolutionary Command and, after the new administration took office on April 15, by the new president in accordance with recommendations of the National Security Council, which in large part consisted of the cabinet. The Institutional Act gave the executive branch control over federal budgets and the right to issue laws in cases where its proposals were not acted on by Congress within thirty days.

Sobral, writing to Castello Branco on April 9, objected to the Institutional Act. Writing about its suspension of tenure rights, he said: "No judge, professor, military officer, or public functionary will dare, under those circumstances, to disobey the government's chief executive." Referring to "the movement of March," Sobral called it the fulfillment of a legal right carried out in defense of the hierarchy and discipline in the military and undertaken to preserve the nation's "constitutional order," being destroyed by a president who had an alliance with a Communist Party that hoped to use the alliance to attain power. But, Sobral continued, the constitutional order was being destroyed by the Institutional Act and Castello Branco's improper candidacy for the presidency. "I appeal to you to decline your candidacy and have it go to one of your military colleagues."[4]

Immediately following the issuance of the Institutional Act, the Revolutionary Command decreed the *cassação* (suspension of political rights and cancellation of mandates) of over one hundred individuals, among them former Presidents Goulart and Quadros and forty federal legislators. The Revolutionary Command also transferred 122 military officers to the reserve.

On April 11, Castello was elected president with the help of Juscelino Kubitschek and members of the PSD, whose José Maria Alkmim was elected vice president. The president-elect telephoned Sobral to say that he had consulted jurists who found that his candidacy did not violate the constitution, whereupon Sobral explained that the constitution, in its prohibition, did not differentiate between popular and indirect elections.[5] Castello, given only a few days to select a cabinet, asked Sobral to recommend possibilities for the Justice Ministry. Sobral suggested Milton Campos, Dario de Almeida Magalhães, and Adroaldo Mesquita da Costa (who had served under President Dutra).[6]

Castello found Milton Campos uninterested in participating in a "revolutionary government." The illustrious lawyer, no favorite of those who considered him "too legalistic" for "revolutionary times," at length acquiesced after Castello said he was needed "to reimplant juridical order in Brazil."[7] However, Castello's appointment of General Costa e Silva to be war minister assured a strong position for "hard-liners," more interested in acting against men associated with recent regimes than in observing legal and constitutional principles. Politicians who had been expelled from office and jailed, such as Pernambuco Governor Miguel Arraes, and others who were threatened, such as Goiás Governor Mauro Borges Teixeira, turned for legal assistance to Sobral, who was determined to help them and innumerable leftists who appealed to him.[8]

Sobral's opposition to the Institutional Act promised to give him a rough time at the Instituto dos Advogados Brasileiros (IAB), whose presidency he was scheduled to assume on April 16. At a session of the Instituto on April 13, a large majority opposed Sobral when he criticized "the juridical monstrosity that attacks the most sacred rights of citizens and gives them no knowledge of the accusations or ability to defend themselves." After Celso Fontenelle's motion to have the IAB express no judgment was adopted, outgoing IAB President Celestino Basílio closed the discussion.[9]

Sobral, in his speech assuming the IAB presidency on April 16, called the overthrow of Goulart legitimate but stressed his opposition to the Institutional Act. Therefore, Basílio insisted on having the membership ratify Celso Fontenelle's "no judgment" motion passed on April 13.[10]

Brazilian President Humberto Castello Branco, in his brief inauguration address on April 15, called on the nation to "move ahead with assurance that the remedy for evil deeds by the extreme Left will not be the birth of a reactionary Right, but of the reforms that have become necessary." Supporters of Kubitschek applauded when Castello said he would turn over his office to his elected successor on January 31, 1966.

After the new president telephoned Sobral to get his opinion about the legal position of political prisoners, Sobral wrote to him: "Can you imagine the insecurity and terror caused by the Military Investigating Commissions in charge of examining those said to have practiced acts of administrative and political corruption or to have held Communist ideologies? Where can you find a law authorizing criminal or administrative proceedings against a civilian officeholder or professor for favoring a Communist ideology?" Sobral also recommended a relaxation of the new government's restriction of credit. The restriction, a part of the battle against inflation, was described by Sobral as "disturbing industry and commerce."[11]

Reports abroad said that Brazil had set up a dictatorship. War Minister Costa e Silva, replying on May 26, told the press that although a possible dictatorship "was in our hands, we preferred to have the support of the people" and therefore Brazil's government was "of the people, by the people, and for the people." Sobral, in a letter to Costa e Silva that appeared in the press early in June, told the war minister that he had shown "not the slightest notion of the meanings of dictatorship, popular backing, or representative government." He cited the war minister's assertion in *O Globo* that new *cassações* would be decreed in accordance with National Security Council recommendations, an assertion confirmed on May 31. Sobral also wrote that the people had not chosen the president of Brazil, and he added: "I cannot tolerate that ambitious politicians and retired military officers persuade respectable women to sign manifestoes calling for the removal of Supreme Court Justices Hermes Lima and Evandro Lins e Silva," Goulart appointees.[12]

"The declarations, interviews, and letters published in the press by Dr. Sobral Pinto" made it necessary, according to IAB members on June 11, to adopt a motion "to reiterate the Institute's statement of April 13, to the effect that the Institutional Act of April 9 and steps taken in accordance with it are not to be judged on account of its eminently historical character, and consequently the Institute does not subscribe to the personal declarations of its president, Dr. Sobral Pinto." Sobral complained that members had met in secret to prepare the proposed motion, which implied disrespect for his authority, and added that if it were adopted, it should be followed by a special meeting to vote for his removal from office. Instead of adopting the proposed motion, the members passed one saying that "clarifications" by Celestino Basílio and Sobral made it clear that the recent pronouncements of Sobral were "exclusively personal." The harmony between supporters and opponents of the Institutional Act, which the new motion sought to bring about, was seen by many members to be difficult to sustain for much longer.[13]

2. Defending Kubitschek (June 1964)

From the moment that victory came to the opponents of Goulart, the hard-liners, led by Costa e Silva, turned their fire on Kubitschek, the PSD presidential candidate who, they believed, represented everything their "revolution" was against. They filled the press with accounts of past electoral deals made on his behalf with the Brazilian Communist Party (PCB) and about his "fortune," said to have been acquired in improper ways. O Estado de S. Paulo, having accused him of not attending Senate sessions, called him Brazil's "most expensive senator," a politician who had secured his Senate seat, in a special election in Goiás in 1961, because he wanted the immunities that went with it.[1]

Old charges about Kubitschek's "illicit fortune" had surfaced in March 1964 when he had prepared to accept his presidential candidacy, and he had at that time asked Sobral to undertake a study of his financial assets so that they might have a "response to the accusations." His request and Sobral's reply accepting it were published in the press on May 14. Commenting on the exchange of letters, Rio's Jornal do Commercio (which had been taken over by the Chateaubriand chain) wrote that Kubitschek, in his letter "begging a favor" of Sobral, discussed a matter that was of little importance compared with his serious sins of having been responsible for "administrative chaos," hyperinflation, Communist infiltration, support for Goulart's career, and everything that the revolution was seeking to remove forever from Brazil.[2]

On May 25 Kubitschek issued a statement in which he argued that by fostering economic development and pan-Americanism, he had prevented the advance of the Communist subversion that "threatened the continent." He accused his detractors, fearful of a "massive vote" in his favor, of seeking to strike down a candidacy and "also the democratic regime itself." Costa e Silva told the press that Kubitschek's pronouncement, "because of its violent language and . . . defiance, appears to me to be much like the speech of Jango Goulart on March 30." Kubitschek, stunned, told the press that "the 'violent language' of my manifesto is much softer than the violent language with which I am assaulted daily."[3]

Sobral, in his letter of June 1 to Costa e Silva, wrote that the adversaries of Kubitschek were renewing their frustrated attempt of 1955 to remove the PSD candidate and that they and "those who are now in absolute power know" that "a free and honest election" would be won by the man who "made Brazil a nation of dynamic work, constructing Brasília, the Furnas and Três Marias hydroelectric projects," and highways all over Brazil, besides "giving Brazil its automobile industry."[4]

For the National Security Council, Costa e Silva drew up a petition calling for a ten-year suspension of Kubitschek's political rights and the cancellation of his mandate in the Senate. Asserting that the destiny of the revolution was at stake, he insisted on the need "to prevent future political maneuvers, already quite well planned, for interrupting the process of restoring moral and political principles." He added that "exemplary acts" of the revolution had been used to punish many secondary figures, and that no justification existed for ignoring "important political figures who were notoriously responsible for the deterioration of our governing system."[5]

Members of the Security Council were consulted individually by Castello Branco and the chief of the presidential *gabinete militar*, General Ernesto Geisel.[6] With reports reaching Kubitschek that a majority of the Council members felt that the revolution made his *cassação* logical, he went to Brasília on June 4 and delivered a dramatic speech in which he exclaimed: "They cancel much more than my political rights: they cancel the political rights of Brazil."[7]

Sobral, on June 5, sent a telegram to Justice Minister Milton Campos and confirmed his sentiments in a letter lest the telegraph system, "in the hands of the military dictatorship," not deliver it. "I cannot," the letter said, "conceive that a man of your character can remain in a government that carries out mean and wretched acts such as the suspension of the political rights, and the cancellation of the mandate, of Juscelino Kubitschek." In a telegram to Castello Branco, Sobral promised to tear up the certificate that made him a voter if the possibility of voting for presidential candidate Kubitschek were denied to the people. Sobral also sent a telegram to the government leader in the Chamber of Deputies, Pedro Aleixo, urging him to persuade Castello Branco to preserve the "untouchable candidacy" of Kubitschek.[8]

São Paulo Governor Ademar de Barros, PSP candidate for president, received a telegram in which Sobral asked him to use his influence to protect the survival of democracy by defending "your most serious competitor, Senator Kubitschek." A cable with a similar message was sent by Sobral to Lacerda, who was in Europe.[9]

When the National Security Council met on June 8, every member except Planning Minister Roberto Campos favored the recommendation of Costa e Silva.[10] The former president lost his political rights and mandate along with forty others, among them two governors and five other senators.

In Rio, where citizens in the streets collected signatures on pro-Kubitschek petitions, Sobral confirmed his vow to tear up his voting certificate. Kubitschek, also in Rio, declared that he was paying the price of having struggled for Brazil's economic independence and of having governed without hatreds. "The gale of insanities," he said, "will sweep away, one by one, all those who helped install this tyranny."[11]

At 11 P.M. that night, June 8, Sobral reached the apartment of Kubitschek, joining Augusto and Ernâni do Amaral Peixoto, Augusto Frederico Schmidt, Negrão de Lima, writer Josué Montello, and others. Kubitschek, giving Sobral an embrace, exclaimed, "Long live Sobral Pinto, the leader of Brazilian democracy." After the visitors applauded and sang the national anthem, Kubitschek and Sobral conferred in another room.[12]

Sobral could not decide whether to advise Kubitschek to leave Brazil or remain to fight for his rights. Writing him on June 9, he suggested departure because of risks, perhaps even physical ones, and because judges would not face up to the dangers they would encounter if they tried to support him. However, on June 10, Sobral altered his view and wrote him two letters. In one he apologized for having made a recommendation without considering that Kubitschek was no ordinary client but was a statesman whose cause was that of "an entire people." Sobral's conclusion, given in the other letter, urged him "to remain and carry out courageously, with your fellow citizens, the greatest struggle of your career, the noble and gigantic one, for the survival of representative democracy in Brazil." The dangers, Sobral wrote, were the price that Providence had placed upon him.[13] Kubitschek, however, departed for Europe a few days after his *cassação*.

The *cassação* of Kubitschek was praised by Gustavo Corção, who called the former president "the public man responsible for Brazil's greatest ills." While Lacerdistas celebrated the removal of the chief electoral opponent of their hero, Guanabara Justice Secretary Alcino Salazar pointed out that Kubitschek's association "with the past situation" did not allow him to "survive politically under the new conditions." In Portugal Lacerda called Kubitschek's *cassação* "an act of political courage" but expressed regret at losing the opportunity to defeat him in the ballot boxes.[14]

O Estado de Minas, a Chateaubriand chain daily, denounced Sobral for supporting Kubitschek, a man who "never raised his voice when Goulart took Brazil to Communism." It wrote that Sobral was afraid of assuming the responsibility of holding public office, and it mocked him for trying to give lessons in civic behavior to "so noble and splendidly spirited" a jurist as Milton Campos and for having "impertinently" told the justice minister to resign. "Let Sobral Pinto withdraw to the insignificance of his egocentrism and not try to prevent Brazil from recovering its morality. Let us put behind us a regime that raided public funds and betrayed democracy more vilely than has ever occurred in Brazil."[15]

Sobral, in his reply, denied being a coward "who appears only at night," and explained that his suggestion to Milton Campos had been made to prevent him from being held partly responsible for the "errors, evils, and outrageous assaults" carried out by the government.[16]

3. The Case of the Nine Chinese (April 1964–November 1965)

After Goulart became president, his administration followed up on understandings reached during his trip to Communist China (People's Republic of China). Arrangements were made for nine Chinese to make official visits to Brazil, and they arrived in Rio in three groups, each with a stated purpose: the promotion of cultural relations, the installation of expositions of Chinese products, and the establishment of an agency for promoting trade and buying cotton.[1] The nine Chinese, only two of whom spoke Portuguese, were befriended by the Sociedade Cultural Sino-Brasileira, whose president was Adão Pereira Nunes, a Rio medical doctor and popular congressman.[2]

On April 3, 1964, following the fall of Goulart, policemen of the

Guanabara DOPS (Departamento de Ordem Política e Social) invaded the apartments used by the Chinese. They arrested all nine, struck some of them, and seized their belongings, including their money.[3] After the Chinese were turned over to the army police, which held them at its First Battalion of Guards, an IPM (Military Police Investigation) sought to determine whether they had violated the national security law. It reported to the Second Auditoria (Judgeship) of the army's First Military Region.

To lawyers who came from abroad to help the Chinese, Sobral explained that they could not practice in Brazil and that, as he was convinced that the Chinese were innocent, he would defend them. He insisted on receiving no legal fee.[4]

According to Guanabara Security Secretary Gustavo Borges, the nine Chinese were Communist spies, intent on using "a Chinese process" to "exterminate" Lacerda, Castello Branco, and others. However, the evidence that was collected was less sensational and consisted of reports that the Chinese had burned papers just before their arrest and that their unburned things included books and other printed material favorable to Communism and a Communist revolution.[5]

A more devastating piece of evidence was made known to the public on May 8. It was a letter in Chinese that the DOPS was said to have found inside a flashlight in the glove compartment of an automobile used by the Chinese. Apparently written by "Comrade Cheng" in Berne, Switzerland, on March 20, 1963, to "Comrade Wang," one of the arrested nine, it said that an important part of the "subterranean work" was to "continue to maintain relations with the leaders of the true Communist Party of Brazil," a reference to the China-line party, which had broken with Luiz Carlos Prestes's Moscow-line PCB in 1961. "Comrade Cheng" told of having spoken in Brazil "about you to these personalities, who are important for the REVOLUTION" and "are willing to be guided by us." The letter gave the names of China-line party leaders João Amazonas, Lincoln Cordeiro Oest, and Maurício Grabois and went on to name "our other important connections, Sergeants Garcia Filho and Paulo Prestes" and Max da Costa Santos, a congressman who, the letter writer said, "supports us strongly."[6]

Sergeant Antônio Garcia Filho had been elected to Congress in 1962, and his inability to take his seat, because of a constitutional clause barring sergeants, had been a reason for an insurrection in Brasília led unsuccessfully by air force Sergeant Antônio Prestes de

Paula in September 1963. Comrade Cheng wrote Comrade Wang that "Paulo Prestes, a born leader, is our most important connection."[7]

Revelation of the letter was followed by a unanimous decision of the Second Auditoria of the First Military Region to decree preventive imprisonment for the nine Chinese and six Brazilians named in the letter.[8] Preventive imprisonment *(prisão preventiva)* decrees were supposed to make sure that suspected criminals would not evade judgments by disappearing, but five of the six Brazilians were already in hiding or outside the country. The sixth, Sergeant Antônio Prestes de Paula, was being held on account of other accusations, and he became another client of Sobral in "the case of the Chinese."

Adão Pereira Nunes and two other members of the Sociedade Cultural Sino-Brasileira, said to have met frequently and secretly with the Chinese, were added to the list of defendants. Raul Lins e Silva, brother of Evandro, defended Adão Pereira Nunes and Sergeant Garcia Filho; Oswaldo Mendonça defended former Congressman Max da Costa Santos; and Evaristo de Morais Filho defended the three leaders of the China-line party.[9]

Sobral, in one of his letters to Castello Branco, called the letter ascribed to Comrade Cheng an "obvious forgery." He maintained that the letter's pre-1956 Chinese orthography was unlikely to have been used in 1963 by an agent of Mao Zedong or Zhou En-lai, and he told *O Jornal* that the letter had been produced because the *autos* (the prosecution's evidence), to which he had gained access, showed absolutely no evidence of the guilt of his Chinese clients. He used his study of the *autos* to deny the charge of Colonel Gustavo Borges that the Chinese had been bribing Miguel Arraes, Sérgio Magalhães, and other politicians, and deny the "literally invented" story about a list of people whom the Chinese planned to put to death. He also rejected the colonel's "absurd" charge about how two hundred Chinese had been sent in gangs to carry out guerrilla activities in the state of Rio de Janeiro.[10]

In November 1964 the nine Chinese were separated into three groups, each group in different barracks, making it difficult for Sobral, especially because one group contained no client who spoke Portuguese. Augusto Frederico Schmidt, in his *O Globo* column, criticized this "imposition of difficulties on the heroic defense by Sobral Pinto." Sarcastically he wrote of how nine Chinese, most of whom spoke no Portuguese, were thought to be able "with 80,000 dollars and instruments of torture and one pistol" to "dominate" Brazil's "defenseless paradise." An editorial in *O Globo* and a column by the *Jornal do Brasil*'s Antônio Callado also gave support to Sobral in the case.[11]

The trial, starting on December 21 at the Permanent Council of Military Justice of the First Military Region's Second Auditoria, attracted a crowd that included representatives of *Pravda* of Moscow, *El Clarin* of Chile, and leftists belonging to the Appeals Court of Paris and to an International Lawyers Group formed to observe the case. The judgment was in the hands of Permanent Council President Arídio Brasil (a colonel in charge of Copacabana Fort), Judge Georgenor Acylino de Lima Torres, and three army captains. Unlike Lima Torres, the four military men had not studied law.[12]

In the presence of the notable lawyers defending the nine Chinese and nine Brazilians (eight of them absent), Prosecutor Rubem Pinheiro de Barros began his four-hour denouncement at 1:15 P.M., the first presentation in a session that lasted until 6:15 the next morning. He pointed out that the Chinese had not purchased one bale of cotton nor installed any exposition of products, and he denied that these matters had been the purpose of meetings with members of the Sociedade Cultural Sino-Brasileira. He presented exhibits that included "photographs of the Cuban revolution" found among the possessions of the Chinese, and he read from the letter of "Comrade Cheng," calling attention to its words "Victory will be ours." He asked for prison sentences of twenty-three years: fifteen for subversion and eight for espionage. He excluded Sergeant Antônio Prestes de Paula because the name "Paulo Prestes," in the letter from Berne, could not be shown to be a clear reference to him.[13]

Max da Costa Santos's lawyer said the mention of the former congressman in the letter constituted no basis for his conviction, and Evaristo de Morais Filho, lawyer of Amazonas, Grabois, and Oest, pointed out that the "illegitimate letter" had been supplied by the DOPS and not by the "honorable military." Raul Lins e Silva asked the judges to "open the five suitcases" said to contain documents proving the guilt of the defendants; they contained, he said, nothing but books.[14]

Concluding the presentation for the defense, Sobral spoke for three and one-half hours. He called the contents of the suitcases just as meaningless as the "23 pieces of evidence," which he described as mere paper clippings and false material furnished by the police of Colonel Gustavo Borges, "an authority who no longer deserves to be considered credible." As for warnings against the Chinese, originating in Formosa ("the so-called Nationalist government of China"), Sobral praised Brazil's Foreign Ministry for having rejected Formosa's "improper intervention."

Emotional and tired, Sobral told the judges that a guilty verdict depended on the disclosure of specific acts and facts that were clear violations of laws about national security and did not depend on "vague and generalized aberrations."[15]

Sobral was still present at 6:15 A.M. when the five judges, after conferring in secret session for three hours, cleared the defendants of the espionage charge but, in a 4 to 1 decision, sentenced the nine Chinese and three members of the Sociedade Cultural Sino-Brasileira to ten years of imprisonment for subversion. The others, Brazilians named in the letter from Berne, were exonerated.[16]

Raul Lins e Silva vowed to appeal on behalf of the three members of the Sociedade Cultural Sino-Brasileira. Sobral, who learned that the single vote against punishments had been given by Auditor (Judge) Lima Torres, the lone civilian and legal expert, expressed confidence in winning an appeal at the Superior Military Tribunal (STM). The government of Communist China declared: "It is time for the Brazilian authorities to get rid of the evil influence of United States imperialism and of the clique of Chiang Kai-shek" of Formosa.[17]

For two months the public remained confused about the fate of the nine Chinese. After Justice Minister Milton Campos expressed himself in favor of pardons by Castello Branco to be followed by immediate expulsions, Sobral, eager to win an appeal, sent the president a telegram rejecting the idea of Milton Campos: "The innocence of the Chinese is so clear that Auditor Lima Torres wanted to absolve them. . . . Innocent people do not get pardoned or expelled."[18]

Milton Campos came around to believing that expulsion could be decreed without a pardon, a view contested by experts, including Sobral, who found expulsion illegal with the ten-year sentences unfulfilled and not overturned. But on February 27 Castello Branco signed the expulsion decree, described by Milton Campos as an act for the defense of public order and the national sovereignty. The STM, in a pronouncement on April 7, handled the illegality question by agreeing that the government had the duty to deport "undesirable foreigners." The Chinese, eager to return home, accepted expulsion.[19]

At Galeão Airport, where Sobral embraced each of his departing clients, students yelled "go home" at them and displayed placards condemning "Peking gold" and "Moscow gold." In their homeland, the returning Chinese were received as heroes, and the government there denounced Brazil's authorities and spoke of Sobral with gratitude and respect.[20]

From China, his recent clients kept in touch with Sobral, sometimes sending gifts. In November 1965 he had to advise them that the STM decided not to rule on their guilt or the return of their money, held in the Bank of Brazil, as long as they remained out of the country.[21]

4.   Lawyer for Miguel Arraes (1964–1965)

Miguel Arraes was deposed from the governorship of Pernambuco on April 1, 1964, and imprisoned at once. He spent nine months at the prison camp on Fernando de Noronha Island, in the company of former Governor Seixas Dória and labor union leaders, and was held later in prisons in Recife.[1]

On May 21 the Council of Justice of the army's Seventh Military Region sentenced Arraes and others to preventive imprisonment in view of information about how "foreign inspiration" had led them to try to alter the nation's political and social order. The Superior Military Tribunal, on March 17, 1965, rejected a habeas corpus petition submitted on Arraes's behalf by Sobral and a Recife lawyer, and so the lawyers turned to the Supreme Court. They argued that the crimes attributed to Arraes were matters of the exclusive competence of civilian justice in Pernambuco and that the duration of *prisão preventiva* was limited to sixty days.[2]

Similar arguments had persuaded the Supreme Court to order the freedom of Seixas Dória. It seemed so likely to order also the release of Arraes that the military late in March 1965 transferred him to Fort Santa Cruz, not far from Rio de Janeiro, to be questioned by Colonel Ferdinando de Carvalho, who headed an IPM investigating Communism in Brazil. Military officers explained that, regardless of a habeas corpus ruling favoring Arraes, he could be kept imprisoned by means of a series of new *prisões preventivas* because of indictments for crimes being uncovered by eight IPMs, including those investigating the PCB, UNE, CGT, and ISEB (the left-leaning Institute of Advanced Brazilian Studies).[3]

By a unanimous decision on April 19 the Supreme Court approved the habeas corpus petition, but General Edson de Figueiredo, interim commander of the First Army, telegraphed Chief Justice Álvaro Ribeiro da Costa to say that Arraes would continue under arrest because he had to testify at an IPM, headed by Colonel Gérson de Pina, investigating the ISEB. Ribeiro da Costa replied with a telegram telling the general he was in rebellion against the sovereignty of the judicial power, and then he consulted Castello Branco. At Laranjeiras Palace in Rio, Castello ordered Edson de Figueiredo and Interim War Minister Décio Escobar to comply with the Supreme Court's decision, and Arraes, much to his surprise, was released on April 22. Sobral, instead of sending his telegram asking Ribeiro da Costa to order the imprisonment of Edson de Figueiredo, sent one to congratulate the chief justice on the courage he had shown, and he sent another one to Castello applauding his decision.[4]

Military officers were furious at Castello Branco and spoke of the chief justice's "sneer for the armed forces" and "contempt for the Revolution." Congressman-Colonel José Costa Cavalcanti declared in Congress, "the Revolution is dead." Lacerda called the liberation of Arraes a demagogic act by criminals "who have turned themselves into judges," and Corção wrote in his column about the "enthusiasm" of some Supreme Court justices for the "Cubanization of Brazil."[5]

Although Arraes had never been associated with ISEB, he reported, as ordered, to Gérson de Pina's IPM on the morning of April 26. There he and Sobral were told by Prosecutor Rubem Pinheiro de Barros that he was being heard not as a witness but as a person indicted for crimes, and he was put in isolation. Threats of his arrest led Sobral to use the lunch break to send telegrams to Castello Branco and Ribeiro da Costa, and, finally, late in the afternoon, Arraes was released.[6]

Lieutenant Colonel Osnelli Martinelli, who prided himself on being "the toughest of the hard-liners," ordered Arraes to report on May 10 to his IPM. It was investigating the "Groups of Eleven Companions," which Brizola had organized aggressively in November 1963 to "free Brazil from international despoilment." Arraes, told by Martinelli that he was testifying as an indicted person, objected, whereupon he was conducted by guards from the IPM, which met at the headquarters of a pension institute, to the barracks of the army police. A captain there, confirming that Arraes was a prisoner under the orders of Colonel Martinelli, told reporters that the former governor had been cited in three IPMs and had had relations with Communists and the "subversive Brizolistas."[7]

Sobral, in a telegram, asked Chief Justice Ribeiro da Costa to get in touch with the commander of the First Army or Castello Branco. Thus a new intervention by Castello, an order to General Edson de Figueiredo, resulted in the liberation of Arraes at 7:00 P.M.[8]

However, Justice Minister Milton Campos announced his opposition to the position taken by the Supreme Court and declared that Arraes should be held for "crimes against the national security." And hard-liners were pleased also to receive reports that Castello was considering asking Congress to enact legislation to make it possible to arrest indicted persons who were at liberty because of habeas corpus decrees. Arraes, deciding not to comply with any further IPM summonses, disappeared.[9]

The police, searching for Arraes, said they had learned that he had recently been in touch with an undesirable person, a new criminal act. In the meantime, Sobral, in touch with two of Arraes's uncles, was seeking to persuade the cautious Chilean ambassador to receive his client as an exile. While doing this, Sobral received an order to appear at the IPM investigation of ISEB. Refusing to do so, he told Gérson de Pina that he was not involved in the matter and did not recognize the colonel's authority to hear him.[10]

The Chilean ambassador finally decided that Arraes was truly in risk of becoming a political prisoner. But the police had seen Sobral entering the Chilean embassy and had positioned men nearby in case Arraes tried to reach it. The former governor chose, instead, to go to the embassy of Algeria, which, unlike Chile, had no understandings with Brazil that regulated the acceptance of exiles and the exchange of information about them.[11]

On May 20, three days before entering the Algerian embassy, Arraes issued a statement that was a sensation. He would not, he declared, turn himself over to "arbitrary imprisonments" or testify further at IPMs, whose purpose was not to find out the truth. He accused Castello Branco of proposing legislation to legitimize his imprisonment in order to placate "military groups of radical tendency," and he accused the officers of the IPMs of wanting to "create conditions indispensable for a new wave of repression, the postponement of elections, and the installment of an arbitrary regime even more formidable than the present one."[12]

Military authorities described the "subversive manifesto" as a call for a counterrevolutionary movement, and hard-liners blamed it on the antirevolutionary attitude of the Supreme Court. The Justice Ministry ruled that a new imprisonment of Arraes would be legal. But Arraes could not be found before he reached the Algerian embassy, and, soon after he arrived there, Castello Branco and Foreign Minister Vasco Leitão da Cunha decided on a safe-conduct that would allow him to depart from Brazil. This news, released by the Foreign Ministry on May 25, disappointed members of the military who wanted Arraes to be treated like Admiral Cândido Aragão, who was confined to the Uruguayan embassy because he could not get a safe-conduct.[13]

On June 16 the former governor and his wife departed for Algeria.

5. Sobral's Clashes with Gérson de Pina and Costa e Silva (mid-1965)

Military officers believed that Sobral might have written "the subversive manifesto" of Arraes, and they felt certain that he had distributed copies. To obtain information, Gérson de Pina sent an army captain to Sobral's office with an order for Sobral's typist to report to his IPM and answer questions. After Sobral forbade her to comply, an assistant of Gérson de Pina spoke about Sobral's probable arrest.[1]

According to the *Diário de Notícias* of May 21, secret agents were searching for Sobral in order to arrest him but could not find him. Sobral, in a telegram to the newspaper, said that his whereabouts were no secret and that to call Arraes's explanation of his conduct a "subversive manifesto" was a demonstration of political passion or ignorance. Replying to a Lacerdista state legislator who had denounced him for distributing the "manifesto," he said that, as Arraes's lawyer, he had distributed copies of "the document composed and signed" by the former governor. "It is ridiculous," he added, "to try to involve me or Arraes in criminal acts of subversion."[2]

Alceu Amoroso Lima, upon learning from a Rádio Globo broadcast on May 20 that Sobral might be imprisoned, prayed that his friend would continue at liberty. Writing to a daughter about the IPM chiefs, he said: "Sobral is really the only person—I repeat, the only person—who confronts them with his head held high and without mincing words."[3]

Congressman Adauto Lúcio Cardoso, learning of threats to imprison Sobral, spoke to Castello Branco on May 21 and received a guarantee that he would remain free. In addition to this news, given him by Adauto, Sobral received telephone messages from men close to Lacerda, informing him that the governor would oppose his arrest.[4]

Eraldo Gueiros Leite, *procurador geral da justiça militar*, suggested that Sobral, instead of being imprisoned, should be reprimanded by the Ordem dos Advogados (OAB) for infractions against the Code of Ethics of Lawyers. Some of the IPM colonels therefore decided to complain to the OAB about Sobral's behavior.[5] At the same time, policemen of the Guanabara DOPS arrested book publisher Ênio Silveira for being a possible contributor to the "manifesto" of Arraes and for having given him shelter before he reached the Algerian embassy. Heleno Fragoso, the book publisher's lawyer, submitted a habeas corpus petition to the STM saying that the case lay outside the realm of military justice.[6]

Sobral added to the controversy by giving, in Belo Horizonte on May 28, a lecture at the law school of the University of Minas Gerais. The audience of about four hundred students was joined by representatives of the army, the federal government's year-old National Information Service (SNI), and the Department of Social Vigilance of Minas Gerais.[7]

During his two-hour lecture, Sobral described the Institutional Act as "entirely foreign to the nation's constituted order" and as having "liquidated the sovereignty of Congress by giving legislative power to a president of the republic who was not elected by the people." What he was doing, he said, was assuming risks on behalf of a regime of law while politicians merely accepted a regime of force, evident at the IPMs. After giving his reasons for refusing to obey the order of Gérson de Pina to appear at the IPM about the ISEB, he said that Ênio Silveira, who may have had relations with the ISEB, had had nothing to do with the "explanation" signed by Arraes. The audience applauded Sobral when he declared: "In Brazil at the present time no one respects a person who defends justice."[8]

The Chateaubriand chain's *O Jornal* criticized much of what Sobral said in his lecture and referred to his "position favorable to subversion." According to the *Jornal do Brasil*, Sobral was "under observation" by hard-line military officers because of reports that he had called the IPM heads "uniformed clowns" in his lecture and had said that "Brazil is being governed by gangsters, liars, and corrupt people but will be liberated soon." Sobral told directors of the *Jornal do Bra-*

sil that these remarks, never made by him, had been reported to the First Army by its observer.[9]

Colonel Gérson de Pina sent First Army Commander Otacílio Terra Ururaí a message asking him to take steps against Sobral for his lecture, with its attacks against the IPM heads and "the army in general." "If things continue as they are," the colonel wrote, "the Revolution will witness a return to corrupt and subversive activities."[10]

After Gérson de Pina ordered law students in Belo Horizonte to appear at his IPM and report about Sobral's lecture, Sobral asked a lawyer who had attended the lecture to furnish a statement denying false reports about what he had said. Then the colonel, in *O Globo*, asserted that Sobral seemed to be "suffering from an obsession," believing that he was being persecuted, whereupon Sobral wrote to Roberto Marinho to say that if Gérson de Pina were practicing his profession, which was medicine, he would recognize that the one with an obsession was himself, the author of witch hunts. Sobral's letter, published in *O Globo*, was read aloud in the São Paulo state legislature by Conceição da Costa Neves.[11]

Learning that Adauto Lúcio Cardoso had assumed the leadership of the government's Bloco Parlamentar Renovador, Sobral told his friend, "You are becoming a backer of those who are implanting a regime with a single power: the executive."[12] The Bloco had done much to put a *udenista* in the presidency of the Chamber of Deputies, in place of Mazzilli, using what Sobral called improper pressure by Castello Branco.[13] And, with the approach of the October 1965 elections, it further discredited itself in Sobral's opinion by helping enact legislation that was supposed to rid the contests of candidates who were corrupt or subversive, and that was used to eliminate members of past administrations.[14] The coming elections were limited to gubernatorial races because already, in July 1964, Congress had postponed the presidential election until 1966.

Although hard-liners found some satisfaction in the "ineligibilities law," they constantly called for setting aside direct elections. When Sobral spoke in a televised interview, on the *Pinga Fogo* program in São Paulo on July 17, he denounced the law and the advocates of indirect elections. Speaking also about the IPMS, he called the application of "IPMs in the civilian sector an abuse, a despotism, an arrogance of military authority. They were instituted to investigate military crimes."[15]

An enormous headline in the *Última Hora* of São Paulo declared

"Costa e Silva against Sobral Pinto." In the paragraphs that followed, the war minister was quoted as answering a reporter's question about Sobral's television interview by saying, "People like Sobral Pinto and Conceição da Costa Neves do not deserve to be given any attention. Now if it were a jurist of the caliber of Vicente Ráo, a reply would be proper."[16]

Sobral, interrogated by *Última Hora* reporters in his São Paulo hotel room, wrote a note for them: "It is hard to believe that General Costa e Silva was as vulgar and rude as stated in your newspaper." From Rio, Sobral sent a telegram to Costa e Silva giving him seventy-two hours in which to confirm or deny the "arrogant, insolent, and scurrilous" remarks, reported as having been made by him. In a letter to *Última Hora*, predicting that the minister would refuse to answer the telegram, Sobral said, "He is too conceited to act in a manner adopted by people who are well bred."[17] Sobral's prediction was correct.

6.   Lawyer for Mauro Borges (1964)

The case of Mauro Borges Teixeira, governor of Goiás, differed from those of Miguel Arraes and Seixas Dória, whose overthrows coincided with the fall of Goulart. Mauro Borges, who had pushed for land redistribution in his state, denounced Goulart's agrarian reform program in mid-March 1964, calling it demagogic, and on March 31 he gave support to the movement that overthrew Goulart.

But Mauro Borges had a far-leftist reputation gained especially from his active role in the Frente de Libertação Nacional, which was formed in October 1961, with Brizola as president and Mauro Borges as secretary general. His state administration contained radical leftists, some of whom were *cassados*. He refused to agree to a proposal that called for him to "cooperate with the revolution of March 31" by dismissing the state cabinet.[1]

In May 1964, when an IPM began investigating the Goiás government, Sobral wrote President Castello Branco about "the political-military plot against the mandate of Governor Mauro Borges." He blamed the plot on those who hated the governor and on *udenistas* who wanted Mauro Borges, a PSD member, to be replaced by a UDN figure, a change that could not, he said, be achieved by the ballot boxes. "Those in power today never cease talking about democracy but they wish to replace the vote of the people with the power of machine guns and bayonets. . . . What is happening in Goiás and everywhere in Brazil is truly sinister."[2]

Retired General Riograndino Kruel, closer to Castello Branco than his brother Amaury Kruel, became head of the Federal Department of Public Security and, in September 1964, was appointed by General Hugo Panasco Alvim, supervisor of IPMS, to take over the IPM investigating subversion in Goiás. Riograndino, regarded by Mauro Borges as his enemy on account of a past land development incident in Goiás, interrogated the governor with especial attention to "subversive propaganda" in the Goiás *Diário Oficial,* where the word "gorillas" had been used to describe adversaries of Brizola and the governor.[3]

Riograndino Kruel, after meeting with Castello Branco on November 13, 1964, declared that Mauro Borges, accused of subversion, corruption, and espionage, would be imprisoned by the military justice system without regard for the state legislature.[4] Justice Minister Milton Campos called Mauro Borges "a constant creator of unrest," and Congressman-Colonel Costa Cavalcanti listed sins of the governor: the close relations of his administration with subversive guerrilla groups and with agents of international Communism, and the use of the state's *Diário Oficial* for subversive propaganda. Senator Pedro Ludovico Teixeira, the seventy-four-year-old father of Mauro Borges and the strongman of Goiás since 1930, infuriated the military with a speech that ridiculed the charges and told of torture by the army's Tenth Infantry Battalion, seeking to obtain confessions.[5]

Sobral Pinto and José Crispim Borges, the Goiás justice secretary, rushed to the Supreme Court on November 13 with a habeas corpus petition that maintained that the military justice system lacked the authority to imprison the governor. On the next day, Antônio Gonçalves de Oliveira, *relator* of the case, issued a provisional ruling to protect Mauro Borges until the court rendered its decision, and he sent a restraining order to the *auditoria* of the Fourth Army and to the Superior Military Tribunal (STM).[6]

The crisis came to a head at this time on account of the theft of rifles and munitions from the army's depot in Anápolis, Goiás. While Mauro Borges blamed the theft on people who sought to disparage his government, Castello and key cabinet ministers met and decided to send troops from Brasília to help local army troops act "rapidly and decisively" to maintain order and prevent "resistance by the governor." In Goiânia, the state capital, Mauro Borges called on his police force to defend the governor's palace. It was joined by volunteers and was cheered in public demonstrations, but it was short of munitions.[7]

After the federal government used planes to "discover centers of resistance," Sobral and José Crispim Borges told Supreme Court Minister Gonçalves de Oliveira that his restraining order was being disrespected. The federals, they complained, had sent army and air force contingents to occupy Goiânia and Anápolis, had immobilized state planes and paralyzed civil aviation in Goiás, and were making flights over the governor's palace and cities, bringing on public panic.[8]

While the decision of the full Supreme Court was awaited, Sobral said that "the overthrow of a governor by a military *auditoria* handling the first step in a legal action" would be "a monstrosity." Costa Cavalcanti added to his list of sins of Mauro Borges: the governor had been associated with Brizola, Darcy Ribeiro, UNE President Aldo Arantes, and the Communist Party state leader, and had sent a representative to the inauguration of Governor Miguel Arraes. Castello Branco asserted that he could count on the fingers of his hand—his "left hand"—the provocative acts of Mauro Borges but that it was up to the Supreme Court (STF) to handle the matter.[9]

Eight STF judges, in a unanimous decision on November 23, upheld the earlier restraining order of *relator* Gonçalves de Oliveira. Ribeiro da Costa, the nonvoting STF president, praised the brilliance of the *relator's* study of the case, and Victor Nunes Leal told the press that he voted as he did "in order to end, once and for all, the absurdity of the military hegemony over all branches of Brazilian justice."[10]

According to the decision, Mauro Borges, as a governor, could not be tried by any justice system, civil or military, without the previous consent of the state legislature in an impeachment trial, and, in the case of his impeachment, the appropriate civilian court was to be used for a judicial trial. Despite the *cassações* of three Goiás assemblymen in May, the governor had the backing of twenty-three of the thirty-nine members of the legislature.[11]

Castello Branco followed the STF decision by issuing a strong note about "the plan of the governor of Goiás to transform his state into a permanent focal point of agitation." In a reference to the movement of April 1, he said: "One of the most fruitful events of the history of the republic will not be defeated by those who want to falsify the law and, in doing so, bring about the destruction of the national revolutionary movement."[12]

The president agreed with his advisers that the only solution was federal intervention in Goiás for "up to sixty days," and after he signed the decree, worded by Milton Campos, he named as interventor Colonel Carlos de Meira Matos, assistant head of the presidential *gabinete militar.* The battle in Congress, whose approval was needed, was directed by Castello Branco, and, although majorities of the PSD and PTB opposed intervention, the PSD supplied so many votes in its favor, enough to obtain approval, that PSD President Ernâni do Amaral Peixoto regarded the occasion as the start of a serious division in his party.[13]

Interventor Meira Matos reached Goiânia on November 30 and replaced hundreds of Mauro Borges's appointees, including the state cabinet. On behalf of two of the dismissed cabinet members who were threatened with imprisonment, Sobral submitted habeas corpus petitions to the STM, and later, at the suggestion of Justice Hermes Lima, he turned to the Supreme Court instead. He also prepared to use, if necessary, the state judiciary, which he said was not under intervention, to assure the return of Mauro Borges after sixty days.[14]

A manifesto issued by Mauro Borges on December 7 denounced "pressures and threats" against his supporters in Congress and the state legislature, and he said that in September he had complained to Castello Branco about the torturing of prisoners in July and August by the head of the IPM and the commander of the army's Tenth Infantry Battalion. He had, he added, called off the defense of the governor's palace when he had learned of the intervention, "an unjust but legal step."[15]

The end of the crisis required more than the intervention. For weeks Castello Branco, Meira Matos, and General Golberi do Couto e Silva, head of the National Information Service (SNI), negotiated with PSD leaders in search of a formula that would place a nonpolitical figure in the governorship before the intervention expired. While Meira Matos held discussions with Iris Resende, head of the Goiás state legislature, Senator Pedro Ludovico Teixeira spoke of "contracting the professional services of Sobral Pinto to give advice to the PSD members of the state legislature."[16]

Sobral, writing to Iris Resende on December 20, called for vigor in resisting efforts of the foes of constitutional order to force the state legislature to declare a vacancy without abiding by regulations governing the removal of a chief executive. The state assembly, according to Sobral, had but one duty in the matter, that of ruling on the IPM material. "Resistance, pacific and virile . . . , will be the bugle call, heard in all corners of Brazil, inspiring everyone to defend public liberties, among them the ability to choose freely their governors and representatives. . . . With this objective I am thinking of raising once more, as in 1955, the banner of legality." This appeal, however, was given little, if any, consideration when Iris Resende, Meira Matos, and Golberi do Couto e Silva sought to reach an agreement on a reason, acceptable to PSD state assemblymen, to be used by the state legislature for declaring Mauro Borges *impedido* (unable to govern).[17]

Early in January 1965 the gubernatorial candidacy of sixty-seven-year-old army Marshal Emílio Rodrigues Ribas Júnior was launched at the suggestion of Castello Branco. The marshal, like Castello, had participated in the Brazilian Expeditionary Force in Italy in World War II, and the acceptance of his name by interested parties was followed by arrangements that put the IPM findings in the hands of the state legislature and the vice governorship in the hands of the PSD. The formalities were completed on January 7 when the Goiás legislature voted to file away the IPM findings and place the marshal in the governorship, which it declared vacant due to "a state of necessity." On January 19 Castello signed a decree ending federal intervention in Goiás.[18]

Early in February, Sobral wrote *O Globo* to put to rest rumors that Mauro Borges had paid him 50 million cruzeiros as a fee. "I received only 500,000 cruzeiros [$300 U.S.] in accordance with my rule not to ask clients to make payments that might be harmful to their personal finances."[19]

7.   José Aparecido's Legal Battle against His *Cassação* (May 1964)

José Aparecido de Oliveira, a popular journalist in Minas Gerais, served in the presidential campaign and administration of Jânio Quadros, was elected in 1962 to Congress on the UDN ticket, and was, in 1963 and early 1964, in the state cabinet of Minas Governor Magalhães Pinto. In Congress he was active in the Nationalist Parliamentary Front. His resignation from the Minas cabinet in the first weeks of March 1964 followed an accusation by General Carlos Luís Guedes, who called him subversive for giving support to the "basic reforms" being advocated by President Goulart.[1]

José Aparecido's *cassação* on April 10 by the anti-Goulart victors was followed by protests by admirers of the thirty-four-year-old congressman and journalist. It was followed also by an invasion by the army police on April 15 of the Belo Horizonte home of José Aparecido and his mother, who were not there at the time. Locked doors and drawers were forced open. Among the things taken was the former congressman's correspondence, including a copy of his letter of 1962 to Jânio Quadros advising that the unrest in Brazil made the moment a good one for his return from Europe. The invaders, seeking to prove subversion, made off with Havana cigars and a miniature of the *Sputnik* that the USSR had sent into orbit, a gift made by astronaut Yuri Gagarin during his visit to Brazil. The miniature, if a cord on it was pulled, would play the music of "The Internationale."[2]

Of all the *cassados*, José Aparecido was alone in taking legal steps against the loss of his mandate and the suspension of his political rights. Friends, including his cousin Geraldo Carneiro, put him in touch with Sobral Pinto.[3]

When Sobral said he was not in accord with José Aparecido's political views, José Aparecido replied: "I did not come here to discuss my views and I do not agree with all of yours." "Your reply," Sobral said, "is one that I like; it reveals character." When José Aparecido explained that friends were urging him to leave Brazil to avoid becoming the victim of violence, Sobral said: "Absolutely not. You are not to leave. You must make a defense."[4]

The defense, a long document signed by Sobral on May 11, 1964, and addressed to a Rio court, opened with a reminder that the Brazilian Civil Code required that defendants be advised of accusations and be given the opportunity to defend themselves. It denied that the petitioner, a believer in reforms, had ever collaborated with movements carried out to disturb social peace, and it cited José Aparecido's hostility to Communism, expressed in a publication in September 1962.[5]

In denying General Guedes's charge that things taken from José Aparecido's home provided evidence of his subversion, Sobral explained that miniature *Sputniks* had been passed out to many public figures during Gagarin's "courtesy visit" to Brazil, and Sobral argued also that the destructive break-in and seizures were illegal acts for which the petitioner should receive compensation. José Aparecido, Sobral pointed out, had never been associated with the CGT or the Frente de Mobilização Popular, and he had, on leaving the Minas government, received statements of praise from Magalhães Pinto and fifty-four state legislators.

Sobral's petition quoted from Castello Branco's inaugural address calling for the nation to move ahead "with assurance that the remedy for evil deeds by the extreme Left will not be the birth of a reactionary Right but of the reforms that have become necessary." In conclusion, it asked that the *procurador geral* of the republic and War Minister Costa e Silva, a signer of the *cassação* of José Aparecido, be advised of the petition so that steps could be taken to assure the petitioner of his rights as expressed in Brazil's Civil Code and as expressed in the United Nations' Universal Declaration of Human Rights.[6]

Costa e Silva and his supporters would not agree to the reversal of any of the *cassação* decrees.

However, José Aparecido's experience in working with Sobral, along with his knowledge of Sobral's other activities, led him to declare later that Sobral was "the only Brazilian with moral authority. . . . Sobral insisted on a moral regency for Brazil. Never has Brazil had a man with so great a moral authority."[7]

8.   Gustavo Borges Denounces SUPRA and Pinheiro Neto (1964–1965)

Another young client of Sobral from Minas was João Pinheiro Neto, member of a family important in the state's history. As Goulart's thirty-three-year-old labor minister in 1962, he had attacked Brazil's monetary policy and criticized men he considered responsible for "maintaining Brazil subordinate" to the program of the International Monetary Fund. In July 1963 he had become head of SUPRA, the federal agency for promoting agrarian reform.[1]

On April 10, 1964, he was *cassado* and on the 15th he was arrested following a *prisão preventiva* decree. Early in June Sobral presented to Lima Torres, *auditor* of the First Military Region, a petition in which João Pinheiro Neto asserted that the charges of subversion, being formulated in an IPM, were "nothing more than vengeance by political victors."

A request was made for the transfer of Pinheiro Neto from Fort Santa Cruz, in Rio de Janeiro state, to a prison in Guanabara, closer to the tribunal that would judge him and more easily reached by his family. According to *Última Hora*, the request was made to facilitate visits by Sobral, "who is in precarious health and is over 70 years old."[2] According to a general who overruled Lima Torres's favorable response to the request, it would be a mistake to move Pinheiro Neto to a prison in Guanabara because throngs of his supporters there would provoke intense agitation. In any event, the time restriction on the *prisão preventiva* was observed and Pinheiro Neto was freed in June.[3]

Learning that his client wished to have his legal staff include retired Supreme Court Justices Nelson Hungria and Orozimbo Nonato, Sobral said he would welcome their collaboration. However, the work of combating the arguments developed in the IPM about SUPRA was done by Pinheiro Neto and Sobral. When Sobral received the first of three 200,000-cruzeiro checks he hesitated to accept it from his friendly client, who was without employment. But Pinheiro Neto called attention to all the cases that Sobral handled without receiving fees and added that his own financial situation would allow him to pay his lawyer without strain.[4]

Sobral studied a *defesa prévia* (first brief) written by Pinheiro Neto and agreed to sign it with several alterations. He eliminated the unfavorable reference to the Marchas da Família led in March 1964 by women in São Paulo and elsewhere. "My idea about this movement differs from yours and I cannot sign something with which I do not agree."[5]

The *razões finais*, presented by Sobral, said that the *autos* contained no indications, let alone proofs, that Pinheiro Neto, as director of SUPRA, had employed violence as an instrument of subversion. They rejected the claim of Colonel Gustavo Borges that Pinheiro Neto had, between July 1963 and March 31, 1964, "used clever, persistent, and insidious propaganda, on which he personally spent vast sums of SUPRA money . . . to agitate the rural population and instill in it a disdain of private property" while he was "closely associated with illegal, spurious entities connected with the PCB."[6]

In particular, the *razões finais* examined Gustavo Borges's declaration that Pinheiro Neto had carried out the expropriations of seven landholdings in order to create, around Guanabara, a semicircle of settlers who plotted with guerrilla groups to bring about uprisings during which vehicle and railroad transportation would be cut off, along with the power and water service in the state. To demolish this "sensational fantasy," Sobral revealed that almost all of the seven expropriations had been decreed before his client had become SUPRA's chief.

Replying to the colonel's contention that Pinheiro Neto had "maintained, without the necessary legalization, nineteen radio stations used to promote social agitation," Sobral provided a declaration by the former administrative secretary of SUPRA that showed that the number of radio stations had been six, of which five had been in operation, and showed that procedures to legalize the six had been under way.[7]

Pinheiro Neto, as SUPRA chief, had visited the city of Governador Valadares in Minas. General José Maria Morais de Barros, a witness for the prosecution, attributed the visit to Pinheiro Neto's work of stirring up indiscipline among rural workers, whereas General Carlos Luís Guedes, another witness for the prosecution, described the visit as one in which Pinheiro Neto met with property owners in a vain effort to sell the idea of agrarian reform—an effort that almost resulted in a physical attack on the SUPRA head by irate landowners.[8] Sobral drew attention to the contradiction in the testimonies of the two generals and went on to point out that the vice president of the landowners association, the Confederação Rural Brasileira, had asserted that "rural subversion" should be blamed on the CGT and not on SUPRA.

Late in 1965, during the trial, Pinheiro Neto spoke in asides to Sobral about "inaccuracies" in the testimony being given by Gustavo Borges, such as statements about SUPRA's spending six million cruzeiros to bring people to the rally of March 13, 1964, and another thirty million to mobilize peasants two days before the military movement of March 31. When the colonel spoke about the "19 clandestine radio stations" and the "semicircle" around Guanabara and what he called its purpose, Sobral made energetic interruptions that were answered by the colonel in language described as "equally vigorous," whereupon Judge Basílio Ribeiro Filho criticized Sobral for giving undue attention to a part of the colonel's preamble rather than to the full meaning of the accusations. The *Diário de Notícias* wrote that Sobral, in his rebuttal to Gustavo Borges, "lost control of himself to such an extent" that a "really serious incident" would have occurred except that the colonel, after "making some contemplative observation," merely smiled and left the room.[9]

The trial ended in 1965, and Pinheiro Neto was absolved in the case about his role with SUPRA. Two other IPMS remained for him, one dealing with his administration of the Labor Ministry and another with his behavior outside the two important posts he had held while Goulart was president. Sobral, apologizing for a delay in preparing some papers, wrote his client about "insufficient time, the volume of my work, and my tiredness. Day and night I continue with this burning resolve to help the persecuted and to struggle against despotism."[10]

Sobral told Pinheiro Neto: "I do not give you the right to leave public life. Young people, above all those with a family tradition like yours, have the duty to struggle and suffer for the good of Brazil."[11]

Although the charges against João Pinheiro Neto in the remaining IPMS were dropped, conditions in Brazil did not allow him to play the role that Sobral had suggested. In 1966 he left for Spain to give lectures.

9. More Minas Clients and a Conflict with Magalhães Pinto about Carone (1964–1965)

Occasionally Sobral found time to go to Juiz de Fora in Minas Gerais to help defendants being judged there by the Permanent Council of Military Justice of the Fourth Military Region.

One of these defendants was Padre Francisco Lage Pessoa, who had combined religious work with activities on behalf of workers and peasants. As a PTB alternate congressman (suplente), he was in Brasília in May 1964 when he was arrested by the Minas Department of Social Vigilance to be held and tried by the army's Fourth Military Region on charges of having received money from North Vietnam for subversive activities and of having worked with Brizola, and with Sinval Bambirra in the labor movement and Francisco Julião in the Peasant Leagues.[1]

In November 1964 Sobral sent word to Francisco Lage that Obregon Gonçalves, a lawyer in Belo Horizonte, could keep in close touch with the padre's IPM cases in Juiz de Fora and Belo Horizonte, and he wrote of his own willingness to cooperate and to go to Juiz de Fora "when absolutely necessary." Sobral helped prepare questions for the defense to ask witnesses, such as the mayor of Sete Lagoas.[2]

Sobral was not at the trial in Juiz de Fora on October 29, 1965, and neither was the padre, who had been freed by a habeas corpus decision. Obregon Gonçalves, in a rather brief presentation, argued that no proof existed to show the receipt of foreign money by his client, but the five judges unanimously found the absent padre guilty of this and other charges and sentenced him to twenty-eight years of imprisonment.[3]

Clodsmith Riani, former head of the CNTI, was also treated harshly by the same court in Juiz de Fora. Although Riani, in mid-October 1965, was released from a *prisão preventiva* sentence by the Superior Military Tribunal (STM), thanks to a letter from Sobral that STM Judge Peri Bevilacqua persuaded the court to regard as a habeas corpus petition, the Council of Justice of the army's Fourth Military Region immediately rearrested him, with the explanation that he was under the orders of Colonel Ferdinando de Carvalho's IPM, investigating Communism in Brazil.

Riani's codefendant Sinval Bambirra was not at the trial, held in Juiz de Fora in December 1965, because he had fled from Brazil, but both Riani and Sobral were there. Sobral argued that the case against Riani was similar to that of the nine Chinese, "in which the accusations are made without proofs."[4] After the court ordered Riani to spend seventeen years in prison, the sentence was reduced by the STM to ten years, and it was reduced still further by the Supreme Court to one year and two months.[5]

Sobral went to Belo Horizonte in February 1965 to defend the right of Jorge Carone Filho to reassume the city's mayorship, from which he had been expelled on January 31 by a vote in which the city council had declared him *"impedido"* (unable to hold the office).

Conflicts between Carone and Governor Magalhães Pinto had occurred early in 1964. The mayor in January 1964 had led a huge street demonstration made up of people who were enraged because the governor wanted to allow a meeting of the Central Única de Trabajadores de América Latina (CUTAL), described by the local archbishop as "a clearly Communist congress." And a month later Carone had joined Mineiros who had protested, with vigor and emotion, against the governor's defense of the right of Brizola to install a chapter of the Frente de Mobilização Popular in Belo Horizonte.[6]

In Rio on February 10, 1965, Carone told the press that he was getting in touch with Sobral and other lawyers because the vote expelling him from office had been a result of improper pressures. It was, he said, ridiculous to remove him on account of "delays in making salary payments to city workers." Lacerda told the press that he could not understand why Magalhães Pinto had replaced Carone with Osvaldo Pieruccetti, whereupon the Minas governor called Carone dishonest and said that the "insolent" Lacerda, "filled with frustration and blind with ambition," did not understand the high ideals of the revolution.[7]

Sobral, in response to an appeal made by Carone on the telephone, agreed to defend his rights, "violently and abusively suppressed by Magalhães Pinto with the cooperation of the federal army in Minas." Then Carone and his father, bringing a 300,000-cruzeiro check, came to Sobral's office. Declining to accept the check, Sobral said that he could not go at once to Belo Horizonte, as his visitors were insisting, and he criticized Carone's press statements, which he said gave too much attention to political aspects of the case and not enough to juridical principles.[8]

On February 22, 1965, Sobral made the trip to Belo Horizonte, taking with him a petition calling for a local court to issue an injunction to annul the city council's resolution of January 31. In his hotel room he told reporters that he would prove the impropriety of the intervention by disclosing a note from the governor to the state security secretary "calling for the encirclement of the mayorship building by the state police," and would reveal the pressure used on city councilmen "to act in violation of the juridical order of the revolution." The Institutional Act, Sobral explained, upheld the legal requirements for declaring a mayor *impedido*, and upheld also a suspension of the validity of the city council vote so that the mayor could defend himself. "Thus Magalhães Pinto lies when he says the removal of Carone was an act of the revolution." It was, Sobral asserted, a "brutal betrayal" of the revolution.[9]

At the court on February 23 to present his petition, Sobral discussed Magalhães Pinto's order to the state troops to occupy the city council and the mayor's office. The governor, commenting that day to the press on the step he had taken, said: "I did not need to consult the president of the republic because I did not consult Castello Branco before I brought about the revolution of March 31."[10]

Magalhães Pinto, Sobral declared, "needed to remove the mayor because Carone is the principal witness of the good relations that the governor had with President João Goulart," and he added that the governor "took advantage of his eleventh-hour adherence to the armed movement of March 31, 1964, in order to make use of slander and lies to remove Carone from the post that was given to him by the vote of the people." The *Correio da Manhã* told its readers on February 24, 1965, that Magalhães Pinto had been "full of fear" when the state capital's mayorship had been in the hands of "the most dangerous witness of the governor's association with certain individuals who were in the administration that was overthrown."[11]

Magalhães Pinto had further comments, given on February 24: "I do not want Sobral Pinto to exercise in Minas the intimidating and defiant influence that he uses elsewhere." He described himself as supported by the sentiment in the city and said that Sobral was damaging the republic with his defense of a cause that was both unpopular and unjust. Sobral, in a reference to the "ridiculous" intimidation charge, told reporters that the only thing he did was make use of the truth. "I am fighting for the sacred right of defense, which has been smashed by Magalhães Pinto in order to serve his ambition and political passion. Belo Horizonte, I observed yesterday, is shocked by the brutal disregard of the law. If Magalhães Pinto is so sure of the legitimacy of his claim, why does he not abide by the legal rules instead of carrying out a disgraceful act of compulsion?"[12]

On February 25, 1965, Jorge Fontana, the judge of the court that heard the case, rejected the petition submitted by Sobral.[13]

In 1966, following the setback, Carone ran for Congress, but because the federal government then made it impossible for him to continue in the race, his wife took his place as a candidate. She was easily elected after campaigning for four days.[14]

10.   A Habeas Corpus for Julião (1965)

Francisco Julião, regarded as the leader of the Peasant Leagues in Brazil's northeast and known for his close relations with Fidel Castro, was elected to Congress from Pernambuco in 1962. He was in hiding on April 10, 1964, when he was *cassado*. Captured by the police near Brasília on June 3, he was transferred late that month to the headquarters of the Fourth Army in Recife. There he was held in solitary confinement for forty days at a battalion of guards before being imprisoned at the barracks of the Recife fire department (*corpo de bombeiros*), where a fellow prisoner was Miguel Arraes. An IPM found thirty-eight reasons for considering Julião guilty of violating the national security law of 1953.[1]

In September 1964 Sobral drew up a habeas corpus petition saying that Julião's *prisão preventiva* had far exceeded the legal limit
of sixty days.[2] When the petition was about to be judged, in April
1965 by the Superior Military Tribunal (STM), Recife lawyer Ailton
Cerqueira disclosed his plan to send a letter to the United Nations
to persuade it to intervene on behalf of Julião, "ill and long held incommunicado." STM Judge João Romeiro Neto, *relator* of the case,
expressed surprise at Cerqueira's proposal and said that he recognized Sobral as the defendant's only lawyer. The judge added that
he was awaiting information about Julião from the army's Seventh
Military Region and that the prisoner would continue to receive no
visitors. Julião's wife Regina de Castro, whom he had married after
separating from Alexina Arruda de Paula in 1963, told the press that
if the habeas corpus petition did not receive the approval of the STM,
she would present a petition to have her husband moved to a medical
clinic lest his high cholesterol count bring on a heart attack.[3]

The STM, in rejecting Sobral's petition by a 7-1 vote on May 19,
1965, pointed out that the IPM of the army's Seventh Military Region
had submitted twenty-nine accusations and therefore Julião should
continue imprisoned regardless of "allegations about excessive time
in prison." General Peri Bevilacqua, author of the dissenting vote,
said that the STM majority was "trying to transform the national
security law" by extending its scope. He cited the time limit for *prisões preventivas* and argued that the case was not appropriate for
military justice.[4]

Sobral emphasized these two points in the habeas corpus petition he presented to the Supreme Court on August 9, 1965, and he
said much more. Julião, he wrote, had sought to organize sugarcane
workers in the northeast in order to force the owners of rural lands
and mills to accept a new form of agricultural production that would
allow workers to receive the sort of wages they deserved. This effort,
he said, quite naturally provoked conflicts that conservatives described as evidences of Communist infiltration and that leftists described as evidences of bourgeois exploitation.[5]

"The reformer," Sobral said, "is not in a position to choose the
companions who offer to help him, and cannot disavow points of
view held by his partners lest he create discouragement and disappointment. And so, with the victory of the movement of March 31,
1964, conservative classes and some army men classified the social
movement fostered by the defendant as one which violated Article 2,

Section III of the national security law of 1953, which prohibits trying to modify, with foreign help, the political or social order established in the constitution."

Calling the charges against his client imprecise and of a general nature, Sobral listed them. Julião, he said, was felt to have adhered to the Marxist-Leninist principles advocated by Red China and to have been closely associated with Fidel Castro in trying to establish a Brazilian socialist republic of the type favored by the Cuban dictator. He was accused of fomenting agitation, of "disputing with Arraes the leadership of Pernambuco," of heading the Cuban Communist line in Brazil, and of having visited Communist countries in order to "receive instructions and material help . . . for changing Brazil's political regime and social structure."[6]

Where, Sobral asked, was the proof that the Peasant Leagues wanted to change Brazil's regime from that provided by the constitution, and where was the proof that Julião sought to make that change in association with any foreign group or had made trips abroad to receive, for that purpose, instructions and material assistance? For handling these vague accusations, Sobral considered the military justice system inappropriate, and he added that "regardless of what is thought about Julião," the length of his *prisão preventiva* "is legally excessive."[7]

The *relator*, Luís Gallotti, opened by rejecting the request of Julião for a special arrangement to allow him to be heard. "In every way," Gallotti said, "the petition is complete, drawn up by a lawyer whose zeal, proficiency, and disinterest in legal fees in defending clients [are] exceeded by no one."[8]

But Gallotti rejected the petition. He said that Julião, a lawyer elected to Congress, had been shown in an IPM as having the ability "to illude uneducated peasants by using Communist hoaxes and lures, thus transforming them into instruments of disorder and subversion." In agreeing with the STM that the case was proper for military justice, Gallotti said that Julião had made trips to Cuba to get financial assistance for subversion and to arrange for his former wife and a daughter to get training there "in the art of guerrilla warfare." "In many cases less serious from the point of view of the nation's security, the Supreme Court has rejected habeas corpus petitions based on the *incompetência* of military justice."

Luís Gallotti quoted jurist Francisco Campos as maintaining that courts had frequently agreed to extensions of *prisões preventivas* where delays had occurred in reaching judgments. Justification for the delay in the case of Julião lay in the fact that Julião had had 38 codefendants, making it necessary for 984 witnesses to be heard in the STM case.

In denying the habeas corpus petition, Gallotti was overruled by all the other STF members who voted: Evandro Lins e Silva, Hermes Lima, Victor Nunes Leal, Gonçalves de Oliveira, and Antônio Vilas Boas.[9]

Evandro Lins e Silva said he could only decide about the *competência* of military justice after further study but that Julião, having been imprisoned for over fourteen months, should be allowed to deal with the case while at liberty. Denial of the habeas corpus, he warned, would result in a series of improper extensions of *prisão preventiva*, and he said that regulations permitted no extension unless the reasons for it were given in the *autos* (the prosecution's evidence), a condition that had not been observed.

Hermes Lima, in agreeing with Evandro, objected to the view of the *relator* of the STM, who had maintained that the *prisão preventiva* could last as long as the minimum punishment for the crime being considered, in this case fifteen years. Victor Nunes Leal argued that *prisão preventiva* was not a tool for holding defendants in prison indefinitely during a search for proving their guilt. He emphasized that the constitution, in establishing the habeas corpus for the prevention of such illegal practices, had also made it a mechanism for avoiding "the abuse of power."[10]

Following the verdict, the lawyers of two other defendants asked the Supreme Court to have it extended to benefit their clients, Ivo Carneiro Valença of the Peasant Leagues and former PCB Congressman Gregório Bezerra. Gallotti joined the other court members in ruling in favor of the lawyers' petitions. "I did so," Gallotti said, "in obedience to the decision about Francisco Julião, in which I was outvoted."[11]

Julião, discussing later his departure from prison, pointed out that President Castello Branco made sure that the Fourth Army would comply with the Supreme Court decision, but that the military in Pernambuco threatened to rearrest him unless he left the state within twenty-four hours. His arrival by plane with his wife in Rio allowed him to become acquainted with his daughter Isabela, who had just had her first birthday. He expressed the hope of receiving treatment for his health but refused to speak about plans or other matters without first consulting Sobral Pinto.[12]

Journalists reported that Julião, at the Rio airport, had said that he would be dwelling at Sobral's home. "Francisco Julião," Sobral wrote the *Diário de Notícias*, "did not look me up, did not seek instructions from me, and is not my guest. It is not the function of a lawyer to furnish instructions to his clients about their personal activities nor to have them living at his residence." Sobral wrote the *Jornal do Brasil:* "I have established a clear distinction between my office and my home."[13]

Late in October 1965, when Julião found refuge in the Mexican embassy, Sobral told the *Jornal do Brasil* that he had had nothing to do with this development. "Julião looked me up only once, two days after arriving in Rio."[14]

The negotiations with the Mexican embassy, which followed refusals of the Yugoslav and Chilean embassies to receive Julião, were carried out by journalist Antônio Callado. Late in December Julião flew to Mexico and there, in Cuernavaca, he gave lectures and wrote.[15]

11. Accepting Appeals to Defend Marighella and Prestes (1964-1965)

Carlos Marighella, an intelligent and physically strong mulatto from Bahia who had been tortured during the Estado Novo, was a PCB congressman in the mid-1940s and, starting in 1957, was a member of the "Bahia group" that helped Luiz Carlos Prestes run the party. Becoming disenchanted with "the peaceful path to power" advocated by Prestes, Marighella felt that the military movement of March 31, 1964, confirmed the validity of his view.[1]

The capture of Marighella by the police of the Guanabara DOPS in a movie theater on May 9, 1964, was dramatic because of the resistance he put up even after one of the men arresting him shot him in the stomach, with bloody results. More policemen were on hand to punch and strike him while he was put in a police car. At the hospital of the penitentiary and later at the headquarters of the DOPS, where he was held in a cell, he was interrogated at length but was often uncooperative. Because his name appeared frequently (133 times) in the notebooks of Prestes, found by the São Paulo police in their unsuccessful search for the PCB's top leader, Marighella was taken for questioning to São Paulo and in July was returned to the DOPS cell in Rio.[2]

When Marighella was in the cell at the DOPS, after his transfer there from the hospital, he told his sixteen-year-old son Carlos Augusto to ask Sobral Pinto to defend him, perhaps, as Carlos Augusto came to feel, because Marighella believed that cases handled by Sobral were apt to create a stir. The boy, together with an aunt, spoke with Sobral, who agreed at once to take the case.[3]

The habeas corpus petition, submitted by Sobral to a Rio court on July 28, 1964, called the eighty-day imprisonment of Marighella by DOPS Director Cecil Borer an illegal act. Sobral described the violent arrest of his client, carried out, he said, on account of "unfounded suspicions" about Marighella's "participation in subversive movements." "With his life in danger from the bullet wound and the beatings . . . , Carlos Marighella was forced to endure long interrogations, during which investigators and members of the DOPS, sometimes using strong-arm methods, were unable to uncover a single act that could even remotely be considered as putting the national security in danger."[4]

Approval of Sobral's petition was rapid and Marighella was set free on July 31, 1964. In publishing his book Por Que Resisti à Prisão in 1965, Marighella told of his ordeal and upheld his combative position in defiance of PCB members who, like Prestes, condemned "radical far leftism."

While PCB leaders, especially Prestes, kept well hidden, the military authorities made use of the Prestes notebooks and papers to build up an IPM case against about sixty individuals including Prestes and Marighella.

A request to defend Prestes was submitted to Sobral in January 1965 by Valério Konder, a PCB member in the 1940s who had helped organize the Continental Congress of Solidarity with Cuba in 1963 and who had been cassado on April 10, 1964. Sobral told Konder he would accept the appeal with the understanding that he would receive no legal fee and provided that Prestes would sign a procuração (official appointment of Sobral to be his lawyer).[5]

On August 18, 1965, a letter written by Prestes on July 10 reached Sobral. In answering the "Cavalier of Hope," Sobral said he wanted to believe what Prestes had written about having always acted in accordance with the laws. He asked whether the notebooks had really been written by him, and he submitted a procuração for Prestes to sign. Sobral said that Prestes's suggested defense, showing that he had committed no crime, would take a lot of time to draw up and that a more expedient defense would be a habeas corpus petition showing that the military justice system was an inappropriate venue. "One final word: human fellowship, mentioned in your letter, is, for me, a mere reflection of my belief in God."[6]

The military trial based on "the Prestes notebooks" was held in São Paulo, with only one defendant present, labor leader Luís Tenório de Lima, who was serving a prison sentence on account of another case. More than ten of the defendants, including Marighella, were represented by lawyer Heleno Fragoso.[7] Sobral, defender of Prestes, presented a long letter he had received from his client, which said that the PCB "had no subversive intent or desire for insurrectional combat. We were convinced that the best and most rapid advance of the revolutionary process in our country was by legal methods and not by illegal ones or subversion." The actual conspirators, according to Prestes, had been the generals who had worked for the 1964 rebellion that had toppled a legal regime. Prestes told of his patriotism and his hopes of improving the lot of the Brazilian masses, and he quoted Pope Paul VI. He asked what his crime had been.[8]

The trial ended in July 1966 with a fourteen-year prison sentence for Prestes and seven-year sentences for PCB stalwarts such as Marighella. Leaders of the China-oriented party, which had favored a violent insurrection, were more fortunate. João Amazonas was sentenced to two years, and Maurício Grabois was absolved because of insufficient evidence against him.[9]

12.   Standing Up for Students Suspended for Indiscipline (1964)

To be minister of education, Castello Branco selected Flávio Suplici de Lacerda, who, as *reitor* (president) of the University of Paraná, had been congratulated by Sobral in 1962 for his stand against "indiscipline by student groups that have become organs of political agitation and social disharmony."[1] As Castello's education minister in 1964, Suplici de Lacerda drew up a project to provide a more legitimate student representation than existed in the student unions. It would require all students to vote in elections for "student directorships" at institutions of learning, and it included plans for the formation of state and national directorships. Strenuous objections were voiced by students active in the UNE (National Union of University

Students) and its local branches. The president of the UME (Union of University Students in Rio) declared that the minister's project sought to eliminate the UNE.[2]

Students belonging to the Centro Acadêmico Cândido de Oliveira (CACO), the association of law students at the University of Brazil, visited Sobral on a Sunday in mid-September 1964. Finding that they shared his ideas about restoring juridical order in Brazil, Sobral accepted their invitation to attend the inauguration of Fernando Barros as president of CACO. He changed his mind, however, after learning that Gustavo Corção had been correct in asserting that Fernando Barros had participated prominently in a radio broadcast of a past political campaign of Brizola. Writing Fernando Barros on September 19, he said that his attendance at the inauguration might cause misunderstandings about the views he held.[3]

Fernando Barros and his supporters were not held in high esteem by the university council, and when the CACO sought to hold an assembly in October, permission was denied by law school Director Hélio Gomes, who said that it was scheduled to interfere with the holding of classes.

The students announced they would hold their assembly at the law school on October 16 "regardless of the consequences."[4] About a hundred of them, preparing to assemble, were met by Hélio Gomes. After he repeated his prohibition, he ordered the removal of wall posters he found objectionable and the departure of the students he was facing. For forty-one students who refused to obey his orders, and for all the CACO officers, he imposed, as punishments, eight-day suspensions from the law school.

The suspensions, he said, would depend on a ratification by the law school faculty. On October 20, when the faculty met, Fernando Barros approached the faculty room with about two hundred irate students, including members of the UME. Prevented by guards from entering the room, they shouted that Hélio Gomes and the faculty were "gorillas." The faculty, in the meantime, agreed with the director that it was necessary to prevent a return to the "subversive tendencies" of the Goulart years. It extended the suspensions from eight to thirty days, shut down the CACO for six months, and approved the director's appointment of a commission, headed by Professor Hélio Tornaghi, to investigate the recent conduct of the CACO.[5]

The CACO turned to Sobral. In response, he prepared two documents, a *memorial* (pronouncement) from the students and a letter from himself to Hélio Gomes, and both were published in the Rio press. The letter, a plea for harmony, said that "we, the professors," should not be influenced by passion resulting from the revolution that overthrew Goulart.[6]

The *memorial*, copies of which Sobral sent to members of the university council, said that the punishments were unjust and in contradiction to all laws because they had been ordered prior to the inquiry that was to be carried out. Furthermore, Hélio Gomes was accused of including, for punishment, students whom he considered to be Communist but who had been absent from the objectionable gatherings and in no way connected with what had gone on.[7]

With the CACO contemplating a student strike, only nineteen of the university's law students, distributed among two classes, were at school on October 22, the day on which press reports told of the discovery of "a powerful bomb" at the school just in time to prevent its explosion. Elsewhere in Rio the UME, along with law student organizations at the Catholic University and the University of Guanabara, expressed their support of the CACO. To show similar support, medical students at the University of São Paulo declared themselves on strike.[8]

Hélio Gomes, replying to Sobral's letter, told the press that the punishments ordered by himself and the faculty were quite in order, and he argued that the CACO directorship represented a minority because its candidate to be orator of the graduating class had been defeated in a vote. The press also carried Sobral's declaration that the punishments were invalid legally because "the right of defense" had been ignored.[9]

A few days later, law Professor Tornaghi announced that his commission had found the punishments "legitimate," and that the CACO students had disrespected, slandered, and disobeyed the school director. "They believe that we are still in the Goulart government where rowdyism reigned. . . . Thanks to the Revolution of 1964 the whole nation has been given a climate of peace and it must reign at the school for the sake of the Revolution's just and democratic ideals."[10]

The views of Tornaghi were maintained in a pronouncement by the university council, and in March 1965 more students were suspended, this time for having shown disrespect for Castello Branco. Sobral wrote university President Pedro Calmon: "You and the council have punished students who booed the president of the republic, but, in December 1963 and early 1964, during the turmoil about the graduating journalism students, you did not act. In those days, support of discipline meant the loss of important jobs. Today, in order to hold on to them, it is necessary to punish."[11]

13. Suzano's Tearful Spell during Sobral's Defense of the "People's Admirals" (1965)

Government support for the UNE, enjoyed before April 1, 1964, had been lost, but the loss was regarded by anti–Castello Branco students as an opportunity to head a movement that had become more noble on account of its freedom from "corrupting" connections in high places.[1] While they pushed ahead in the hope of revamping the whole structure of society, the "admirals of the people," often their allies in the tumultuous times of Goulart, experienced days of grief that were somewhat assuaged by Sobral and other lawyers.

Admiral Cândido Aragão, who had headed the marine corps when he and the marines had adhered to the sailors' mutiny in March 1964, was locked up in a fort on April 2 and was so badly mistreated that he lost sight in one eye and suffered other health problems. A habeas corpus decision in his favor was granted by the Superior Military Tribunal (STM) in August 1964, but the court was persuaded a few days later, by navy officers who hated him, to order his reimprisonment. He spent much time in the embassy of Uruguay because, as his lawyer Wilson Lopes dos Santos told the press in October 1965, the Castello Branco government refused to grant him a safe-conduct to leave Brazil, as requested by the embassy. So many Brazilians were in the embassy that it was described as "a prison whose jailer is the ambassador."[2]

Among the "red admirals" defended by Sobral was Pedro Paulo de Araújo Suzano, whose appointment to be navy minister in July 1962 so enraged antileftist admirals that six of them resigned from their posts. He was navy chief of staff on March 27, 1964, when sailors in Rio, jubilantly celebrating the outcome of their mutiny, carried him and Cândido Aragão on their shoulders.[3]

Suzano was *cassado* on April 14, 1964, and charged with favoring indiscipline and cooperating with the Sailors' Association.

The most dramatic moments in the "Case of the Admirals" occurred on November 9, 1965, when Suzano, who had been in poor health, broke down following a four-hour defense speech by Sobral. The speech was given in Rio in the court of the STM, where twelve high-ranking navy officers were being defended by Sobral, Raul Lins e Silva, Alfredo Tranjan, Evaristo de Morais Filho, José Valladão, and Wilson Lopes dos Santos.[4]

Sobral declared that "these defendants are as honorable as you judges and are here on account of hatred, passion, and ignorance." He called the accusations a collection of old newspaper articles, one of which reported that Luiz Carlos Prestes had said "we have already achieved the power and only lack taking over the government." After asserting that the prosecution was attempting to use "these second-hand and thirdhand articles" to revive the political climate of the past, he pointed out that the prosecution could just as well accuse Castello Branco's planning minister Roberto Campos of being a Moscow agent because "he is shown in the newspapers today as full of smiles as he cuts a cake at the side of the Russian ambassador in a ceremony to commemorate the 48th anniversary of the Bolshevik Revolution."[5]

Sobral went on to tell the STM judges, "You must understand one thing: the so-called ascension of the masses is an inevitable occurrence and has to be handled in a way to prevent the masses from falling into the hands of the Communists, and this can be done by favoring those who receive the support of the masses." Kubitschek's political associates, opposed by the military, were mentioned as having that support. "But Brazil's elite, the bourgeoisie and most of the members of the armed forces, do not understand this and describe people who have popular backing as being corrupt and subversive."

Sobral, calling Suzano one of those men who attracted the masses, reminded the judges that his client had become known as "father of the sailors" and that Corporal José Anselmo dos Santos had said that these words, along with Suzano's name, should be displayed prominently in all Brazilian navy barracks.[6]

Suzano was so deeply moved by the recollection that he was overcome by a tearful spell. After an STM doctor tried to deal with the defendant's "emotional crisis," the court suspended its work for a day and Suzano was taken to his home. All the lawyers in the courtroom embraced Sobral and so did some of the judges. When the court reconvened, Suzano was acquitted.[7]

PART III

A Second Institutional Act Crushes Democracy (October 1965)

1. Kubitschek Returns, Ignoring Warnings from Sobral and Others (October 4, 1965)

The government's austere financial policy, making steady but slow progress against inflation, was unpopular and was attacked fiercely by ambitious UDN Governors Carlos Lacerda and Magalhães Pinto. Financial restraints, painful for wage earners and businessmen, gave ammunition to those who argued that the direct elections of eleven governors, if carried out as scheduled on October 3, 1965, would bring about a return of the "corrupt and subversive." Press organs, such as *O Estado de S. Paulo, O Globo,* and the *Jornal do Brasil,* questioned the wisdom of holding direct elections so soon. However, on February 13, 1965, President Castello Branco asserted that "the Revolution that is restoring democracy in Brazil should not fear elections but, rather, should guarantee them."[1]

Hard-line Colonels Gérson de Pina and Osnelli Martinelli, in a display of anger at the administration's refusal to allow them to arrest men suspected of corruption and subversion, resigned from their IPM posts in June 1965. After Martinelli was punished with thirty days of imprisonment in Copacabana Fort for his attack on the government, Magalhães Pinto condemned the punishment. Lacerda joined Gustavo Borges and Gérson de Pina in a visit to the imprisoned colonel and then rudely called Castello Branco "an angel of Conde de Lage Street" (famed for prostitution). The Liga Democratica Radical (LIDER), headed by Martinelli, issued a manifesto saying that it should be understood that Castello Branco was "nothing more than a delegate of the Supreme Command of the Revolution and must not act contrary to the revolutionary ideals, which are above those of the constitution itself."[2]

During the heated electioneering in Guanabara, Governor Lacerda campaigned for gubernatorial candidate Carlos Flexa Ribeiro (UDN), who had been the state's successful education secretary. The governor, hoping to win the presidency in 1966, warned voters that if the UDN were defeated in 1965 by the forces that had been eliminated in 1964, a direct presidential election in 1966 would not occur. With Flexa's chief opponent, Negrão de Lima (PSD-PTB), making headway by orating about the "financial crisis" and Lacerda's "insane acts," Lacerda and Raphael de Almeida Magalhães sought to split the opposition by working for the entry of other candidates, especially the popular broadcaster Alziro Zarur, "father" of the Legion of Goodwill.[3]

Sobral, describing himself as a friend of both Flexa and Negrão who would not be voting, told Lacerda that Zarur was a "horrifying hoodwinker." He mentioned Lacerda's past condemnation of the Communist principle that the end justifies the means when he wrote the governor that he had no right to ally himself with Zarur simply for the sake of victory.[4]

Alceu Amoroso Lima, favoring Negrão, said that Lacerda was wrong to worry about Communism and that what Brazil had to worry about was fascism or the Portuguese type of rightism represented by Lacerda. Gustavo Corção, on the other hand, supported Flexa Ribeiro and warned his readers that a Negrão victory would mean a return of the "trash" expelled in 1964. Sobral, writing Corção, asked whether that trash was any worse than the "profanities and hoaxes" of Zarur. "With Flexa Ribeiro threatening us with the reign of Zarur's Legion of Goodwill, why do you remain silent about this sinister danger?"[5]

The "sinister danger" was eliminated because men in Castello Branco's administration, wishing to set back Lacerda's presidential aspirations, decided to contest the candidacies of Zarur and another broadcaster and found minor technical reasons for disqualifying them.[6]

Ferdinando de Carvalho believed that the candidacy to be disqualified was that of Negrão de Lima. Convinced that Negrão had purchased Communist electoral support, the hard-line colonel planned to make a dramatic revelation of the details on television. But the Castello Branco government stepped in to prevent the IPM study of Communism from becoming involved in current politics.[7]

After hard-liners spoke of preventing the inaugurations of Kubitschek associates if they won governorships, Castello Branco assured the nation that the inaugurations would take place. He added that, regardless of the election results, nothing would be allowed to prevent a "continuation of the Revolution of March 31, 1964." In the meantime, in France, Kubitschek increased the anger of his foes by making statements about how the election results would completely change the situation in Brazil; the former president was quoted as saying that he was contemplating a return to Brazil shortly after the elections in order to renew his political activities and "consolidate democracy."[8]

Negrão de Lima and PSD President Ernâni do Amaral Peixoto tried to persuade Kubitschek to stay away. They shared the view that his arrival in Brazil, coinciding closely with the likely victories of his friends Negrão de Lima and Israel Pinheiro in Guanabara and Minas, would intensify the determination of hard-liners to act against the inaugurations of the Juscelinistas.[9]

The UDN's Adauto Lúcio Cardoso brought Sobral a warning against the return of Kubitschek and said that Sobral was the only person who could convince Kubitschek not to come. Claiming to speak for the UDN opponents of the former president, Adauto said that President Castello Branco would be unable to prevent military enemies of Kubitschek from humiliating the former president, who might even be imprisoned by them. Sobral believed that Adauto, the deliverer of an earlier message from the president at the time of threats to Sobral's freedom, was speaking on behalf of Castello Branco and describing problems the president felt he would have, and so Sobral told Adauto that he would telephone the message to Kubitschek and advise against his return provided he could say that the message came from Adauto's friend, Castello Branco. Adauto agreed, but when Sobral spoke with Kubitschek, Kubitschek refused to believe that the warning came from the president.[10] In any event, Kubitschek was eager to return.

Lacerda, having collapsed from exhaustion while campaigning for Flexa Ribeiro on September 30, was in a hospital on October 2, when it became known that Kubitschek would reach Rio on October 4, the day after the elections. The governor and Gustavo Borges issued a note to the press calling on Castello to reply to "this affront" to the revolution. Sobral, in a telegram to Lacerda, said that Kubitschek, in returning, was simply carrying out a legitimate right and was not affronting anyone.[11]

At Rio's Galeão Airport, where Kubitschek and his wife Sarah disembarked at 9:00 A.M. on October 4, the former president was greeted by a sea of welcoming placards and a throng of five thousand that included Negrão de Lima and Sobral. The car in which he was taken to his apartment in the Ipanema district was followed by over a hundred cars, making for a victory parade that received an especially enthusiastic reception along Rio Branco Avenue, where paper streamers were thrown from windows and people shouted greetings. "Operation Return" was described as a great success by the Paris press, which called Kubitschek "the man of the day."[12]

At his apartment Kubitschek explained to reporters that he planned to cooperate with the redemocratization of Brazil, demonstrating the same patience and serenity that he had shown while suffering in exile. "I hope," he said, "never again to leave this country." Writer Josué Montello told the reporters that Kubitschek would travel the next day to Belo Horizonte. And Sobral, referring to the summonses from colonels for Kubitschek to report to IPMS, told the newsmen that Kubitschek had a right to reject the summonses just as he had done.[13] Kubitschek, however, was disposed to cooperate with the IPMS, although the order from Colonel Joaquim Portella Ferreira Alves, new head of the IPM investigating the ISEB, was inconvenient, requiring his presence at the barracks of the army police at 2:30 that very day of his return.

Analyses of the elections, published late on October 4 and the next day, made it clear that Negrão de Lima and Israel Pinheiro had won in Guanabara and Minas. The outcomes, together with Kubitschek's triumphant arrival, were resented by an estimated 80 percent of the military officers in the Rio area.[14] A manifesto, distributed in the barracks on the evening of October 4, condemned Castello Branco and said that the inauguration of Negrão would be "a premeditated malevolent act, a defiance of the Revolution." With young officers at the barracks at Vila Militar planning to take direct action against Negrão's inauguration, Rio was full of rumors about plans to destroy the ballot boxes and carry out a coup to replace the "too theoretical" Castello Branco with hard-liner Costa e Silva.[15]

2. The IPMS, Sobral Tells Castello, "Make Kubitschek's Life a Hell" (October 4–15, 1965)

Juscelino Kubitschek, accompanied by Sarah and their two daughters, reported at the army police barracks at 2:30 on October 4 to answer questions about subversion in the extinct ISEB (Institute of

Advanced Brazilian Studies). Sobral was there but the former president testified alone. The IPM ruled that no lawyer should be with him because the IPM was not a judicial body. Sobral said his decision not to be at his friend's side was his own, made because Kubitschek did not need him. The decision, he said, had nothing to do with any order of Colonel Portella Ferreira Alves.[1]

During the interrogation, which lasted for two and one-half hours, the colonel produced a message written in the 1950s to the National Security Council by Kubitschek's justice minister, Armando Falcão, giving reasons why the ISEB should be closed down.[2] Kubitschek, who said he knew nothing about the message or the institute's activities, was ordered to report early the next morning at Ferdinando de Carvalho's IPM about Brazilian Communism and then return the following day to the investigation of the ISEB.

Colonel Portella Ferreira Alves told the press that the documents of the IPM "seriously incriminate" Kubitschek in the "Communist penetration of the ISEB" and that as the former president was an indicted person and not a mere witness, a decision about imprisoning him on orders of the head of the First Army would follow further questioning at a series of sessions. The press also reported that most of the fifty-six IPMs containing references to Kubitschek had made their way to the courts for judgments, leaving only four or five that required his presence.[3]

At Ferdinando de Carvalho's IPM, Kubitschek testified on October 5 from 9:00 A.M. until 3:00 P.M. Following an order that Kubitschek report on October 6 and 7 to the IPMs about the ISEB and Communism, Sobral sent a long telegram to President Castello Branco in which he said that the IPM colonels were turning the former president's life into a "veritable hell" *(inferno)* caused by their resentment of his return to Brazil, "his legitimate right."[4]

Sobral told Castello Branco to remember that his own election to the presidency by Congress in April 1964 had been made possible by PSD votes, thanks to the "loyal and sincere cooperation of Juscelino Kubitschek, incontestable chief" of that party. "The wheel of fortune is capricious and tomorrow Your Excellency may suffer from attacks and humiliations similar to those being hurled today against the creator of the Belém-Brasília highway, civilizer of the previously abandoned interior."

Sobral mentioned "insignificant and improper" investigations being carried out by colonels, former subordinates of Kubitschek, whose position had made him head of the armed forces in the past, and he called the threat of imprisonment of Kubitschek an attack on the constitution, a defiance of the Supreme Court, and a display of disrespect for the "prerogatives held by the former president even when out of office." "I am sure you will bring an end to these acts which so capriciously harm your authority." On the next day, October 7, Sobral sent telegrams to the colonels of the IPMS investigating the ISEB and Communism to acquaint them with his telegram to Castello Branco.[5]

The telegram to Castello Branco brought an unfriendly response in a telegram from Luís Viana Filho, head of the presidential *gabinete civil*. It was a message from the president saying that Kubitschek, not listed in the military hierarchy and with his political rights suspended, had no special privilege *(foro privilegiado)* and was required to submit to legal and necessary questioning like all Brazilians. "As for the whim of the wheel of fortune, known by everyone to be capricious, the president, besides being willing to submit himself to inquiries that might be in store for him, always asks God to keep him from robbing the people and from betraying the nation's security."[6]

In a new telegram to the president, sent on October 11, Sobral was especially critical of the "deplorable insinuations" in the final words of the message signed by Viana Filho. "The people, whom you declare to have been robbed, have been giving, in their enthusiastic applause for the *cassado* politician, an adequate reply to your unjust and revolting aggression. I did not ask for privileges for the former president but simply a show of moral sensibility and respect for personal dignity, attitudes that prevail in all governments which do not place their confidence in machine guns and in factious passion. The suspension of the political rights of the former president cannot wipe out his signature on your appointment to generalship. . . . Prerogatives based on positions once held are guaranteed by the Supreme Court in jurisprudence that destroys the sophistic argumentation in your reply signed by Minister Luís Viana Filho."[7]

Sobral took heart from Rubem Braga's article, "The IPMS and Sr. Juscelino," published the next day in the *Diário de Notícias*. "The interrogations," the columnist wrote, "are not held for the purpose of learning anything because the investigators, knowing that it is nonsense to accuse Sr. Kubitschek of subversion, simply seek to force him to face a long and ruthless vexation."

Rubem Braga went on to say that it was common knowledge that Kubitschek had the right to a special prerogative and that the people questioning him "are not qualified to judge the acts of a president of the republic." Braga, although describing himself as a longtime political opponent of Kubitschek, called for respect for a man who, after being chosen president by the popular vote, had turned the presidency over to an adversary also chosen by the popular vote. "The IPM colonels may think they are humiliating Juscelino Kubitschek and reducing his prestige. Perhaps they do not perceive that they are increasing his popularity, bringing him the sympathy and backing of the masses and also of all serious people."[8]

In a telegram sent to Castello Branco on October 12, Sobral said that Rubem Braga's article was "required reading." Messages that Sobral sent to Luís Viana Filho referred to Braga's article and to the ideas of Ruy Barbosa, bygone "apostle of civil order," about whom Sobral was preparing a speech for an IAB meeting. Because Luís Viana Filho was a biographer of Ruy Barbosa, Sobral told him he could not fail to understand the importance of legal principles even though, like others who had taken over the government in April 1964, he had become interested in pushing adversaries aside, often at the cost of destroying the law. "Eager for power, you and your companions invented a revolution, which exists in name only, and speak about democracy, forgetting that the term depends on voting."[9]

War Minister Costa e Silva told hotheaded young hard-liners at the Vila Militar barracks to turn from their plans to act against Castello Branco and the inauguration of Negrão de Lima because the revolution would definitely go forward. To make the war minister's pledge a reality and placate the powerful hard line, the presidency prepared to submit for a congressional vote a program to reform the national security law and the judiciary, curtail the activities of the *cassados,* and facilitate federal intervention in the states. The proposals would give military justice clear authority to handle cases of civilians who violated the national security law, would abolish the *foro privilegiado* in the case of all who had governed but were out of office, and would exclude from judicial review all steps carried out under the Institutional Act. While hard-liners awaited the enactment of the measures by Congress, Governors Magalhães Pinto and Lacerda, ridiculing Castello Branco, said the measures were insufficiently revolutionary. Magalhães Pinto called them "innocuous," and Lacerda spoke of Castello's "drivel" and "clownish series of little laws."[10]

Sobral sent a telegram to the PTB calling for its congressmen to be firm in fighting against the plans of the government "to liquidate the federation and democracy and to legitimize the tutelage of the armed forces over the civil power." He sent a copy to Kubitschek.[11]

Kubitschek could find satisfaction in speeches made on his behalf in Congress and in a message signed by many congressmen who, "rejoicing at his return," believed that any "affront" to him would be more harmful to Brazil than to the former president, who had governed "with vision and devotion to the constitution." Other signs of support came from the invitations of students to honor their classes with his graduating speeches and from columnists. Sobral, pleased with a column about "military radicalism" in the *Correio da Manhã*, told its author, Hermano Alves: "Seldom have I come across an analysis about the political situation as perfect as yours."[12]

After a weekend in Belo Horizonte, Kubitschek returned to Rio on October 11 for daily sessions at the IPMs, one of which, directed by Ferdinando de Carvalho, lasted from 3:00 P.M. until 2:00 A.M. Because Kubitschek, with his denials or lack of information, seemed uncooperative, the colonel said later that he would use future sessions, which would be even longer, to "break the barrier of silence of the former president."[13]

Kubitschek's return from Belo Horizonte coincided with the formation of another IPM, this one to investigate an interview he was said to have given, in the plane which flew him from France, to a reporter of the Chilean Communist daily *El Siglo*. Eraldo Gueiros Leite, *procurador geral da justiça militar*, called the interview "offensive to the national interests," but Kubitschek, testifying at the new IPM, run by Colonel Oswaldo Ferraro de Carvalho, denied having ever spoken about Brazilian affairs to the press while he was out of the country. In Chile, a new issue of *El Siglo* published a photograph of Kubitschek and its reporter on the plane and a headline about "the truth which the gorillas want to gag, as Brazil's former president told me while flying to Rio de Janeiro."[14]

On October 16, Kubitschek was reported by *Última Hora* as having set a record of fifty-six hours of testifying before IPMs.

3. Turning to the Supreme Court for the Protection of Kubitschek (late October 1965)

Telegrams from Sobral were sent in abundance in October 1965, and some of them, such as those to Castello Branco, appeared in the press. His telegram of October 18 to Ernâni do Amaral Peixoto urged the PSD leader to organize the party to defeat the proposed statute that would regulate the activities of the *cassados* and to demonstrate that Congress had the independence necessary to reject "odious measures" that would bring shame to Brazil.[1]

Chief Justice Álvaro Ribeiro da Costa, assailing the government's plan to increase the Supreme Court membership from eleven to sixteen, asserted on October 19 that the armed forces had no right to express their opinion on the subject, "although this has been happening, something never seen in truly civilized nations," and he added that "the time has come for the armed forces to understand that in democratic regimes they do not exercise the role of mentors of the nation."[2]

A telegram from Sobral congratulated Ribeiro da Costa for his forthrightness, lucidity, and patriotism.[3] But Costa e Silva, speaking with emotion on October 22 at army maneuvers in São Paulo state in the presence of Castello Branco and other authorities, called the assertion of the head of the Supreme Court "the greatest injustice ever practiced against the Brazilian soldier." He also said: "We left the barracks at the call of the people and we shall return to them only when the people so determine." The war minister was wildly acclaimed by most of his audience and was given support the next day when local army commanders met in Rio to declare that, with Congress reluctant to act, "a solution of force is the only one capable of reinvigorating and consolidating the ideals of the Revolution." Sobral, however, sent the war minister a telegram saying that in threatening the nation he had used expressions at the São Paulo army maneuvers that resembled those used by Mussolini after assuming power in 1922.[4]

Juracy Magalhães, who had been serving as ambassador in Washington, replaced Milton Campos as justice minister on October 19 and worked with politicians to gain congressional approval of the government's proposed measures. Sobral, in a telegram to him, said that his training for his new post had been inadequate but he saw hope in Juracy's civic spirit. Recalling praise of Kubitschek expressed by Juracy in the past, he asked the new justice minister to persuade Castello Branco and the military to bring an end to the "intolerable treatment" of Kubitschek, "the illustrious public figure" who was being handled as though he were "a common criminal." Also on October 20 Sobral sent a telegram praising former congressman Mário Martins for his recent *Jornal do Brasil* column and asking him to send copies of it to every congressman and senator.[5]

First Army Commander Otacílio Terra Ururaí was reported

to have ordered Ferdinando de Carvalho to deal aggressively with Kubitschek, considered by the military to be giving "difficulties" to the colonel's investigation. In another of his telegrams sent on October 20, Sobral appealed to the general for better treatment of Kubitschek, "the illustrious signer of thousands of officer appointments in the armed forces." And then Sobral sent a letter to Ferdinando de Carvalho to complain about newspaper stories that described Kubitschek as being "afraid of the truth and seeking to keep it hidden." "At the illegal and unjust IPMS," Sobral wrote, "the conduct of the former president reveals just the opposite. What he cannot do is invent crimes he did not commit and provide affirmations about things he cannot remember, perfectly understandable in the case of a former president."[6] Speaking on the *Pinga Fogo* television program, Sobral criticized the IPM colonels for their conduct. Fearing that Congress might approve the administration's projects to fortify the revolution, he told his audience that the Institutional Act had turned Congress into a mere machine for "registering the pretensions of the executive."[7]

On October 19 Sobral presented a habeas corpus appeal to the Supreme Court. Already, when Kubitschek was in France a month earlier, Cândido de Oliveira Neto had gone to the court with such an appeal because of the inclusion of Kubitschek's name on the list of those who, according to Colonel Portella Ferreira Alves, had to appear at the investigation of the ISEB for having committed crimes against the political and social order. Cândido's response to the demand that Kubitschek appear, indicted for crimes, within ten days (or suffer punishment for not appearing) had been to cite legal reasons why the Supreme Court was the only body able to receive, in the first instance, a case against a former president for crimes committed during his term of office.[8]

Like Cândido, Sobral cited Section 1 of Constitutional Article 101, and he used it to say that "for common crimes that might have been carried out during his term, the petitioner can only be tried and judged by the Supreme Court on account of the prerogative of his office, a prerogative that is his even after leaving office." Sobral also wrote a great deal about the "use of power" and the "violence" of the IPMS, which, he said, were bringing "endless torments" to the former president. He included some of his messages to Castello Branco and the column by Rubem Braga. Explaining that the eleven-hour IPM session of October 16 brought to sixty hours the time spent by

Kubitschek in testifying, he wrote that one of the colonels had been quoted as saying that he would question Kubitschek "500 times, if necessary."

In conclusion, the appeal asked that the *relator* of the case grant at once an injunction *(liminar)* to end the interrogations until the full court could rule on the petition. He argued that the questioning, without parallel in Brazil's history, was "already sufficient to get at the facts, if that is the objective" of those "trying to intimidate" his client.[9]

To present this document to the Supreme Court, Cândido de Oliveira Neto was in Brasília on October 23 when it became known that Sarah Kubitschek, at 3:00 A.M., had found her husband suffering chest pains and that his doctor, Aloysio Alves, had forbidden him to testify that day at the investigation of the ISEB because of his "circulatory disturbance." Cândido declared that Kubitschek might die at the hands of his inquisitors, and he added that the former president had authorized delivery of the new habeas corpus petition "only on account of the grave condition of his health" and not because he was refusing to continue giving clarifications to the IPMS, "improper though these interrogations are."[10]

In Rio, Sarah Kubitschek declared, "the colonels are responsible, before the nation, for the life of Juscelino." Colonel Portella Ferreira Alves, in reply, told the *Diário de Notícias:* "We are the ones who are threatened by a heart attack and not the former president, who keeps answering all questions with a simple 'yes,' 'no,' or 'I don't remember,' whereas we are the ones who have been losing hours and hours carrying out research of material, contained in twenty volumes, to come up with the questions."[11]

After it became known that Kubitschek would not appear on October 27 at the IPM investigating Communism in Brazil, Ferdinando de Carvalho named a commission of army doctors to examine him. The commission decided that Kubitschek should not be interrogated for fifteen days.[12]

The Supreme Court, upon receiving the habeas corpus appeal, ordered the colonels to submit information within five days and named Hahnemann Guimarães to be *relator* and to rule quickly on the request for the injunction. Rejection of the injunction, made known on October 26, was no surprise to those who recalled that the majority opinion in the case of Arraes, written by Evandro Lins e Silva, had granted the habeas corpus because the imprisonment time had been excessive but had required the former governor to testify at IPMS regardless of any *foro especial*.[13]

The rejection of the injunction coincided with a speech in Congress in which Aliomar Baleeiro (UDN), favoring the proposed limitation on the activities of the *cassados*, blamed "the crisis" largely on the return to Brazil of Kubitschek, described by the orator as lacking in probity and dignified behavior.[14]

4. A New Institutional Act Ends Democracy (October 27, 1965)

Justice Minister Juracy Magalhães, seeking to persuade Congress to vote for the administration's program, announced that its failure to do so would force the government to issue a new institutional act, more radical than the proposals sent to Congress. But many congressmen, such as PSD Mineiros bent on protecting Kubitschek's prerogatives, could not vote for proposals that they considered too radical, and they were joined by congressmen who, like the followers of Lacerda, said the proposals were not radical enough. Many shared the view of Congressman Wilson Martins, who called on Congress to demonstrate "a worthy position" by rejecting proposals submitted by "those who humiliate us."[1]

Agreeing with Wilson Martins, Sobral sent a telegram to Congressman Adauto Lúcio Cardoso to remind him of the pledge they had made, when founding Resistência Democratica in 1945, to uphold democratic practices. Adauto, by this time, had joined Francisco Campos, Luís Viana Filho, and Carlos Medeiros Silva in submitting suggestions to Professor Nehemias Gueiros, who was drafting the proposed institutional act mentioned by Juracy Magalhães.[2]

In a telegram to Juracy, Sobral called the minister's talk about a new institutional act "a threat against the adversaries of authoritarianism." Also he admonished Juracy for not having replied to his appeal on behalf of Kubitschek. The reply this time was not slow in coming, and it distressed Sobral by declaring that Kubitschek was "responsible for the present crisis."[3]

Castello Branco became convinced of the impossibility of the government's obtaining the necessary 205 votes in the lower house, and messages from the military told of the need to attend to the demands for revolutionary measures being made by the vast majority of its officers. So many of them were resolved to act with troops that Milton Campos believed that Castello would not be able to continue in office unless the proposals became law. Columnist Carlos Castello Branco pictured the "idealistic" president as faced with the choice of "probable overthrow" or the issuance of Institutional Act Number Two.[4]

When at length the president agreed to the Ato's promulgation, he insisted, against the advice of his supporters, on the inclusion of a clause to make it impossible for him to continue in office after the end of his term in March 1967. Pernambuco Governor Paulo Guerra told Castello Branco: "With this clause the command will go to Costa e Silva."[5]

Institutional Act Number Two, announced in a ceremony attended on October 27 by the president and his cabinet, was to remain in effect until Castello Branco left office. It closed down all political parties (in preparation for a two-party system), made the presidential election indirect by Congress, renewed the government's authority to suspend the political rights of individuals and cancel their mandates, increased from eleven to sixteen the number of Supreme Court justices, and made it easier for the president to declare a state of siege and intervene in the states. Further, the new institutional act (Ato 2) would suspend the constitutional guarantees of tenure (such as those held by judges), would end "special immunities" on account of positions once held, and would curtail the activities of the *cassados* and, "if necessary," their movements. The judicial system was not to pass judgment on steps taken in accordance with the first institutional act or the new one. The president would be able to issue "decree laws about the national security" and complementary acts to the new Ato, including ones that would force legislatures into recess; during such a recess of Congress the president could legislate by issuing decree laws.[6]

Castello Branco and Juracy Magalhães, who were among the signers of the new Ato, also signed Ato Complementar No. 1, calling for the imprisonment of *cassados* who participated in political activities or pronounced on political matters, and equal punishments for anyone who helped the *cassados* to do so. Press or broadcasting organs that issued political remarks of the *cassados* were to be fined.[7]

Hard-line General Afonso de Albuquerque Lima, who had become chief of staff of the First Army, spoke with satisfaction about the success of "our group" in "forcing" Ato 2 on the president and about the group's success in "pressing" for Castello to accept the hard-line war minister, Costa e Silva, as the next president, a choice that the *Jornal do Brasil* found to be the wish of 85 percent of the army. But Albuquerque Lima's remark about "all the power" being "in the hands of our group"[8] was somewhat off the mark in the months that followed the issuance of Ato 2, which gave immense power to the executive branch.

Fully as important as the steps taken against the "enemies of the revolution" after October 27 were those taken to curb the hard-line radicals. Castello Branco, telling the military to get out of politics, transferred hard-liners from command posts in the First Army. LIDER, the organization of Colonel Osnelli Martinelli and his group, was closed down, and the inaugurations of the elected governors were achieved. The last of the plans to overthrow Castello Branco, discussed by Admiral Sílvio Heck and Governor Magalhães Pinto, was abandoned.[9]

PART IV

The Last Months of 1965

1. Sobral Resigns as IAB President (October 28, 1965)

For Sobral Pinto, as head of the Instituto dos Advogados Brasileiros (IAB), the new institutional act brought insurmountable difficulties. Already his problems with the IAB had been made evident back in May 1965 when his proposed motion to congratulate the Supreme Court for issuing a habeas corpus decision had been rejected at a meeting where a majority wished to avoid acting in a manner that might be interpreted as censuring the president of the republic.[1]

On October 14, after the IAB decided to set up a commission to study the reforms that Castello Branco submitted to Congress to fortify the revolution, Sobral told the IAB that the proposed reforms were an attack on the "constituted organization of the nation" and would have "fatal consequences for Brazilian democracy, which I love and defend along with individual liberties."[2] The work of the study commission, headed by Professor Celestino Basílio, was discussed at an IAB meeting on October 21, and, at the meeting a week later, the discussion was about Institutional Act Number Two.

Sobral, speaking at the October 28 meeting, pointed out that the IAB had the responsibility of disseminating information about matters of law and justice and that he, as its head, found himself with the duty of declaring that the president of the republic, who had promised to defend and abide by the constitution, had abusively issued an act that crushed the sovereignty of Congress, altered the constitutions of the Supreme Court and Federal Court of Appeals, suspended the tenure of all Brazil's judges, and made the National Security Council the supreme organ of the republic, along with conferring on Castello Branco attributes of absolute power. "Law has lost its authority and justice its power. The democratic regime has disappeared and juridical order has been torn to shreds."[3]

Maria Rita de Andrade, in opposing the declaration of Sobral, was backed by Celestino Basílio and Thomas Leonardos, supporters of Ato 2. They maintained that it was a "political act, beyond the range of juridical analysis" and was, besides, "a consequence of necessity." This view was overwhelmingly favored, with Sobral's position receiving only two votes, and subsequently the IAB adopted a motion expressing its support of the government. Sobral resigned as IAB president, saying he could not continue representing an institution of lawyers that favored a situation that he would have to continue to attack.[4]

With this announcement Sobral left the meeting, and Celestino Basílio, speaking of his veneration of Sobral, arranged to have a commission visit him and urge his return to the organization's presidency. But the commission failed in its mission, and at the next IAB meeting some of the officers who had served with him, including First Secretary Gabriel Costa Carvalho, also left their posts. Because Alceu Amoroso Lima had written a column harshly berating the IAB for not supporting Sobral's view, Alceu was criticized. One of the lawyers asserted that Alceu had moved from the extreme Right to the extreme Left and was "serving the Communist cause."[5]

2.   Kubitschek Leaves for the United States (November 10, 1965)

Among those who were invited to fill the five new Supreme Court positions were Adauto Lúcio Cardoso, Milton Campos, and Pedro Aleixo, but they declined in protest against some of the provisions of the new institutional act. Two of those who accepted, José Eduardo Prado Kelly and Carlos Medeiros Silva, received letters from Sobral expressing surprise at their agreement to fill vacancies "implanted by the military dictatorship." Sobral wrote that the vacancies, created in violation of the constitution and in opposition to the views of the Supreme Court, had been filled without regard for the role of Congress in the matter and for the sole purpose of serving "the Revolution," said to have been set back by the justices appointed by Kubitschek and Goulart. A second letter to Prado Kelly, following the new justice's criticism of the first, brought a friendly response, appropriate for Sobral's seventy-second birthday, November 5, 1965.[1]

Little warmth characterized Sobral's exchanges with Justice Minister Juracy Magalhães, reported in the press. They coincided with a series of pronouncements in which Juracy told the public that the government, armed with the new institutional act, would concentrate its attacks on Communists and subversives, guilty of disturbing the peace, and would apply sanctions against all violators of the new regulations.[2]

Sobral had expressed "revulsion" at Juracy's charges against Kubitschek, and so Juracy, in a telegram to Sobral, said he, too, was filled with "revulsion"—"revulsion brought about by the fits of fury of those who seek to maintain a climate of tension so great that it is harmful to the efficient work of the honorable President Castello Branco. Rest assured that I shall not retreat in the defense of order, which will bring more benefits than the false liberty being defended demagogically."[3]

Sobral, replying in a telegram on November 5, said that "the climate of tension is caused by the federal administration and above all by the justice minister, who, instead of governing within the principles of justice, distributes each day . . . announcements of sanctions to be taken against his disarmed and defenseless fellow citizens." Describing himself as no conspirator but, rather, an upholder of order, Sobral wrote that the minister's threats would not silence his voice. He added: "In the opinion of the oppressors, the demagogues are those who demand the restoration of liberty, outlawed in the nation."[4]

While Sobral exchanged published messages with Juracy Magalhães, the press reported that Kubitschek would be accused of "cheating on his income tax and other grave matters." As Sobral correctly foresaw, the petitions submitted on Kubitschek's behalf would be denied by the Supreme Court as unsustainable under the second institutional act. Declaring that "courts, justice, and laws no longer exist," he advised Kubitschek to depart from Brazil.[5]

A good reason for departure lay in the threats of imprisonment. According to one of them, which was made known to Kubitschek by an army major, Kubitschek was likely to be held under guard at the army's central hospital following a new examination of his health by the commission of army doctors, and later, while under arrest, judged by military officers for his "crimes." An army colonel who had been helped by Kubitschek in the past advised him in no uncertain terms to leave the country or be arrested.[6]

Permission for Kubitschek to leave Brazil as a voluntary exile was given, Kubitschek said later, by President Castello Branco.[7] The negotiations for it and the arrangements for the departure involved quite a few people, including Vice President José Maria Alkmim, troubleshooter for Kubitschek in the past. Raphael de Almeida Magalhães, who had become governor of Guanabara following the resignation of Lacerda, cooperated with Kubitschek and Alkmim, and the United States embassy provided Alkmim with visas so that Kubitschek and Sarah could disembark in New York on November 10.[8]

At Kennedy Airport, Kubitschek said: "I made the trip in order not to be imprisoned. What is happening in Brazil is of utmost importance for Latin America. The recent decrees of the government, above all Institutional Act Number Two, wipe out all democratic expression." His exile, he said, could last for one month or for twenty years.[9]

These comments on Brazilian political matters, disturbing to Juracy Magalhães, were explained by Sobral in a telegram telling the justice minister that Kubitschek, during his first exile, had been no less silent than former Brazilian President Washington Luiz, famous for his silence on such matters following his exile in 1930. But the recent victors, Sobral said, were unlike those of 1930, because they made it a crime for oppositionists in Brazil to express themselves and so the advocates of liberty had become obliged to turn to the foreign press. He also wrote that while Washington Luiz had found his career ended, Kubitschek had a role to play as a participant in the struggle for the return of democracy.[10]

With the appearance in the United States press of articles about Kubitschek's alleged corruption, the exile sought Sobral's advice about taking legal steps. Sobral, in reply, expressed the belief that "the author of the campaign is General Costa e Silva." Justice in the United States, he added, would be likely to side with the victim of the work of "a powerful publicity organization such as the one that presently attacks you." He pointed out that the legal expenses would be very great and that while they would be paid by the company found guilty of slander if Kubitschek won the case, "you will, if you lose, have to explain the origin of the money you will have to pay, creating pretexts for new attacks on your personal honesty."

"The allegation of corruption," Sobral wrote, "is cruel, perfidious, and treacherous when carried out by able, unscrupulous persons." Supposing that the right of response to accusations existed in the United States and would not, if used, interfere with possible future legal action, he urged Kubitschek to make it known at once that he had not been convicted of any corruption and that no proof existed of his having permitted Communist infiltration in his administration in return for votes.[11]

3. A Disturbance at the Opening of the Inter-American Conference (November 1965)

At 5:30 P.M. on November 17, Castello Branco reached Rio's Hotel Glória to open the Second Special Inter-American Conference. Just outside the entrance, he was confronted by nine members of "the intellectual set" who raised placards and shouted, "Down with the dictatorship; we want liberty."[1]

The eight men who planned the protest (they were joined by another) were journalists Carlos Heitor Cony, Antônio Callado, and Márcio Moreira Alves, theater director Flávio Rangel, three cinema actors, and Jaime de Azevedo Rodrigues, a diplomat who had been *cassado*. Although the cautious Brazilian Communist Party (PCB) had refused to join them for a mass demonstration, they were determined to make the delegates from abroad aware of the situation in Brazil.[2]

Outside the Hotel Glória security agents, using force, arrested the protesters and turned them over to the War Ministry, which ordered them to be held incommunicado at the barracks of the Military Police. There they were interrogated collectively and individually by Colonel José Maria de Andrada Serpa and his men. General Riograndino Kruel, head of the Federal Department of Public Security, was upset because of the lack of prior knowledge of the disturbance, and he ordered permanent vigilance over all *cassados* "lest we be surprised again."[3]

Friends and relatives of some of the prisoners sent messages to Sobral Pinto. Quickly he submitted a habeas corpus petition to the head of the Superior Military Tribunal, complaining that "abusive treatment, ordered by the commander of the First Army," was used against citizens who, in the presence of the president, had exercised "their civic right of objection to the dictatorial regime imposed on the country."[4]

Learning on November 19 that the Minas state legislature had adopted a resolution condemning the protesters, Sobral sent a telegram to one of the legislators to deny that "the peaceful and legal manifestation" was "a Communist attack on the president of the republic." He said, "The ones who discredit the nation before foreigners are the representatives of the people who, in order to save their legislative mandates, threatened by the oppressors, bow submissively to the will of those who have all the power."[5]

After about four hundred writers and artists released a manifesto defending the prisoners who had "peacefully expressed their love of democracy," Sobral sent material for the *Correio da Manhã* and the *Jornal do Brasil* to publish about the wrongs "being endured by Antônio Callado, Carlos Heitor Cony, Márcio Moreira Alves, and their companions." He warned the executives of the *Jornal do Brasil* that "violent acts" such as those he was condemning "could in the future strike at the liberty of your newspaper and radio broadcasting station."[6]

Luís Viana Filho, head of the Brazilian delegation to the Inter-American Conference, received a telegram from Sobral about a project of the Brazilian delegation that would give the Inter-American Commission on Human Rights the authority to intervene in nations where those rights were violated. "Let me remind you that those rights are presently being violated by our government, which subscribed to the Universal Declaration of Human Rights at the United Nations on December 10, 1948. And let me further remind you that Law 4319 [of March 1964] guarantees in Brazil the rights defined in the above-mentioned Universal Declaration."[7]

In Alagoinhas, Bahia, Castello Branco delivered a speech with a warning against "any force in the military that might consider itself autonomous," and he declared that the government had the power to defeat any conspiracy. Because his speech followed the example of Ruy Barbosa in praising Alagoinhas, Sobral sent the president a telegram advising him to imitate "the noble statesman" in a more significant way. He should, Sobral said, adopt Ruy Barbosa's demand that the legislative, judicial, and executive branches be independent and sovereign, and he should arrange for the Justice Ministry to provide justice instead of "the regime of threats and force instituted by Juracy Magalhães."[8]

Juracy Magalhães favored harsh measures against those who had demonstrated outside the Hotel Glória, and he was particularly angry at former diplomat Jaime de Azevedo Rodrigues, a *cassado*, and at Carlos Heitor Cony, who had written unflattering articles about the new regime as early as April 1964. The press carried the news that "every one of the eight intellectuals" would be *cassado* and that Cony and Jaime de Azevedo Rodrigues would be confined geographically to an area in Mato Grosso state.[9] The retired diplomat remained, like journalist Antônio Callado and cinema actor Glauber Rocha, a client of Sobral, but, as Sobral advised STM Judge João Romeiro Neto, the other members of the original group of protesters were by this time being defended by other lawyers.[10]

At the Military Police barracks the arrested protesters signed a letter saying that they had wanted to bring the dictatorial aspects of the regime to the attention of international opinion. The final judgment, reflecting Castello Branco's opposition to severity in the punishments, found the protesters guilty merely of interfering with traffic at the time and place of an international meeting. Colonel José Maria de Andrada Serpa, according to Carlos Heitor Cony's recollection, followed orders when he released a note to the press saying that the protesters' plans had not included violence against the regime. They were set free on December 1.[11]

On December 3, Sobral submitted a document to the STM to withdraw his habeas corpus petition, no longer necessary. He used the document to present arguments such as he had given to Luís Viana Filho about the obligation of Brazil to adhere to the Universal Declaration of Human Rights and to the list of those rights presented to the recent conference by the Inter-American Commission on Human Rights. He wrote that the curbing of those rights was a "criminal act," and he went on to say that in the United States police protection had been given to "a dramatic manifestation with placards" in opposition to the Vietnam War.[12]

4.   Closing 1965 with a Tribute to Schmidt

Late in November, Guanabara Governor Raphael de Almeida Magalhães inaugurated the school that Lacerda had named the Ginásio Estadual Sobral Pinto. Sobral wrote to thank Raphael for his kind words at the ceremony and, at the same time, to criticize him for planning to resign the governorship several days before the inauguration of Negrão de Lima in order not to have to transfer the state to the recent election victor. Commenting on this "unjustifiable affront" to a man who had been a friend of Dario de Almeida Magalhães in the past, Sobral wrote: "Personal tolerance of adversaries is a demonstration of a culture characteristic of a civilized mentality."[1]

Sobral had advice also for Governor-elect Negrão de Lima after announcements named the participants in his incoming administration. Much as he admired the intelligence of the future state secretary of education, Benjamin Moraes Filho, he opposed his selection, feeling the appointment would further the status of Protestantism.[2]

Above all, Sobral disliked the choice of Lino de Sá Pereira to be *procurador geral da fazenda* (public finance), a choice that he told Negrão filled his eyes with tears. Sá Pereira, Sobral pointed out, had been dismissed from ruling on the estate of Paulo Bittencourt "because he betrayed the interests of Guanabara state in order to benefit Niomar Moniz Sodré," who claimed to have inherited the *Correio da Manhã*.[3]

While Sobral was defending the victims of the coup of 1964, he was, as before, devoting time to the case of Paulo Bittencourt's daughter Sybil against Niomar. "You cannot," he wrote Negrão, "put the exceedingly important *procuradoria da fazenda* in the hands of a submissive instrument of the unscrupulous will of this terrible woman, Niomar." He described Niomar as terrifying everyone in Brazil. "The Supreme Court justices, except for Hahnemann Guimarães, bow before her illegal and dishonest demands." Negrão, Sobral added, was full of fear lest he suffer from "a wretched campaign in the newspaper that was usurped by that woman."[4]

Commenting on the "frailty of our public men," Sobral discussed how Juscelino Kubitschek, given by Niomar the choice of "siding with her and the *Correio da Manhã*" or with Sobral and his legal defense work, did not vacillate: "He chose Niomar." "You asked me," Sobral reminded Negrão, "to accept this capitulation of Juscelino. But with the arrival of the bitter and hazardous hour, all of you felt unable to do without my legal help, which I gave with the care you know so well."[5]

Sobral was in Juiz de Fora in mid-December, arguing the case of labor leader Clodsmith Riani, and therefore was not at the Conselho Federal of the Ordem dos Advogados do Brasil (OAB) when it received a surprise "courtesy visit" by Juracy Magalhães, brought to the meeting by Maria Rita de Andrade. Learning later that the justice minister had used the occasion to explain why lawyers should support the work of his ministry, Sobral wrote Juracy to say that if he had been present he would have given the reasons that made it impossible for him, as a lawyer, to support that work. "I would have said that your appeal was not really an expression of esteem for lawyers and their leading organ but was a display of disrespect for these defenders of legality." He attributed to Juracy the "inglorious task" of trying to justify Institutional Act Number Two, which removed tenure guarantees for judges at all levels, transforming them into submissive instruments of executive power.[6]

In the same vein, Sobral wrote to the president-elect of the IAB, José Ribeiro de Castro Filho. Advising him how to reply to an invitation to serve on a Justice Ministry commission, Sobral told him to declare categorically that "acceptance of the invitation does not imply approval of the orientation of the government" and to use his position on the commission to fight "for the restoration of the rights that have been violated and for the reparation of injustices carried out against innocent compatriots."[7]

Among the "injustices" that Sobral tried to reverse in December were the charges against the director of production of Mannesmann do Brasil, a steel company whose excessive emission of promissory notes during the Goulart administration had led to a scandal. Sobral convinced the general investigating the case that his client was innocent.[8]

As had happened in the past, Sobral felt that his position separated him from friends who were supporters of the military regime. To one of them, a Catholic priest who had stopped writing or telephoning him, Sobral wrote in November: "The excommunication that the colonels decreed against me has built up a wall between me and my close friends."[9] He was, however, the recipient of honors. Journalists covering the activities of the Guanabara state assembly praised him at the end of the year. And in Curitiba, Sobral was honored by the graduating law students of the Catholic University of Paraná.

Brasil em Marcha magazine listed Sobral as one of the "best of 1965" and called him "the Champion of Liberties in Brazil" who argued on behalf of political outcasts and the restoration of liberties. In view of these words, Sobral asked the magazine's publisher how it could include, also among "the best," Marshal Castello Branco, General Juracy Magalhães, and General Costa e Silva. Sobral went on to say that these were the very men who, "fancying themselves to be the administrators of Brazil," persecuted and oppressed their fellow citizens who turned to Sobral for the help that was praised in the article.[10]

The annual December 31 lunch of Sobral and old friends was held at the Mesbla Restaurant, continuing a tradition begun in 1933 by Alceu Amoroso Lima, Sobral, Augusto Frederico Schmidt, Hamilton Nogueira, and Catholic leader Wagner Dutra. After the number attending had risen from five to nine, it was reduced to six, as Sobral explained, "by politics and deaths."[11] With the death of Schmidt on February 8, 1965, only five were at the Mesbla Restaurant at the end of that year: Sobral, Alceu, Hamilton Nogueira, José Carlos de Mello e Souza, and Rubens Porto.

Thoughts in memory of Augusto Frederico Schmidt, written by Sobral, were read aloud by Alceu Amoroso Lima at the lunch: "We have lost someone who was more than poet, citizen, and patriot because he was, above all, the faithful friend, always present in times that were both good and bad. We have lost our unforgettable and boisterous Schmidt, as less recently we lost the intelligent, discerning Wagner.

"We do not know whether they see and hear us. . . . It is certain, however, that at this moment they will be asking God, the Virgin, and the Saints to whom we are devoted to watch over our souls, our spirits, and our desires, keeping them, during the obstacles and dangers of our earthly journey, always guided by the compass of our Faith in Jesus Christ and our Love of God the All Powerful, leading us to love our neighbors as ourselves."[12]

PART V

From Ato Three (1966) to Ato Five (1968)

1. Opposing Indirect Gubernatorial Elections and the *Cassação* of Ademar de Barros (1966)

By early 1966 President Castello Branco came around to agreeing with military leaders that direct elections for governors might be harmful to the work of the revolution, and therefore in February Institutional Act Number Three was issued to place the elections in the hands of the state legislatures. Sobral described Ato 3 as an affront to the nation and a confession by the government of its lack of popular support.[1]

At a meeting of the Instituto dos Advogados Brasileiros (IAB) held later in February, Sobral argued that Castello Branco did not have the authority to issue institutional and complementary acts. And he proposed that the government, in order to overcome "the institutional crisis," arrange for a popular election for a constitutional assembly.[2]

Institutional Act Number Three gave Governor Ademar de Barros the opportunity to purchase votes of the São Paulo state legislators who would elect the next governor in September. Reports that he would do this and had plans to issue vast amounts of state bonds, injurious to the federal government's financial policy, made it seem likely that he would be *cassado*.[3] Sobral, in São Paulo in March to study the notebooks of Luiz Carlos Prestes, told the press that although he was no political ally of Ademar, he was at the governor's side in seeking the return of order in Brazil. "Any attack against the mandate of Ademar de Barros," he said, "is an attack against the rights of Brazilian citizens and the autonomy of São Paulo." Thus Sobral irritated *O Estado de S. Paulo*, run by Ademar-hating Júlio de Mesquita Filho.[4]

In June, when Sobral was again in São Paulo, this time to defend

Prestes in a military court, Ademar was *cassado*, in accordance with a decision of Castello Branco. At the military court, Sobral gave the journalists a written declaration saying that Castello had struck down a mandate of the people of the great state, which had become the slave of the capricious will of an army marshal. He added that if Ademar had committed crimes, appropriate laws existed for dealing with them.[5]

Sobral's emotional four-hour oral argument on behalf of Prestes did not prevent the hidden PCB leader from being given a fourteen-year prison sentence. Nevertheless, Sobral kept receiving a flood of appeals for legal help, and these he accepted while handling old cases such as those of Sybil Bittencourt, Clodsmith Riani, former diplomat Jaime de Azevedo Rodrigues, and the absent Kubitschek, who was being investigated by an IPM about the CNTI (National Confederation of Workers in Industry).[6] In July Sobral obtained the freedom of Mauro Borges, the former governor of Goiás who was jailed in Rio Grande do Sul after being *cassado*.[7] Later in 1966 Sobral agreed to defend Tarsan de Castro, who was said to have trained guerrilla fighters while serving as Governor Mauro Borges's education secretary, and who had found asylum in the Uruguayan embassy after escaping from a fort. Sobral was also a part of the team formed to defend Herbert José de Sousa, director of Ação Popular, made up in large part of young militants eager to overthrow the capitalist system.[8]

Late in May 1966 War Minister Costa e Silva was overwhelmingly chosen to be the presidential candidate of the government party, the ARENA (Aliança Renovadora Nacional), and, after that, the IAB arranged for him to have a debate with Sobral. The press looked forward to the debate, scheduled for August, and before it was to take place Sobral sent the general questions for him to answer about his plans for governing. Would he protect human rights? Would he abolish the "present system" of punishing people without giving them the right of defense? Would he restore direct elections? With the date of the debate drawing near, Costa e Silva said he would not participate. He said that students planning to attend and support Sobral would create bedlam at the affair and that the questions in Sobral's letters revealed Sobral's incompatibility with him.[9]

Sobral's name was among those of six civilians being considered by the opposition party, the MDB (Movimento Democrático Brasileiro), as possible candidates to oppose Costa e Silva. The MDB asked Tancredo Neves to persuade Sobral to accept and to travel around

Brazil, giving speeches in reply to those of the official candidate. However, following the *cassação* of Ademar de Barros in June, the MDB announced that it was not interested in competing in indirect elections; the presidential candidacy of Costa e Silva, who promised to "humanize the Revolution," was left unopposed. Proposals to have Sobral run on the MDB ticket in the senatorial race, a direct election, were discontinued because Sobral said he had not been consulted and did not wish to run.[10]

2. Advising Kubitschek to Return Only after March 15, 1967 (1966)

In October 1966, Adauto Lúcio Cardoso, president of the Chamber of Deputies, thought he had a commitment from Castello Branco not to *cassar* congressmen. He was so upset by a decree of October 12 that violated his understanding that he declared it invalid in the case of the six congressmen who were *cassados* by the decree. Five of the six would not leave the Chamber, slept there at night, and issued statements against the government. When Castello asked Supreme Court Justice Aliomar Baleeiro to try to persuade Adauto to desist from protecting them, the name of Sobral came up, prompting Castello to tell Baleeiro that Sobral "is a diabolic creature who dominates Adauto." Also dominating Adauto, Castello said, was the recent Housing Bank president, Sandra Cavalcanti, a close friend of the violently anti-Castello Carlos Lacerda.[1]

Adauto remained intransigent, and on October 20 Ato Complementar 23, signed by Castello, the military ministers, and the ministers of justice and foreign affairs, declared Congress in recess until November 22. After troops under Colonel Carlos de Meira Matos forced Congress to close, Sobral sent a telegram to Castello to remind him that, as army chief of staff in March 1964, he had issued a warning against "the dictatorial pretensions of João Goulart."[2]

Sobral, in a telegram to Adauto, said that the brutal new *ato complementar* required a "radical change" in Adauto's relations with the government. Writing to Adauto a few days later, he expressed his disappointment in him. Explaining to the congressman that he was suffering from "dreadful neuralgic pains" (on the side of his face, the left, that had not undergone surgery in New York in 1954), he said he was handicapped in making the energetic attack on the government that he wanted Adauto to make.[3] Adauto, however, remained silent. In January 1967 Castello named him to the Supreme Court, where he replaced the retiring Álvaro Ribeiro da Costa. Thus Castello fulfilled a promise he had made to Adauto before the crisis of October 1966.

During the crisis brought on by Adauto in October, Lacerda prepared a manifesto to launch the Frente Ampla to oppose the military regime and to bring about direct presidential elections. Kubitschek, who was in the United States, agreed to be a joint signer, but he became hesitant a little later upon receiving warnings that, if he did so, steps against his friends would be extended beyond the *cassações* of October 12 and prosecutors might call for the confiscation of his own properties. Sobral, writing to Kubitschek on October 14, urged him not to leave off participating in the Frente Ampla, which he described as a "necessity," like the Liga de Defesa da Legalidade, organized by himself in 1955.[4] But Kubitschek, while on his speaking tour in the United States, decided not to be a joint signer, and the Frente's manifesto, finally made public on October 27, was signed by Lacerda alone.

In Lisbon on November 19, Kubitschek warmly received his old foe Lacerda and issued with him an antigovernment statement praising the objectives of the Frente Ampla. In Brazil, after that, charges of "illicit enrichment" were brought against Kubitschek amidst much publicity. The former president had told the foreign press that the charges were based on his having received, as "an homage of the people of Brasília, a piece of land worth about two thousand dollars," but in Brasília in November an attorney of NOVACAP (the government company that built Brasília) went to the courts to accuse Kubitschek of having received "two mansions" from friends.[5]

Sobral wrote Kubitschek that the accusation was a mere reflection of hatred that would get nowhere in the Federal Court of Appeals, and he turned for assistance to Minas Governor Israel Pinheiro, a schoolmate of his who had headed NOVACAP under Kubitschek. Answering one of Kubitschek's questions, Sobral told him not to return to Brazil "at this moment when you will be given serious troubles, perhaps imprisonment or confinement." He told Kubitschek to be patient and await the "new climate" that would come with the replacement of Castello Branco on March 15, 1967, by Costa e Silva. "Have faith in the future. It belongs to you." Within two years, Sobral wrote, the military would find itself unable to continue enslaving the nation.[6]

The Federal Court of Appeals was on vacation until mid-February, and, as Sobral advised Kubitschek, so was the Supreme Court, scheduled to decide whether to hear a new charge, this one related to Kubitschek's ownership of his Rio apartment. Sobral called the new charge nothing more than an opportunity for Alcino Salazar, *procurador geral da república,* to draw up a document for insulting Kubitschek.[7]

Sobral, still suffering from facial pains, joined Cândido de Oliveira Neto on January 21, 1967, in answering more of Kubitschek's questions. By that time Congress, authorized by Institutional Act Number Four, was in the process of giving Brazil a new constitution, which would be effective on March 15 with the expiration of the institutional acts and the inauguration of Costa e Silva. The constitution reflected some alterations made by Congress to Castello Branco's proposals but left unaltered the indirect election of presidents and a strong declaration of individual rights. Sobral, noting the powerful role to be given to the president, described the constitution as "of the dictatorial type" but capable of improving the situation because of the articles protecting individual rights and the independence of the judiciary.[8]

In their joint letter, Sobral and Cândido wrote Kubitschek regarding the expiration on March 15 of the institutional and complementary acts "that make Castello Branco an absolute dictator. We shall have courts in which we shall be able to defend you." Referring to the case of an automobile given to President Kubitschek, the lawyers assured him that if this matter were to result in an IPM, the procedure, carried out by the nation's *procuradoria,* would be a proper one, in which he could testify briefly and leave it up to his lawyers to give fuller information.[9]

Castello Branco, who had assumed the presidency with a determination to reform everything, issued so many decree laws during his last month in office that Sobral sent him a telegram on March 6 calling "the torrent" an attack on the sovereignty of Congress.[10] The most important decree law, issued on March 13, was a new national security law, with broad definitions of crimes, among them the furnishing of false or biased news dangerous to the prestige of Brazil. The new law gave military justice the authority to judge civilians for the crimes it listed and was described by Sobral as allowing a simple denouncement for subversion to prevent a person from exercising his profession until he proved his innocence. São Paulo's *Jornal da*

Tarde accused Castello of liquidating the democratic process with the new security law.[11]

In the face of all the changes being enacted, Sobral occasionally remarked that the change most needed in Brazil was a change in the mentality of the men in power.[12] However, with the takeover by hard-liners on March 15, 1967, the change he wanted was not realized.

3. While Kubitschek, Back in Brazil, Is Threatened, Hélio Fernandes Is Interned (1967)

Juscelino Kubitschek, hopeful that the new presidential adminis-tration would bring about the "complete reestablishment of politi-cal and juridical order,"[1] returned to Brazil on April 9, 1967. Sobral, however, had become far from hopeful. Writing to Dario de Almeida Magalhães about the "military enslavement" of Brazil, brought about, he said, by the National Security Council, the National War College, and the SNI (National Information Service), he called the days the "most bitter" of his life, symbolized by the black clothing he always wore following the death of his daughter Maria do Carmo in 1956. He was depressed also by the overwhelming defeat of his candidacy for the presidency of the Conselho Federal of the OAB; in telling Dario that he was "everywhere attacked," he added "especially by the lawyers."[2]

Finding the new administration determined to have Kubitschek interrogated, Sobral dealt with a summons by explaining to a gen-eral that physicians had found Kubitschek too ill to leave his home. Arrangements were made for the inquiry to take place in the former president's residence in May.[3]

The influence of the hard line was clear after Hélio Fernandes, in the *Tribuna da Imprensa*, vilified the character of Castello Branco following the late president's death in July 1967 in a plane crash. Military Club President Augusto César Moniz de Aragão convinced Costa e Silva and Justice Minister Luís Antônio da Gama e Silva that the fury of the military against Hélio Fernandes would lead to a seri-ous crisis if the journalist were not punished, and therefore Costa e Silva authorized Gama e Silva to confine Hélio Fernandes on Fer-nando de Noronha Island, off the northeastern coast.[4]

Sobral, although critical of the cruel language in the Fernandes article, condemned the "illegal capitulation" of the government. In the first of two telegrams to Gama e Silva, he described the confinement as proof of the existence of a military dictatorship. In the second he said, "You say that Hélio Fernandes should be grateful for the confinement because it prevented his being assailed and perhaps assassinated by furious military men. Strange logic by a justice minister who should have arranged to protect the threatened journalist and insisted that the ministers of the armed forces punish officers for their crime of making the threats."[5]

The journalist, after losing a 6-5 decision in the Federal Court of Appeals, was moved to Pirassununga, São Paulo, to complete the two months of confinement.

The Hélio Fernandes case led to so bitter an exchange between Lacerda and Military Club President Moniz de Aragão that the justice minister barred Lacerda from further use of television. But General Moniz de Aragão avoided a debate with Sobral by returning, unanswered, Sobral's telegrams to him. The six telegrams, all published in the press, began with a reply to the general's article about Hélio Fernandes in *O Globo* and described the article as violating the army's disciplinary regulations. Subsequently Sobral denounced the "vulgar" acts of returning, unanswered, telegrams about liberty of the press, the civilian nature of the Fernandes case, and the sins of the military.[6]

Early in September 1967 Kubitschek attended a meeting of the Frente Ampla with Lacerda, Congressman Renato Archer, and others at Archer's home. The federal police, on instructions from Gama e Silva, ordered Kubitschek to testify on September 11 about the meeting. The inquiry was brief because Kubitschek, although he made an appearance, refused to say anything. After it ended, Kubitschek was acclaimed by the people in the streets, and he issued a manifesto, distributed by Sobral and read aloud in the Chamber of Deputies by Hermano Alves. In it he said that he had been inspired by Costa e Silva's promises to establish justice in Brazil and that, ever since returning in April, he had been contributing to the peace by remaining silent. As for the questions put to him at the inquiry, he was, he said, exercising his legal right to remain silent. "Silence is the only means of protest that I have at this time."[7]

With Gama e Silva maintaining that the *atos complementares*, including the statute governing the behavior of the *cassados*, remained in effect, the press speculated about a confinement of Kubitschek. Kubitschek, at the same time, went to Houston, Texas, on account of a health problem of one of his two daughters.

During the six weeks that Kubitschek was away, Lacerda made

a trip to Montevideo and had a friendly meeting with Goulart. The resulting "Pact of Montevideo," with its joint statement of praise for the Frente Ampla, was heavily assaulted by many who had supported either Lacerda or Goulart in their past battles against each other. But the new alliance was defended by Sobral, who reminded Brazilians that all advocates of democracy should work together.[8]

Following Kubitschek's return to Brazil on October 25, Gama e Silva declared that if he should disturb the peace again, "I shall order him to spend sixty days confined in Brasília." Sobral told the press that the disturber of the peace was not Kubitschek but was the government, with its "revolting" accusations. Gama e Silva's charge, he said, was so ridiculous that it was a laughing matter.[9]

4.   The Student Movement in the First Half of 1968

During Costa e Silva's first year in office, Sobral became a member of a legal team to help Nelson Carneiro after the prodivorce congressman used a revolver in the Chamber of Deputies building to wound another congressman, said to have been threatening him.[1] At the same time, Sobral defended a former Nazi, Franz Stangl, who was threatened with extradition from Brazil to Europe for activities there during World War II. Although Sobral hated the activities, he maintained that they had been performed on account of orders from superiors and had not been illegal until the war's victors, at Nuremberg, had mistakenly issued convictions for what had been done before the crimes were defined.[2] In taking still another position that aroused controversy, Sobral described the United States intervention in Vietnam as legitimate. But when students were arrested in Recife for campaigning against the Vietnam War, he called their campaign no reason to find them subversive.[3]

Most importantly, Sobral gave support to students in Rio who had become displeased with Governor Negrão de Lima because of the dilapidated condition of the Calabouço student restaurant. A group of them, headed by Elinor Mendes de Brito, called on Sobral in January 1968 to complain that members of their Frente Unida dos Estudantes do Calabouço had been arrested while they roamed the streets, seeking donations for repairing the restaurant. They told Sobral that the police, while beating students, had broken an arm of one of them, had seized the money that had been collected, and had threatened to have the DOPS start an investigation of cases of "disobedience."[4]

Agreeing to represent the students, Sobral offered to try to work things out with Negrão de Lima. On January 24 he prepared an appropriate letter, and he delivered it when he called on the governor. Although Negrão, in Sobral's presence, telephoned the security secretary, General Dario Coelho, and asked him to call off the investigation, this was not done. Because the students continued to be threatened with arrest, Sobral visited with Negrão again. Negrão, after telephoning the general once more, told Sobral to advise the students to ignore the arrest orders.

On January 31 Sobral brought Negrão another letter, listing the repairs that he found necessary after he inspected the restaurant. The governor, during this conversation and another one a week later, spoke of getting the necessary funds from the federal government. He asked Sobral to tell the students to be patient because it would take three or four weeks to get the work started. During these weeks, students who had jobs found it difficult to keep them because the police told their employers that they were wanted by the DOPS. Sobral made three more calls on Negrão and wrote to him again on March 11.[5]

Late in March, when it was clear that nothing was being done about the restaurant, the Frente Unida dos Estudantes do Calabouço organized more demonstrations.

Soldiers of the Guanabara Military Police, trying to prevent a parade of hundreds of protesting students on March 28, shot and killed eighteen-year-old Edson Luís de Lima Souto and wounded others. Students brought Edson's corpse to the state legislative building. The vicinity, that evening and night, became filled with people and irate speeches.[6]

Sobral was at home in bed at 9:00 P.M., suffering from his neuralgia, when he received a message from Elinor Mendes de Brito about what had happened. Taking pills for the pain, he hastened to the legislature. There he told the press that the measures promised him by Negrão "were not taken and this is the result."[7]

At the legislature Sobral was assisted by its president, José Bonifácio Diniz de Andrada, when he argued that Edson's corpse should receive a proper autopsy at the Instituto Medical Legal. He gave his word of honor about its quick return to the legislature and arranged that the trip to the Instituto be accompanied by students, journalists, and others. But most of the students, in a state of frenzy, called Sobral's suggestion a maneuver to get the body out of the legislature.[8] Sobral, his promise discredited, returned home after midnight, and the students succeeded in having the autopsy carried out at the legislature.

Demonstrations to protest the killing occurred in many parts of Brazil. The funeral procession of tens of thousands in Rio on March 29 was notable for scuffles between young people and men in uniform who said·they were preventing depredations. Negrão de Lima forbade a mass rally planned for April 1, but his ruling was defied by thousands of civilians, many with clubs and stones and some with revolvers. The state Military Police, with the help of federal troops, dominated the situation only after skirmishes during which shops were pillaged, vehicles were damaged, and scores of civilians and policemen were wounded. About 230 arrests were made. Sobral, seeking legal protection of Elinor Mendes de Brito and others, declared: "Now, when the person killed is a civilian student, the armed forces mobilize throughout the country to prevent manifestations demanding punishment of the assassins."[9]

During a parade in Rio that followed the Seventh Day Mass at Candelária Church for the soul of Edson, the authorities prevented a repetition of the disorders of April 1. Zealous members of a force of ten thousand military policemen, some on horseback, used swords, billies, and tear gas, and rounded up a reported five hundred people.[10]

Students in Brazil became bold in demonstrating, and their leaders made it clear that their aim was to overthrow the capitalist structure of society. They jeered at bourgeois politicians such as the "opportunistic" ones of the Frente Ampla, "sham populists" moved by "personal ambition."[11] And they rejected the peaceful stance of the PCB, which was objecting to the urban guerrilla activities undertaken by Carlos Marighella and others who had left the party.

Costa e Silva was told that the student movement was the work of PCB infiltrators, and so he authorized Gama e Silva to have the governors work against student rallies. He also agreed that the Frente Ampla, planning to organize antigovernment demonstrations, should be closed down. The justice minister's directive of April 5, banning the Frente Ampla, was described by the *Folha de S. Paulo* as an act against an "incompetent movement." Sobral called the directive a "confirmation of a military dictatorship."[12]

"I'm scourged by the neuralgia and have no rest on account of the students," Sobral wrote Dario de Almeida Magalhães in April 1968. To help fourteen students, arrested that month in Rio for distributing pamphlets, he drew up a habeas corpus petition.[13] Arrests like these, in Rio and elsewhere, did nothing to slow down the momentum of the activities of the students and the intellectuals who supported them. In São Paulo on May Day, students and their allies distributed leaflets of urban guerrilla groups and of Trotskyite revolutionaries, and they shouted against the "wage freeze" that infuriated workers. At São Paulo's Praça da Sé they brought about a conflict that wounded Governor Roberto de Abreu Sodré in the head, preventing him from giving a speech.[14]

Sobral, in the *Tribuna Estudantil*, said that nothing in the past could compare with the student movement and that to try to smash it by the force of arms was stupid. He regretted the dangerous misunderstanding between the "generation ruling Brazil" and the "new generation," eager for drastic reforms. Noting the demands of young people for a "reform of Brazil's social structure," he said that a suitable message for the students could be provided "only by a divine force, which exists here and is able to make itself heard. It is the renovating Church, the Church of the Second Vatican Council."[15]

The Second Vatican Council (1962–1965) emphasized the mission of the Catholic Church for social justice and for the improvement of the lot of the poor, and it called on the laity to play an important role. But Sobral, who had been named president of the Centro Dom Vital by Cardinal Jaime Câmara in August 1967, found the conflicting reactions of Alceu Amoroso Lima and Gustavo Corção to Vatican II an impediment to his hope of reviving the Centro. The ultraconservative Corção, in his *O Globo* columns, condemned leftism and the "modernist wave" and attacked Alceu violently. Although Alceu had views that pleased Sobral, he was, in Sobral's opinion, too much on the side of socialism and positions of Communists who attacked United States "imperialism."[16]

5. The Formation of the Human Rights Council and the Defense of More Clients (second half of 1968)

Former President Jânio Quadros, who attacked the military regime, was described by São Paulo student leader José Dirceu as a mere populist demagogue. He was described by Justice Minister Gama e Silva as a violator of *atos complementares* that had been decreed in 1965 to restrict the activities of the *cassados*. After Quadros spoke to reporters in July 1968 about the need for a "reconstitution of po-litical and juridical values, destroyed by the government," Gama e Silva condemned him to 120 days of confinement in Corumbá, on the Bolivian border. Sobral, in an eight-page letter to Costa e Silva that appeared in the press, said that the Constitution of 1967 had ended the institutional and complementary acts. The confinement of Quadros, he wrote, revealed the "arbitrary and dictatorial men-tality" of those who had taken over the power.[1]

Sobral, in his letter, informed Costa e Silva about Law 4,319 of March 16, 1964, which called for the formation of a Council to De-fend Human Rights (Conselho de Defesa dos Direitos da Pessoa Humana—CDDPH). This *conselho* was to consist of the justice min-ister, the majority and minority leaders of both houses of Congress, and the heads of the OAB's Conselho Federal, the ABI (Brazilian Press Association), and the Brazilian Association of Education; these eight members were to choose a ninth, a professor of constitutional law. Its duty was to investigate human rights violations and arrange that violators be punished.[2]

Following the administration of Castello Branco, when nothing was done to implement Law 4,319, Sobral became the great cam-paigner for its implementation. In legal defense arguments and in communications to government officials he wrote about it, often along with references to Brazil's participation in human rights decla-rations of the United Nations and the American republics. Above all, he worked to have the lawyers' associations and especially the OAB exert pro-CDDPH pressure on the government, and he convinced the OAB that the CDDPH should include an adviser from the IAB (Insti-tuto dos Advogados Brasileiros).[3]

On August 13, 1968, after Justice Minister Gama e Silva ignored various messages sent to him by the OAB, Sobral persuaded the OAB to have its president, Samuel Duarte, tell Gama e Silva that if he would not issue, within thirty days, a convocation of the CDDPH, the OAB would arrange for the CDDPH to come into existence at the OAB headquarters. Sobral, on the next day, sought to have Press Associa-tion President Danton Jobim cooperate with the OAB's position.[4]

Early in September Gama e Silva agreed to install the CDDPH. The *Jornal do Brasil*, praising the justice minister for his efforts leading to this development, was reprimanded by Sobral in a letter explaining the role of the OAB. Writing to a law partner of Dario, Sobral called the installation "largely the result of my work." When Sobral sent a telegram to Costa e Silva to advise that ill health would prevent his attendance in November at the installation ceremony, he added that much more was required of Brazil than the ceremony: Brazil would have to adhere to the letter and spirit of the human rights resolutions of the UN and American republics that condemned "measures of exception decreed by the armed forces" of Brazil.[5]

During his battle for the installation of the CDDPH, Sobral had opportunities to call attention to violations of human rights. He learned that theatrical director Flávio Rangel and architect Bernardo Figueiredo had been held incommunicado for seventy-two hours and shorn of their hair, and therefore he sent a telegram to Navy Minister Augusto Rademaker Grünewald demanding punishment for the navy men responsible for the acts.[6]

Opening a more important case, Sobral sent a telegram to Army Minister Aurélio de Lyra Tavares asking for information about the whereabouts of petroleum workers' leader Paulo Rangel Sampaio Fernandes, who had been seized when an army major and six of his men had invaded the Duque de Caxias refinery workers' union, in Rio de Janeiro state, on July 19, 1968, making off also with the union's list of members. Senator Mário Martins, turning to First Army Commander Siseno Sarmento, joined Sobral in seeking information about the labor leader, and it was learned, four days after his arrest, that he was in an army barrack, but, being incommunicado, was unaware of the habeas corpus petition already presented to the STM by Sobral on his behalf.[7]

At the trial on July 29, Sobral told the court that the prisoner, accused of subversion and of wanting to form another union in Belo Horizonte, had been arrested in order to create a "climate of fear" in the working class. After STM Judge Peri Bevilacqua maintained that the matter was one for the Labor Ministry, not the military, the court, in a unanimous decision, upheld the petition submitted by Sobral.[8]

Even more publicity was given to the case of Gregório Bezerra, a PCB organizer of rural workers who was arrested in the northeast in April 1964. He refused in February 1967 to continue being represented by a legal team that had been assigned to defend him, and said "Sobral Pinto alone merits my confidence." The team, which included Cândido de Oliveira Neto, therefore withdrew, and Sobral set out to try to persuade the STM that the sixty-seven-year-old Bezerra should be released from prison by means of a rejection or drastic reduction of the nineteen-year sentence already decreed by the *auditoria* of the Seventh Military Region in Recife.[9] Bezerra, before being elected to Congress on the PCB ticket in 1945, had been among those receiving amnesty for his participation in the Communist uprising of 1935, but many army men could not forget that he was held responsible for the killing of an army officer during the uprising.

Sobral, at the STM trial of Bezerra in January 1968, heatedly interrupted the presentation of Eraldo Gueiros Leite, *procurador geral* of military justice, and was told by presiding Judge Olímpio Mourão Filho to calm down. When the judges voted, Peri Bevilacqua said Bezerra's sentence should be reduced to two years, which would set him free, but a majority of eight, including Generals Ernesto Geisel and Otacílio Uraraí and Brigadeiro Gabriel Grün Moss, voted for ten years. Sobral's stay of execution petition to the STM was rejected in October 1968, and so Sobral said he would turn to the Supreme Court.[10] But what brought about Bezerra's freedom and exile was the government's release in 1969 of fifteen prisoners in exchange for the freedom of the United States ambassador, kidnapped by leftists belonging to urban guerrilla groups.

Sobral's difficulties in the Bezerra case did not diminish his confidence in handling cases of men influential during the Goulart regime. After one such client, labor leader Clodsmith Riani, was set free in June 1968,[11] Sobral worked with optimism on cases of Paulo de Tarso Santos, who had resigned as Goulart's minister of education in October 1963 when Goulart was disappointing the far leftists of the Frente de Mobilização Popular. Sobral informed Paulo de Tarso, who was in Chile, that the courts would find him innocent, and he encouraged him to return soon to Brazil, following the example of Darcy Ribeiro, who came from Uruguay in October 1968.[12] Paulo de Tarso, however, remained in Chile.

Deaths in 1968 of old friends José Fernando Carneiro, active in Catholic lay work, and Affonso Penna Júnior, Sobral's neighbor and benefactor in the past, followed the death of another old friend, Vargas police chief Coriolano de Góes, late in 1967. In a sorrowful mood Sobral wrote to a former law school classmate, listing members of their class who had died, among them brilliant lawyer Mário Bulhões Pedreira.[13] Perhaps the personal setback that most distressed Sobral and his wife Maria José was the determination of their daughter Ruth, who had been doing legal work in Sobral's office, to marry Sobral's longtime office companion Wilson Salazar after Wilson separated from his wife. Sobral and Maria José could not, as Sobral explained to a niece, do anything that might give the impression that they recognized a union "condemned by the Church." Their love for her continued, but they made it clear that they strongly reproved the step she took.[14]

6. Institutional Act Five and the Imprisonment of Sobral (December 1968)

In September 1968 Sobral was telling the STM that there was no excuse for the police roundup, in the streets of Belo Horizonte, of students accused of seeking contributions to help pay for the forth-coming thirtieth Congress of the UNE. Dismayed to find three of the judges conversing instead of paying attention to his words, he spoke harshly: "I have the right to be heard. I am not talking to a bunch of fish." The judges, when they voted, rebuked Sobral for his conduct and rejected his arguments.[1]

When the thirtieth UNE Congress was held in October near the town of Ibiúna, São Paulo, it was invaded by the São Paulo police. The arrest of 739 students, among them the top leaders, was a crippling blow to the student movement. Sobral was approached by the families of eight of the students who had been transferred to Rio and were held incommunicado by the Guanabara Military Police, and he asked STM President Olímpio Mourão Filho to arrange for him to see the students, his clients.[2]

At the time of the arrests near Ibiúna, Gama e Silva and Costa e Silva demanded that Congress revoke the parliamentary immunities of Márcio Moreira Alves so that he could be tried by the Supreme Court for saying in Congress that army men were "executioners" who were "beating up and machine gunning the young people."[3] In October, while debate about this hard-line demand became the chief topic in Brazil, Sobral, in a telegram to Décio Miranda, *procurador geral da república*, urged him to oppose the planned "violence against Congress." In another telegram, Sobral assured Márcio Moreira Alves that his mandate should be considered untouchable but for "the militaristic regime that enslaves the civilian power."[4]

With Gama e Silva rumored to be ready to promulgate a drastic *ato adicional* if Congress were disobedient, Sobral spoke to the press about the "insane" reaction of the military to Moreira Alves's speeches. And he complained that his own "frequent telegrams" to the justice minister and the president never brought replies.[5]

In November 1968, when the Marighella terrorist group in São Paulo was carrying out assaults on banks, the Rio police tried to show that Marighella, with the help of a young resident of Rio, was responsible for the robbery of cash from a vehicle of the Guanabara State Retirement Institute. Sobral, calling the charge ridiculous, denounced a resulting *prisão preventiva* decree against Marighella, who was already being sought to serve a prison sentence. Marighella, he said, was too intelligent to believe that with a few million cruzeiros he could carry out a revolution in Brazil. "Besides, he is dedicated to the doctrine of Marx, which opposes terrorism, a tool of the anarchists. Marighella deserves more respect."[6]

In December Sobral was defending three French priests, whose association with Ação Popular and possession of "subversive" papers had brought about their arrest in Minas Gerais and likely expulsion from Brazil.[7] He interrupted the work to attend the Third National Conference of Lawyers, held in Recife between December 7 and 13. Speeches and comments made at the conference were not much to the liking of Justice Minister Gama e Silva, who presided at the installation of the conference. Samuel Duarte, president of the OAB, called for amnesty for individuals who had been imprisoned or *cassados* following the movement of March 31, 1964. Sobral declared that only the despotism of the military could bring about the cancellation of the parliamentary immunities of Márcio Moreira Alves.[8]

In Goiânia on December 13, Sobral was given a warm reception by the students and faculty of the law school of the Federal University of Goiás, where he was scheduled to address the graduating class on the 14th. Because Congress had defied the government in a secret vote about the case of Moreira Alves on the afternoon of December 12, Sobral told his greeters that a flood of rumors made him fearful of the consequences.[9]

On the night of the 13th, Sobral's fears were realized. The justice minister, in a proclamation that was broadcast, disclosed the details of a new institutional act, Number Five, that had been approved by the president and all the National Security Council members except for Vice President Pedro Aleixo. Ato 5 allowed the president to place Congress in recess, and this was done at once by the issuance of a complementary act. Also the new institutional act renewed *cassações*, ended the use of habeas corpus for political crimes, and gave the central government the right to remove personnel, including judges, from their posts, and to intervene in states and close local legislatures.[10] It was followed immediately by a strict censorship and hundreds of imprisonments. Quickly Kubitschek was placed in barracks in Niterói and Lacerda in barracks in the city of Rio, where one of his cell mates was Hélio Fernandes.

Sobral, on the morning of the 14th, was informed by the director of the law school in Goiânia that a colonel had asked whether Sobral would denounce Ato 5 when he addressed the students. Sobral replied that the director could tell the authorities that he would be discreet in order to avoid any disturbance to the ceremony of the young people.[11]

However, on that evening, when Sobral was preparing to leave his hotel room to speak at the ceremony, a police agent, accompanied by four sturdy men, commanded Sobral to accompany him "on orders of the president of the republic." Sobral refused, calling the order illegal, and was seized by the men. While being taken to a car he kept repeating, "What a notable achievement of the military regime, the violent arrest of an honorable citizen who has committed no crime." At the local army barracks, the commander told him, "Your purpose is to get Communists released from prison, a demonstration of your lack of patriotism." Sobral called the commander ignorant, unaware that it was the judges who released persecuted Communists after verifying abuses of power revealed by lawyers. "As for patriotism, I could give lessons to you and your army colleagues." Later an officer there told Sobral that he was being imprisoned because of his words of praise, given on December 11, for Supreme Court Justice Antônio Gonçalves de Oliveira, a Kubitschek appointee who became the court's president.[12]

In a drive of about three hours, Sobral was taken by four men to the barracks of the army police in Brasília, reached at 1:30 on the morning of Sunday the 15th. The commander there, Colonel Epitácio Cardoso de Brito, treated the prisoner well. Sobral spent the rest of the night in the apartment reserved for the officer of the day and then attended Mass at the colonel's invitation and breakfasted at the officers' dining room before returning to the apartment.

In the apartment he received visitors thanks to an authorization obtained from the army's regional commander by Procurador Geral Décio Miranda. Among the visitors were members of the Brasília section of the OAB and the local representative of Sobral's law firm.

During the night they had been advised of his whereabouts by a lawyer who had witnessed Sobral's transfer to Brasília, and one of them, at 3:00 A.M., had advised Décio Miranda. Now Sobral asked the visitors to get word to his wife that he was being treated well.[13]

On Monday, December 16, Sobral was transferred to the recently built prison at the barracks. He occupied a cell that was not locked, and so did the other prisoners, Carlos Castello Branco (whose column in the *Jornal do Brasil* was banned), Octacilio Lopes (of the *Diário de Notícias*), and four congressmen. They ate in the restaurant for officers, and at other times held discussions in the corridors of the prison. On Monday night, when the journalists were absent, giving official testimonies, Sobral and the congressmen were joined by the commander, Colonel Epitácio Cardoso de Brito, who said he admired Sobral. The colonel tried to justify the activities of the armed forces, whereupon Sobral defended the patriotism of the civilians and said that they were better prepared to govern than the military, accustomed to giving orders.[14] Perhaps remarks made during this discussion led to the much repeated story about how an army officer, explaining to Sobral that Ato 5 had the purpose of establishing *democracia à brasileira*, heard the stubborn lawyer reply that he was familiar with turkey being served *à brasileira* but that "democracy is universal, without adjectives."[15]

Tuesday the 17th was notable for the large number of visitors received by all the prisoners and for the release of Congressman José Carlos Guerra and the journalists. Sobral, ordered late in the afternoon to appear before a colonel who was receiving testimonies, refused to cooperate. Asked for a written statement giving his reasons for not testifying, he wrote of owing an accounting to no one except himself and added that his "abusive and illegal" arrest in Goiânia should have been followed by his release with apologies instead of inquiries about why he would not testify.[16]

In the officers' restaurant, Sobral had supper with Colonel Epitácio and the colonel who had been collecting testimonies and was told by both that he had been placed at liberty. He spent the night at the home of the head of the OAB in Brasília, and on the 18th, before returning home, appeared at the Federal Court of Appeals to plead, unsuccessfully, the case of a teacher.[17]

When Sobral wrote to the IAB on December 26 about his experience as a prisoner in Brasília, he called its attention to lawyers arrested in Rio, Heleno Fragoso, Evaristo de Morais Filho, Celso do

Nascimento, Celso do Nascimento Filho, and Vivaldo Ramos de Vasconcellos, "all arrested for defending students and Brazilian citizens accused of subversion. These imprisonments were possible only on account of Institutional Act Number Five."[18]

Lacerda had been set free after a week but had been *cassado*. Kubitschek, complaining of physical ailments, was released after two weeks. For a month he was under house arrest with no visitors allowed, and then he went to the United States for medical treatment. In March 1969 he returned to Brazil, where he kept apart from political matters and became associated with financial ventures. But his lawyers were kept busy because, in August 1969, a new investigation of his "illicit enrichment" was begun.[19]

PART VI

The Repression Reaches Its Pinnacle (1969–1971)

1. The Forced Retirement of Three Supreme Court Judges (January 1969)

Following the promulgation of Institutional Act Number Five, Celestino Basílio proposed that the IAB refrain from judging it. Sobral called the proposal immoral, thus disturbing its backers.[1] In the end, the IAB rejected Basílio's proposal and issued a careful statement of support of the government "in its effort to bring about juridical order." It expressed the hope that the decree laws to be issued would be limited to "cases of national security and the proper functioning of government finances." The OAB was silent about Ato 5.[2]

On the other hand, the Brazilian bishops presented Costa e Silva with a message condemning torture, censorship, violations of human rights, and the suppression of habeas corpus. Sobral called the message, issued by the CNBB (Conferência Nacional dos Bispos do Brasil) in February 1969, "the first voice raised in the country against the military despotism." After the CNBB message was attacked by Ernâni Sátiro, the government leader in Congress, Sobral told the congressman that the bishops' message should have come from members of Congress or of the law courts.[3]

At the request of the *Jornal do Brasil*'s José Machado, head of the union of journalists, Sobral agreed to visit and assist journalists who had been imprisoned after the issuance of Ato 5. But he told Machado that, much as he deplored the imprisonment of Niomar Moniz Sodré, he could give her no legal assistance because of his involvement in a case against her.[4] Niomar, whose speech to graduating journalism students in Recife on December 21 had praised young people for opposing the regime, was arrested in Rio on January 7 because articles in the *Correio da Manhã* were said to have violated the national security law. For months she put up with house arrest, but was absolved in November 1969 in a decision that brought hearty congratulations from Sobral to her criminal lawyer, Heleno Fragoso.[5]

Using Ato 5 in January 1969, Costa e Silva decreed the retirement of Supreme Court Judges Evandro Lins e Silva, Victor Nunes Leal, and Hermes Lima, and of STM Judge Peri Bevilacqua. In protest, Supreme Court President Gonçalves de Oliveira retired from the court and so did Judge Antônio Carlos Lafayette de Andrada, the next in line to be president. Sobral, hoping that the OAB would join in the protest, sent telegrams to OAB Conselho Federal President Samuel Duarte and the leader of its Guanabara section, but he was left in doubt about whether his telegrams were transmitted. A notice from a telegraph agency advised him of its refusal to transmit his telegrams to the judges who had been forced to retire.[6]

Supreme Court Judge Luís Gallotti, seeking to avoid a direct confrontation between the court and the military, accepted the court's presidency on a provisional basis, but his statement to the press seemed to Sobral to be critical of Gonçalves de Oliveira and Lafayette de Andrada. In letters to Gallotti, Sobral wrote that the Supreme Court and Congress had only one honorable option, collective resignations, and he called Gallotti's statement to the press an expression of conformity with the executive's dictatorial act. Commenting on the imprisonment of Darcy Ribeiro, Sobral told Gallotti that Justice Minister Gama e Silva had added to the sins of corruption and subversion a third reason for jailings: "refusal to accept the present regime."[7]

Costa e Silva, after conferring with Gallotti, issued Institutional Act Number Six on February 1. It reduced the membership of the Supreme Court from sixteen to eleven and demonstrated, according to Gallotti, that Costa e Silva had not dismissed judges in order to replace them with his supporters.[8]

Three of the students who had been jailed in São Paulo following the police invasion of the thirtieth UNE Congress appealed to Sobral for legal help, and he said he would make the necessary trips to São Paulo if they would appoint a lawyer there with whom he could collaborate.[9] At the same time he agreed with a friend in Minas, Antônio Lara Resende, that Satan was at work among many of the young people. "The document you sent is precious for me. It reveals that where there are young people there is rebellion, contempt for tradition, neglect of the experience of older people. The phenomenon is alarming. . . . Revolt against the present and past. And the boastful assertion that only the young people are in possession of the secret of the future. Such a spirit cannot result from human forces alone. The world unfortunately lacks belief in the existence of the Devil."[10]

Young lawyers who took over the directorship of the Brasília section of the OAB were also accused by Sobral of paying no attention to the experience of older people. He was shocked at their failure to consult him before naming new directors of the Brasília section and deciding that the section should give its support to Laudo de Almeida Camargo to succeed Conselho Federal President Samuel Duarte. He wrote Antônio Carlos Osório, head of the Brasília section, that this "discourteous maneuver," ignoring his "51 years of legal activities," was "incredible," and he was therefore determined not to vote for Laudo Camargo and would submit his irrevocable resignation from the section's directorship, thus removing himself from the Conselho Federal of the OAB.[11]

In rejecting an appeal from Osório that he withdraw his resignation, Sobral wrote that harmony should prevail in the section's leadership. He also took exception to Osório's "insinuation" that he, Sobral, considered himself to have a "monopoly" in providing "the correct and courageous position for the defense of the prerogatives of lawyers." Calling such an idea "ridiculous," he wrote that he had always been "modest, humble, and simple."[12]

In April 1969 Laudo Camargo was elected to the presidency of the OAB's Conselho Federal by a wide margin. His relatively young age, he felt, was responsible for Sobral's opposition to his election.[13] But Sobral may have objected to his lack of aggressive opposition to Ato 5.

2.   An IPM Investigates the Bishop of Volta Redonda (late 1969)

In August 1969 it became known that Costa e Silva was planning to reconvene Congress in September and seek its approval of a reform of the constitution that he would make known. During the discussion in the press about the matter, Sobral told a Rio magazine that the moment was inopportune for a constitutional reform. "The men in power do not accept the Universal Declaration of Human

Rights, proclaimed by the United Nations with the participation of Brazil."[1]

The military ministers objected to the plan to reopen Congress, and members of the National Security Council found faults with the proposed constitutional reform, presented to Costa e Silva by Vice President Pedro Aleixo.[2] However, before these problems could be resolved Costa e Silva suffered a massive stroke that left him completely incapacitated and brought on his death in December. On August 28, the day of Costa e Silva's collapse, the military ministers assumed charge of the government, and their takeover, thrusting aside the rights of Vice President Pedro Aleixo, was given official status by the issuance of Institutional Act Number Twelve, signed by the cabinet on August 31.

Sobral, writing to lawyer José Ribeiro de Castro Filho on September 1, said that he had been hoping that Costa e Silva would convince his companions in arms that after five years of arbitrary acts, a restoration of juridical order should be brought about, but by civilians and not by the military.[3]

The junta of the military ministers, called by Sobral a "military triumvirate," had to deal with the kidnapping on September 4 of the American ambassador by members of guerrilla groups. To achieve his release, it freed fifteen imprisoned leftists and arranged for them to leave Brazil. Their banishment was legitimized by Institutional Act Number Thirteen, and in Institutional Act Number Fourteen the punishments for violating the national security law were broadened to include death or perpetual imprisonment. These penalties were included in a new national security law (Decree Law 898 of September 18) and in a new constitution (constitutional amendment of October 17), signed by the military ministers. This new Constitution of 1969 incorporated Institutional Act Number Five and features of subsequent Atos.

Proponents of democracy could take comfort from the promises of Third Army Commander Emílio Garrastazu Médici, chosen early in October by the military leaders to be named president of Brazil by a reconvened Congress on October 28. On October 7, following his selection, he had declared emphatically that he would restore democracy fully and give Brazil abundant liberty, "free labor unions, a free press, and a free Church." Following his inauguration on October 30, he stressed the necessity of closer dialogue with students, the press, and the clergy in the march to democracy.[4] Subsequently, however, the justice minister, Alfredo Buzaid, received telegrams from Sobral denouncing new imprisonments. Sobral also told him that the law creating the Conselho de Defesa dos Direitos da Pessoa Humana (CDDPH) should cease to be "a dead letter."[5]

In November 1969 the *Diário de Notícias* called on its readers to make suggestions for the new president, and therefore Sobral wrote the newspaper's João Ribeiro Dantas to say that Médici should send Congress a message asking it "to suppress constitutional Article 182," which "maintains Institutional Act Number Five and the subsequent Acts." With the failure of Dantas to publish the suggestion, Sobral sent it directly to Médici. Writing Dario de Almeida Magalhães, Sobral said, "Médici won't be pleased with my advice," and he added that Dario was wrong in believing that democracy would return thanks to Médici and the military. "The return will come about because the nation will soon rebel against all this humiliation."[6]

While the *junta militar* issued decrees, institutional acts, and a constitution, and agreed on placing Médici in the presidency, the IPM investigating the CNTI reimprisoned Riani, and army men brought accusations against the bishop of Volta Redonda (in Rio de Janeiro state), leading to a case that was widely discussed.[7]

The bishop of Volta Redonda, Waldyr Calheiros, and priests associated with him had been giving support to workers at the government's steel plant and had accused army men of having tortured workers. An IPM prosecuting attorney accused the bishop and eleven of the priests of committing crimes listed in the national security law and the military and civilian penal codes. Sobral, lawyer for Dom Waldyr, compared the case with that of bishops whose imprisonments were said to have shaken the empire in the previous century. In December 1969 he advised Nelson Barbosa Sampaio, *procurador geral* of military justice, to turn to the army minister to prevent putting the bishop on trial as "a Communist and common agitator." "I do not think Pope Paul VI will put up with such an affront." The bishop and the priests, Sobral said, had been following recommendations of popes about social justice, and findings against Dom Waldyr would amount to a prohibition against the acceptance of those recommendations.[8]

The findings of the IPM, sent in December to General Tasso Villar de Aquino of the Second Auditoria of the First Military Region, concluded that Dom Waldyr and the eleven priests should be tried in court. Sobral hastened to ask the papal nuncio, Dom Umberto

Mozzoni, to seek an understanding with Brazil's foreign minister. A copy of the letter to the nuncio, full of praise for the courage of Dom Waldyr, was sent by Sobral to Procurador Geral Nelson Barbosa Sampaio with the admonition that he not confuse a bishop, "successor of the apostles," with a priest. "He is seen as practically a Pope in his diocese."[9]

In February 1970 Cardinal Jaime de Barros Câmara had good news for Sobral. Arrangements in "the case of Dom Waldyr" had been worked out in a manner satisfactory for the bishop.[10]

3. Prominent Rio Lawyers Are among the Imprisoned (November 1970)

Repression during the Médici administration was more severe than it had been during the administrations of his predecessors. The flow of Sobral's complaints to Justice Minister Alfredo Buzaid continued early in 1970 when a lawyer in Belém was interrupted while defending clients and was rushed off to prison because he used words offensive to the armed forces.[1] A more serious denouncement by Sobral, sent to the justice minister and other members of the CDDPH, followed the discovery in May, in a thicket in São Paulo, of the body of labor leader Olavo Hansen, who had been arrested, along with eighteen workers, during a May Day rally, and tortured before dying. Sobral, who was giving arguments against the death penalty to the press, spoke of the Hansen case in his interview with *Veja* magazine. "Absolute silence," he said, had followed his communications about it to OAB leader Laudo Camargo and other members of the CDDPH.[2]

Diversion for Sobral consisted of keeping abreast of the games of his favorite local soccer team, América. And, like most Brazilians in mid-1970, he followed the international contests of the Seleção Brasileira, competing for the World Cup. In letters, often written to law partner Tito Lívio Cavalcanti de Medeiros, he sent suggestions and criticisms about the play of the Seleção. As Brazil advanced in the playoffs, he was nervous and found reasons for pessimism. "I cannot," he wrote Tito, "have confidence in the present masters of Brazilian *futebol.*" In June, after Brazil won the World Cup in Mexico, he wrote Tito: "I must confess that you were right in believing in our Seleção from the start."[3]

The World Cup victory was used by government propaganda, along with what historian Thomas E. Skidmore has called "the catchy marching tune 'Pra Frente Brasil' ('Forward Brazil')," to garner votes for the ARENA in the congressional elections of November 1970.[4] The government's election victory was lopsided. After the outcome was acclaimed by ARENA President Filinto Müller, who was returned to the Senate, Sobral wrote Müller about the large number of voters whose protests had been in the form of ballots that were intentionally nullified or deposited in blank form. And Sobral quoted Barbosa Lima Sobrinho's observation: "Many governors acted as electoral chiefs, imposing threats on the voters."[5]

In November, prior to the election, the police and federal agents rounded up for imprisonment thousands of opponents of the regime.[6] Lawyer Heleno Fragoso, one of the multitude of peaceful opponents, was seized at his home in Rio and taken, with a black hood over his head, to solitary confinement in a cold and sparsely furnished cell in which he could hear, from an adjoining cell, the voices of fellow lawyers George Tavares and Augusto Sussekind de Moraes Rêgo. On the night of the second day, he was taken, again with a hood over his head, on a long automobile ride and eventually set free on one of the hills in Rio. This was after Arnaldo Sussekind, who had been Castello Branco's labor minister, complained about the disappearance of his relative Augusto and the others, leading OAB Conselho Federal President Laudo Camargo to seek, from First Army officials, the release of the lawyers.[7]

Heleno Fragoso, who was an officer of the OAB, has written that after this experience of the three lawyers late in 1970, "the OAB adopted a uniform and firm position of opposition to the government." "All of us were inspired by the exceptional example of Sobral Pinto, who embodies, more than any other person, the virtues of our profession," Heleno said in one of his books.[8]

At the time of the roundup of leftists, Sobral was in a hospital for a month-long treatment for his neuralgia. There he wrote a note to Heleno Fragoso to express his "revulsion" at the "savage violence" against him, and, after the treatment, Heleno Fragoso visited Sobral at his home. Heleno reported that the Brasília section of the OAB had given overwhelming support to a "Sobral Pinto slate." As for the movement to make Heleno the head of the OAB Conselho Federal, Sobral told his visitor that he would support him but for his commitment to José Ribeiro de Castro Filho.[9]

José Cavalcanti Neves, longtime head of the Pernambuco section of the OAB, won the Conselho Federal presidency, and, at the OAB Guanabara section, Ribeiro de Castro Filho headed the winning slate. The section returned Sobral to the OAB's Conselho Federal, which he had left in his dispute with the Brasília section. It was a Conselho Federal that, under the new leadership of José Cavalcanti Neves, turned from silence about Ato 5 to attacking it.[10]

Already Sobral had welcomed the replacement of IAB President Thomas Leonardos by Miguel Seabra Fagundes in April 1970. In a correspondence in which Leonardos and Sobral criticized each other, Sobral praised the aggressive speech of incoming IAB President Fagundes, a denouncement of governments based on force, and called it a contradiction of the mentality of Leonardos, "complacent about the government's use of force."[11]

4.   Sobral, the Brazilian Presidency Decides, Is Afflicted by Senility (June 1971)

Despite the killing of Marighella by the São Paulo police early in the Médici administration, the urban guerrillas were active throughout 1970. In 1971, however, the government's repression brought these activities to an end. Luiz Carlos Prestes, who had called them ineffective, was in Moscow, and Brazilian defense lawyers, such as Sobral, Heleno Fragoso, and Evaristo de Morais Filho, were busy defending former activists, accused of having planned to kidnap top government officials.[1]

Gastão Ribeiro, prosecuting attorney of the air force, studied the IPM of the ISEB and, in May 1971, brought charges of subversion against Quadros, Goulart, and approximately forty individuals influential during the Goulart administration. He also drew up a case against Sobral, whom he considered guilty of having refused to testify at the IPM and of having cooperated with Arraes in issuing a "manifesto" and in evading demands of the authorities.[2]

In a letter to Gastão Ribeiro, published in the *Jornal do Brasil*, Sobral answered the charges and discussed the prosecuting attorney's remarks about how Sobral, taking advantage of a good reputation built up in the past, had been using intimidating methods to create a public opinion in opposition to worthy persons and in favor of the guilty ones. "I am not," Sobral wrote, "the only lawyer struggling to defend justice in the military courts. In seeking to put me in prison, you wish to intimidate and terrorize all these lawyers. I accept your provocation." However, before a trial could begin, José Bezerra Filho, of the Second Auditoria of the air force, rejected the petition of Gastão Ribeiro in a decision that called Brazil "at peace juridically" and that was critical of "digging up facts buried long ago."[3]

On June 18, 1971, after Judge Bezerra wrote his decision, Sobral sent eight pages to President Médici to admonish him for having ended in Brasília the *cartório* functions (registering real estate transactions) of César Prates, appointed by Kubitschek. Sobral described Prates as remaining loyal to Kubitschek, "a statesman of great vision," and he said that admirers of Prates's work refused to join Sobral in publicly backing Prates lest they, in turn, lose their positions. Sobral's letter, critical of recent constitutions and of institutional and complementary acts, reminded Médici of how Italy, Germany, and Russia had fallen in the past to the fascists, Nazis, and "iron rule."[4]

Sobral's letter was returned to him with a card from the Correspondence Service of the presidency bearing a note that the letter, "written by someone clearly afflicted by signs of senility," was "completely unrelated to the national reality." On June 28 Sobral returned the original letter to Médici together with twenty-eight pages in which he commented on passages that he found underlined or otherwise marked in it, and he argued that some of them revealed "robust virility" and not senility. Opinions about Sobral, expressed by Filinto Müller, Hélio Fernandes, Dario de Almeida Magalhães, and others contributed to the length of what was written by Sobral, who added that he was not seeking to glorify himself but to "demonstrate the immensity of the incredible injustice carried out against me."[5]

Sobral did not mention that the OAB was making plans for a ceremony at which he would become the first recipient of its Ruy Barbosa Gold Medal, for "outstanding contributions to the law, justice, and the profession." In 1957 the OAB had accepted Nehemias Gueiros's idea of creating the award, the top honor of the OAB, but not until 1970 was a commission of former Conselho Federal presidents formed to name a recipient.[6] The commission, which included Gueiros, unanimously chose Sobral, and in March 1971 the official notification reached Sobral, along with a request from Nehemias Gueiros for biographical data. Gueiros, preparing a speech for the ceremony, received an abundance of data, appropriate, he felt, "for a biography," and was able to quote from Lacerda's decree naming the Sobral Pinto School, articles by Dario de Almeida Magalhães and literary critic Luiz Delgado, a letter from Sobral to Adauto Lúcio Cardoso, and journalist Araken Távora's book about Sobral, *O Advogado da Liberdade*, published in 1966.[7]

At the suggestion of Conselho Federal President José Cavalcanti Neves, the date of the ceremony was finally set for November 5, 1971, the birthday of both Ruy Barbosa and Sobral (Sobral would become seventy-eight). In the meantime Sobral received, by mail, the José Verissimo Medal of the Academy of Letters of the state of Pará, and a number of requests that he honor graduating classes in December.[8]

5. A Trip to Europe and Receipt of the Ruy Barbosa Medal (late 1971)

In September 1969 Niomar Moniz Sodré made an arrangement to rent for five years her interest in the *Correio da Manhã* to a group whose policy, it soon became clear in the newspaper, was not anti-government.[1] In the same year Sybil Bittencourt, accepting the advice of Dario de Almeida Magalhães and Sobral, concluded the agreement with Niomar that gave Sybil ownership of the newspaper's physical plant. In 1970, while Dario and Sobral awaited their legal fee from Sybil, Sobral borrowed money, mostly from Dario but also from Gabriel Costa Carvalho.[2]

The legal fee was received in mid-1971, and Dario, calling Sobral to his office, presented him with a large check, half of the fee. When Sobral sent a deposit to Dario's account to pay off his debt, he added an amount equal to 10 percent with the explanation that Dario had done most of the work.[3]

"We are conspiring against you," Dario remarked to Sobral in jest later in July before offering to finance a vacation trip for him. It was not, as Sobral supposed, a trip to the Amazon area, such as had delighted Dario a little earlier, but a round-trip passage by air to take him to Rome and Paris, together with a check for one thousand dollars.[4] Before leaving Brazil on September 18, Sobral informed Eugênio de Araújo Sales, who had become cardinal in Rio after the death of Dom Jaime Câmara, that in Rome he would speak with Church authorities about the case of the will of the late Gabriela Bezanoni Lage Lillo, whose bequest to the Church was being defended by Sobral and challenged by members of her family.[5]

At the Vatican's state secretariat Sobral discussed the contested will, and on September 22 he joined thousands at a public audience where Pope Paul VI blessed the flock and absent family members of all who were present.[6]

Finding his "isolation unbearable," Sobral was making plans to return to Brazil on September 23. But he was rescued by Tina Polvani, of the tourist agency he was using. Calling his early departure absurd, she arranged for him to join tourist groups. Thus in pleasant company he saw the great sights of Rome, traveled on tourist buses to Florence and Milan, and, after a "magnificent" train trip to Paris, became a member of groups that were "intelligently organized" to use buses in Spain and Portugal. Filled with admiration for the tourist agencies in Europe, he concluded that Brazil was backward, failing to do what was done in Europe because "our public men, when they go there, do not learn what is good and can be transplanted."[7]

After returning to Brazil on October 19, Sobral told José Barreto Filho that "during the entire excursion" he was free of facial pains, "thanks to the Virgin, to whom I prayed constantly," but, he added, then they returned.[8] They interfered with his attendance later at graduating ceremonies, but not with the presentation of the OAB's Ruy Barbosa Medal at the ceremony held at the auditorium of the Brazilian Press Association on November 5.

After Conselho Federal President José Cavalcanti Neves opened the ceremony with praise for Sobral's bravery, competence, integrity, and idealism, Nehemias Gueiros embarked on the main speech, with its long quotations. Coming closest to analyzing the personality of Sobral were thoughts of Dario, published in 1967 and repeated now by Gueiros. Dario described Sobral as more than a liberal. "He is a libertarian who never abandoned respect for order" and whose determination to be completely free, and thus generously at the side of freedom for all, kept him apart from any power, interest, or expediency.

"And in this tough bondage to liberty, this affectionate, sentimental person cultivates friendships tenderly, finding them a shelter for his sensitiveness in the brief pauses in his immense and heartbreaking struggles; but he never capitulates, even in the face of the warmest of relationships." Dario called this behavior that strained dear friendships "true heroism" and added that Sobral's fiery passion for justice was nothing like the common love for it "but is a devouring, volcanic, and obsessive passion, keeping his soul inflamed by the certainty that the only noble destiny lies in its pursuit."

In remarks about Sobral's personal indifference to money, Dario explained that Sobral was incapable of the slightest envy of, or resentment against, people who were rich. Understanding and experience, Dario said, had led Sobral to appreciate that material prosperity, licitly obtained, was legitimate and was beneficial for advancing the collective well-being.

"The radicalism of his fidelity to himself and his beliefs frequently leaves Sobral feeling isolated in the midst of the indifference of those who are untouched by his cravings and agonies. . . . The coldness of this solitude makes it evident that Sobral's self-exaltation comes not from pride or vanity, but from a desperate effort to move apathetic souls by example. And this solitude is purifying and fruitful, preventing the corruptive action of compromises and accommodations, and maintaining in full force the personality of the paladin who marches apparently without converts and followers because he alone, all by himself, represents a legion."[9]

Sobral, in response to the speeches, reminded the audience that Ruy Barbosa, in addressing a graduating class before World War I, had said that the best lesson he had for his audience, based on all of his experience, could be summed up in five words: "No Justice exists without God." Ruy Barbosa, according to Sobral, had proved his point by describing the behavior of mankind, drowned in material things and destructive havoc, and had concluded that "peace and Justice do not reign because mankind does not believe."[10]

Speaking for himself Sobral said he lacked the requisites for receiving the medal. Listing the requisites, he spoke of honesty, independence, and bravery, and added that a correct knowledge of law, jurisprudence, and legislation was also a necessity. Justice and the courts, Sobral added, should be strictly obedient to the law, and the nation's executive should at all times submit to the decisions of judges and the courts.[11]

The CDDPH, described and praised in Sobral's remarks, was about to be modified in a manner that disturbed its supporters. The proposal of ARENA Senator Rui Santos, which became Law 5,763 on December 15, 1971, ruled that the Conselho's sessions should be limited to six annually and should be secret unless otherwise determined by a majority of its members. The new law increased the CDDPH's membership from nine to thirteen by adding representatives of the Foreign Relations Ministry, the office of the *procurador geral da república*, and the Federal Council for Culture, along with a professor of penal law at a federal university.[12]

PART VII

The Repression Continues (1972–1977)

1. The Sobrals' Fiftieth Wedding Anniversary (1972)

For the religious service to observe the fiftieth anniversary of the marriage of Sobral and Maria José, the family gathered on February 11, 1972, at the chapel of the Casa da Previdência, where Sobral usually worshipped. Among the participating churchmen were Cardinal Eugênio Sales, who called the couple "a model of Christianity," and Waldyr Calheiros, the bishop of Volta Redonda whom Sobral had defended.[1]

Juscelino Kubitschek, unable to be in Rio, wrote Sobral a gracious letter on February 9 in which he said that on the 8th he had attended the Mass that marked the seventh anniversary of the death of "our mutual friend Schmidt, through whom I came to know you in one of the most dramatic hours of my political career." Kubitschek recalled being taken by Schmidt in 1955 to a rally at which Sobral defended the right of Kubitschek to run for the presidency. "In that hour, when all the negative forces threatened that right, there appeared on the scene, one man alone, using a moral authority that he transformed into a symbol in defense of the law. I saw you defending the ideas defended by other men of your stature, Jefferson, Lincoln, Churchill, and Ruy Barbosa."[2]

Kubitschek wrote that all Brazilians admired Sobral for his positions, nobility, courage, and civic valor, "but, unlike me, they lack the closeness to you that is necessary for understanding the true magnitude of your kindness and extraordinary moral qualities." "In order that it not be supposed that your defense of legality had any personal motive, you did not accept the offer which would have honored you and the Supreme Court." It was in this letter that Kubitschek reminded Sobral of the crisis of November 1956, when disturbances by "the military and politicians" created the "most serious situation of my presidency" and when Sobral, Kubitschek wrote, persuaded War Minister Lott to withdraw his decision to resign.

"When adversity fell upon me, you appeared again, defending me against iniquitous accusations and facing dangers so that you could be at the side of one who was persecuted and stripped of all power. I could write pages and pages about you, my noble friend, to explain the esteem, admiration, and friendship I have for you."[3]

To interview Sobral, a *Politika* reporter called on him at his home in the Laranjeiras district. The home, acquired in 1935 with a loan from Affonso Penna Júnior and enlarged in 1957 with a loan from Regine Feigl, was described by the reporter as a large, attractive old house in which Sobral lived with his wife, his son Alberto, and Alberto's wife.

Replying to the reporter's inquiry about how to handle a client addicted to drugs, Sobral emphasized the need to understand the social conditions that caused the addiction. "Even in a pathological case, I would work to have the individual receive treatment. For curing or punishing an addict, a prison cell is most inappropriate." Asked about Women's Lib, Sobral told the reporter: "I believe that the emancipation of women should be carried out at home. I consider that the great disorder of the modern world is the result of their leaving the home. The emancipation should be to enable them to give their children ideas that are intelligent and compassionate. To have women competing with men is positively a catastrophe."[4]

Sobral spoke of his fondness for classical music, especially that of Beethoven, Chopin, and Liszt, but pointed out that listening to music brought him sorrow because it reminded him so much of his music-loving son José Luiz, whom he had lost in 1961. Brazilian authors whom he favored were José Lins de Rego and Octavio de Faria. "But I do not like the works of my friend Jorge Amado. Poets I like are Carlos Drummond de Andrade and my friend Manuel Bandeira." Jacques Maritain ("who modernized Saint Thomas Aquinas") and Leon Bloy met with Sobral's approval, but when he was asked about Friedrich Nietzsche, Jean-Paul Sartre, and Arthur Schopenhauer, he said that "all of them" were "crazy." "I dislike psychoanalysis and psychology; in any case, I find Freud more coherent than Jung."[5]

His library, he added, included "complete collections of Sherlock Holmes and Maurice Leblanc" detective stories, which he "adored."

2.   Persuading the OAB Not to Withdraw from the CDDPH (August–September 1973)

Sobral, occasionally described as the OAB's "great elector," wrote to Conselho Federal President José Cavalcanti Neves in December 1972 to oppose his bid to be reelected. Sobral's choice was José Ribeiro de Castro Filho, and he defeated Neves in a close vote after delegates of several of the OAB sections that favored Neves decided to forsake their commitments to their sections and adopt Sobral's anti-reelection thesis.[1]

Early in September 1973, after the OAB objected to the alterations of the Conselho de Defesa dos Direitos da Pessoa Humana (CDDPH) enacted by the Rui Santos law of 1971, Sobral wrote Justice Minister Buzaid to tell him to reject the recommendation of advisers who maintained that the CDDPH should be closed down because it was not functioning and had been created in 1964 by legislation that they sought to show to be unconstitutional. Sobral quoted portions of the legislation that made it a crime to try to prevent the CDDPH from functioning. He also quoted clauses from the legislation that gave it the ability to punish those who were responsible for tortures and other mistreatments of individuals. He hoped in this way to convince Buzaid that ineffectiveness should not be blamed on the law but on the members of the CDDPH.[2]

The OAB Conselho Federal was determined to adopt the proposal of Carlos de Araújo Lima to have the OAB withdraw from the CDDPH as a protest against its inertia. Heleno Fragoso felt that such a withdrawal would be the "most eloquent" way to express disapproval of the CDDPH. Conselho Federal President Ribeiro de Castro Filho, supporting withdrawal, cited the failure of the CDDPH or Buzaid to respond to complaints about the abduction of lawyer José Carlos Brandão Monteiro by federal agents. A study by Conselheiro Danilo Marcondes de Souza, who also liked the idea of withdrawal, resulted in a report about the CDDPH's failures.[3]

Sobral, whose role to prevent withdrawal was decisive, was in Ribeirão Preto, São Paulo, late in August 1973, and there he told the local *O Diário* that the participation of the OAB representative at the CDDPH would allow the OAB to protest against "the monstrous annihilation" of human dignity and against the secret nature of the CDDPH sessions, made possible by the Rui Santos law. "The absence of the OAB would leave the government deaf to the possibility of punishments of those responsible for the tortures and assassinations, carried out daily all over Brazil." "The violence of the Estado Novo was sporadic; today violence is institutional."[4]

On September 28, 1973, when the OAB Conselho Federal met to settle the matter of withdrawal, Sobral, in arguments with Heleno Fragoso, said the OAB should not "cowardly" renounce its responsibilities, defined in the law. To those who argued that the existence of the CDDPH was being used by the government to make a good impression on the United Nations and other foreign groups, Sobral pointed out that participation in the CDDPH would help the OAB contradict lies. "The liberty of peoples is obtained through struggles," he asserted.[5]

Like Sobral's anti-reelection thesis, his anti-withdrawal thesis was achieved by a narrow margin. In a 10-9 vote the sections decided that the OAB Conselho Federal president should attend all CDDPH sessions, thus setting aside a compromise that would have him attend only those that seemed likely to deal with "matters of real public interest." He was instructed to use the sessions to denounce the failings of the CDDPH and to report fully on all matters discussed at them "so that they can be revealed later in the press."[6]

Ribeiro de Castro Filho, fearless in his defense of the rights of lawyers and all that the CDDPH stood for, had no opportunity to attend sessions of the CDDPH in 1974 because none took place.[7]

3. Sobral, Irritated, Leaves the Fifth OAB Conference (August 1974)

During the Médici administration the economy prospered to such an extent that foreign bankers spoke of "the Brazilian economic miracle." But Sobral declared late in October 1973: "I do not accept economic development that is achieved without harmony with individual liberty." He was speaking in Porto Alegre to journalists and members of the local OAB who had honored him, and he went on to discuss how lawyers suffered from restrictions, including the inability to communicate with clients, and how journalists suffered from the inability "to write what they think." He called for a popular movement to restore individual rights. "The movement must be a peaceful one, without terror," he emphasized.[1]

Sobral returned to Rio in time for a magnificent Mass at the Can-

delária Church on the morning of November 5, his eightieth birthday, and for the receipt that evening of the most prestigious honor of
the Instituto dos Advogados Brasileiros (IAB), its Teixeira de Freitas
Medal.

The church service, with Cardinal Eugênio Sales participating,
was attended by about four hundred, including officers of the lawyers' associations, members of the Superior Military Tribunal, well-
known Catholics such as Alceu Amoroso Lima, and even children
from the Sobral Pinto School. Surprising Sobral, Archbishop Hélder
Câmara came from Pernambuco. "Never," Sobral said later, "have
I received so many compliments as during the hour following the
Mass."[2]

Among the speakers at the ceremony of the IAB, attended by about
two hundred, were the OAB's José Ribeiro de Castro Filho and the
IAB's official orator Otávio Alvarenga. Upon accepting the Teixeira
de Freitas Medal, Sobral said that "never, during my struggle of over
50 years, did I dream of receiving this, the foremost reward for Brazilian legal activity."[3]

On the same day at the Brazilian Academy of Letters, historian
José Honório Rodrigues delivered an address calling Sobral the successor of Father Antônio Vieira, the seventeenth-century "defender
of Indians," and of Ruy Barbosa, "defender of public liberties and
individual guarantees." "No one in contemporary life has better
represented this sacred spirit of humanism" than "this courageous,
fearless Mineiro from Barbacena."[4]

Sobral continued to be grieved by the deaths of friends. Lawyer
Cândido de Oliveira Neto died in 1973. Especially sorrowful was the
death in 1974 of Cecy (Cecília Silva), who, at Sobral's home, had typed
his letters from the 1920s until 1972.

Adauto Lúcio Cardoso, who had been close to Sobral since the
days of the Vargas Estado Novo, died in mid-1974. In 1971 he had resigned from the Supreme Court, indignant that all of its other members had disagreed with his contention that a Médici decree law
imposing prior censorship of books and periodicals was unconstitutional. Sobral called the death of his longtime friend an "irreparable
loss." "One of Adauto's greatest moments occurred when he founded
Resistência Democrática with a few friends during the Estado Novo
in order to do away at once with the dictatorship."[5]

In July 1974 Sobral took steps to reactivate the Centro Dom Vital
and to revive its journal, *A Ordem*, which had not appeared for ten
years. And in August he participated in the debates at the Hotel

Glória's convention center, where the Fifth National Conference of the OAB discussed "The Lawyer and Human Rights."[6]

The Fifth Conference applauded enthusiastically a speech of Miguel Seabra Fagundes proposing that the conference denounce to the executive, legislative, and judicial powers the many human rights violations. The antigovernment spirit of the delegates may have been responsible for the absence of Armando Falcão, who had become justice minister with the start of the new presidential administration of General Ernesto Geisel, ARENA's candidate in an indirect election.

The conference became agitated when the presiding officer, Ribeiro de Castro Filho, alienated the supporters of theses that he dismissed as being outside the scope of the agenda. One of them called for replacing the "inefficient" CDDPH with a new *conselho*, unconnected with the executive power. In the case of a thesis that would substitute the *mandado de segurança* (injunction) in political cases where the habeas corpus could not be used, Sobral called the sponsor "crazy," and Ribeiro de Castro Filho irritated delegates by telling the sponsor to stop speaking.[7]

The supporters of a popular thesis for legalizing divorce described it as "based entirely" on the Universal Declaration of Human Rights. The Minas delegation, the only one to oppose it, said it was out of order. After the thesis was adopted, Sobral said that it meant "the destruction of the family," and, visibly upset, he departed from the conference. To reporters he announced that he was resigning from the OAB's Conselho Federal. They quoted him as saying, "I cannot remain at the side of colleagues determined to follow paths other than mine."[8]

Lawyers from Bahia had brought a gold medal for Sobral and for some of the other "eminent participants." They called on him at his residence and found, they said later, that he was "just as discourteous" as he had been during the debates at the conference. They decided against awarding him their medal.[9]

Sobral did not leave the OAB's Conselho Federal but remained an active member, representing lawyers of the state of Rio de Janeiro because the state of Guanabara had disappeared, being incorporated into its neighboring state by a federal law in June 1974. When the reorganized Rio de Janeiro section voted for officers in March 1975 it chose Sobral as one of its three representatives on the OAB Conselho Federal.[10]

Early in 1975 Sobral met at his home with Ribeiro de Castro Filho,

Nehemias Gueiros, Laudo de Camargo, and others to plan the campaign that brought the presidency of the Conselho Federal to Caio Mário da Silva Pereira, a lawyer from Belo Horizonte.[11]

4. A Stronger MDB but "Rule by Law Is Still a Mere Hope" (1974–1975)

In October 1974 Congressman Francisco Pinto of the Bahia MDB was deprived of his seat in Congress and condemned to imprisonment by the military justice system. His speeches in defense of individual rights contained attacks on Chile's new president, Augusto Pinochet, that were found by the justice minister and a military prosecutor to be in violation of the national security law. The failure of the Supreme Court to uphold Francisco Pinto's rights was denounced by Sobral in a letter to Pinto that was applauded by oppositionists in Congress after it was read there by one of Bahia's congressmen. But when another MDB congressman attempted to disclose a manifesto of Francisco Pinto, he was unsuccessful because the presiding officer, who belonged to the ARENA, cited internal regulations and forbade the reading.[1]

The prestige of the MDB soared in the next month when the 1974 congressional elections increased its representation in Congress from 87 to 165 and decreased that of the ARENA from 223 to 199; the state legislatures of São Paulo, Minas, Rio de Janeiro, and Paraná became MDB-dominated.[2] While Senator Franco Montoro, chief organizer of the MDB campaign, was being congratulated for his party's strong showing, Sobral sent him a letter full of advice. It was important, Sobral told him, to have the opposition set aside personal interests and collaborate peacefully with the military power to bring about gradually a series of steps that would begin with the reestablishment of legislative sovereignty and be followed by the elimination, by President Geisel, of the undesirable features of Institutional Act Number Five. Sobral concluded his letter by praising the ARENA's Carlos Alberto Carvalho Pinto, who had lost his Senate seat, for admitting that the election was clearly "a condemnation of Brazil's political structures, installed by military force."[3]

MDB President Ulysses Guimarães called for the MDB to initiate a "national debate" about constitutional reforms. Sobral, who had declined Guimarães's invitation to join the MDB and run for office in 1978,[4] had no hesitation in participating in the debate, and he did so as a member of the OAB's Conselho Federal. Described by the press in July 1975 as a bit bent with age but full of vigor and "banging the table" for emphasis, he presented a "Plan of Action" to the OAB. Speaking to a reporter later, he said that his plan was approved unanimously after a "somewhat tense" discussion and would be forwarded in the name of the OAB directly to President Geisel, unlike previous appeals, made to "intermediaries." It would attack no one, would show respect for the authorities, and would insist on the need for restoration of habeas corpus and full autonomy for judges.[5]

Sobral was defending prisoners in São Paulo who had been badly mistreated after being abducted by the DOI-CODI (Destacamento de Operações e Informações/Centro de Operações de Defesa Interna), made up of civilian police and military security officers and assisted financially by businessmen.[6] He wrote on November 7, 1975, to President Geisel that his legal work had put him in touch with several dozens of these unfortunate citizens, held for long periods. "Generally, after being seized, they are taken to places that are not revealed and are the victims of indescribable tortures, which leave gruesome marks." He told Geisel that Castello Branco had persuaded Congress to pass Law 4,898 of December 9, 1965, making such treatments illegal, but that it, like the CDDPH, was a dead letter.[7]

Law students who would graduate late in 1975 at the Catholic University of Minas Gerais proposed that the university create a Sobral Pinto Medal and award it annually to the person who, while practicing law, was outstanding in the defense of human rights. The university accepted the idea. Representatives of the university officers, the faculty, and graduating law students were to select in future years the recipients of the medal, bearing in mind the example of Sobral. At the graduation ceremony in Belo Horizonte on December 12, 1975, Sobral was presented with the first of the medals. He spoke of his emotion and added: "Only the generosity of the young people of the university's law school could discover virtues in me that my conscience tells me I do not have."[8]

On the other hand, Sobral found no end of virtues in the 1975 recipient of the OAB's Ruy Barbosa Medal: Dario de Almeida Magalhães. Sobral, whose speech at the ceremony was filled with proliberty quotations expressed by Dario in the past, called attention to Dario's struggle against the Vargas dictatorship and his successful fight in 1950 to keep the OAB outside of the government supervision that was exercised on other class or professional organizations. Dario, in his long speech accepting the medal, agreed with Sobral's contention that material progress did not require the elimination of the rights of citizens. He called on those in power to bring an end to the rule of force. "The restoration of a state ruled by law," he said, "is still a mere hope or promise; but I believe that the president of the republic is sincerely trying to bring it about."[9]

5.   Defending Oswaldo Pacheco (1976)

The tripling of the price of petroleum by OPEC (Organization of Petroleum Exporting Countries) in 1973 brought about financial and economic conditions that were unfavorable for Brazil after Ernesto Geisel became president. During his term in office (1974–1979) the gross domestic product declined, important financial institutions declared themselves in bankruptcy, Brazil's foreign debt doubled, and the annual inflation rate jumped from 16 percent to over 40 percent.[1] Such changes weakened the arguments of those who had pointed to the Brazilian "economic miracle" of the Médici administration as a benefit resulting from the ability of the military regime to prevent disturbances by discontented oppositionists.

The repression continued. The death in a São Paulo prison of journalist Vladimir Herzog in 1975 was followed in January 1976 by that of another mistreated São Paulo prisoner, metalworker Manoel Fiel Filho, and people doubted that President Geisel could control the military security apparatus. Sobral, in São Paulo early in October 1976 to receive an award from lawyers there, told the Paulistas that the situation was worse than anything he had seen in his sixty years of practicing law. "Ruy Barbosa would have died ten times on account of what goes on in Brazil today."[2]

However, Justice Minister Armando Falcão described Brazil as "living in complete democracy and ruled by law," and President Geisel lauded those who worked with optimism and confidence in themselves and in the government. Sobral, addressing Falcão in a letter published in the *Folha de S. Paulo*, wrote of legislators and judges who could suddenly be thrown out of their positions. "What kind of democracy is this where the executive power can deprive citizens of their political rights . . . and where anybody can, from one moment to the next, be jailed and held rigorously incommunicado?" Also in

October 1976 Sobral wrote to Geisel to say that it was unfair of him to refer to critics of the government as "defeatists and demagogues." "The ones who lack confidence in the people," Sobral told Geisel, "are your comrades in arms who promulgated Ato 5. Unlike us, they believe that the people lack the ability to elect their representatives, the governors, and the president."[3]

Sobral was in Belo Horizonte in December to witness the 1976 award of the Sobral Pinto Medal. The recipient, Edgar da Mata Machado, author of seven books and editor of the antigovernment weekly *Movimento*, had been deprived of his political rights and his MDB congressional seat in January 1969 and later been forced to give up teaching at the Catholic University of Minas because of an order by the Ministry of Education.[4]

Nineteen seventy-six saw the loss by death of Juscelino Kubitschek and João Goulart, and in May 1977 Carlos Lacerda died. All were younger than Sobral, Kubitschek being seventy-three, Goulart fifty-seven, and Lacerda sixty-two. The body of Kubitschek, victim of a vehicle accident in August, was viewed by many thousands in Rio's *Manchete* building and was accompanied by another large crowd when it was buried in Brasília after Geisel decreed three days of official mourning. Sobral regretted that Kubitschek had not been permitted to be reelected president to "complete his mission as a statesman."[5]

Goulart, victim of a heart attack in Uruguay in December, was buried in his birthplace, São Borja, Rio Grande do Sul, at a service attended by an estimated thirty thousand. Sobral, at a meeting of the OAB, proposed an expression of sorrow, and it was approved.[6]

Carlos Lacerda, the last of the "big three" associated with the Frente Ampla, died of infective endocarditis in Rio in May 1977. Among those making statements about him following the crowded Seventh Day Mass at Candelária Church was Sobral, who reprimanded the military regime for having pushed aside leaders of real merit such as Kubitschek and Lacerda.[7]

Sobral's clients in São Paulo in 1975 and 1976 included Oswaldo Pacheco, one of the Communists abducted in 1975 by the DOI-CODI. Pacheco's role in the CGT (General Labor Command) during the hectic days of March 1964 had made him an important national figure. Arrested in April 1964, he was set free later that year and traveled to countries in Latin America and to Russia and countries in Eastern Europe. With a false name he entered Brazil in Rio Grande do Sul in 1967 and, starting in 1971, participated in labor union work in São Paulo state. Following his arrest in 1975 he and others were investigated by an IPM and then, in November 1975, sentenced to imprisonments by an *auditoria* of the military justice system. Pacheco was ordered to serve a three-and-one-half-year term for violating the national security law after his accusers said that he had visited Russia, used a false name, and sought to revive the PCB, sometimes with the help of clandestine printing presses. His two principal codefendants, whose lawyers worked closely with Sobral, "confessed" to having participated in labor union work favorable to the PCB and also received three-and-one-half-year sentences. These defendants, the lawyers complained, had been tortured after being abducted.[8]

Sobral's appeal on behalf of Pacheco, made to the STM in February 1976, was full of denouncements of the strong-arm methods used by the DOI-CODI. He said that during months when Pacheco had been held at the mercy of his torturers, in a secret place, he had been forced to make a confession, which he later retracted, and that marks on his body remained during the 1975 trial as evidence of his ordeal. A minor codefendant, Sobral added, had been so "filled with terror" by tortures that he had untruthfully said "yes" when he had been shown a photograph of Pacheco and asked if it was of a person who had conversed about a real estate matter of interest to the PCB.[9]

But for that "yes," Sobral pointed out, no codefendant had mentioned, in testimony, Pacheco's name. He explained that many a government official had, like Pacheco, visited Russia, and he found legal reasons to reject the "confession" of Pacheco. Concluding that mere guesswork and no solid evidence had been submitted to show that Pacheco had sought to reactivate the PCB, Sobral wrote that the use of a false name, necessary on account of the "permanent persecution" of his client, was a crime under the penal code but not under the national security law. According to Sobral, the true violators of the national security law were those who ignored the requirements for reporting imprisonments to the judiciary, for limiting the time of imprisonments prior to judicial action, and for limiting periods in which prisoners remained incommunicado.[10]

In December 1977 the STM upheld the three-and-one-half-year prison sentence of Pacheco and one of his two major codefendants. It reduced to two years the sentence of the other, journalist Renato Cupertino. All three defendants, the STM asserted, had tried to reorganize the PCB.[11]

6. Geisel's "April Package" and the Legalization of Divorce (1977)

Ernesto Geisel, on the third anniversary of becoming president, declared that Brazil, in its political development, should make use of its own model, as it had done, he said, in the economic and social areas. "We must not copy what others do, because conditions differ."[1]

Sobral, on March 29, 1977, used twelve pages to tell Geisel that it was wrong not to set up in Brazil the sort of institutions that had brought cultural advances to "civilized nations." In sending Dario de Almeida Magalhães a copy of his letter to Geisel, Sobral told his friend that medical administrator Oswaldo Cruz had won the battle against yellow fever in Brazil at the start of the century by insisting on applying American techniques rather than Brazilian ones; and, Sobral said, political thought could benefit from copying what foreigners could offer, just as in the case of telephones, telegraphic communications, the radio, and television. Sobral assured Dario that he would write further to Geisel. That he expected no replies was made clear when he told the press that the only post-1964 president to answer his letters had been Castello Branco.[2]

Late in March 1977 Congress failed to provide the two-thirds vote for enacting the administration's amendment for reforming the judiciary. Calling the MDB a "dictatorial minority," Geisel decreed a recess of Congress on April 1, and, during the recess, which lasted for two weeks, he used presidential decrees to enact the judiciary reform amendment and, at the same time, alter political practices in order to keep the ARENA on top. The alterations, known as the "April Package," also ruled that constitutional amendments would require an absolute majority of votes in Congress and not a two-thirds majority.[3]

Supreme Court President Carlos Thompson Flores congratulated Geisel for the judiciary reform amendment, but leading lawyers attacked it, saying that genuine reform would revive habeas corpus and guarantees for the judiciary. Sobral's long report to the OAB's Conselho Federal was regarded by many lawyers as the first careful analysis of the illegality of the step taken by Geisel, who, Sobral pointed out, could legislate while Congress was on forced recess, in accordance with Ato 5, but could not amend the constitution.[4] OAB Conselho Federal President Raymundo Faoro released a statement saying that Brazil's lawyers repudiated the forced recess of Congress along with the judiciary reform, "already rejected by the Brazilian people through their representatives."[5]

Enactment of constitutional amendments by an absolute majority made it possible for divorce to become legal in Brazil. While an appropriate amendment, long advocated by Senator Nelson Carneiro, made its way through Congress in June 1977, the OAB Conselho Federal voted to support the popular change. Sobral, indignant, concluded an irate speech at the OAB by saying, "I'll never set foot in here again." In his raised hand he held a rolled-up newspaper, and, for emphasis, he brought it down, intending to bang a table with it, but by mistake it hit the head of a nearby lawyer.[6]

Lawyers who worked in Sobral's office were surprised to receive a letter from him saying that no divorce case would be permitted in the office. "Of course your conscience can give you the right to handle such cases, immoral in my opinion. But, if that happens, I must, I regret, bring an end to your collaboration, which, until now, has been so dedicated, useful, and precious for me."[7]

Speaking to the press, Sobral said that Geisel was responsible for divorce in Brazil because of his Lutheran beliefs and because of his alteration of the rules about amending the constitution.[8]

Sobral also said that redemocratization was not likely to be achieved by government initiative. Speaking to reporters at the STM, where he won the freedom of Communist Ruth Simis, he declared that the men in power had "no interest in democratic normalization."[9] Thus he showed a lack of faith in the "mission" of Senate President Petrônio Portella, who had been authorized by Geisel to seek understandings with prominent oppositionists about political reforms for achieving *distensão,* or *abertura* (opening Brazil for democracy). Initially Portella's work was hindered by the "April Package" and then in June 1977 because MDB congressional leader José de Alencar Furtado was *cassado* by Geisel for denouncing the president in a broadcast. Only Portella's intervention saved MDB President Ulysses Guimarães from a similar fate. Starting in September, however, things went better for Portella, and he began collecting the opinions of Raymundo Faoro and eminent jurists of the past.[10] Things improved immeasurably after October 12, when Geisel dismissed the hard-line leader, Army Minister Sylvio Frota, thus strengthening his position over military opponents of *abertura.*

Replying in December 1977 to one of the questions of reporters of the *Jornal de Brasília,* Sobral said, "I have the impression that the president has begun to feel that changes are necessary." In the course of answering the questions, Sobral recalled that Geisel, as a STM judge, had never acted in a friendly way toward him.[11]

In December Sobral told the press that the Superior Military Tribunal (STM) was "the best court in Brazil," thus repeating a remark made in August. He explained that although the STM lacked an understanding of "the great Communist leaders, such as Julião, Prestes, Gregório Bezerra, and Oswaldo Pacheco," it acted "magnificently" in handling the cases of less prominent defendants.[12] Furthermore, he described it as a court with an interest in human rights. It had, he said, ordered an investigation of the tortures suffered by one of his clients, a captain, and had also called for the investigation of the circumstances leading to the death of Congressman Rubens de Paiva, a former member of the Nationalist Parliamentary Front who had been seized by the DOI-CODI.[13]

Luís Gallotti was displeased with remarks of Sobral that seemed to belittle the Supreme Court. Sobral, replying to the justice's complaint, explained that all he had done, in recent remarks to reporters, was praise the STM for the fearless way in which it had demanded that authorities reveal where prisoners were being held and the reasons for holding them. "I called no one a coward. Neither I nor my colleagues are among those who make unjust attacks on the Supreme Court. The attackers are those who uphold Ato 5, which deprives the court of its autonomy."[14]

PART VIII

Abertura (1978–1985)

1. Geisel Reforms the Constitution and Makes General Figueiredo His Successor (1978)

In 1978 Sobral became the lawyer for Rio *favela* dwellers who re-fused to be transferred from their shacks in the Morro de Vidigal to the Santa Cruz area, distant from the jobs they picked up in the city. And he helped the Centro Dom Vital observe, in November, the fifti-eth anniversary of the death of its founder, Jackson de Figueiredo. Sobral's speech was critical of those who believed that one could be, at the same time, a good Christian and a member of the Masonic Order.[1]

A Catholic intellectual friend of Sobral's who passed away in 1978 was the eighty-one-year-old Gustavo Corção, whose writings had supported the military regime. Sobral attributed Corção's position to his hatred of Communism. São Paulo's Archbishop-Cardinal Paulo Evaristo Arns, who worked ardently against the military repres-sion, attributed Corção's position to old age. Dom Hélder Câmara said that in eternity Corção would return to being the Corção who had been at the side of Alceu Amoroso Lima in the 1940s and 1950s. Another friend who died in 1978 was Nehemias Gueiros, creator of the OAB's Ruy Barbosa Medal. He was known as the chief author of Institutional Act Number Two, and some words of Sobral, praising his memory, were reported in a manner that Sobral had to correct in order not to seem to favor the Ato.[2]

Most of the headlines about Sobral in 1978 concerned political affairs. Early in the year he disapproved of Geisel's work to have the indirect presidential election of October won by General João Batista Figueiredo, head of the SNI (National Information Service). Brazil, So-bral said, could not put up with a system in which the army was an armed political party and in which the authorities placed no faith in the will of the people. When Senator Magalhães Pinto offered to run against General Figueiredo, Sobral praised the ideas advanced by the Minas politician and gave him advice about how to present them to the public.[3]

In February 1978 the inauguration of the new headquarters of the Minas OAB brought hundreds of lawyers and magistrates to Belo Horizonte. They gave a standing ovation to Sobral, who used the occasion to express support for Cardinal Arns, who had been arguing that Justice Minister Armando Falcão was mistaken in saying that all exiles, except the 128 who had been officially "banished," should feel free to return to Brazil. "Thousands," Sobral said, feared to return lest they be imprisoned and perhaps tortured. He referred to pending legal cases against them and added that it was up to the Supreme Court to judge the cases with honesty. Later, while arguing a case before the Supreme Court, Sobral's criticisms of its members were felt, by a young lawyer who accompanied him, to be a contributing factor to his loss of the case.[4]

Senator Petrônio Portella, becoming the most important elaborator of *abertura*, gathered the opinions of lawyers, of Cardinal Eugênio Sales and the bishops (the CNBB), and even of metalworker Luís Inácio da Silva ("Lula"), strike leader in São Paulo. The OAB's Raymundo Faoro, whom he consulted frequently, declared later that the Petrônio Portella mission was the cornerstone for achieving the transition from the authoritarian regime.[5]

Petrônio Portella, like Geisel, insisted that the steps desired by the opposition be accompanied by "safeguards," and therefore the constitutional reforms, presented to Congress by Geisel on June 23, 1978, included clauses about "emergency measures" and a "state of emergency" or "state of siege," which the executive could use without congressional consent. Otherwise, the proposed reforms were welcome because they did away with all the institutional acts, returned habeas corpus to its historic status, ended penalties of death and perpetual imprisonment, lifted censorship, and reinstituted job security.

The Instituto dos Advogados Brasileiros (IAB) authorized Sobral to report on the proposals, and on July 5 he completed a twenty-page study. Adopted by the IAB and given wide publicity, it objected to limitations placed on congressional immunities, the retention of indirect elections of governors and the president, and the idea of waiting until March 15, 1979, for the effective date. Sobral also maintained that a sufficient "safeguard" of public order existed in the 1969 Constitution's provision for invoking a state of siege, subject to congressional consent, and that the reform should not give the executive authority to enact a state of emergency.[6] In October Congress approved Geisel's proposals, and they were made effective January 1, 1979.

In the meantime the MDB chose a general, Euler Bentes Monteiro, to contest the presidential candidacy of General Figueiredo, and Sobral supported him, although he would have preferred a civilian. The pro-Euler movement, called the Frente Nacional de Redemocratização, was born in June 1978, thanks in large part to the efforts of MDB Senate leader Paulo Brossard, General Euler's running mate. The launching, at the São Paulo state legislative building, was attended by three thousand enthusiastic oppositionists, such as MDB President Ulysses Guimarães, Senator Magalhães Pinto, Congressman Tancredo Neves, and sociologist Fernando Henrique Cardoso, senatorial candidate in São Paulo. A government spokesman called the Frente illegal, and the Federal Police prohibited radio and television broadcasts from mentioning it.[7]

In the October 14 indirect presidential election, General Figueiredo was victorious. Although the MDB did well in the popular elections for Congress in November, the "April Package" rules, such as increased representation for the less heavily populated states, controlled by the ARENA, and indirect elections of one-third of the senators, gave the ARENA majorities in both houses. Sobral declared that the ARENA would long remember "the thrashing it received" in important states such as São Paulo, Rio de Janeiro, and Rio Grande do Sul.[8]

President-elect Figueiredo proposed "conciliation" between the government forces and the opposition, but leaders of the opposition rejected the proposal. Raymundo Faoro, speaking for the OAB, warned that Figueiredo's objective was to divide the MDB and weaken the opposition precisely when public opinion was becoming effective.[9] Sobral argued that in 1945 it had been public opinion that had "destroyed" Vargas's Estado Novo. He said that recently proposed "improvements," such as the use of habeas corpus for political cases, were "tricks" to quiet public opinion. "Only idiots," he told the press, would accept conciliation, "being offered in order to uphold dictatorship."[10] He set out once again to defend Luiz Carlos Prestes, because the name of the absent "Cavalier of Hope" was among sixty-four being accused of "reorganizing the PCB," in a new case at an *auditoria* of the navy.[11]

Honors were awarded to Sobral in 1978. When he went to Manaus in August to attend the closing sessions of Lawyers' Week, the OAB of Amazonas voted to present his name to Stockholm as a candidate for the Nobel Peace Prize. The state legislative assembly endorsed the proposal, and the Municipal Council, its galleries filled with Sobral's admirers, heard speeches supporting the decision to make him an honorary citizen of Manaus. Visitors who flocked to his hotel room included the governor. At the Amazonas Theater he was introduced as having become the symbol of human rights long before United States President Jimmy Carter. His speech called for peaceful changes brought about by public opinion.[12]

Opportunities for Sobral to sway public opinion were plentiful. In Vitória on December 8 he spoke to the Association of Magistrates of the State of Espírito Santo, which awarded him its Muniz Freire Prize in recognition of his struggle for law and liberty. He told his audience that the Brazilian executive power could issue a new Ato 5 at any moment, and he demanded an immediate return of the military to the barracks.[13]

From Vitória he went to Belo Horizonte for the ceremony that awarded the Sobral Pinto Medal to Alceu Amoroso Lima. Speaking to the press there, Sobral said, "I find no hope in the mentality of General Figueiredo, but I base my hopes on the Brazilian people." He went on to Barbacena, Minas Gerais, his birthplace. There he became a member of the Academy of Letters of Barbacena and attended a ceremony at which his picture was placed on a wall in the meeting room of the Municipal Council. Addressing the councilmen for two hours, he ridiculed the "bionic senators" chosen by indirect election. Military officers, he said, had an important role to play in upholding civil order, but, in seeking to run Brazil, they were losing respect and "bringing about their own ruin."[14]

2. Sobral Pinto, Brazil's "Intellectual" of 1978 (1979)

Officers of the Catholic University of Minas Gerais, after accepting in 1975 the idea of law students to establish the Sobral Pinto Medal, sought documents from Sobral to support their decision. Sobral supplied copies of letters and telegrams sent to Castello Branco, Costa e Silva, Médici, Ernesto Geisel, and others, as well as some of his studies about Institutional Act Number Five and the Conselho de Defesa dos Direitos da Pessoa Humana (CDDPH). The university insisted on having the documents appear in book form, and the result was *Lições de Liberdade* (a title chosen by the university), which was published by the university and Editora Comunicação in Belo Horizonte and was offered to the public there on December 12, 1977.[1] Ary Quintella, a writer of fiction and nonfiction who edited the work, included useful notes about the life of Sobral.

The book was a success. With the sale of all the copies within a month and a half, a second edition, slightly enlarged, was published in May 1978.[2]

Admirers of the author decided to add Sobral's name, early in 1979, to those of others who were felt to have published literary works in 1978 that made them worthy of being selected as Brazil's outstanding intellectual of that year.[3]

The annual contest had originated in 1963 after the União Brasileira de Escritores (UBE) of São Paulo came up with the idea of having the selection made by votes of members of the Brazilian Academy of Letters and the São Paulo Academy of Letters, presidents of UBE sections throughout Brazil, and representatives of the Ministry of Education and associations and publications considered to be playing a role in culture.[4] The organizers accepted the idea of writer Mário Donato for the trophy: a statuette of "Juca Pato," a fictional little individual, roundheaded and bald and persecuted by the powerful, made famous from the 1920s to the 1940s by the drawings and writings of Benedito Bastos Barreto, known as Belmonte. The *Folha de S. Paulo* sponsored the yearly selection, which began in 1963 with the victory of Francisco San Tiago Dantas in a hard-fought contest. Among those who obtained the most votes in subsequent years were Alceu Amoroso Lima, Érico Verissimo, Jorge Amado, Josué Montello, and Juscelino Kubitschek (author of autobiographical volumes).[5]

Candidacies were presented in petitions signed by members of the UBE. Sobral learned about his candidacy from press reports, which, early in February 1979, put him in second place with 17 votes, behind the 28 votes received for Gilberto Freyre, whose well-known *Casa Grande e Senzala (The Master and the Slaves)* had appeared in 1933. Its publisher, Augusto Frederico Schmidt, had been accused by Freyre of not paying him proper royalties and had been defended by Sobral.[6]

With three books reportedly published in 1978, Freyre was making his third try for the Juca Pato award, and he remained in the lead until late in February 1979, when the Women's Movement for Amnesty came out for Sobral on account of "his struggle for liberty and his moral qualities." Besides the two leaders, four other candidates had been inscribed, but they attracted few votes, and one of the four, novelist Josué Guimarães, announced early in March that he wanted Sobral to win. Eduardo de Oliveira, a well-established poet, declared: "As a black writer, I vote for the intellectual Sobral Pinto, . . . who never hesitated to place his talent in defense of the oppressed, among whom are a majority of the Afrobrazilians."[7]

The voting closed on March 10, 1979, with Sobral ahead of Gilberto Freyre, 234 votes to 213. The final outcome was delayed by protests from Freyre's supporters, who argued that reasons given for votes for Sobral showed that the contest had ceased to reflect its literary purpose. Brazil's so-called "Oscar" was described in the *Diário de S. Paulo* as having become a *prémio político*, with Freyre pictured as a "rightist" in opposition to the "leftist" stance of Sobral.[8]

Specifically, the Freyre supporters argued that Sobral's *Lições de Liberdade* had appeared in 1977, not 1978, and that the UBE had admitted that its list of Rio intellectuals eligible to vote had been incomplete. Besides, the 49 votes by small radio broadcasting stations in the interior were questioned, especially after one man, owner of ten stations, had cast 10 votes for Sobral. Votes by six magazines, such as one put out by the Clube Monte Libano, were described as lacking validity.[9]

UBE President Raymundo Magalhães Júnior, eminent biographer, asserted that Sobral "is a worthy representative of the intellectual class and won honestly despite the complaints." In Congress, Rio de Janeiro's Congressman Álvaro Valle (ARENA) proclaimed Sobral to be "an intellectual in the best sense of the word, deserving the prize." He called him a defender of principles who, at times, "refuses to reach understandings with political reality." Josué Guimarães, in an article in the *Folha de S. Paulo*, rejoiced to find that the opinion of the majority coincided with his own opinion about Sobral, "who combines talent with independence."[10]

Speaking with modesty to a reporter, Sobral said, "Imagine me receiving the same prize that Alceu received!" It was pleasing, Sobral also said, to find so many notable people interested in reestablishing a climate respectful of human rights. Upon receiving the Juca Pato trophy at the ceremony held on May 25, 1979, at the UBE of São

Paulo, Sobral expressed his gratitude for those whose votes, he said, had strengthened his convictions and had elevated his name "undeservedly" to the "pinnacle of fame," something for which he had never dared to hope.[11]

The success of *Lições de Liberdade* led to the publication in mid-1979 of Sobral's *Por que defendo os Comunistas,* also by Editora Comunicação and the Catholic University of Minas Gerais, and also with the valuable assistance of Ary Quintella. This volume, with letters written in 1937 and 1938 about the imprisoned Luiz Carlos Prestes and "Harry Berger" (a German Communist tortured in Brazil), led Alceu Amoroso Lima to publish a column about both of Sobral's books. These collections of documents, Alceu wrote, "are a treasury of pugnacity, juridical culture, love of justice and liberty, and intrepid faith. Reading them is the best possible lesson about civil liberties and character."[12]

Tuna Espinheiro, well-known producer of short cinema documentaries, went from Bahia to Rio to film a twenty-minute motion picture about Sobral. The result, an interview with the main character and briefer interviews with Raymundo Faoro, Heleno Fragoso, Alceu Amoroso Lima, and history writer Hélio Silva, was exhibited to the producer's friends in Salvador, but before it was presented at the Sixth Festival of Short Films in Rio it suffered from cuts by censors, who argued, in September 1979, that it was more about Luiz Carlos Prestes than about Sobral.[13]

Another award for Sobral was the Osvaldo Vergara Trophy of the Rio Grande do Sul section of the OAB. In Porto Alegre in September to receive it, Sobral spoke to lawyers and journalists about the gains furnished by *"abertura política."* He praised the army for fulfilling its role of upholding order and said it had done so in acting against Goulart in 1964, but he lamented the occupation of the presidency by generals, not elected by the people. Sobral also had much to say about the imprisonments of strike leaders in 1979, with special mention of bank workers in Rio Grande do Sul and Rio de Janeiro. Calling the arrests an "abuse of authority," he said, "we have always had such abuses." They had occurred, he added, even under Juscelino Kubitschek, whose administration he described as "the best that Brazil ever had."[14]

Press interviews with Sobral had become frequent, and in them he repeated his convictions. Sometimes his interviewers mentioned his daily after-lunch taxi rides to his Debret Street office, his black clothing and hat, his umbrella, and his "totally white hair." A spread in São Paulo's *Shopping News* in November called attention to the eighty-sixth birthday of "the hard worker" who, it reported, felt optimistic about the future of Brazil.[15]

3. *Abertura,* Further Advanced by Amnesty (August 1979)

Sobral was asked by one of his press interviewers in April 1979 whether his trip to Brasília on March 14 had been made for the purpose of witnessing, along with so many others, the inauguration of President Figueiredo. He had come, Sobral explained, to examine, at the Superior Military Tribunal, the papers that had resulted in the 1966 sentencing of Luiz Carlos Prestes to serve fourteen years in prison.[1]

From Prestes, who was in Europe, Sobral had received no *procuração* (legal authorization) in October 1978 when the *auditoria* of the navy had brought accusations against more than forty "Communist intellectuals," including Prestes, but Sobral had been accepted by the *auditoria* as a participant in the defense of the whole group. He had argued that accusations such as those based on the Prestes notebooks seized by the São Paulo police in 1964 were not proofs of plans to "reconstitute the PCB," and the lawyers of other defendants had followed Sobral's lead. The result had been the acquittals of all the "intellectuals."[2]

Now in March 1979 these acquittals were being appealed by the accusers, and Prestes, feeling that the climate had much improved, had sent a *procuração* to Sobral. Sobral, finding in Brasília that the papers about the Prestes case filled twenty-five volumes, decided to take copies of them to Rio. He would, he said, spend a few weeks studying them to make up his mind on whether to handle the 1966 imprisonment sentence with an appeal for reversing the decision or with a habeas corpus petition.[3]

In August 1979 Congress approved the extensive amnesty bill of Justice Minister Petrônio Portella and the extinction of all *cassações.* Therefore on August 30 the Superior Military Tribunal decreed amnesty for 326 persons who had been convicted of committing political crimes, including Prestes and Brizola. Even those who had been legally "banished," following the release of kidnapped ambassadors in 1969 and 1970, received amnesty from the military justice system.[4]

Oswaldo Pacheco was liberated. Brizola entered Brazil in Rio Grande do Sul and talked about reviving the old Vargas PTB because, with *abertura,* there would be a number of parties, as had existed before the two-party system installed by the military. Miguel Arraes, after a stay in Recife, came to Rio, saying that the first thing he would do would be to thank Sobral for all that he had done for him. He spoke also to Raymundo Faoro and Alceu Amoroso Lima and addressed the Rio de Janeiro state assembly. Gregório Bezerra, in Recife, was visited by scores of people and paid a "courtesy call" on the state assembly there.[5]

Prestes's return to Brazil from Paris occurred on October 20, 1979. Among the reported five thousand who greeted him at Rio's Galeão Airport were his daughter Anita Leocádia, who had returned a little earlier, and his sisters. Sobral was on hand and so were Bezerra and officers of the Brazilian Communist Party (PCB). The eighty-one-year-old "Cavalier of Hope" was given red roses, and admirers shouted, "From north to south, from east to west, all the people call for Luiz Carlos Prestes." He climbed onto the top of a pickup truck at the airport to address the crowd and declared that his first words were "in praise of all those who have fallen in defense of democratic liberties in Brazil." He invited Sobral to join him on the truck, and Sobral did just that.[6]

4.   Sobral, Opponent of Liberation Theology, Is Honored by the Pope (1980–1981)

The 1980 school year of the Pontifícia Universidade Católica (PUC) of Rio de Janeiro opened on March 12 with a ceremony that was attended by Cardinal Eugênio Sales and other dignitaries and was addressed by Sobral. "Recently," Sobral told his audience, "the PUC has been facing, as is happening in all nations, an immense, terrible, and sinister danger: the infiltration of the Marxist philosophy in its courses." The address was filled with denunciations of Marxism.[1]

Dom Eugênio Sales, pleased with what Sobral said, gave orders to have the address published in the *Boletim* of the archdiocese.[2] But it led to controversy. The CNBB (National Conference of Brazilian Bishops) said that Sobral misinterpreted the work of the Church for social and economic reforms, and it denied that this work of priests and bishops was characterized by Marxism. Officers of the PUC asserted that Sobral had merely issued a warning and had not affirmed the existence of infiltration. The education minister said that Sobral had been discussing a specific situation at the Rio PUC and that it would be a mistake to talk about any danger of Marxism in universities elsewhere.[3] But when Sobral discussed his PUC address with the press, he made it clear that priests and even bishops, along with lay Catholics, had caused "segments of the Church to adopt Marxist positions that we cannot accept."[4]

On the afternoon of March 13, 1980, the day after the address at the PUC, someone placed a time bomb, wrapped in a shoe box, under the sofa in the waiting room next to Sobral's work room on the third floor of the Debret Street office building in downtown Rio. Curiously, an anonymous telephone call, answered by Benedita Novais, the secretary, told about the bomb and said it would explode in twenty minutes (at 5:10 P.M.). Sobral, believing that "if they want to kill us, they would not warn us," was unworried and went on with his work. But after lawyer Jarbas Macedo de Camargo Penteado and a janitor moved the box to the street below, a police inspector, who disassembled the apparently homemade contraption, found that it was set to go off at 6:00 P.M.[5]

Sobral, who had already received threats in telephone calls to his home, testified that he had no idea why he had been threatened. Eduardo Seabra Fagundes, president of the OAB's Conselho Federal, guessed that the bomb threat was unrelated to Sobral's address at the PUC. "It was, I think, a provocation by people wanting to disrupt Brazil."[6]

Brazil was suffering from a campaign of violence by opponents of *abertura* in which most of the approximately forty assaults, estimated to have occurred between January 1980 and April 1981, were inflicted by bombs.[7] More serious than the threat of March 13, 1980, was the explosion on August 27, 1980, that occurred at the headquarters of the OAB when Lyda Monteiro da Silva, longtime OAB secretary, opened a package addressed to Eduardo Seabra Fagundes. It wrecked her office and killed her. Although Seabra Fagundes called for a police investigation, two days passed before it began. An independent investigation, set in motion by the OAB, eventually sought to incriminate Ronald Watters, said to be a "far rightist" previously involved in terrorist activities, but he was absolved because of insufficient proof.[8] This failure to punish culprits was typical of the so-called investigations of these violent crimes, including the most sensational one, that of April 30, 1981, when a bomb, apparently intended to terrify a RioCentro theater audience, exploded prematurely, killing one of its purveyors and wounding the other, members of the DOI-CODI.[9]

Sobral in 1981 continued to condemn Liberation Theology for its Marxism. Writing to Cardinal Eugênio Sales in March 1981, he complained of the activities of advocates of "progressive" Catholicism, Frei (Brother) Carlos Alberto Betto, Frei Leonardo Boff, Frei Clodovis Boff, and Cláudio Hummes, the bishop of the ABC industrialized zone in São Paulo. These Catholics, Sobral noted, were lecturing about changes in the doctrine of Christianity at an "extension course" at a Protestant institution within the archdiocese of the cardinal.[10] The position of Sobral, critic of Leonardo Boff's writings, was described as "exemplary" by Dom Eugênio Sales, but it upset Dom Hélder Câmara, who sent a copy of one of his talks to Sobral. Sobral, writing to Henrique Hargreaves, accused Dom Hélder of "upholding the ridiculous idea that, just as Saint Thomas Aquinas had given support to Aristotle's philosophy, a new Saint Thomas Aquinas will appear to support Marxism."[11]

The rise of "progressivism" in the Catholic Church hurt the Centro Dom Vital. Sobral, its president, sorrowfully accepted the resignation of Professor Antônio de Rezende Silva from the position of vice president of the Centro in charge of publishing A Ordem. Telling Hargreaves that Rezende Silva, a PUC professor, supported progressivism, Sobral wrote that teaching deficiencies in seminaries and in the Catholic universities caused "priests and bishops, in many places, to be entirely unprepared for the struggle against Marxism."[12]

The Liberation Theology of the progressives, Sobral learned unhappily from Vicente Scherer, archbishop of Porto Alegre, led priests to refuse to carry out the service of Mass for the souls of rich people even though they had devoted their lives to following the preachings of Jesus Christ. Scherer, who had been combating Marxism, had been kept in his position three years beyond the usual retirement age of seventy-five, but was now being retired, leading Sobral to observe that forced retirements should be based on "loss of lucidity," not age.[13]

It shocked Sobral to read, late in 1981, an article in IstoÉ magazine, "Ultimatum to Dom Eugênio." The article quoted Father Daniel de

Castro as saying that the "progressive clergy's opposition" to the cardinal "is a struggle for human rights and liberty of expression." In the past, Sobral reminded *IstoÉ*, Daniel de Castro had been accused by the authorities of subversion and had been saved from imprisonment only because Dom Eugênio had given him refuge in the cardinal's palace, a step that had been followed by the successful effort of Eny Raymundo Moreira, an office companion of Sobral, to win the Catholic padre's legal case. Sobral told *IstoÉ* that the clergy of the archdiocese, at a recent meeting that included Daniel de Castro, had unanimously repudiated the magazine's article. Dom Eugênio, Sobral also wrote, was not a conservative. Sobral described him as dedicating himself to carrying out faithfully the directives of the Pope.[14]

During a part of 1980 and some months of 1981, Sobral was ill, and he was interned from time to time in the São José Hospital with acute asthmatic problems. He delegated his law partner Tito Lívio Cavalcanti de Medeiros to go to São Paulo and read his speech turning over the Juca Pato trophy to his successor, and, also in mid-1980, he had to miss being at the Holy Communion celebrated by Pope John Paul II in Rio de Janeiro.[15]

Sobral was in the São José Hospital on the night of February 15, 1981, when he received a telephone call from Cardinal Eugênio Sales saying that the Pope had awarded Sobral the title of Commanding Cavalier of the Order of Saint Gregory the Great. Confirming this message, a letter from Papal Nuncio Carmine Rocco advised Sobral of the award, dated December 18, 1980, in recognition of the Pope's high regard for his "faithfulness to the Church and dauntless defense of great causes of Justice." Sobral's son Alberto told reporters of the joy of Sobral, who, Alberto added, had received four blood transfusions and would soon leave the hospital.[16]

Sandra Cavalcanti, who was contemplating a run for the governorship of Rio de Janeiro, wrote, in her *Última Hora* column, of the ecstasy she felt on learning of the award. "I love Sobral Pinto. I can say this with an open heart, overflowing with admiration and gratitude because he is one of those who turn us into believers in what is good." Sobral gave Tito Lívio the letter from the nuncio and a copy of the article by Sandra Cavalcanti with the explanation that it was proper that they be in the hands of a law companion and friend of thirty years whose "ability, loyalty, and dynamism have been precious."[17]

On June 25, 1981, Sobral's family gathered with an estimated three hundred persons at the cardinal's palace in Rio to be present when Eugênio Sales officially conferred the lofty papal title on him. Sobral, in response, spoke with humility about himself and discussed the letters of Pope Gregory XVI, written in 1821 with the purpose of creating the Order as a tribute to his predecessor. Sobral spoke also of the need for "authority and liberty" to be pursued in harmony, neither getting out of hand. This "wisdom," he said, was being forgotten. "The Church itself, on account of the unfortunate influence of profane infiltration in a part of its clergy and lay members, certainly of a temporary nature, is suffering."[18]

5. *Abertura* Remains Incomplete (1981–1982)

With the OAB's Conselho Federal scheduled to elect new officers late in March 1981, Sobral and José Ribeiro de Castro Filho issued a "manifesto" in February containing a "vehement appeal" in favor of the election of Bernardo Cabral, of Amazonas, to be president, and Mário Sérgio Duarte Garcia, of São Paulo, to be vice president. The signers said that their appeal, made without consulting their colleagues, was addressed to all the OAB sections except for the one in Brasília, already committed to vote for José Paulo Sepúlveda Pertence to be the Conselho president. When the election took place, the sections adhered, by a 19 to 7 vote, to the recommendations made in February by Sobral and Ribeiro da Costa Filho, although outgoing President Eduardo Seabra Fagundes and his father Miguel supported the loser, Sepúlveda Pertence. Bernardo Cabral, who had been congressional vice leader of the MDB before being *cassado* in February 1969, took office early in April 1981 following introductory remarks by Sobral and Ribeiro de Castro Filho.[1]

"Lawyers' Day," August 11, was observed by the São Paulo OAB with the presentation of the title of "exemplary lawyer" to Sobral. In his acceptance speech he blamed the severe economic recession and "massive unemployment" on the "incompetence, incapacity, and ignorance" of the government. Speaking early in September to the *Folha de S. Paulo*, Sobral called Congress cowardly. "If it lacks the courage to fight for its own prerogatives, how can we expect it to revoke the absurd national security law?"[2]

A man of courage, in the opinion of Sobral, was Ribeiro de Castro Filho, and he wished to have him receive the Sobral Pinto Medal of the Catholic University of Minas Gerais. In November 1981 he wrote a strong letter to the university's Professor Valmir Catão insisting on his wish and the removal of the name already chosen without his being consulted. He wrote that "as long as I am alive the medal should not go to anyone not approved by me," and he reminded the professor that Alceu Amoroso Lima had been awarded the medal in 1978 because he, Sobral, had made the choice. In his letter, he praised the work of his new nominee, sometimes personally risky, on behalf of prisoners who had been mistreated and tortured, and who had sometimes simply "disappeared." In addition, he wrote, Ribeiro de Castro Filho had so forcefully opposed a decree for ending the OAB's autonomy that it had been withdrawn.[3]

The medal was given to Ribeiro de Castro Filho, and, for the ceremony, Sobral was joined by Bernardo Cabral in Belo Horizonte in December 1981. While there, Bernardo Cabral and Sobral denounced the plans of the government to provide difficulties for the opposition with new rules for the elections of federal and state legislators in November 1982, when the people would also choose governors directly.[4] Because each state would furnish six representatives to join all the federal legislators to form the electoral college, the local elections would play a role in determining the outcome of the indirect presidential election of January 1985.

In 1980 the ARENA politicians had formed the PDS (Partido Democrático Social) as the government party. Late in 1981 the party's leaders, such as PDS President José Sarney, backed a proposed rule that would prevent an opposition party, the PP (Partido Popular of Senator Tancredo Neves and Congressman Magalhães Pinto), from incorporating itself, prior to the 1982 elections, into the PMDB (Partido do Movimento Democrático Brasileiro), successor to the MDB. Other opposition parties, such as the Partido dos Trabalhadores (PT, headed by Luís Inácio da Silva, known as Lula) and the Partido Democrático Trabalhista (PDT, headed by Brizola), joined the PP and PMDB (headed by Congressman Ulysses Guimarães) in denouncing the government's proposed election rules. Tancredo Neves said, "Sobral Pinto was marvelous and spoke for the people."[5]

In 1981 the PT's Lula was sentenced by a military court for violating the national security law by leading a metalworkers' strike in São Paulo.[6] He and his lawyer Luís Eduardo Greenhaldt, who appealed the three-and-one-half-year sentence, received votes late in 1981 for "outstanding contributions to justice" in the contest for the so-called "Bertrand Russell Prize," established by advertising executive Carlito Maia and the Brazilian Press Association of São Paulo. The votes, by newspapers, magazines, and television stations, gave the prize to Sobral, whose 297 votes surpassed the 232 received by Lula. The "Mahatma Gandhi Peace Prize" was won by São Paulo Cardinal Arns, with 366 votes, and the "Charles Chaplin Liberty Prize" went to Alceu Amoroso Lima, with 297 votes.[7]

The military government's attempt to tinker with election rules and its opposition to direct presidential elections, along with the use it made of the national security law, contributed to the evidence that *abertura* was not complete. Among the national security law cases that angered Sobral in 1982 was the case that resulted in the conviction of two French priests, for their alleged roles in land disputes, and cases arising from statements made by journalist Hélio Fernandes and by the head of the Goiás OAB.

In accusing Hélio Fernandes of violating the national security law, the authorities were said to be seeking to prevent his becoming a PMDB senatorial candidate. Sobral called the charge against the journalist "absurd." Regarding the French missionaries, whose conviction was being appealed by Heleno Fragoso, Luís Eduardo Greenhaldt, and others, Sobral and former Justice Minister Miguel Seabra Fagundes spoke persuasively at the OAB's Conselho Federal. In support of the priests, threatened with expulsion, Bernardo Cabral sent a telegram to the justice minister, Ibrahim Abi-Ackel.[8]

The sin attributed to Wanderley de Medeiros, head of the Goiás OAB, was his statement in Rio to young men being admitted to the bar: "The Supreme Court, in the few cases it accepts, has transformed itself from acting as the guardian of liberty to acting as a rancid appendage of the executive, and it issues illegal judgments in order to convict citizens."[9]

When the army's Third Auditoria heard the case of Wanderley de Medeiros in Rio in August 1982, Sobral and then Heleno Fragoso delivered the concluding defense arguments, emphasizing that the national security law was irrelevant to the case at hand. Unanimously the court's judges agreed that the case belonged in a civilian court and not the military justice system.[10]

In the meantime the Military Police of the state of São Paulo undertook an investigation of the "political tendencies of the directors of the subsections of the OAB in São Paulo." This led the OAB's Conselho Federal to send the justice minister a protest, in which amazement was expressed at the choice of the São Paulo Military Police for such an assignment.[11]

Sobral was among those who attended the July 15, 1982, meeting of the CDDPH at the office of the justice minister in Brasília. On returning to Rio, he suffered severe pains in his heart and went to the São José Hospital. There, in the words of his daughter Ruth, surgeons "inserted a valve to free him from having to receive a series of medicines, which, besides not being altogether effective, caused him to have to put up with much interference in his active life."[12]

His recovery, however, was not complete. Following a lunch in a restaurant on November 5, offered by colleagues to observe his eighty-ninth birthday, he had to seek help from his doctors. His daughter Idalina made it known that other commemorations would be postponed.[13]

In the direct elections held that month, the governorships of Minas Gerais and São Paulo were won by PMDB candidates Tancredo Neves and Franco Montoro. "Social Democrat" Brizola (PDT) and his running mate Darcy Ribeiro were victorious in the state of Rio de Janeiro. But, although the opposition parties received a few more seats than the PDS in the Chamber of Deputies, the government party remained in control of the Senate and the electoral college that would choose the next president of Brazil in January 1985.

6. Honors Heaped on the Ninety-Year-Old Sobral (late 1983)

The biennial election for officers of the OAB's Conselho Federal, held in March 1983, was a close, hotly contested one after the Conselho's vice president, Mário Sérgio Duarte Garcia of São Paulo, belatedly opposed the presidential candidacy of Alcides Munoz Neto, criminal lawyer in Paraná. Sobral, described by Mário Sérgio as "a great elector," worked with others to overcome the initial advantage of Munoz, whom Sobral criticized for offering to pay for trips of *conselheiros* to Rio to be at his expected inauguration. Supporters of Mário Sérgio argued that Munoz would be less forceful than they wanted in defying the military.[1]

After the OAB sections gave thirteen votes to each contestant, the tie was broken by a switch favorable to Mário Sérgio Duarte Garcia. Then Sobral wrote letters to reply to charges made against the victor by Munoz in what Mário Sérgio called a "defamatory campaign." On May 31 *O Globo* carried Sobral's detailed explanations to show that Munoz's defeat could not, as charged, be attributed to financial assistance sent by the Conselho Federal to the poorer OAB sections.[2]

Mário Sérgio, during his two-year administration of the OAB's Conselho Federal, found President Figueiredo uninterested in having a dialogue with the OAB, and he found Justice Minister Ibrahim Abi-Ackel, who presided at the few meetings of the CDDPH, to be a polite listener who made promises that went unfulfilled. Listing past heads of the OAB who had acted "fearlessly" for democracy, Mário Sérgio named José Ribeiro de Castro Filho (recipient of the 1982 Ruy Barbosa Medal), José Cavalcanti Neves, Raymundo Faoro, and Eduardo Seabra Fagundes.[3]

For Sobral, a long and close association ended with the death in August 1983 of ninety-year-old Alceu Amoroso Lima, who had been suffering from cancer. Sobral, speaking at the graveside in the name of the OAB, called Alceu "the most important man of the twentieth century" and "a present from God to the nation," and he concluded emotionally with words to his departed friend, "Until we soon meet again." Vice Governor Darcy Ribeiro spoke in the name of the people and government of Rio de Janeiro. Among the approximately 150 mourners were Governor Brizola and Luiz Carlos Prestes, who had become political allies after Prestes's break with the Brazilian Communist Party (PCB) in 1980.[4]

In September Brizola set up a state human rights council. Sobral was invited to be a member but he declined, saying that his ideas differed from the "senseless socialist" ideas preached by the governor. Sobral also said that Vice Governor Darcy Ribeiro, "a friend of mine, calls himself a socialist, but for me socialism and Communism are the same thing. I have a horror of socialism. Russia is socialist. Socialism is incompatible with liberty."[5]

Asked by the press if he believed that women, by leaving the home, were causing the disintegration of the family, Sobral replied in the affirmative and praised his wife Maria José for her spirit of renunciation and for all that she did to make life good at home, all very simple, without luxuries, and without any complaints on her part. "If she had not had that spirit of renunciation, I could not have done what I have done."[6]

Shortly before the Mass at the Candelária Church for Sobral's ninetieth birthday on November 5, 1983, Maria José broke her long public silence. She said, in reply to reporters, that her husband "deserves this tribute. He has dedicated his life to his work and his family. He has always been doing things without any concern for his personal interest. He might have been rich but he has nothing." Commenting on remarks about her pleasing appearance, she said that this was not something put on for the occasion. Without referring to the fact that it was also her birthday, her eighty-seventh, she spoke about her health, saying, "Sometimes I have problems with my back, but I'm in good shape."[7]

Following the Mass, attended by a reported five hundred, Cardinal Eugênio Sales called on a lay Catholic leader to read aloud a message from the Pope prepared for the occasion. Sobral, surprised and deeply moved, embraced Dom Eugênio. At a time when so many in Brazil were praising him, Sobral was also especially touched by a warm letter from poet Carlos Drummond de Andrade that ended with words "You, who unite love and justice, are rigorously a good Christian."[8]

Among the large number of notables at the Mass was the secretary of culture of Minas, Congressman José Aparecido de Oliveira, who had, with Sobral's help in 1964, legally contested *cassação*. José Aparecido, representative of Governor Tancredo Neves at the Mass, spoke on November 7 at a lunch at which Professor Cândido Mendes de Almeida announced the formation of the Forum Sobral Pinto, to be a part of the Cândido Mendes College in Rio, and the establishment of the Sobral Pinto Prize of five thousand dollars, to be given every two years to the most outstanding Brazilian lawyer, selected by a commission that would include Dom Eugênio Sales and José Aparecido. São Paulo Governor Franco Montoro, who also spoke at the lunch, revealed that his entry into politics had been inspired by Sobral.[9]

In São Paulo a few days later, Sobral joined Franco Montoro and other distinguished oppositionists in launching a campaign for making the presidential election direct. The launching was followed by a ceremony at which the governor awarded Sobral the title of commander of the Order of Ipiranga, previously awarded by Franco Montoro only to the king of Spain. Sobral, who had been selected on account of "his courage as a jurist and his outstanding work in defending human rights," spoke to the Paulista press about the virtues of Tancredo Neves, "firm and prudent." "When he speaks of the need of a consensus, it is because he feels that a direct confrontation with the military, still very strong, would be dangerous." Some caution, Sobral added, would benefit the nation while the armed forces "are becoming convinced that they lack the capacity to govern the country."[10]

In Brasília, where members of the Chamber of Deputies were preparing to have a session to honor the memory of Carlos Marighella, the Senate resolved to honor Sobral Pinto by making him "the third person ever to address the Senate without a mandate" (after Lúcio Costa, creator of the pilot plan for building Brasília, and Pelé, the soccer star). Sobral, in his two-hour Senate speech, given to the filled chamber on November 24, reviewed his past effort to emulate Ruy Barbosa, and he said that if the senators and congressmen had been bold in facing risks, the situation would be better than it was.[11]

From the Senate, Sobral went to the Chamber of Deputies because Ulysses Guimarães and others had decided to follow the example of the Senate. In contrast to the lack of interest shown for a speech by PMDB Congressman Jorge Carone Filho (whom Sobral had defended in 1964), the lower house quickly filled up for Sobral, who said he was repeating his plea, made in the Senate, for a national union to defend democracy.[12] A little later he told the press that Brazil needed three things: (1) direct presidential elections, (2) a constitutional assembly, and (3) a modification of the economic program of Planning Minister Antônio Delfim Neto. He opposed any demonstration of hostility to the armed forces but said they should cease trying to run Brazil and should return to maintaining order and upholding respect for laws and judicial decisions.[13]

In Belo Horizonte on December 7, Sobral lunched with Tancredo Neves, and on the 9th he received from the governor the state's foremost medal, the Grande Medalha da Inconfidência, and from the Minas legislature the Medal of the Order of Legislative Merit. Sobral was greeted by a former client, Clodsmith Riani, who was among those who witnessed his receipt of honors in Belo Horizonte. Following the ceremonies, a meal, attended by OAB leaders and politicians, was given in Sobral's honor at the Governor's Palace, and, after the meal, Sobral made a courtesy visit to the mother of José Aparecido de Oliveira.[14]

Back in Rio on December 10, Sobral learned that the OAB was sponsoring a talk by Archbishop Hélder Câmara. At the meeting Sobral remained long enough to embrace his friend, but he left before the well-known progressive Catholic, addressing about a hundred listeners, called for the extinction of the International Monetary

Fund, which, Dom Hélder said, was responsible for crushing the Brazilian people and contributing to hunger and misery.[15]

7. Sobral Faces a Noisy "Direct Elections" Multitude (April 10, 1984)

In Congress in 1983 the PMDB's Dante de Oliveira proposed a constitutional amendment that would make the approaching presidential election a direct one by the people.

With the vote on the amendment scheduled for April 25, 1984, its many supporters held a rally on April 10 in the square in front of Candelária Church in Rio. Commenting on the presence of "a million participants" and their demand, Sobral said that "nothing like it" had ever occurred in Brazil.[1] The throng came to hear more than forty orators, among them the presidents of the PMDB, PDT, and PT (Ulysses Guimarães, Armindo Doutel de Andrade, and Lula), Governors Tancredo Neves, Franco Montoro, and Brizola, the congressional leaders of the opposition parties, and Sobral Pinto, Barbosa Lima Sobrinho, and jurist Afonso Arinos de Melo Franco (three "special guests" invited by the host, Brizola).[2]

The multitude, when Sobral arose to face it, was shouting, singing, waving "*Diretas Já*" placards, and, Sobral felt, showing a lack of respect for the military. "Figueiredo, the time has come for you to cry" were the words in a refrain being chanted about the president, who was on a visit to Spain.[3] Lifting a finger and speaking with firmness, Sobral called for silence, "so I can be heard." The multitude, becoming silent at once, heard Sobral's clear words: "In any civilized nation the armed forces are given respect because they guarantee internal order and protection from abroad." He went on to receive hearty applause when he added, "It is important, however, that we place in the presidency a civilian, who will handle the armed forces so that they abide by the constitution that calls on them to respect the law and human rights. Also, it is important that this multitude understand how every citizen who loves his country should behave." Especially pleasing to the enormous audience was Sobral's emphatically given quotation from the constitution: "All power is derived from the people and is to be carried out in their name."[4]

After Sobral returned to his seat, Tancredo Neves spoke to him, saying, "I don't understand how, with a crowd like this, you got everyone to become silent to hear you." According to an article by Hélio Fernandes, Sobral, seated near Brizola, complained to the governor during someone's violent attack on those in power, and the governor acted immediately to have the speeches "return to their earlier tone, vehement but not offensive." Speaking later to reporters, Sobral said that after the warning given in his own speech, the crowd displayed maturity. Reports about the rally were almost unanimous in praising its orderliness, and they frequently described Sobral as the most loudly applauded orator. One commentator, disappointed in what he called the "weakness" of the governors' speeches, said that Lula, who introduced Goulart's daughter to the crowd, received the most applause.[5]

Sobral, thrilled by the rally, told the press that the people would record the names of all those in Congress who, failing in their duty, opposed the Dante de Oliveira amendment. He added that the rally "liquidated the presidential hopes" of PDS candidates General Mário Andreazza, the minister of the interior, and Congressman Paulo Maluf, former governor of São Paulo.[6] But Justice Minister Abi-Ackel said that the political demonstration, "the largest in the history of Rio de Janeiro" and "carried out in perfect order, a sort of civic entertainment," had not brought about the alteration of a single vote by members of the government parties in Congress. While other cities prepared to hold direct election rallies, and while Vice President Aureliano Chaves (PDS) repeated his oft expressed support for a direct presidential election, the SNI (National Information Service) released a study to show that the Dante de Oliveira amendment would be defeated and that, even if it were adopted, a direct election would not bring the presidency to Brizola. Maluf supporters had been warning of a Brizola victory to arouse fear in the military of a direct election.[7]

A week before the congressional vote, President Figueiredo signed a decree establishing emergency measures in Brasília and the principal cities in Goiás in order to protect Congress from any "popular coercion" in favor of the Dante de Oliveira amendment. Ulysses Guimarães and other oppositionists, fearing that the decree would be used against the opposition, turned to Sobral, who delivered an injunction petition to the Supreme Court. At about the same time, April 24, the press published Sobral's letter to General Rubem Ludwig, chief of the presidential *gabinete militar*, to upbraid him for describing "*Diretas Já*" advocates as being of the type who would bring about gangster-like violence.[8]

Violence, it turned out, was practiced on April 24 by the troops of the military commander in Brasília, General Newton Cruz. Students, after a visit to Congress, were accused of having disturbed it. Tear gas was used during the arrest of students, journalists, and two congressmen. "You are a Communist," the general shouted at Congressman Aldo Arantes (PMDB). The National Federation of Journalists in Brasília was invaded by troops. But on April 25, Sobral's petition to the Supreme Court was rejected. The court said the enactment of emergency measures was constitutional, and it observed that the documents presented to it had not furnished concrete information about any act to prove that the government used the measures to threaten Congress.[9]

On the 25th almost half the congressmen voted for the Dante de Oliveira amendment, fewer than the two-thirds vote needed to send the proposal to the Senate for its consideration. Brazilians abided by appeals for calm, made by Franco Montoro and others.[10]

Late in July Sobral agreed to be honorary president of the Movimento Nacional Tancredo Neves, for electing Tancredo to the Brazilian presidency on the PMDB ticket, but he made it clear that he would leave the Movimento if it failed to fully respect its opponents.[11] At about the same time the Movimento gained strength in the electoral college because of the adherence of politicians who had been important in the PDS. Among them were Vice President Aureliano Chaves and Senator Marco Maciel, founders of the new Frente Liberal, which made an alliance with the PMDB and supplied one of its group, recent PDS President José Sarney, to be the running mate of Tancredo.

8. The Election and Death of Tancredo Neves (early 1985)

A reporter interviewing Sobral in 1984 asked him about a remark of his daughter Gilda: "My father acts morally like a man of the 19th Century, is living the 20th Century intensely, and has his thinking turned to the 21st Century." "Exactly," he replied. "My juridical, religious, and political formation is of the 19th Century, and I live the present intensely, dynamically. . . . Furthermore, I believe that the 21st Century will bring a return of that juridical order and religious thinking that existed in the 17th and 18th Centuries."[1]

A bit later, also in 1984, the ninety-year-old Sobral made headlines by facing a jury for the first time in fifteen years. He sought to prove that a youthful member of a family he had known for forty years should not be found guilty of attempted murder because of his use of a knife during a barroom brawl. With Tito Lívio at his side, he delivered arguments that were applauded by spectators. After he won the case, he was surrounded by law students seeking his autograph.[2]

On his ninety-first birthday, November 5, 1984, Sobral autographed copies of his new book, *Teologia da Libertação*, at a session arranged by Editora Lidador in Rio. The book, with an introduction by Cardinal Eugênio Sales, contained some of Sobral's writings in opposition to those who, he wrote, "contend that Marx is as important as the Bible or more so."[3]

In the next month Sobral was in Brasília to be honored by the new Partido da Frente Liberal (PFL), ally of the PMDB. At the Brasília airport he was often embraced and sometimes kissed by children and adults, and he posed with them for the photographs they wanted. He condemned the "totally inept and illegal" inquiry that reached no conclusion in determining who was responsible for the murder of a *Correio Braziliense* journalist who had been accusing the police in Brasília of participating in "death squads."[4]

On January 15, 1985, Tancredo Neves received 480 of the 686 electoral college votes, thus defeating the PDS's Paulo Maluf. But a serious illness of Tancredo made it necessary for his running mate, José Sarney, to be named acting president on March 15. Following a series of operations, Tancredo died on April 21 in a São Paulo hospital, and Sarney became full-fledged president the next day.

Sobral, speaking to the press on April 22, said that he had been glued to the scenes of mourning shown on television. "Never have I found in the history of Brazil nor witnessed in my life a spectacle as moving, as edifying. All the people weeping and praying in the streets of São Paulo. Not to be compared with it was the mourning following the death of Getúlio Vargas, which was limited to his supporters. Today it is the entire nation."

Sobral expressed no doubt that the people would renew, more forcefully than ever, the campaign for direct presidential elections. He praised the "words of humility and firmness" of Sarney upon assuming the presidency, "bringing to all Brazilians the certainty that the program of Tancredo will be carried out."[5]

PART IX

Epilogue (1985–1991)

1. Mayorship Elections Disappoint (November 1985)

When Sobral had spoken to Tancredo Neves about arrangements for a constitutional assembly, he had suggested that the Congress, to be elected in November 1986, act simultaneously as an ordinary Congress and a constitutional assembly, thus avoiding a period of executive decree laws, as had existed while the Constitutional Assembly of 1946 had devoted itself exclusively to writing a constitution.[1] Tancredo's ideas on the matter coincided with those of Sobral and were presented by President Sarney in a message asking Congress to enact the necessary constitutional amendment. The message, calling for the Constitutional Assembly to start work on February 1, 1987, was signed by Sarney in June 1985 in the presence of Sobral and other special guests. Sobral, who had been inducted by Sarney into the Order of Rio Branco in May 1985 (along with almost eighty others), was a warm supporter of Sarney, and he defended the president's message of June about the Constitutional Assembly during the debates that preceded the congressional vote in its favor in November.[2]

With his usual forcefulness, Sobral expressed his opinions about some of the elections for mayors to be held on November 15, 1985, especially those in Rio and São Paulo. Participation by Sobral in the Rio election began in August, when he gave his support to the mayorship campaign of Congressman Álvaro Valle, who had become president of the small Partido Liberal (PL) after a brief association with the Partido da Frente Liberal (PFL). Sobral received hearty applause when, at the side of Valle, he helped launch his friend's candidacy in the presence of about three hundred PL people at a Rio theater. In October he was photographed "campaigning in the streets" because Valle met him when he emerged from a bank near his Debret Street office and the two of them set to work handing out election propaganda.[3]

Reporters, sometimes calling Sobral "the most important electoral chief" of Valle, gave Valle little chance in the field of six, whose leading candidates were Roberto Saturnino Braga, of Brizola's PDT, and Rubem Medina, of the PFL. Sobral admitted that his candidate lacked money. Brizola's main interest, Sobral added, was to reach the presidency, and he criticized Brizola for advocating that a direct presidential election coincide with the congressional elections of 1986.[4]

Jânio Quadros, candidate of the PFL and PTB for the mayorship of São Paulo, was harshly condemned by Sobral, who maintained that the former president, by resigning in 1961, had delivered the presidency to the "completely unprepared" Goulart, stimulator of Communism and leftism, leading to twenty years of military dictatorship. When Sobral accepted the Mauá Medal, awarded on his ninety-second birthday at a lunch of the Commercial Association of Rio de Janeiro, he astonished his audience by asserting: "If Jânio Quadros wins the mayorship, I'll be convinced that the Brazilian people do not know how to vote and never should vote." He also asserted that if Brazil were given "the choice between Jânio and the military dictatorship, perhaps the former would have brought more evil to Brazil."[5]

Sobral's attacks against Quadros pleased Senator Fernando Henrique Cardoso, the São Paulo mayorship candidate of the PMDB and Brazil's two Communist parties (the PCB and the party that split from it in 1961). Cardoso, who had been a close friend of Tancredo Neves, resented the decision of the PFL to back Quadros. In the polls he had a slight lead over Quadros when he invited Sobral to join him in São Paulo for his closing rally. Sobral, in explaining to reporters why he would be unable to accept the invitation from the candidate he favored in São Paulo, referred to physical weaknesses, such as those that had prevented him, since reaching the age of eighty-five, from making his daily walk to the Mass at the chapel near his home. Furthermore, he said, his efforts to help candidates were not effective, as had been demonstrated by the defeat in 1982 of Rio de Janeiro gubernatorial candidate Sandra Cavalcanti.[6]

With the Conselho de Defesa da Mulher (Council for Defending Women) complaining about Sobral's "failure to adhere to the evolution of the role of women in society," newspapers wrote that Cardoso's invitation to Sobral had been made "despite the protest of the candidate's *comitê feminino.*"[7]

Sobral in 1985 continued to alienate the many admirers of the Catholic Left. Speaking at the inauguration of a Catholic seminary, he described Liberation Theology and "progressivism" in the Catholic Church as undermining the authority of the Church and of Pope John Paul II, who, he said, exceeded all his predecessors in dynamism, spiritual work, and pastoral work. When the Vatican condemned Leonardo Boff to one year of silence, much to the sorrow of Cardinal Arns of São Paulo and the cardinal of Fortaleza, Sobral declared that this punitive step should have been taken earlier.[8]

The soaring inflation, bringing unpopularity to Sarney and the government party, the PMDB, was blamed by Sobral on the military regime, creator of an enormous foreign debt. He praised the austerity used by President Campos Salles between 1898 and 1902 to "rescue Brazil," and he called on everyone, particularly those in government, to cooperate with Sarney in such a program.[9] Although he argued for the elimination of "all superfluous expenses," such as those associated with the inaugurations of public works, he participated in the celebration to observe the eightieth anniversary of Rio Branco Avenue. Surrounded by photographers and a large crowd, he cut the first slice of a gigantic cake displayed on the avenue.[10]

The November 15, 1985, elections for mayors took place a week later. The victor in Rio, Saturnino Braga (of Brizola's PDT), received twice the vote of his closest rival, the PFL candidate, and Álvaro Valle received little more than 7 percent. Jânio Quadros, with more than 1.5 million votes in São Paulo, narrowly defeated Fernando Henrique Cardoso in a race in which the PT's Eduardo Matarazzo Suplicy received over 800,000 votes. Sobral, disappointed, said, "We must pray and ask God to protect Brazil."[11]

Sobral had been maintaining that orderly nations, like England and the United States, had few political parties, and thus were unlike the less orderly France, Spain, and Italy. After Brazil's mayorship elections, he complained that the anarchy created by so many parties and candidates left the "great masses" with no understanding of the true causes of Brazil's problems. Speaking about Sarney, whose prestige had been damaged by the strong showing of the opposition, Sobral attacked "demagogues" who questioned the legality of his mandate or who wished to shorten it in order to have a quick choice of president by the people.[12]

Newspapermen photographed Sobral next to Sarney late in

November when the president signed international accords placing Brazil at the side of all sorts of individual rights (human, civil, political, social, cultural, and economic).[13] Then Sobral went to his birthplace, Barbacena, Minas Gerais, for the awarding of the city's Medal of the Order of Sobral Pinto to Paulo Brossard, *consultor-geral da república*, and Carlos Castello Branco, prominent journalist. The main oration, mostly about Sobral, was delivered by José Aparecido de Oliveira, governor of the Federal District.

"Brazilians," José Aparecido declared, "are fascinated by Sobral Pinto, a unique personality at the permanent service of the rights of men and women. This Mineiro from Barbacena, this Ruy Barbosa of our times, led the pro-civilian campaign during all the years when liberties were besieged by authoritarianism, and he became a vanguard of resistance in favor of human rights." Asserting that "the authoritarian monolith trembled before this free man," the speaker recalled his own unique judicial protest, made with Sobral's help, against the destruction in 1964 of his congressional mandate. He recalled also that in 1984 Sobral had presented to Tancredo Neves the same award that was being given to Paulo Brossard and Carlos Castello Branco. In closing, José Aparecido referred to Sobral as "the most respected Brazilian of our time."[14]

2.   "Patron" of the PL in the 1986 Elections

On February 28, 1986, the Sarney administration launched the Cruzado Plan (named for the new currency) for ending inflation, largely by means of price and wage freezes. The plan, presented by Finance Minister Dilson Funaro, was opposed by Governor Brizola and by the PT and the labor unions of the CUT (Central Única dos Trabalhadores), associated with Lula, but it was popular and got off to an effective start. It was helpful to the candidates of the government party, the PMDB, in the campaigns that led to the November 15, 1986, elections for governors and the Congress that would act as a constitutional assembly.

In the São Paulo governorship race the PMDB candidate, Vice Governor Orestes Quércia, had several opponents, the strongest being industrialist Antônio Ermírio de Morais, who ran on the PTB ticket and received support from São Paulo's two PMDB Senate candidates, Fernando Henrique Cardoso and Mário Covas.[1]

In April 1986 Antônio Ermírio was taken by Álvaro Valle to visit Sobral, who was at home recovering from four weeks of facial neuralgia pains. Sobral spoke of the legal work he had done for Antônio Ermírio's father in the late 1950s, and he gladly endorsed the industrialist's candidacy. A little later Antônio Ermírio announced the alliance he was making with the PL, "a party whose honorary president is Sobral Pinto."[2] He was also supported by the Labor Party (PTB), Socialist Party (PSB), and PMDB dissidents.

In May Sobral participated in a PL television program (wearing, at the producer's suggestion, a light-colored suit). The program, according to O Globo, attracted more viewers than any similar one and had a peak audience (3.6 million viewers) when Sobral made his appearance.[3] Following this broadcast, leaders of the major parties in Congress decided to have a daily distribution of free broadcasting time for electioneering, with the amount of time for each party to depend on how many representatives it had in the two houses of Congress and in the state assemblies. Sobral, calling the ruling "a disgrace," declared indignantly that each party should have an equal amount of free broadcasting time.[4]

In Minas the PMDB launched the gubernatorial candidacy of Newton Cardoso, recently a mayor, and therefore Senator Itamar Franco, seeking to win the governorship, left the PMDB and joined the PL. Itamar Franco, at the PL convention that nominated him in August, received a telegram of support from Sobral, who explained that he could not participate in the convention's activities because his wife was ill.[5] In September, Sobral's own illness prevented his presence at a pro-Itamar rally in Barbacena, but the participants heard José Aparecido de Oliveira, governor of the Federal District, read a letter from Sobral praising Itamar ("austere and dynamic") and asserting that, while campaigning, Itamar should make no references to the private lives of his adversaries.[6] Itamar's PL candidacy had by then received the support of the PFL, PTB, PCB, Brizola's PDT, and the PSB (Socialist Party).

In Rio de Janeiro, where Álvaro Valle was running for reelection to Congress, the candidate to succeed Governor Brizola was the vice governor, Darcy Ribeiro (PDT). Darcy's opponent, Wellington Moreira Franco (with a sociology doctorate earned in Paris), was candidate of the PMDB and eleven other parties. Sobral, distressed by the "anarchy" and meaninglessness that he attributed to the many parties, said, without much enthusiasm, that he would vote for Wellington

Moreira Franco, and he held out little hope for a sensible constitutional assembly.[7]

In July Sobral met with the PMDB leaders of Paraná when he went with Tito Lívio Cavalcanti de Medeiros to Curitiba to award, at the Federal University of Paraná, the Sobral Pinto Prize for the Defense of Consumers. One of those who joined Sobral in presiding at the ceremony was Senator Álvaro Dias, PMDB candidate for governor, and one of the two recipients of the prize was the recent governor, José Richa, PMDB candidate for the Senate.[8]

By this time Carlos Alberto Cruz Filho, head of the Municipal Council of Campinas, São Paulo, had learned from Stockholm of the acceptance of his request that Sobral's name be inscribed as a candidate for the 1986 Nobel Peace Prize.[9] The president of the Brazilian Senate, José Fragelli (PMDB), agreed to head a movement to support the selection of Sobral and said that the work would begin after the forthcoming award of an honorary doctor's degree to Sobral by the University of São Paulo, which was observing its five hundredth anniversary. The degree, bestowed on Sobral on August 14, was only the fourth such degree to be awarded by the university in ten years.[10]

Early in November, shortly before the elections, Sobral published a signed message, written, he said, "when the attention of the whole nation is turned, above all, to the governorship race in São Paulo." Sobral warned Paulistas not to make the mistake of failing to elect Antônio Ermírio de Morais, "intelligent and dynamic" and a Christian devoted to honest work. In the message, Sobral pointed out that President Sarney, striving conscientiously to implant authentic democracy, had inherited the worst of situations, characterized by indiscipline and disorder—a situation that could not be straightened out in two or three years. The solution, Sobral added, would depend on the election of good governors, especially in São Paulo.[11]

Thanks to the Cruzado Plan's curtailment of price increases, the elections provided an overwhelming victory for the PMDB. The PMDB won twenty-two of the twenty-three governorship races and could expect to have 303 members, including senators, among the total of 559 constitution writers (representing thirteen parties).

In São Paulo Orestes Quércia won the governorship, and the PMDB senatorial contestants, Mário Covas and Fernando Henrique Cardoso, also were winners. In Minas, Newton Cardoso narrowly defeated Itamar Franco, and in Rio de Janeiro Wellington Moreira

Franco triumphed over Darcy Ribeiro. Adding to the discomfiture of Brizola, Álvaro Valle, the PL's defender of private enterprise, emerged as the congressional candidate with the most votes in the state.

Ulysses Guimarães, president of the PMDB, said that Sarney need not fear the party's victory, but he added that Sarney should leave office after four years, meaning that a presidential election should take place in 1988.[12] Neither this prospect nor the installation of a parliamentary form of government, the wish of many PMDB leaders, appealed to Sarney. Sobral, in statements to the press, said that the constitution writers should preserve the presidential system and allow Sarney to complete a five-year term.[13]

One week after the elections, the Sarney administration abandoned the price and wage freezes of the Cruzado Plan. They had resulted in severe shortages in the shops, insufficient tax receipts, and such a depletion of foreign exchange revenues that Brazil in February 1987 stopped servicing its foreign debt. Beginning late in 1986, inflation became acute and Sarney lost his popularity.

3. The Deaths of Sobral's Wife and His Daughter Lourdes (1987–1988)

Sobral, in the first part of 1987, became increasingly worried about the health of Maria José. At the age of ninety his wife suffered from ills brought on by the years. In May, when she could not feed herself and occasionally lost consciousness, she was interned at the São José Hospital. After ten days in the hospital she died there on May 27.[1]

For months Sobral had been suffering from pulmonary complications, and his children thought it best that he not deliver a eulogy at the burial at the family plot at the John the Baptist Cemetery, an occasion attended by about 150 mourners, including Rio's assistant bishop, Romeu Vicente, long a family friend.[2]

But Sobral, with a doctor at his side, spoke there, saying, "This moment requires a testimony. You were strong and admirable at home and in the Church, admirable as a daughter, wife, mother, and grandmother, always modest, unpretentious, and loving." Sobral recalled Maria José's last words, "I believe," spoken in the hospital after Sobral had asked, "Do you believe that, after God and the Virgin Mary, you are the one who has been the chief support of my life?" Sobral recalled also the past Sunday visits that the two of them had made to the graves of their children Maria do Carmo and José Luiz "at this same place"—visits that, he said, would now be made by himself alone. His voice choking, he concluded, "My love, until we are soon together again."[3]

Speaking about his wife to a reporter, Sobral mentioned the congeniality that had brought her many friends. She had adored, he said, the Brazilian national anthem and used to sing it whenever she heard it played. Her votes for electoral candidates, he said, had been made without regard for his own choices. He could have added that she had not shared her husband's interest in politics, had not been close to his politically active friends, and had disliked discussions about political matters.[4]

Replying to a letter of condolence from Dario de Almeida Magalhães, Sobral wrote: "I feel totally adrift. I am a sailboat in an ocean overwhelmed by a terrible submarine earthquake. What can I do? Where can I go? My faith assures me that we shall be together in eternity. But until then how can I endure the hallucinating pain of the unbearable separation? Keenly my memory makes me always aware of the inexorable words of Dante 'No pain equals the one that is suffered in adversity when days of happiness are recalled.' This is my indescribable torment. No one can imagine what Maria meant to me. She was everything, everything, everything. . . . How can I go on without her at my side, gentle, peaceful, and trustful?"[5]

A new personal tragedy began for Sobral a few months later when his daughter Lourdes suffered from swelling in an arm where a lymphocytic cancer had been dormant for years. Doctors, deciding to operate, found her condition hopeless and told her husband, Eduardo Portella Neto, a successful careerist in government, that she could expect to survive no more than six months. Efforts of the family to keep the news from the enfeebled Sobral were to no avail because he spoke with Lourdes's doctor. "Pray for your aunt," he told Maria do Carmo's son Roberto, "because her condition is beyond hope." She died in February 1988.[6]

4. Sobral, "Man of Vision" (late 1987)

At the cardinal's São Joaquim Palace in July 1987, Dom Eugênio Sales presided at a ceremony at which the president of Rio's Pontifícia Universidade Católica (PUC) honored five of the university's benefactors. Of the five, only Sobral and *O Globo*'s Roberto Marinho were present because Regine Feigl was in poor health and Alceu Amoroso Lima and a businessman, also to be honored posthumously, had died. Applause followed the announcement that the university's administrative buildings would be given the name of Sobral Pinto.[1]

At the lunch of the Commercial Association of Rio to observe Sobral's birthday, his ninety-fourth, the president of the Brazilian Academy of Letters called Sobral "the symbol of Brazilian liberalism." Sobral spoke of unfortunate developments that had accompanied the "radical transformations of customs." A little later, on November 13, Sobral issued a manifesto to the nation expressing the need for unity in the face of the "extremely grave political and economic situation." Attacks against President Sarney, his ministers, or other political leaders, Sobral said, "only increase the moral anarchy and the political and social disorder that are taking the nation to a terribly dangerous future."[2]

A bit of controversy followed the announcement late in November of the four winners of the annual "Man of Vision" award, chosen by Henry Maksoud, businessman and president of *Visão* magazine, from names suggested by the magazine's staff and readers. The winners were Sobral, law professor Ives Gandra da Silva, São Paulo Art Museum Director Pietro Maria Bardi, and Ronaldo Caiado, head of the União Democrática Ruralista, which was defending land properties being invaded by landless peasants or being threatened by redistribution plans. The selections did not leave Sobral immune from cutting remarks by writers unsympathetic to the annual event known as "the landmark for the defense of capitalism and free enterprise," but the selection of Caiado was the most controversial and led Sobral to declare that it was "not a crime" to be among those who opposed the Left.[3]

At a lunch on December 14 at São Paulo's Maksoud Plaza Hotel, approximately a thousand guests heard improvised speeches given by the award's recipients. Bardi, speaking of the art museum and Assis Chateaubriand, amused the audience, whereas Professor Gandra attacked the Sarney government's anti-inflation plans, such as the Cruzado Plan of February 1986, the short-lived plan of June 1987 of Finance Minister Luiz Carlos Bresser Pereira, and a new one being formulated by Bresser's successor, Maílson da Nóbrega, to combat, again with unsustainable price-wage freezes, the huge new increase in the cost of living. Gandra described the "fiscal packages" as socialist and said that the constitution being written was the worst of any he had ever known.[4]

Like Gandra, Caiado was one of the two speakers most heartily applauded. He blamed the producing class for not doing enough politically to struggle against a situation in which it had few defenders. "The hour has come for us, the producers, to show that we are the real, authentic leaders, the true *progressistas* of the nation." He denounced corruption and the government's arbitrary state-enhancing, confiscatory interventions.[5]

Sobral, the final speaker, was applauded from time to time. He opened by referring to tragedies that brought darkness to him at what should have been a lustrous moment. One of these tragedies, he said, was the loss of Maria José, unfortunately not alive to learn about his award, an award owed chiefly to her "because she sustained me the most after God, the Virgin Mary, and the Holy Church of Rome—of the Rome of the popes and not of the *progressistas* who are destroying the Church."

Turning to another tragedy, "the disorder" in Brazil, Sobral denied being a conservative, "as has been said ceaselessly ever since I was chosen to be here, a charge made because I do not tolerate upholding, in the name of the Church, Liberation Theology, which is Marxist, materialistic, and atheistic." He pointed out that he was not one of those who praised an old order that had failed to give workers the rights they deserved. Nevertheless, he spoke with longing about a past world that had been an organized one, with property rights guaranteed and with the three government powers assuming their proper functions and bringing riches and civilization to the nation. "Families, too, used to be admirably organized. . . . Women today do not understand that their grandeur and strength lie in their modesty." Also critical of politicians, Sobral said, "today they believe in nothing." The Constitutional Assembly, he said, should not include so many people "who do not even know what a constitution is." And he added that a person from the *favelas* might indeed be serious and honest, "but never, as has happened in Brazil, should he be elected vice president of the Constitutional Assembly."[6]

"In this disorder, this anarchy of ideas, this immorality that presents itself openly everywhere, on the beaches, on television, in the drawing rooms and the streets, in this infernal paganism that presently degrades Brazilian society, what should we do?" Good, intelligent, courageous men, he said, should join forces, take positions, and work to have humanity guided by fundamental moral principles, giving Brazil "the future that it deserves, a future that ennobles every citizen."[7]

5. Complaining about the Work of the Constitutional Assembly (1987–1988)

The Congress, meeting as a Constitutional Assembly on February 1, 1987, chose Ulysses Guimarães as its presiding officer and Senator Mário Covas as floor leader of the PMDB, and it set up commissions to draft articles for the new constitution and a ninety-three-member Systematization Commission to coordinate the work and produce a final draft to be sent to the full Assembly for its approval. This important commission, whose president was Afonso Arinos de Melo Franco and whose *relator* Bernardo Cabral was a key figure, revised its original five-hundred-article project to one with about three hundred articles, and, in November 1987, it concluded its labors with a project that called for a parliamentary system of government and a term for Sarney that would end after he had been in office four years.[1]

Sarney, opposing these provisions and opposing also a sizeable part of the PMDB leadership that had favored them, built up a Centrão (Big Center) position in the Assembly by the distribution of favors there. Governors such as Quércia of São Paulo and Newton Cardoso of Minas were allotted generous federal financial assistance for their ambitious state programs and used their influence on constitutional assemblymen. The military expressed its traditional opposition to the parliamentary system and its hostility to a 1988 presidential election, much desired by Brizola. In January 1988 the Centrão achieved a major victory because the Assembly, defying floor leader Covas, changed the rules and procedures, making each article of the Systematization Commission's project subject to approval by the Assembly's majority and allowing for the inclusion of substitute articles.[2]

While the Systematization Commission carried on its work in 1987, Sobral criticized it. He called a presidential election in 1988 a "crime against the nation" that satisfied only demagogues. To those who argued that Sarney's term was "illegitimate," Sobral replied that this was not so, and he asserted that Sarney should complete a five-year term. *O Estado de S. Paulo* wrote that Sobral, valorous defender in 1984 of an immediate direct presidential election, had undergone a radical change.[3]

Sobral believed that both the national security law and the press law were necessary and should be reformed but not discarded.[4] In June 1987, after a former adviser of Brizola was accused of stirring up a crowd in Rio to show hostility to a visit by Sarney, the president charged the troublemaker with violating the national security law. This step by Sarney was criticized by influential members of the OAB, including Carlos Maurício Martins Rodrigues, head of its Rio de Janeiro section, who called the use of the national security law a "retrogression" and a failure to abide by "the promises of the New Republic" of the postmilitary days. Sobral, however, declared that it was entirely proper to turn to the national security law, "the only arm of defense of the government." Much of the complaining, he said, could be attributed to subversives.[5]

Commenting late in October 1987 on the work of the constitution writers, Sobral said that it represented a struggle between the PMDB and the PFL for public offices and the wishes of leftists to have agitation that would bring them to power. He called the draft of the Systematization Commission a "disaster" and "rubbish" *(uma porcaria)*, conceived by people who could not distinguish between material appropriate for ordinary legislation and material appropriate for a constitution. He concluded that the constitution writers would do well to abandon "the disorder existing in Brasília" and limit their work to writing a single short article: "Article 1, The Constitution of 1946 is reestablished."[6]

The full Constitutional Assembly, revising in the first half of 1988 the project received from the Systematization Commission, defeated the parliamentary system and ruled on March 22 that the next presidential election would occur in November 1989. Mário Covas, Fernando Henrique Cardoso, and Franco Montoro, all from São Paulo, and Senator José Richa, from Paraná, left the PMDB in June 1988 to form a new party, the PSDB (Partido da Social Democracia Brasileira), whose program, presented on July 6, sought to appeal to voters with inclinations to the left of ideas being favored by the PMDB. Ulysses Guimarães, remaining at the head of the PMDB and skirmishing occasionally with Sarney, contributed much to the last steps of the work that resulted in the promulgation of the Constitution of October 5, 1988.[7]

The constitution provided benefits to workers such as a work week of forty-four hours instead of forty-eight and work shifts of six hours instead of eight where factory operations were continuous. It gave preferential treatment to Brazilian companies over foreign ones, excluded foreign companies from mining, and placed a 12 percent cap on real (inflation-adjusted) annual interest rates. It mandated that a specific percentage of the federal tax revenues was to be spent on education, and, perhaps more importantly, that specific percentages were to go directly to the states and municipalities. When Finance Minister Maílson da Nóbrega's anti-inflation plan of January 1989 met with failure, he blamed the Constitution of 1988. Afonso Arinos de Melo Franco forecast difficulties for future presidents and questioned the need of pregnant women to have as much as 120 days' maternity leave, without loss of job or of salary, and the need of their husbands to have "paternity leave." Economists guessed that labor benefits would contribute to the inflation by increasing production costs by 35 percent.[8]

Sobral, speaking at the University of Minas Gerais in December 1988, told a journalist that "this constitution cannot be put into effect. It will require a great many complementary laws. It contains more bad things than good things." Asked for examples, he said that an evaluation could not be made briefly. But, before the journalist left, he criticized Paragraph 3 of Article 226 of the constitution for its description of "the family" as "the stable union between a man and woman" without the requirement of marriage.[9]

6. A Legal Case of Fernando Collor de Mello (1987–1988)

Contributing to the PMDB's landslide victory of 1986 was the election to the Alagoas governorship of the thirty-eight-year-old Fernando Collor de Mello, whose father Arnon de Mello had been Sobral's client in 1963 (after a Senate shooting). Fernando, upon taking office in March 1987, made it known that he would not obey a state decree law of 1983 that handsomely increased the salaries of bureaucrats, including members of the state's Tribunal of Justice and Tribunal of Accounts. Fernando's argument that the decree law was unconstitutional was presented to the Supreme Court (STF) by the *procurador geral da república* and brought about a temporary ruling issued in the governor's favor by the *relator* late in March 1987. However, on November 25, the full court decided that the salary increases, although regrettable in view of the state's deplorable financial situation, were not unconstitutional.[1]

Collor called the STF's decision "immoral" and refused to make the payments, whereupon the state Tribunal of Justice called for federal intervention in Alagoas. Opposition members of the state legislature, led by the PFL, sought the impeachment of Collor and persuaded the legislature to nullify his plan to reduce the number of state secretaryships and dismiss ten thousand bureaucrats.[2]

Such battles in Alagoas brought Collor fame as the foe of the "maharajahs." At the same time he denounced corruption in the administration of President Sarney, who, he said, was spending public money to get the constitution writers to give him five years in office. Sarney threatened to sue him, and, after the decision of March 22, 1988, which gave Sarney his five years, Collor left the PMDB, thus abandoning his plan to challenge Ulysses Guimarães for the party's nomination for president of Brazil.[3]

Collor, in a letter dated February 29, 1988, turned to Sobral for legal assistance to uphold his resolve not to pay to "highly ranked state officials" the amounts stipulated in the decree law of 1983, and for assistance also in dealing with the authors of "slanders and defamations." Collor mentioned a reference in the press to a "dossier" said to have been drawn up against him by the government's National Information Service (SNI).[4]

In the first part of March 1988 Sobral received two visits from Collor and one from the *procurador geral* of Alagoas. As Sobral made clear in a letter written to the governor on March 7, he felt that Collor should abide by the Supreme Court decision of November 25, 1987. He should, Sobral said, issue at once a public statement to advise that, as long as the state legislature failed to revoke the decree law of 1983, the state would consider the salary enhancements payable but that the payments would have to wait until a way could be found to obtain the funds. When Collor told Sobral that the decree law of 1983 was immoral, Sobral said that the question of its morality would not serve as a means of getting it annulled.[5]

Collor, rejecting Sobral's advice, declared on television and to journalists that he would not make the "immoral" payments to the "maharajahs." Sobral reacted by writing Collor on March 9 to say that he would be unable to represent him because "the orientation of cases given to me to handle is decided by me." When the governor's secretary telephoned Tito Lívio Cavalcanti de Medeiros to ask whether Sobral would defend the governor at the SNI, Sobral let it be known that he would not do so because Collor "is a person who does not accept the orientation of his lawyer."[6]

Collor turned to Dario de Almeida Magalhães and found satisfaction. Dario argued successfully that the role of the Supreme Court in jurisprudence was such that it could not bring about an intervention in the state based on the refusal of Alagoas to make the payments that Collor was contesting. Sobral called Dario's argument "brilliant and convincing," but also he found it an unfortunate device for allowing states to evade payments of their debts. The proper way for Alagoas to avoid intervention, Sobral wrote Dario, was for it to recognize the debt and tell the Supreme Court how it would raise the money to pay it and how long this would take. If, Sobral added, the debt remained unpaid after this time period, then it would be up to the Supreme Court to declare intervention and call on the federal executive to take the necessary steps. "This," he told Dario, "is the constitutional duty of the Supreme Court. Unfortunately the jurisprudence of the Supreme Court, cited by you, and many other decisions made in the name of justice do not allow me to have confidence in the judiciary. This, my letter, is a cry of anguish."[7]

7. Sobral Rejects a Pension and Handles His Last Legal Cases (1987–1990)

Late in 1987, Dario persuaded Governor Wellington Moreira Franco that it would be appropriate to have the Rio de Janeiro state legislature authorize a lifetime monthly pension for Sobral, to be granted in return for Sobral's becoming available for occasional consultations as honorary public defender of the state. Sobral, informed of the plan by Dario, said that he would be pleased to accept the position but would not accept the pension. Dario insisted on the pension, and Sobral appeared for a while to be hesitant about contradicting the wishes of his eminent friend. But early in 1988, after Dario's departure for a visit to Europe, Sobral made it clear to two lawyers, who shared Dario's view, that he would not accept the pension. In support of his decision he cited the unexpected receipt of a share of a large legal fee following the recent settlement of an old case of the

Rio de Janeiro Dock Company that made it possible for him to live modestly but comfortably.[1]

One of the two lawyers showed Sobral the governor's message to the legislature. The message, delivered on February 4, 1988, praised the man who, while "rejecting fees and material seductions," had "exceeded all others in providing outstanding public services" and had become "the symbol of Brazil's legal profession and the public defender of Brazil and its people."[2]

In the legislature in mid-March the PMDB leader referred to the governor's message and brought the matter up for a vote. The idea was supported by all but the PDT representatives and one member of the PFL. Its adoption, granting a monthly pension of 211,000 cruzados (the currency made effective in 1986), was followed by Sobral's expression of gratitude and explanation of his refusal to accept it. "It contradicts my moral principles," he said.[3]

In a letter thanking a legislator for her speech in his favor, Sobral praised his colleagues who, in the past, had joined him and acted courageously in defending victims of dictatorial practices.[4] In April, after reading the law for the pension that was published after the legislature's vote, Sobral wrote to the governor to explain his rejection of the pension and to plead that his example be followed by sacrifices on the part of all government officials, who, he said, would have to reduce at once all government expenses in order to combat the "rampant, unrestrained, intolerable inflation" that was making it impossible for wage earners to pay what they owed and was bringing about "unemployment, hunger, and misery." He described the situation as a "dramatic prerevolutionary" one, characterized by a "climate of violence in which nothing is respected" and "the violators of authority remain unpunished," a condition of agitation that "has led some countries to install inhuman totalitarian regimes."[5]

Dom Eugênio Sales, more pleased than Collor with Sobral's professional work, was represented in legal petitions signed by Sobral and other lawyers. In one of them the cardinal argued for the unconstitutionality of a municipal law, issued in July 1987 by Rio de Janeiro Mayor Saturnino Braga, that made it obligatory, rather than optional, for doctors of the city's health service to carry out abortions where pregnant women had been raped or were in danger of death. Again, in February 1989, Sobral was a representative of Dom Eugênio when the cardinal sought a ruling to prevent the use of images of Jesus Christ and Saint Sebastian in carnival parade displays that featured "women who are almost totally nude."[6]

Sobral and Tito Lívio turned to a São Paulo court with legal arguments in defense of José Aparecido de Oliveira in September 1989.
This friend of Sarney's and Sobral's, while serving as Sarney's minister of culture after his three years (1985–1988) as governor of the
Federal District, "indignantly" rejected "false" charges against him
related to a Federal District construction deal made years before he
became governor.[7] Sobral also showed a keen interest in the defense
of Eduardo Portella Neto, who had married his daughter Lourdes,
after some of Portella's government work became the subject of an
investigation carried out in the Ministry of Transport. Defending his
son-in-law from "unjust persecution," Sobral wrote letters to Sarney
after learning from José Aparecido that the president would "resolve
Portella's problem." Three letters went unanswered, and so Sobral,
during Sarney's last months in office, asked José Aparecido to deliver
to the president his fourth letter on the subject.[8]

The ninety-six-year-old Sobral appeared in court in August 1990 to
defend the reintegration into the Brazilian air force of a former first
lieutenant who had been deprived of his rank in 1980 for improper
behavior, such as signing bad checks. Sobral was accompanied by
one of his grandsons, Carlos Alberto Sobral Pinto, a lawyer, who told
the press that this would probably be Sobral's last court appearance
because his grandfather was "very tired." Sobral, *O Globo* reported,
was handicapped by a hearing difficulty but had delivered a vigorous
argument, praised by the judge, the opposing lawyer, and law students who were there. As for Carlos Alberto's observation about the
improbability of more court appearances by Sobral, it was rejected
by Sobral, who declared, "Whenever there is a right to be defended or
an injustice to be opposed, I shall be available if I am asked."[9]

8. "Dumfounded" by *Futebol's* Collapse, Catholic Voodooism, and Cardinal Arns (1988–1989)

Sobral's views about Brazilian soccer were published in a sports publication, *Segundo Tempo*, in May 1988 under a headline "God is punishing the América [soccer team] because of its emblem, the devil."
Describing himself as "dumfounded" to have learned about the emblem, he recalled his long interest in the team, starting in 1912 "when
América was a decent, honorable club. . . . Because I no longer follow the América, I have no right to attribute its decadence to this or
that cause, but it seems to me that bad administrations of the team

have been responsible for its collapse." He blamed professionalism for turning players into worshipers of money above all else, and he added that the directors of the federation of *futebol* and its clubs achieved their positions by buying votes. "We need to replace these directors with men of character, such as those in the directorships in the old days. Today no one in *futebol* merits my respect."[1]

When Sobral, also in the first half of 1988, wrote his admirer Dom Marcos Barbosa to praise his articles attacking Liberation Theology, he said he had been unable to contribute much to the campaign because of pains that "terribly paralyzed" his movements.[2] In his letter he went on to tell of his fear that the CNBB, being guided by its ecumenical adviser, was embracing the "alarming" practice of black voodoo rites. It was shocking, he wrote Dom Marcos, to learn that a black Catholic padre had carried out a "sacred Mass" featuring the rattling of tambourines and the "dancelike shaking of bodies" while canticles were sung about matters that were related to slavery and that expressed "worship of pagan idols of African ancestry." The black padre, according to reports that reached Sobral, had said that the Virgin Mary could be considered by blacks to be a black, and had also said that "churches, often built with stolen money, are associated with a history of white domination."

"Where," Sobral asked, "are we headed when the CNBB has such advisers? Already we have priests and bishops who favor materialistic Marxism and who encourage land invasions and the legitimizing of prostitution, calling it a profession. They disparage the hierarchy by establishing the so-called Popular Church."[3]

A year later, in March 1989, Sobral wrote at length to São Paulo's Cardinal Paulo Evaristo Arns to express his "astonishment and distress" to learn of the cardinal's warm letter to Fidel Castro. Among the passages in Arns's letter that Sobral quoted were these: "Christian faith has discovered in the conquests of the Cuban Revolution signs of the Kingdom of God," "You are daily in my prayers, and I pray God to grant you the favor of forever directing the destinies of your nation," "We know of the heroism and sacrifices with which the people of your nation have resisted foreign aggressions, eradicating misery and illiteracy and chronic social problems," and "Cuba today can feel pride in being an example of social justice in our continent, so impoverished by foreign debts."[4]

Sobral asked whether "the Kingdom of God" existed in a society where "a dictatorial government preaches and imposes materialism and atheism." He denied the existence of social justice without God and said that it and other justices were direct corollaries of the will of God. Writing that to govern with justice was not simply the provision of material welfare, he quoted from the Bible: "Man does not live by bread alone, but by every word that proceedeth out of the mouth of God." Arns, Sobral wrote, should, in his daily prayers, ask that Castro become enlightened in order to teach his people of the existence of God and the supernatural life.[5]

As Sobral advised Arns, he planned to send copies of their correspondence to Catholic leaders and others, among them Eugênio Sales and the nuncio of the Pope. In a letter addressed to Pope John Paul II to acquaint him with the correspondence, Sobral wrote that the Catholic Church, deeply wounded by the Progressive Church and its Marxist Liberation Theology, was preaching "revolution against the economic and agrarian structures of Brazil." "The letter of Cardinal Arns will greatly increase the confusion in the Church unless Rome does something to neutralize its dramatic effects."[6]

Sobral also sent copies of the correspondence to influential Cardinal Lucas Moreira Neves, a friend of the Pope who had returned to Brazil in 1987, after a long stay at the Vatican, to become archbishop of Salvador and Brazil's highest-ranking archbishop. Like Sobral, Lucas Neves had denounced the 1988 movie *The Last Temptation of Christ*, which, as Sobral had written President Sarney, showed Christ yielding to the "attractions of sex, lechery, and even adultery." Lucas Neves, while rejecting the labels of conservative or progressive, was viewed by conservatives as a candidate who might defeat the progressive wing that held sway in the CNBB.[7]

Cardinal Arns, in his reply to Sobral, appeared to be displeased that copies of their correspondence were being distributed by Sobral, whereupon Sobral advised Arns that he had done this only in the cases of the Pope, Cardinal Lucas Neves, and Cardinal Eugênio Sales, and he promised in the future to abide by Arns's wishes except for informing Dom Eugênio of the second letter he was now writing to Arns. In it, Sobral accepted Arns's decision that "the matter be closed." Arns, Sobral told Dom Eugênio, "did not reply to a single one of the points made by me. He limited himself to explaining that a dialogue with Fidel Castro was useful to the Church, a subject not mentioned in my letter to him. I cannot argue further with him, because he prohibits this with his declaration that the matter is closed."[8]

9. The Presidential Election of Late 1989

Asked by the press about Brazil's republic, which had reached its one hundredth anniversary in 1989, Sobral had good words for Presidents Campos Salles, Rodrigues Alves, Affonso Penna, Dutra, and Kubitschek. He condemned Vargas for his dictatorship but spoke well of his work on behalf of workers' rights and the labor and electoral justice systems. The current situation, Sobral said, was deplorable on account of the widespread indiscipline, but would be improved if the people, voting for a president in November for the first time since 1960, would elect the PL's Guilherme Afif Domingos, a candidate whose "spiritual and cultural background" would place Brazil "on the path of Christian civilization."[1]

The contest of twenty-four presidential candidates opened in 1989 with the public opinion polls showing Brizola (PDT) and Lula (PT) in the lead. But starting in April they fell behind Fernando Collor de Mello, the youthful, handsome, and athletic candidate of the small, new PRN (Partido de Reconstrução Nacional), who denounced corruption and became the hope of those who feared the leftism of Brizola and Lula. Afif Domingos, the popular congressman from São Paulo who defended the interests of small businessmen, was in fourth place in the polls for a while.

Sobral, hoping that the PDC (Partido Democrata Cristão) would join the PL in supporting Afif, wrote in June to Senator Mauro Borges, president of the PDC. In the letter Sobral referred to the "unprecedented moral, political, and social crises" and added: "I believe that my views of the situation and of the qualities required of the next president are shared by the party that you head."[2] Mauro Borges, however, remained a supporter of Brizola. The PDC continued to be split among adherents of Afif, Collor, and Brizola.

"Is Lula prepared to be president?" was a question that the *Jornal do Brasil* put to some well-known citizens. According to Sobral's reply, published on November 5, "Brazil will become worthless if Lula is elected. It is not enough to be honest and a lathe operator. Lula lacks education and culture. To have such a person in the presidency is inconceivable."[3]

When Sobral spoke to the press that day, his ninety-sixth birthday, he said that the monarchy had been overthrown long before Brazil was ready to become a republic, with tragic results during the one hundred years that followed. Speaking of "the transformation of the city," he called attention to the destruction of houses to make way for apartments, "the big enemies of families. . . . My great-grandchildren who live in apartments like to remain in my residence because I have a garden there."[4]

In the election of November 15 Collor received over 20 million votes, or about 28.5 percent of the total, well ahead of Lula's 16 percent and Brizola's 15.5 percent. Commenting on the outcome, in which Afif's 3,271,000 votes placed the PL candidate in sixth place, Sobral told the press that Brazilians had voted "rottenly." "But," he added, "nothing surprises me anymore. Half the people elected to the Constitutional Assembly were incompetent."[5]

Prior to the runoff of December 14 between Collor and Lula, a reader of the *Jornal do Brasil* published a letter taking exception to Sobral's early November observation that Brazil would become worthless if it elected Lula. The writer, calling Sobral biased and superficial, said that if erudition was what mattered, Brazil should be among the foremost nations because Sarney was a member of the Brazilian Academy of Letters. "Sobral Pinto gives no attention to intelligence and self-education. In the Constitutional Assembly Lula was more active than Afif. The PT includes men who are competent in their professions and an honest appraisal should be based on the program of Lula." Sobral, in a reply published before the runoff, denied having ever, in his long life, been biased against persons or ideologies, doctrines, or political movements. "My divergence with Lula is based on his lack of the necessary culture, knowledge, and political experience. . . . He has always been involved in the problems of his class."[6]

Also before the runoff, the *Jornal do Brasil* published Sobral's reply to another of its questions, this one asking whether Collor was prepared to be president. Sobral, asserting that Collor was not prepared, explained: "He is young and lacks a significant political past. . . . He was elected to Congress on the ticket of the PDS, the party associated with the military. His governorship, which he did not complete, was not outstanding."[7]

In the runoff Collor received about 35 million votes and Lula received about 31 million. Sobral, explaining to José Aparecido de Oliveira why he voted for Collor, wrote that "the election of Lula would have been the end of the world." "But," Sobral also wrote, "Collor unfortunately seems to me to be without the culture, experience, and the governing fiber that are required to begin to resolve the moral, political, economic, social, and religious crises of our people."[8]

Following the various inflation-fighting plans of the Sarney administration, with their unmanageable freezes of prices and wages, the country, when Collor assumed the presidency on March 15, 1990, was suffering from an inflation rate amounting to about 80 percent per month. Sobral, in a letter to Sarney about the Sarney administration, wrote that he could not "give an opinion about the economic sector, which is too complex," but he agreed with *O Globo* that Sarney had inherited a "calamitous" situation from his predecessors. Sobral confessed to having believed, early in Sarney's administration, that the president was being too tolerant in dealing with the indiscipline of political parties, the working classes, and the unions. However, he went on to tell Sarney that a better examination of the situation "convinced me later that Your Excellency, in failing to repress all that disorder, wished, with your tolerance, to defend and protect the principle of liberty, so completely disrespected in the regime that governed for twenty years. For this truly notable service, the nation is indebted to you, as *O Globo* has pointed out."[9]

10. Sobral's Ninety-seventh Birthday (1990) and the "Sobral Pinto Lawyers Congress" (1991)

Fernando Collor de Mello took over the Brazilian presidency on March 15, 1990, and, on the 16th, Zélia Cardoso de Mello, Collor's *ministra da economia*, disclosed the Plano Collor for combating inflation. In addition to reducing government personnel and ministries, increasing taxes, and freezing wages and prices, it drastically cut the availability of cash by blocking for eighteen months the use of those portions of bank accounts, including savings accounts, that exceeded fifty thousand cruzeiros (the name given by Collor to the cruzado novo, the currency created late in the previous administration). Fifty thousand cruzeiros was worth about $1,200 U.S. currency.[1]

Even these steps, some of them found to be unconstitutional by courts, did not prevent inflation's return. In September 1990, when the monthly inflation rate was reported to exceed 13 percent, a romance between Zélia and Justice Minister Bernardo Cabral, a married man, was creating a sensation, and on October 15 Cabral was dismissed by Collor. Sobral told the press that this private matter should not have been given publicity, and he argued that the continuation of Zélia in her post demonstrated that the dismissal of his friend Bernardo Cabral was not related to the romance. Sobral could have pointed out that Cabral had opposed the wishes of Collor regarding candidacies, in the October 1990 elections, for the governorship of the Federal District.[2]

As in recent years, Sobral's birthday in November 1990, this one his ninety-seventh, was observed with enthusiasm by the Sociedade dos Amigos da Rua Carioca (SARCA), which attributed to Sobral a key role in preserving, in the 1960s, this downtown street and its shops from a destruction desired by Governor Lacerda, eager to build an expressway. Members of SARCA were joined on November 5, 1990, on Carioca Street by hundreds of students, many of them from the Sobral Pinto School, and by a band that played martial music. Sobral, accompanied by his daughter Ruth, cut the four-hundred-kilogram SARCA birthday cake, which was distributed to the public. In his remarks, Sobral expressed his regret at not being accompanied by Tancredo Neves, "who would have been ideal for Brazil." After about an hour, he departed, saying that he had promised to attend a lunch being given in his honor by former office companions.[3]

Later in November 1990 Sobral gave his support to Sérgio Sveiter, candidate for president of the Rio de Janeiro section of the OAB, and he authorized Ruth to cast his vote, later that month, for Sveiter. In December Sobral wrote to the *reitor* of the Federal University of Santa Catarina to say that he best not make "the long trip" to be present at a ceremony to give him an honorary degree.[4]

Sérgio Sveiter won his contest, and he organized the Seventh Conference of Lawyers of the State of Rio de Janeiro, to be known as the "Sobral Pinto Congress" and held at the Hotel Glória between September 30 and October 4, 1991. The conference, with its thirteen panels for discussing many matters, such as Brazil's form of government, the economic crisis, and Collor's drive to amend the constitution, attracted leading jurists and political figures. At the speakers' table, Sobral Pinto, patron of the meetings, was joined by Senator Mário Covas (PSDB, São Paulo), critical of Collor, and Bahia Governor Antônio Carlos Magalhães (PFL), defender of the idea that "the economic crisis" would induce everyone, including politicians, to agree on the need, expressed by Collor, for changes in the constitution. Also photographed with Sobral at the speakers' table was São Paulo

Congressman Antônio Cunha Bueno, who favored a monarchy for Brazil.[5]

"A serious attack of grippe," brought on by the air-conditioning in the main meeting room of the lawyers' conference, was cited by Sobral as making it impossible for him to attend the closing session. From his bed at home he sent a message to explain his absence and to authorize his "beloved daughter Ruth Sobral Pinto Salazar, our esteemed colleague," to tell of the gratitude he felt for the "excessive honors" given to him.[6]

11.   Ill with Pneumonia (October–November 1991)

On October 5, Sobral was interned at the São José Hospital, where he was found to be suffering from pneumonia.[1] Thus he was unable to see Pope John Paul II, who, Sobral had written in September, was about to make his second visit to Brazil in order to bless many people in its extensive territory who had missed the opportunity during his short visit in 1980 (when illness had also kept Sobral from seeing the Pope).[2]

Sobral returned on October 16 to his Pereira da Silva Street home. The former visitors' room on the first floor was converted into a bedroom for him, and arrangements were made for two male nurses, associated with Rio's Santa Casa de Misericórdia, to alternate in helping him.[3]

Residing in the house were Luzia Dias Sobral Pinto, who had married Sobral's son Alberto, and the couple's sons, Carlos Alberto (26), and Rogério (24). Other grandchildren and Sobral's daughters Idalina Ribeiro (68), Ruth Salazar (64), and Gilda (54) lived in Rio and provided comforts for the invalid. Gilda, a psychologist, had separated from her husband, who had found a new wife. Alberto (59), after his separation from Luzia, had left the Sobral home in 1988 and had also found a new wife, a resident of Espírito Santo. But he was in Rio during his father's last years. He ran unsuccessfully for the Rio City Council in 1990 and at the same time was involved in a lawsuit that he and over three hundred former members of the local transit department were pursuing to protest their dismissal by the department. Sobral had tried to assist them with their case in August 1991.[4]

A constant visitor was Tito Lívio Cavalcanti de Medeiros. Always helpful to Sobral, he had invested, in inflation-protection securities,

Sobral's share of the legal fee of the Rio de Janeiro Dock Company, alluded to by Sobral when he had rejected a pension from the state.[5] Late in 1991, Tito Lívio read from newspapers to Sobral and assisted him in handling correspondence.

In letters sent in October 1991 to Education Minister José Goldemberg, President Collor, and Justice Minister Jarbas Passarinho, Sobral condemned the education minister for dismissing Professor Jerônimo Rodrigues de Morais Neto from his position of delegate in Rio of the Education Ministry. Sobral attributed the dismissal of his friend to "the mediocre people who are taking over the important positions in the Education Ministry." And, as a reaction to what he called Goldemberg's "lack of consideration," he said he was returning to the University of São Paulo the honorary doctorate presented to him when Goldemberg had been the university's *reitor.* Goldemberg, at the ceremony inducting the new *delegado,* declared that the dismissal that had upset Sobral had had nothing to do with the honorary degree, "the university's highest honor," awarded when Goldemberg acted as agent in his capacity of *reitor.*[6]

One of the letters received by Sobral was an invitation, dated November 4, 1991, sent by the members of the Cândido Mendes Law School Class of 1971, known as the "Class of Sobral Pinto" because of Sobral's participation as its patron when it had held its graduation exercises. Sobral's presence at the twentieth anniversary Mass and dinner on November 29, 1991, had to be declined because he was confined to his bed.[7]

The observation of Sobral's ninety-eighth birthday took place on November 5 at his home. Participating in the Mass there that evening were Dom Marcos Barbosa, of the São Bento Monastery, and Sobral's confessor, Chaplain Assis Lopes of the Candelária Church. Then a meal featuring Sobral's favorite dish of shrimps in sauce was served to the gathering of about forty persons, mostly family members. The press reported the presence of special friends, lawyers Dario de Almeida Magalhães and Evandro Lins e Silva and medical doctor Nélson de Azevedo Alves, although the presence of visitors had been discouraged. It reported also on Sobral's sorrow at the absence of his wife, whose birthday it also was, and about how he missed the usual November 5 celebration by SARCA. He was described as arguing that his doctor, Felipe Sanguiliane, ought to have allowed him to carry out his routine of work at his Debret Street office. Thanking the group for its presence, he told of his wish that young Brazilians remain faithful to the Catholic tradition, adhering to teachings about spirituality and devoting themselves to work and to loving people.[8]

12.   Death and Burial (November 30–December 1, 1991)

On November 16 Sobral was interned at a clinic for treatment for dehydration. When he was taken back to his home on November 19 he was very frail. In the week that began on November 24, he felt, according to Ruth, that the frailty would only increase and that he was approaching death and would welcome it. He showed so little appetite for his meals (fruits, soup, tea, and milk) that Chaplain Assis Lopes, in response to an appeal from the family, made a visit on November 29 to persuade him to eat more.[1]

During the night that followed, Sobral asked Luzia and Ruth to pray that he might be taken without delay to heaven. He asked the same of Gilda, whose nighttime visit brought her a reminder that she had forgotten to bring to the house, which lacked air-conditioning, a fan, an oversight that was promptly corrected because Tito Lívio, in his usual 11 P.M. telephone call to Luzia, had learned of the need for a fan and had supplied one. Gilda, returning with a fan after midnight, found her father too weak to speak and able only to use gestures, which seemed to her to indicate that they were separating for the last time.[2]

The disappearance of vital signs, according to nurse Adilson Fonseca, began at 6:30 A.M. on November 30, and at about 7:00 A.M. Sobral died peacefully.[3]

As Sobral had wished, his body was taken to the chapel of the Casa da Previdência on Pereira da Silva Street, where he had worshiped for fifty-two years. There at 11:00 A.M. the first of a series of Masses was conducted by Assis Lopes. Other Masses at the chapel were attended by notables, such as Leonel Brizola, who had been reelected governor in 1990, Rio Mayor Marcelo Alencar, Press Association President Barbosa Lima Sobrinho, Academy of Letters President Austregésilo de Athayde, former Justice Minister Oscar Dias Corrêa, and members of the family of Luiz Carlos Prestes, who had died in the previous year. Among the telegrams received were some from admirers in China, who had been defended by Sobral in Brazil in 1964.[4]

Brizola decreed three days of official mourning in the state of Rio de Janeiro, whereas President Collor, who had quarreled with Sobral before his successful campaign for the presidency, left it up to his spokesman, Cláudio Humberto Rosa e Silva, to make a statement. According to Cláudio Humberto, Sobral was "one of the most notable Brazilians in our history," and Collor, lamenting Sobral's death, "always deeply respected the exemplary Christian conduct of the jurist."[5]

Before the coffin was taken from the chapel on Sunday morning, December 1, to the family burial plot at the John the Baptist Cemetery, it was draped with flags of Brazil, the América Futebol Clube, the OAB, and SARCA.[6] It was received at the cemetery by about two hundred persons, including José Aparecido de Oliveira and Cardinal Eugênio Sales, who had been in Salvador, Bahia, when he had learned of Sobral's death. José Sarney, who was also at the cemetery, compared Sobral to Ruy Barbosa and felt it fitting to use some erudite words inspired in 1917 by the death of French sculptor Auguste Rodin: "With his death, it seems that all the great men have died."[7]

The press noted the presence of lawyers Evaristo de Morais Filho, Evandro Lins e Silva, and Evandro's nephew Técio Lins e Silva, famed for having defended victims of Institutional Act Number Five, and it reported on the splendor with which the band of SARCA rendered "Oh, Minas Gerais" and "Chopin's Funeral March." Among the nine speakers who paid tribute to Sobral before the burial were his daughter Ruth, Tito Lívio, Professor Cândido Mendes de Almeida, and Flávio Tavares, a former political prisoner who had come from Buenos Aires to be present and who declared that Sobral, his lawyer in the past, had "always been immortal." Other speakers were IAB President José Luiz Villares, OAB Conselho Federal President Marcelo Lavenère Machado, and OAB Rio de Janeiro Section President Sérgio Sveiter.[8]

Pronouncements by prominent Brazilians about the life and virtues of Sobral filled the newspapers. Famed architect Oscar Niemeyer felt that Sobral had been "a person of greatest importance in the nation." When Sérgio Sveiter, also filled with admiration, said that Sobral was "without any doubt the greatest of all the lawyers in the history of Brazil,"[9] he was expressing an opinion that some others also expressed and that might be said to have depended on what one was looking for in a lawyer.

Behind all of this admiration lay a fact noted by Evaristo de Morais

Filho. Recalling the group of lawyers who had struggled for democratic causes during the military regime, he pointed out that "Sobral Pinto was our leader."

Academy of Letters President Austregésilo de Athayde described the death of Sobral Pinto as "the disappearance of one of the legendary figures of contemporary Brazilian life."[10]

NOTES

HSP letters, telegrams, and legal papers refer to these documents written by Sobral Pinto in Rio de Janeiro, unless another place is indicated. Copies of them are in the collection possessed by his family in Rio de Janeiro. In the notes the names of the recipients of the documents are spelled as Sobral Pinto wrote them.

Publication information about books is given with their first mention. In the case of newspapers and magazines, locations are given when they are first mentioned, and occasionally are repeated. Where no publication places are shown for newspapers *O Dia*, *Última Hora*, and the *Diário de Notícias*, the place is Rio de Janeiro, and references to their publications elsewhere are shown where appropriate. In some cases the names of newspapers make publication places obvious.

Where the word "interview" is followed by no information about publication, the interview was with JWFD.

Introduction

1. Alceu Amoroso Lima, *Cartas do Pai* (São Paulo: Instituto Moreira Salles, 2003), p. 501.

2. Dario de Almeida Magalhães in *Digesto Econômico* (São Paulo), no. 196 (July–August 1967), pp. 136–142.

3. Heleno Cláudio Fragoso, *Advocacia da Liberdade* (Rio de Janeiro: Forense, 1984), p. 147.

4. *O Estado de Minas* (Belo Horizonte), February 16, 1986. Academia Brasileira de Letras, Sessão do dia 5.11.73, in HSP papers.

5. *Jornal do Brasil*, December 1, 1991.

I. Prologue

1. DENOUNCING THE DUTRA ADMINISTRATION'S REPRESSION OF COMMUNISM (1946–1948)

1. HSP, letters to Luiz Carlos Prestes, April 25, May 2, 7, 1947.

2. HSP, letter to José Pereira Lima, May 2, 1946.

3. "Fortalecendo o governo," *Correio da Noite* (Rio de Janeiro), May 26, 1947. Resistência Democrática, "Advertência à Nação," *Diário de Notícias* (Rio de Janeiro), May 11, 1947.

4. HSP, letter to Hamilton Nogueira, October 28, 1947. *Correio da Manhã* (Rio de Janeiro), October 30, 1947.

5. *Diário do Congresso Nacional*, p. 7609 (November 1, 1947). HSP in *O Jornal* (Rio de Janeiro), November 2, 9, 1947.

6. Partido Comunista Brasileiro entry in *Dicionário Histórico-Biográfico Brasileiro, 1930-1983* (Rio de Janeiro: Editora Forense-Universitária, 1984).

7. Manifesto of Luiz Carlos Prestes, January 28, 1948, published at that time in the *Tribuna Popular* (Rio de Janeiro daily associated with the Brazilian Communist Party).

2. SOBRAL'S RELATIONS WITH CATHOLIC LEADERS (1947-1950)

1. HSP, letter to Alceu (Amoroso Lima), April 7, 1947. HSP, letters to Eminência (Cardinal Jaime de Barros Câmara) and Adroaldo (Mesquita da Costa), November 19, 1947.

2. HSP, letters to Hildebrando Leal, June 13, 18, 1947. HSP, letter to Padre (José) Távora, January 22, 1948.

3. *Correio da Manhã*, November 28, 1947. HSP, letter to Alceu, November 29, 1947. HSP, letters to Eminência, December 1, 1947, and n.d.

4. HSP, letter to Alceu, January 20, 1948. HSP, letter to Eminência, February 23, 1948. HSP, letter to Padre Hélder (Câmara), January 21, 1948.

5. HSP, letters to Eminência and John F. Parr, February 14, 1948. HSP, letters to Padre Hélder (Câmara), February 16, 23, March 2, 1948. HSP, letters to (Richard) Pattee, July 5, 16, 27, 1948. Hélder Câmara, letter to HSP, Rio de Janeiro, March 24, 1948 (in HSP papers).

6. HSP, letter to Alceu, April 1, 1948. HSP, letter to (José Maria Moss) Tapajóz, May 2, 1950. HSP, José Vieira Coelho, and Gabriel Costa Carvalho, legal arguments in *Jornal do Commercio* (Rio de Janeiro), June 4, July 30, November 19, December 3, 1950.

3. SOBRAL'S RELATIONS WITH THE UDN (1947-1950)

1. HSP, letter to Amarílio de Vasconcellos, August 28, 1947. HSP, letter to João Alberto Lins de Barros, September 10, 1947.

2. HSP, letter to Carlos (Lacerda), June 26, 1947.

3. *Correio da Manhã*, April 18, 20, 21, 1948. Afonso Arinos de Melo Franco, interview, Rio de Janeiro, July 29, 1984.

4. HSP, telegrams to José Américo de Almeida and Hamilton Nogueira, April 22, 1948. HSP, letter to Adroaldo (Mesquita da Costa), April 23, 1948.

5. "Atividades do Centro D. Vital," *A Ordem* (Rio de Janeiro Catholic journal), vol. 41, no. 5 (May 1949). P. B. (Paulo Bittencourt), "Na Tribuna da Imprensa," *Correio da Manhã*, May 1, 1949.

6. HSP, letters to Carlos (Lacerda) and (Emílio) Ippolito, December 31, 1949.

7. HSP, letter to Dario (de Almeida Magalhães), February 14, 1950, and HSP, letter to José, February 8, 1950. (Both from Fazenda São Lourenço.)

8. HSP, letters from Fazenda São Lourenço to Dario, February 14, 1950, to Carlos (Lacerda), February 18, 1950, to (José Fernando) Carneiro, February 20, 1950, to Adaucto (Lucio Cardoso), February 25, 1950. HSP, letter to Carlos (Lacerda), March 14, 1950. HSP, letter to Alceu (Amoroso Lima), April 18, 1950.

9. HSP, letter to Hamilton (Nogueira), March 14, 1950.

10. HSP, letters to General (Pedro Aurélio de) Góes Monteiro, March 20, 24, 1950. *O Estado de S. Paulo*, April 12, 19, 1950.

11. HSP, letter to (Gustavo) Corção, June 23, 1950.

12. *Tribuna da Imprensa* (Rio de Janeiro), June 20, 22, 1950. HSP, letter to Carlos (Lacerda), June 26, 1950.

13. *Tribuna da Imprensa*, August 3, October 2, 1950.

14. *O Estado de S. Paulo*, September 14, 16, 19, 22, 24, 1950.

15. HSP, letter to Wilson (Salazar), October 6, 1950. HSP, letter to (Aliomar) Baleeiro, December 20, 1950.

16. HSP, letter to (Gustavo) Corção, October 7, 1950.

17. HSP, letter to Baleeiro, December 20, 1950.

4. SOBRAL'S RELATIONS WITH LACERDA (1951–1954)

1. HSP, telegrams to Carlos Lacerda, March 2, 3, 1951. HSP, letter to Carlos (Lacerda), June 23, 1951.

2. Carlos Lacerda in *Tribuna da Imprensa*, June 8, July 14, 15, 1951. HSP in *Tribuna da Imprensa*, June 12, 26, 28, 29, 30, July 2 to 9, 1951. HSP, letters to Carlos (Lacerda), July 10, 19, 23, 1951. HSP in *Jornal do Commercio*, July 14, 1951.

3. HSP, letters to Carlos (Lacerda) and (Augusto Frederico) Schmidt, January 26, 1952.

4. HSP, letters to Alceu (Amoroso Lima), February 8, March 15, 1952, January 9, 1953. Carlos Lacerda, "Relatório aos Acionistas," *Tribuna da Imprensa*, March 14, 1952.

5. *Tribuna da Imprensa*, December 2, 1952. HSP, letter to Alceu, January 9, 1953.

6. HSP, letters to Carlos, December 8, 15, 29, 1953. HSP, notes recording "Diálogo telefônico entre Carlos Lacerda e Sobral Pinto, 29 de Dezembro, 1953" (typed on December 30). HSP, letters to Dario (de Almeida Magalhães), January 14, April 5, 1954.

7. HSP, message to Dario, conveyed by Gilda Sobral Pinto, April 12, 1954 (in HSP papers). HSP, letters to Alceu, February 10, 20, March 20, 1954.

8. HSP, letter to Dario, April 14, 1954.

9. Ibid. HSP, letters to (Gustavo) Corção, Alceu, and (José Fernando) Carneiro, April 19, 1954.

10. *Tribuna da Imprensa*, July 6, 9, 15, 17–18, 19, 1954. *Última Hora* (Rio de Janeiro), May 31, July 15, 1954.

11. *Última Hora*, May 31, 1954.

12. HSP, letters to (Alfredo) Tranjan, Lutero Vargas, and Carlos (Lacerda), July 5, 1954. Lutero Vargas in *Última Hora*, July 12, 1954.

13. Carlos Lacerda in *Tribuna da Imprensa*, July 12, 1954. HSP, letter to Lutero Vargas, July 13, 1954.

14. *Tribuna da Imprensa*, July 27, 1954. HSP, "Defesa Prévia de Carlos Lacerda," July 29, 1954 (in HSP papers).

5. LEGAL CASES OF REGINE FEIGL AND OTHERS (1951–1954)

1. HSP, letter to Affonso Penna Júnior, December 31, 1946. HSP, letter to Othon Ribas, December 16, 1948. HSP, letters to Haroldo (Valladão), November 18, 19, 1949.

2. HSP, letters to (Jorge Dyott) Fontenelle, July 11, August 20, 1951. HSP, letter to Cecy (Cecília Silva), August 29, 1951. HSP, letter to Dario (de Almeida Magalhães), September 4, 1951. HSP, letters to Alceu (Amoroso Lima), November 17, 24, 1951.

3. HSP, letters to Alceu, November 17, December 7, 1951. HSP, letter to his daughter Maria do Carmo, December 28, 1951.

4. HSP, letters to Júlio César Leite, July 10, 17, 27, 1953. HSP, letter to Alceu, August 1, 1953. HSP, letter to (Luís) Gallotti, August 6, 1953.

5. HSP, letter to *Diário de Notícias*, October 24, 1953, and article in *Jornal do Commercio*, April 11, 1954. HSP, letter to Gallotti, April 23, 1954. HSP, letter to João (de Alencar Athayde), August 30, 1954.

6. Regine Feigl, statement to HSP, in HSP, letter to (Henrique) Hargreaves, July 15, 1954. HSP, letter to Affonso Penna Júnior, December 5, 1952.

7. HSP, letter to Desembargador Oliveira e Silva, July 16, 1954.

8. HSP, letter to (Anésio) Frota Aguiar, August 13, 1954.

9. HSP, letter to Tribunal de Contas do Distrito Federal Presidente Benjamin Reis, March 18, 1954. HSP, letter to Antonico, April 20, 1954.

10. Regine Feigl, statement to HSP, given in HSP, letter to Hargreaves, July 15, 1954.

11. HSP, letters to Lindolpho (Pio da Silva Dias) and Padre Antão, July 3, 1954. HSP, letter to Eminência (Jaime Câmara), n.d.

12. HSP, letter to Hargreaves, July 15, 1954. HSP, letter to Mme Feigl, October 8, 1954. HSP, cable to Professor Feigl e Sra., October 16, 1954.

6. VARGAS'S SUICIDE, FOLLOWED BY MILITARY OPPOSITION TO KUBITSCHEK (1954–1955)

1. HSP, letter to Castro Lima, August 20, 1954. See also HSP, letters to (Manuel) Ordoñez (September 11, 1954), (Aquinaldo) Caiado de Castro (February 26, 1955), and Alceu (Amoroso Lima) (November 14, 1955) regarding August 1954.

2. Tristão de Athayde (Alceu Amoroso Lima), "Sangue e Lama," *Diário de Notícias*, August 29, 1954.

3. HSP, in *Gazeta Judiciária* (Rio de Janeiro), August 31, 1954. *Tribuna da Imprensa*, October 1, September 3, 1954.

4. João Café Filho, *Do Sindicato ao Catete* (Rio de Janeiro: Livraria José Olympio Editora, 1966), vol. 2, p. 365.

5. *Tribuna da Imprensa,* September 11–12, 13, 14, 1954.

6. Café Filho, *Do Sindicato ao Catete,* vol. 2, p. 494.

7. Ibid., vol. 2, pp. 496–497. Juscelino Kubitschek, *A Escalada Política: Meu Caminho para Brasília* (Rio de Janeiro: Bloch Editores, 1976), vol. 2, pp. 343–344. Joffre Gomes da Costa, *Marechal Henrique Lott* (Rio de Janeiro: n.p., 1960), p. 231.

8. HSP, letter to João Café Filho, January 28, 1955. HSP, letter to Raul Fernandes, January 27, 1955.

9. HSP, letter to Adaucto (Lucio Cardoso), February 3, 1955. HSP, letter to Afonso Arinos de Melo Franco, March 18, 1955.

10. HSP, letter to Otto (Lara Resende), April 22, 1955.

11. HSP, letters to Dario (de Almeida Magalhães) and Adaucto, April 26, 1955.

12. Juarez Távora, interviews, Rio de Janeiro, October 5, 1966, October 20, November 27, 1967, and documents shown to JWFD. Viriato de Castro, *O Fenômeno Jânio Quadros* (São Paulo: Palácio do Livro, 1959), p. 131.

13. HSP, letter to Adaucto, October 28, 1958.

7. THE KUBITSCHEK CANDIDACY AND SOBRAL'S LEAGUE TO DEFEND LEGALITY (1955)

1. *Correio da Manhã,* August 6, 1955.

2. *O Estado de S. Paulo,* August 9, 11, 12, 1955. HSP, letter to (José Maria) Alkmim, August 13, 1955.

3. *Diário Carioca* (Rio de Janeiro), August 23, 1955. *Correio da Manhã,* August 24, 1955. *O Estado de S. Paulo,* August 25, 1955.

4. *Correio da Manhã,* August 25, 27, 28, 30, 1955. *Jornada,* ano 1, no. 1 (Rio de Janeiro, September 1955). *O Estado de S. Paulo,* September 4, 8, 1955.

5. *Tribuna da Imprensa,* August 26, 1955.

6. HSP, letter to Eminência, September 14, 1955, and "Declaração," September 21, 1955 (in HSP papers).

7. HSP, letter to Rafael (Corrêa de Oliveira), October 27, 1955.

8. *Correio da Manhã,* October 8, 9, 16, 20, 1955. *Jornal do Commercio,* October 17–18, 1955.

9. Afonso Arinos de Melo Franco, *A Escalada: Memórias* (Rio de Janeiro: Livraria José Olympio Editora, 1965), pp. 375–376. *Correio da Manhã,* October 19, 23, 1955.

10. HSP, letters to Rafael, October 27, November 4, 1955.

11. Henrique Lott, interview, Rio de Janeiro, August 27, 1963.

12. HSP, letter to Alceu (Amoroso Lima), November 14, 1955. Ministério da Guerra, *Depoimento do Advogado Dr. H. Sobral Pinto, a respeito dos acontecimentos dos dias 11 e 21 de novembro de 1955* (Rio de Janeiro: Secretaria Geral do Ministério da Guerra, Imprensa Militar, 1956), p. 14. *Correio da Manhã,* November 8, 1955.

13. Gomes da Costa, *Marechal Henrique Lott*, p. 287. HSP in *Correio da Manhã*, November 10, 1955.
14. Lott, interview, August 27, 1963. Gomes da Costa, *Marechal Henrique Lott*, pp. 288–289. Lucas Lopes, interview, Rio de Janeiro, October 30, 1965.

8. LOTT'S COUPS AGAINST LUZ AND CAFÉ FILHO (NOVEMBER 1955)

1. Henrique Lott, interview, August 27, 1963. Odílio Denys, interview, Rio de Janeiro, December 14, 1965. Gomes da Costa, *Marechal Henrique Lott*, p. 303.
2. *Correio da Manhã*, November 12, 13, 1955. HSP, letter to Alceu (Amoroso Lima), November 14, 1955.
3. HSP, telegrams to Hilcar Leite, Herbert Moses, and Nereu Ramos, November 11, 1955. HSP, letter to Raphael (de Almeida Magalhães), January 18, 1956.
4. HSP, letter to Raphael, January 18, 1956.
5. HSP, letter to Otto (Lara Resende), November 25, 1955.
6. *Correio da Manhã*, December 4, 1955. HSP, letters to (Antônio Lara) Resende and Alceu, November 29, 1955.
7. HSP, letter to (Raimundo de) Magalhães Júnior, February 21, 1956.
8. Ibid.

9. SOBRAL'S ACTIVITIES FOLLOWING KUBITSCHEK'S INAUGURATION (1956–1958)

1. *Uma Vida Cristã: In Memoriam Maria do Carmo Sobral Pinto Ribeiro* (Rio de Janeiro: n.p. [1956]), pp. 9–12.
2. *Correio da Manhã*, April 4, 1956 (showing the letters).
3. HSP, letter to Victor (Nunes Leal), January 9, 1957.
4. HSP, telegram to Presidente da República, April 7, 1956.
5. HSP, telegrams to Henrique Lott and Juscelino Kubitschek, August 24, 1956.
6. HSP, letters to Adaucto (Lucio Cardoso), August 4, 6, 23, 1956, October 8, 1959. HSP, letter to Dario (de Almeida Magalhães), August 23, 1956. HSP, letters to Carlos (Lacerda), August 23, 28, 1956.
7. HSP, letter to Carlos, August 28, 1956.
8. HSP, letter to Carlos, October 22, 1956.
9. HSP, letter to Evandro (Lins e Silva), July 24, 1956.
10. Gomes da Costa, *Marechal Henrique Lott*, p. 376.
11. Ibid. *O Estado de S. Paulo*, November 22, 24, 1956.
12. Claudio Bojunga, *JK: O artista do impossível* (Rio de Janeiro: Editora Objetiva, 2001), pp. 384–386.
13. Ibid. Juscelino Kubitschek de Oliveira, letter to HSP, February 9, 1972 (in HSP papers).
14. Tristão de Athayde (Alceu Amoroso Lima) in *Diário de Notícias*, December 2, 1956. HSP, letter to Alceu, December 3, 1956.
15. HSP, letters to Victor (Nunes Leal), April 9, 25, 1957.

16. *Diário de Notícias,* April 27, 1957. HSP, letter to João Portella R. Dantas, May 2, 1957. HSP, letter to Adaucto, April 29, 1957.

17. *Maquis,* no. 30 (Rio de Janeiro, first half of August 1957), no. 33 (second half of September 1957), and no. 35 (second half of October 1957).

10. SOBRAL BREAKS WITH HIS CLIENT, JÂNIO QUADROS (1959)

1. HSP, "O processo contra o Embaixador Francisco de Assis Chateaubriand Bandeira de Mello," August 31, 1958 (in HSP papers).

2. Fernando Morais, *Chatô: O Rei do Brasil* (São Paulo: Companhia de Letras, 1994), pp. 594–598. *Jornal do Commercio,* July 20, 1958. HSP, letter to Dario (de Almeida Magalhães), June 6, 1957.

3. HSP, letter to (Luís) Gallotti, July 29, 1958.

4. Morais, *Chatô,* p. 592. HSP, letters to J. E. Macedo Soares and (José Maria) Alkmim, November 18, 1957.

5. HSP, letter to Oscar Pedroso Horta, July 17, 1958. HSP, brief of Jânio Quadros to Carlos Cirilo Júnior, August 25, 1958 (in HSP papers).

6. HSP, letter to (Luís) Gallotti and copies for other justices, July 29, 1958.

7. HSP, brief to Cirilo Júnior, August 25, 1958, and letter to Oscar Pedroso Horta, August 28, 1958.

8. HSP, letters to Jânio Quadros, October 20, 1958, September 1, 1959. HSP, letter to Oscar Pedroso Horta, October 23, 1958.

9. HSP, letter to Adaucto (Lucio Cardoso), October 8, 1959.

10. Jânio Quadros, letter to HSP, Paris, August 8, 1959, quoted in HSP, letter to Jânio Quadros, December 16, 1959, and Jânio Quadros, letter to HSP, August 29, 1959, quoted in HSP, letter to Dario, December 1, 1959.

11. HSP, letters to Victor (Nunes Leal), April 29, May 2, 1959. HSP, letter to Juscelino Kubitschek de Oliveira, May 6, 1959. HSP, letter to Gabriel (Costa Carvalho), September 10, 1959.

12. HSP, letter to (Henrique) Teixeira Lott, June 15, 1959.

13. HSP, letters to Jânio Quadros, August 29, September 17, 1959.

14. HSP, letters to Jânio Quadros, September 1, 17, 1959.

15. Jânio Quadros, letter to HSP, September 2, 1959, quoted in HSP, letter to Jânio Quadros, December 16, 1959. HSP, letters to Jânio Quadros, October 7, 24, 1959.

16. Assis Chateaubriand, "A Vingança do Urso," *O Jornal,* November 29, 1959.

17. HSP, letter to Dario, December 1, 1959.

18. HSP, letter to Jânio Quadros, December 16, 1959, and quotations in it from Jânio Quadros, letter to HSP, December 11, 1959.

19. HSP, letters to Eminência, October 5, November 4, 1959 (the latter includes text of Jaime de Barros Câmara, letter received by HSP).

20. HSP, letter to Eminência, November 4, 1959.

11. ELECTIONS AND CONTROVERSIES ABOUT BRASÍLIA AND RIO'S CITY COUNCIL (1960)

1. HSP, letters to Dario (de Almeida Magalhães), December 3, 1959, January 2, 1960.

2. HSP, letters to *Diário de Notícias*, March 14, 18, 1960. HSP, letters to Afonso Arinos (de Melo Franco) and Paulo de Tarso Santos, March 26, 1960. HSP, letter to Adaucto (Lucio Cardoso), March 27, 1960. HSP, letter to Octavio Mangabeira, March 16, 1960.

3. *Correio da Manhã*, April 1, 2, 7, 1960. *Tribuna da Imprensa*, April 7, 1960.

4. HSP, letters to Gabriel (Costa Carvalho), March 24, May 3, 1960. HSP, letters to Eugênio Gudin, March 30, April 2, 6, 1960. HSP, letters to Alceu (Amoroso Lima), April 28, August 13, 1960. HSP, letter to Adaucto, May 4, 1960. HSP, letters to (Gustavo) Corção, July 7, 12, 1960. *Tribuna da Imprensa*, April 2, 5–6, 1960. *Correio da Manhã*, April 5, 22, 1960.

5. HSP, letter to Gabriel, May 3, 1960. HSP, letter to Hahnemann (Guimarães), April 9, 1960.

6. HSP, letter to Gabriel, May 3, 1960.

7. HSP, letters to Supreme Court justices, June 15, 1960. HSP, letter to Nelson (Hungria), September 2, 1960.

8. HSP, letter to Adaucto, September 23, 1960. HSP, telegram to Adaucto Cardoso, October 3, 1960. HSP, letters to Alceu, July 8, August 13, 1960.

9. HSP, letter to Adaucto, October 13, 1960.

10. HSP, legal brief to Presidente do Tribunal de Justiça do Estado da Guanabara, December 30, 1960, and HSP, legal document to Cândido de Oliveira Neto, January 4, 1961 (in HSP papers). *Tribuna da Imprensa*, January 9, 19, February 1, 2, 1961. *Diário de Notícias*, February 3, 1961.

11. HSP, letters to Raphael (de Almeida Magalhães), February 2, 16, 1961. HSP, letter to Mme Feigl, May 17, 1961.

12. *O Globo* (Rio de Janeiro), March 17, 1961, January 20, 1962. *Jornal do Brasil* (Rio de Janeiro), August 1, 2, 1961.

12. THE IMPERIOUSNESS OF PRESIDENT QUADROS AND HIS RESIGNATION (1961)

1. HSP, letter to (Henrique) Hargreaves, March 4, 1961. HSP, letter to Adaucto (Lucio Cardoso), August 25, 1961. HSP, letter to M. F. do Nascimento Brito, May 23, 1961 (published in *Jornal do Brasil*, May 24).

2. *O Globo*, April 1, 1961. HSP, document to Frederico de Barros Barreto, July 10, 1961. HSP, letter to Artur Bernardes Filho, March 29, 1961.

3. HSP, letter to Roberto Marinho, February 9, 1961. HSP, letter to (Antônio Joaquim) Peixoto (de Castro Júnior), April 28, 1961. Empreendedora Civil, Ltda, letter to Jânio Quadros, Rio de Janeiro, April 26, 1961 (in HSP papers).

4. José Tocqueville de Carvalho Filho, petition to Oscar Pedroso Horta, Rio de Janeiro, February 10, 1961. José Tocqueville de Carvalho Filho, "Con-

sulta," Rio de Janeiro, April 25, 1961, and draft of letter, Juscelino Kubitschek de Oliveira to HSP, Rio de Janeiro, September 12, 1961 (both in HSP papers). HSP, letter to (Manuel) Ordoñez, April 27, 1961. HSP, letter to J. V. (de) Faria Lima, May 10, 1961. "Irregularidades no BNDE," *Diário de Notícias*, February 7, 1961.

5. Roberto Sobral Pinto Ribeiro, interview, Rio de Janeiro, January 3, 2001. Antonio Carlos Villaça, interview, Rio de Janeiro, January 10, 2001. *O Globo*, June 9, 1961. HSP, letter to Alceu (Amoroso Lima), June 10, 1961. HSP, letter to (Augusto Frederico) Schmidt, June 21, 1961.

6. Antonio Carlos Villaça, interview with Daphne F. Rodger, August 17, 1985.

7. HSP, letter to Carlos (Lacerda), February 18, 1963. HSP, letter to Raphael (de Almeida Magalhães), December 7, 1961.

8. HSP, letters to Alceu, August 24, 25, 1961. HSP, letter to Adaucto, August 25, 1961.

9. Carlos Lacerda, "Rosas e Pedras do Meu Caminho," Chapter 11, *Manchete* (Rio de Janeiro magazine), June 24, 1967, p. 116.

10. *O Globo*, August 25, 1961.

11. Pedro Geraldo de Almeida, interview, Rio de Janeiro, November 4, 1965. Genivel Rabelo, "O Inquérito," *PN (Política e Nogócios)* magazine, Rio de Janeiro, October 7, 1961. See also Mário Victor, *Cinco anos que abalaram o Brasil* (Rio de Janeiro: Editôra Civilização Brasileira, 1965), p. 309.

12. These words were spoken on August 26, 1961 (see Carlos Castello Branco, "O Dia Seguinte," *Realidade* [São Paulo magazine], vol. 2, no. 20 [November 1967]).

13. Carlos Castello Branco, "O Dia Seguinte."

14. HSP, "Pela Legalidade," August 26, 1961 (in HSP papers). HSP, letter to José Vicente, September 4, 1961.

15. HSP, document to General do Exército Tristão de Alencar Araripe, president of the Superior Military Tribunal, September 8, 1961.

16. HSP, letter to (Francisco) Negrão (de Lima), September 8, 1961. Mineiro: of the state of Minas Gerais.

13. ACTIVITIES OF SOBRAL DURING GOULART'S FIRST YEARS (1961–1963)

1. HSP, letter to (Francisco) San Tiago Dantas, November 22, 1961.

2. *Jornal do Brasil* and *Tribuna da Imprensa*, July 6, 1962.

3. HSP, letter to Herbert Levy and Ernâni do Amaral Peixoto, July 12, 1962 (published in the *Diário Carioca*, July 15).

4. HSP, letter to Roberto Lyra, August 16, 1962.

5. HSP, letters to Alceu (Amoroso Lima), July 19, August 4, 1962. *O Globo* and *Última Hora*, July 16, 1962.

6. HSP, letters to Nelson de Mello, August 7, 8, 1962.

7. HSP, letter to Carlos (Lacerda), n.d.

8. HSP, letters to Miguel Arraes, December 17, 1962, February 8, 1963.

9. HSP, telegram to Miguel Arraes, July 25, 1963. HSP, letter to Hélio Fernandes, August 5, 1963.

10. Luís Tenório de Lima, interview, São Paulo, November 21, 1968.

11. *Análise e Perspectiva Econômica* (APEC), a Rio de Janeiro publication, August 27, 1963. *O Estado de S. Paulo*, August 17, 1963.

12. *O Globo, O Estado de S. Paulo*, and *Correio da Manhã*, July 9, 1963. *Jornal do Brasil*, July 9, 10, 11, 1963. HSP, letter to Darcy Ribeiro, July 9, 1963.

13. HSP, letter to Carlos (Lacerda), July 15, 1963.

14. HSP, letter to Evandro (Lins e Silva), August 9, 1963.

15. HSP, letter to Dario (de Almeida Magalhães), August 16, 1963. HSP, letter to Tude, November 11, 1963.

16. HSP, letter to Dario, August 16, 1963. HSP, letters to José Bonifácio de Andrada, September 9, 18, 1963. HSP, letter to Lourival Batista, September 10, 1963. HSP, letters to J. Seixas Dória, September 2, 13, 1963. HSP, telegram to Orlando (Vieira) Dantas, October 16, 1963. HSP, letters to Tito Lívio (Cavalcanti de Medeiros), September 11, 1963, February 18, 1964.

17. *O Estado de S. Paulo*, January 7, 1964. HSP, letters to Arnon (de Mello) and Virgílio, August 1, 1964.

18. HSP, letters to Carlos Alberto Dunshee de Abrantes, September 24, October 14, 1963. HSP, letters to Haryberto (de Miranda Jordão), September 12, 1963. HSP, letter to Otto Gil, September 27, 1963. HSP, letter to Celestino (Basílio), Haroldo (Valladão), Júlio Mello, Teófilo Azevedo, and (Fernandes) Couto, September 27, 1963.

19. HSP, letter to Jair Dantas Ribeiro, Sílvio Motta, and Anísio Botelho, October 1, 1963.

20. Gilberto Crockatt de Sá, interview, Rio de Janeiro, December 12, 1968. Luís Fernando Bocaiuva Cunha, interview, Rio de Janeiro, December 5, 1968. Luís Tenório de Lima, interview, November 21, 1968.

21. Abelardo Jurema, *Sexta-Feira, 13: Os Últimos Dias do Governo João Goulart*, 2nd ed. (Rio de Janeiro: Edições O Cruzeiro, 1964), pp. 131–132, 126–127. Gilberto Crockatt de Sá, interview, December 12, 1968. Luís Tenório de Lima, interview, November 21, 1968.

22. Telegram to Ranieri Mazzilli, signed by HSP and other lawyers, n.d.

23. João Cândido Maia Neto, interview, Montevideo, November 18, 1967. João Goulart, in *Manchete*, November 30, 1963.

24. HSP, letter to Armando Falcão, October 16, 1963.

25. Decree of Carlos Lacerda, Rio de Janeiro, November 5, 1963, in *Diário Oficial* of Guanabara state, November 8. HSP, letters to Laercio Dias de Moura, March 5, 21, April 1, 1963.

26. Arthur José Poerner, *O Poder Jovem* (Rio de Janeiro: Editôra Civilização Brasileira, 1968), pp. 224–225.

27. HSP, letter to Eremildo (Vianna), September 20, 1963. HSP, letter to Oscar de Oliveira, Paulo de Góes, and Waldemar Areno, September 20, 1963. HSP, letters to Jair Dantas Ribeiro, September 19, 24, 1963.

28. *Tribuna da Imprensa*, December 30, 1963. HSP, letter to Corpo Docente da Faculdade Nacional de Filosofia e aos meus amigos, December 28, 1963.

29. *Diário de Notícias, Jornal do Brasil, Tribuna da Imprensa*, and *O Es-*

tado de S. Paulo, December 31, 1963. *Novos Rumos* (Rio de Janeiro weekly newspaper of the Brazilian Communist Party), January 3–9, 1964.
30. HSP, letter to Abelardo Jurema, January 4, 1964. *Jornal do Brasil*, December 31, 1963.
31. *Jornal do Brasil*, January 2, 1964.

14. GOULART BRINGS ABOUT A MILITARY DENOUEMENT; "INEXPLICABLY" IT DISAPPOINTS HIM (MARCH 1964)

1. HSP in *Tribuna da Imprensa*, March 31, 1964.
2. Gilberto Crockatt de Sá, interviews, Rio de Janeiro, October 9, 11, 1967, December 12, 17, 1968. *O Estado de S. Paulo*, December 27, 1963, January 7, 11, 12, 1964.
3. Ernâni do Amaral Peixoto, interview, Brasília, October 15, 1965.
4. HSP, letters to Amaury Kruel, Justino Alves Bastos, and Benjamim Galhardo, January 22, 1964. "Sobral alerta chefes do Exército," *O Estado de S. Paulo*, January 23, 1964.
5. HSP, letter to (Henrique) Hargreaves, February 19, 1964. HSP, letter to Alceu (Amoroso Lima), February 14, 1964.
6. Victor, *Cinco anos que abalaram o Brasil*, pp. 474–475. Hélio Silva, *1964: Golpe ou Contragolpe* (Rio de Janeiro: Editôra Civilização Brasileira, 1975), pp. 234, 457–466.
7. Ibid. *Correio da Manhã, Tribuna da Imprensa*, and *O Estado de S. Paulo*, March 14, 1964.
8. Araújo Netto, "A Paisagem," in Alberto Dines et al., *Os Idos de Março e a Queda em Abril*, 2nd ed. (Rio de Janeiro: José Alvaro Editor, 1964), p. 61. Coleção Memória do Brasil, *História Política do Brasil: Revolução de 64* (Rio de Janeiro: Editora Rio, n.d.), pp. 211, 214 (quoting newspapers).
9. HSP, letter to General de Exército Arthur da Costa e Silva, June 1, 1964. "Núcleos de Resistência Legal," signed by HSP, March 19, 1964 (in HSP papers). *O Globo* and *Diário Popular* (São Paulo), March 19, 1964.
10. Sálvio de Almeida Prado, interview, São Paulo, November 18, 1965. Victor, *Cinco anos que abalaram o Brasil*, p. 487.
11. Victor, *Cinco anos que abalaram o Brasil*, pp. 487–488. Wilson Figueiredo, "A Margem Esquerda," in Dines et al., *Os Idos de Março*, pp. 213–216. *Correio da Manhã*, March 20, 1964. HSP, letter to Alceu, March 21, 1964.
12. CAMDE officers, interview, Rio de Janeiro, December 18, 1965. *Correio da Manhã*, March 21, 1964.
13. Luís Tenório de Lima, interview, São Paulo, November 21, 1968.
14. Hélder Câmara entry in *Dicionário Histórico-Biográfico Brasileiro, 1930–1983*.
15. HSP, letter to Hélder (Câmara), March 25, 1964. HSP, letter to Eminência (Carlos de Vasconcellos Mota), March 24, 1964.
16. *Tribuna da Imprensa*, March 25, 1964. *Correio da Manhã*, March 26, 1964. *O Estado de S. Paulo*, March 25, 26, 1964. Victor, *Cinco anos que abalaram o Brasil*, p. 494. Jurema, *Sexta-Feira 13*, pp. 152–155.
17. Jurema, *Sexta-Feira 13*, p. 152.

18. *O Estado de S. Paulo,* March 27, 1964. Araújo Netto, "A Paisagem," in Dines et al., *Os Idos de Março,* pp. 54–56.

19. Araújo Netto, "A Paisagem," pp. 56–58. Dante Pelacani, interview, São Paulo, November 24, 1968.

20. Jurema, *Sexta-Feira 13,* p. 162.

21. Carlos Castello Branco, "Da Conspiração a Revolução," in Dines et al., *Os Idos de Março,* p. 303. Araújo Netto, "A Paisagem," p. 61.

22. Antônio Carlos Muricy, *Os Motivos da Revolução Democrática Brasileira: Palestras Pronunciadas na Televisão Canal 2 nos Dias 19 e 25 de Maio de 1964* (Recife: Imprensa Oficial, n.d.), pp. 36–37. Siseno Sarmento, interview, São Paulo, November 21, 1967.

23. Haroldo Veloso, interview, Marietta, Georgia, January 6–7, 1966. *O Estado de S. Paulo,* March 29, 1964. Wilson Figueiredo, "A Margem Esquerda," in Dines et al., *Os Idos de Março,* p. 235.

24. "Entrevista Sobral Pinto: Por uma Constituição," *Veja* (São Paulo magazine), June 1, 1977.

25. HSP, letter to (Henrique) Hargreaves, April 6, 1964. HSP, "Declaração à *Tribuna da Imprensa,*" March 31, 1964 (in HSP papers).

26. Jurema, *Sexta-Feira 13,* pp. 167–173, 176.

27. Ibid., pp. 173–176. Victor, *Cinco anos que abalaram o Brasil,* p. 506.

28. Jurema, *Sexta-Feira 13,* p. 174. *Correio da Manhã,* March 31, 1964.

29. Olímpio Mourão Filho, interview, Rio de Janeiro, October 9, 1965. "General Guedes Relata o Comêço do Movimento," *Correio da Manhã,* April 3, 1964. José Stacchini, *Março 64: Mobilização da Audácia* (São Paulo: Companhia Editôra Nacional, 1965), p. 64.

30. Olímpio Mourão Filho, interview, October 9, 1965. *O Jornal,* April 1, 1964.

31. Pedro Gomes, "Minas: Do Diálogo ao 'Front,'" in Dines et al., *Os Idos de Março,* p. 91. Oswaldo Pieruccetti, letter to JWFD, Belo Horizonte, January 18, 1968. Stacchini, *Março 64,* p. 77.

32. Amaury Kruel, interviews, São Paulo, November 16, 30, 1965, Guanabara state, October 21, 1967. *O Jornal,* April 1, 1964.

33. HSP, letter to (Henrique) Hargreaves, April 2, 1964. Carlos Lacerda, interview, Rio de Janeiro, October 11, 1967. Carlos Lacerda, *Depoimento* (Rio de Janeiro: Editora Nova Fronteira, 1977), pp. 285–286.

34. Armando de Abreu in transcription of Salvador Mandim tape for the Sociedade dos Amigos de Carlos Lacerda (in papers of JWFD), p. 26. Antônio Dias Rebello Filho, *Carlos Lacerda, Meu Amigo,* 2nd ed. (Rio de Janeiro: Editora Record, 1981), p. 124. HSP, letter to (Henrique) Hargreaves, April 2, 1964.

35. José Guimarães Neiva Moreira, *O pilão da madrugada: Um depoimento à José Louzeiro* (Rio de Janeiro: Editora Terceira Mundo, 1989), pp. 172–175. Jurema, *Sexta-Feira 13,* pp. 188–190.

36. Odílio Denys, "Denis Conta Tudo," *Fatos & Fotos* (Rio de Janeiro magazine), May 2, 1964. Olímpio Mourão Filho, interview, October 9, 1965.

37. *O Estado de S. Paulo,* April 2, 1964. Abelardo Jurema, interview, Rio de Janeiro, July 27, 1976.

38. *O Jornal* and *O Estado de S. Paulo*, April 2, 1964. Gustavo Borges, "Operação Salame," Part III, *O Cruzeiro* (Rio de Janeiro magazine), June 20, 1964.

39. HSP, letter to Diretor de o *Diário de Notícias*, December 23, 1964.

40. Courtesy of Professor Michael L. Conniff, who, in 1987, consulted polls of May 1964.

41. F. Zenha Machado, *Os Últimas Dias do Governo de Vargas* (Rio de Janeiro: Editôra Lux Ltda, 1955), pp. 81–82.

42. HSP, letter to Hargreaves, April 2, 1964.

II. Defending Men Punished by the New Regime (1964–1965)

1. SOBRAL OPPOSES THE INSTITUTIONAL ACT AND CASTELLO BRANCO'S ELECTION (APRIL 1964)

1. *O Globo*, April 3, 1964. HSP, "Entrevista a O GLOBO sobre a eleição do Presidente e Vice-Presidente da República" (in HSP papers).

2. HSP, letter to (Henrique) Hargreaves, April 6, 1964.

3. Carlos Medeiros Silva, interview, Rio de Janeiro, November 12, 1975. Francisco Campos, interview, Rio de Janeiro, December 14, 1965.

4. HSP, letter to General H. Castello Branco, April 9, 1964.

5. HSP, letter to Paulo Vial Corrêa, editor-in-chief, *O Jornal*, May 31, 1965.

6. "Entrevista Sobral Pinto: Por uma Constituição," *Veja*, June 1, 1977.

7. Luís Viana Filho, *O Governo Castelo Branco* (Rio de Janeiro: Livraria José Olympio Editora, 1975), p. 65. Raphael de Almeida Magalhães, interview, Rio de Janeiro, November 19, 1975.

8. HSP, letter to Hargreaves, April 6, 1964.

9. Instituto dos Advogados Brasileiros, *Instituto dos Advogados Brasileiros, 150 Anos de História, 1843–1993* (Rio de Janeiro: Editora Destaque, 1995), pp. 230–232.

10. Ibid.

11. HSP, letter to Presidente Marechal Castello Branco, May 15, 1964.

12. HSP, letter to General de Exército Arthur da Costa e Silva, June 1, 1964, including a Costa e Silva quotation.

13. Instituto dos Advogados Brasileiros, *Instituto dos Advogados Brasileiros, 150 Anos de História, 1843–1993*, pp. 232–233.

2. DEFENDING KUBITSCHEK (JUNE 1964)

1. *O Estado de S. Paulo*, May 17, 22, 24, 1964.

2. Juscelino Kubitschek de Oliveira, letter to HSP, March 12, 1964, and reply of HSP, both in *Correio Braziliense* (Brasília), May 14, 1964. *Jornal do Commercio*, editorial, May 15, 1964.

3. *O Estado de S. Paulo*, May 26, 27, 28, 1964.

4. HSP, letter to Arthur da Costa e Silva, June 1, 1964.

5. Viana Filho, *O Governo Castelo Branco*, p. 95.

6. Vasco Leitão da Cunha, interview, Rio de Janeiro, November 23, 1974.

7. Carlos Heitor Cony, *JK: Memorial do Exílio* (Rio de Janeiro: Edições Bloch, 1982), p. 86.

8. HSP, letter to Milton Campos, June 5, 1964. HSP, telegram to Presidente Marechal Castello Branco, n.d. HSP, telegram to Deputado Pedro Aleixo, n.d.

9. HSP, telegram to Ademar de Barros, reported in *Última Hora*, June 8, 1964. HSP, cable to Carlos Lacerda, n.d.

10. Ernâni do Amaral Peixoto, interview, Rio de Janeiro, December 20, 1975. Paulo V. Castello Branco, interview, Rio de Janeiro, December 21, 1975.

11. *Folha de S. Paulo*, June 8, 9, 1964. *Diário de Notícias*, June 9, 1964.

12. *Diário de Notícias*, *O Globo*, and *A Notícia* (Rio de Janeiro), June 9, 1964.

13. HSP, two letters to Senator Juscelino Kubitschek de Oliveira, June 10, 1964.

14. *Folha de S. Paulo*, June 10, 1964. *Jornal do Brasil* and *O Estado de S. Paulo*, June 18, 1964.

15. "Savonarola Caolho," editorial, *O Estado de Minas*, June 21, 1964.

16. HSP, letter to Diretor do *Estado de Minas*, July 9, 1964.

3. THE CASE OF THE NINE CHINESE (APRIL 1964–NOVEMBER 1965)

1. HSP, letter to Gustavo Corção, August 31, 1965. Nine Chinese, document for Auditor da 2a Auditoria da 1a Região Militar, May 26, 1964 (in HSP papers). HSP, letter to Marechal Castello Branco, July 17, 1964. *Jornal do Brasil*, August 20, 1964.

2. *Jornal do Brasil*, August 20, 1964. HSP, letter to Presidente Eduardo Frei (of Chile), October 31, 1964. *Diário de Notícias*, November 4, 1964. *Diário Carioca*, October 23, 1964.

3. *O Globo*, October 13, 1964. *Jornal do Brasil*, May 9, 1964.

4. HSP, letter to Roberto Marinho, December 29, 1964.

5. Ibid. *Correio da Manhã*, April 3, 4, 1964. *O Jornal*, April 4, 5, 1964. HSP, letter to Embaixador do Paquistano, November 5, 1964.

6. "A Carta," *Jornal do Brasil*, July 12, 1964.

7. Ibid. *Jornal do Brasil*, December 24, 1964.

8. *Jornal do Brasil*, August 20, 1964.

9. *O Dia* (Rio de Janeiro), December 22, 1964.

10. HSP, letter to Marechal Humberto Castello Branco, July 17, 1964. Antônio Callado in *Jornal do Brasil*, July 12, 1964. *O Globo*, May 19, 1964. *Tribuna da Imprensa*, October 23, 1964. HSP, letter to Paulo Vial Corrêa, of *O Jornal*, September 19, 1964. HSP, letter to Roberto Marinho, December 29, 1964.

11. Augusto Frederico Schmidt in *O Globo*, November 17, December 22, 1964. HSP, letter to Roberto Marinho, November 17, 1964.

12. *O Jornal* and *O Globo*, December 22, 1964. HSP, letter to the nine Chinese, March 5, 1965.

13. Ibid. *Última Hora* and *O Dia*, December 22, 1964.
14. *O Jornal* and *Última Hora*, December 22, 1964.
15. *Última Hora* and *A Notícia* (Rio de Janeiro), December 22, 1964.
16. *Última Hora*, December 22, 1964. *Diário de Notícias*, December 23, 1964.
17. *Jornal do Brasil*, December 23, 24, 1964, February 5, 1965. HSP, letter to the nine Chinese, March 5, 1965. *Jornal do Commercio*, December 23, 24, 1964. *Diário de Notícias*, December 24, 1964.
18. *Tribuna da Imprensa*, December 23, 1964. HSP, telegram to Presidente Castello Branco, January 6, 1965. *Diário de Minas*, February 5, 1965.
19. *Folha de S. Paulo*, February 8, 1965. *Jornal do Brasil*, February 9, 10, April 8, 1965. *Correio da Manhã*, February 27, 1965. HSP, letters to the nine Chinese, February 27, March 5, 1965.
20. *Jornal do Brasil*, April 18, 23, 1965.
21. HSP, letter to the nine Chinese, November 26, 1965. *Jornal do Brasil*, October 9, 1965.

4. LAWYER FOR MIGUEL ARRAES (1964–1965)

1. Adirson de Barros, *Ascensão e Queda de Miguel Arraes* (Rio de Janeiro: Editôra Equador, 1965), pp. 153–162.
2. Jardel Noronha de Oliveira and Odaléa Martins, *Os IPMS e o Habeas Corpus no Supremo Tribunal Federal* (São Paulo: Sugestões Literárias, 1967), vol. 2, pp. 457–466.
3. Ibid., vol. 2, p. 459. *Jornal do Brasil*, March 30, April 1, 1965. *O Globo*, March 31, 1965.
4. *O Estado de S. Paulo*, April 22, 25, 1965. HSP, letter to General Edson de Figueiredo, April 23, 1965. HSP, telegrams to A. Ribeiro da Costa and President Castello Branco, April 24, 1965.
5. *O Estado de S. Paulo*, April 22, 23, 24, 1965. Paulo Guerra, interview, Brasília, November 11, 1965. HSP, letter to (Gustavo) Corção, April 30, 1965. Gustavo Corção, letter to HSP, Rio de Janeiro, May 2, 1965 (in HSP papers).
6. HSP, telegrams to President Castello Branco and A. Ribeiro da Costa, April 26, 1965. *Jornal do Brasil*, April 27, 1965.
7. *Jornal do Brasil*, May 9, 11, 1965.
8. HSP, telegram to A. Ribeiro da Costa, May 10, 1965. HSP, letter to Embaixador do Chile, May 12, 1965. *Jornal do Brasil*, May 11, 1965.
9. *Jornal do Brasil*, May 11, 15, 16, 1965. *O Estado de S. Paulo*, April 23, 25, 1965. HSP, letter to Embaixador do México, May 12, 1965.
10. HSP, letter to José and Antônio Arraes, May 18, 1965. HSP, letters to Embaixador do Chile, May 12, 17, 1965. *Jornal do Brasil*, May 29, 1965. HSP, *Lições de Liberdade*, 2nd ed. (Belo Horizonte: Universidade Católica de Minas Gerais and Editora Comunicação, May 1978), pp. 81–84. (The first edition was published in 1977.)
11. *Jornal do Brasil*, May 29, 1965. HSP, letter to José and Antônio Arraes, May 18, 1965. HSP, letter to Embaixador do Chile, Hector Correia, May 25, 1965.

12. *Jornal do Brasil,* May 21, 1965.
13. Ibid., May 25, 26, June 5, 1965.

5. SOBRAL'S CLASHES WITH GÉRSON DE PINA AND COSTA E SILVA (MID-1965)

1. *Tribuna da Imprensa,* June 4, 1965. HSP, letter to Roberto Marinho, June 11, 1965.
2. HSP, telegram to the director of *Diário de Notícias,* May 21, 1965. HSP, letters to (Emílio) Nina Ribeiro, May 22, 27, 1965.
3. Alceu Amoroso Lima, *Cartas do pai* (São Paulo: Instituto Moreira Salles, 2003), p. 501.
4. HSP, letter to Adaucto (Lucio Cardoso), May 22, 1965. HSP, letter to Carlos (Lacerda), May 22, 1965.
5. *Jornal do Brasil,* May 22, 1965. *Folha da Tarde* (Porto Alegre), May 25, 1965.
6. *Jornal do Brasil,* May 29, 1965.
7. Ibid., May 27, 29, 1965.
8. Ibid., May 29, 1965. *Correio Braziliense,* May 30, 1965.
9. HSP, letter to Paulo Vial Corrêa (of *O Jornal*), May 31, 1965. HSP, letter to General Edson de Figueiredo, June 2, 1965. HSP, letter to M. F. do Nascimento Brito and Celso de Souza e Silva, June 2, 1965.
10. *Tribuna da Imprensa,* June 4, 7, 1965.
11. HSP, letter to Carlos Infante Filho, June 11, 1965. HSP, letter to Roberto Marinho, June 11, 1965. HSP, telegram to Conceição da Costa Neves, July 1, 1965.
12. HSP, letters to Adaucto, July 13, 14, 1965.
13. HSP, letter to President Marechal Humberto de Alencar Castello Branco, March 29, 1965. *O Estado de S. Paulo,* February 19, 1965.
14. HSP, letter to Armando Falcão, July 14, 1965.
15. *Diário de S. Paulo* and *Jornal do Brasil,* July 18, 1965.
16. *Última Hora* (São Paulo edition), July 19, 1965.
17. HSP, telegram to General Costa e Silva, July 21, 1965. HSP, letter to Celso Kinjô, July 21, 1965.

6. LAWYER FOR MAURO BORGES (1964)

1. Mauro Borges entry in *Dicionário Histórico-Biográfico Brasileiro, 1930–1983.*
2. HSP, letter to Presidente Marechal Humberto Castello Branco, May 20, 1964.
3. Humberto Castello Branco in *Diário de Notícias,* November 21, 1964. Mauro Borges, *O Golpe em Goiás: História de uma grande triação* (Rio de Janeiro: Editôra Civilização Brasileira, 1965), pp. 156–157, 161, 190–215. *O Estado de S. Paulo,* November 6, 1964.
4. *O Estado de S. Paulo* and *Diário de Notícias,* November 14, 1964.
5. *Diário de Notícias,* November 14, 1964. *O Estado de S. Paulo,* October 27, November 17, 18, 1964. Borges, *O Golpe em Goiás,* pp. 153–155.

6. Noronha de Oliveira and Martins, *Os IPMS e o Habeas Corpus no Supremo Tribunal Federal*, vol. 1, p. 221. *Diário de Notícias*, November 15, 1964.

7. *Última Hora*, November 17, 1964. *A Gazeta* (São Paulo), November 18, 1964. *O Estado de S. Paulo*, November 15, 1964. Robert W. Dean, telegram from Brasília to Secretary of State, November 16, 1964, in National Security Files, LBJ Library, Austin, Texas. Borges, *O Golpe em Goiás*, pp. 151, 161–165.

8. *A Gazeta* (São Paulo), November 18, 1964. *Diário de Notícias*, November 19, 1964.

9. *Diário de Notícias*, November 20, 21, 22, 1964. *Última Hora*, November 17, 1964.

10. Noronha de Oliveira and Martins, *Os IPMS e o Habeas Corpus no Supremo Tribunal Federal*, vol. 1, pp. 212–271. *Diário de Notícias*, November 24, 1964. *O Estado de S. Paulo*, November 24, 25, 1964.

11. Noronha de Oliveira and Martins, *Os IPMS e o Habeas Corpus no Supremo Tribunal Federal*, vol. 1, pp. 212–271. Borges, *O Golpe em Goiás*, p. 172. *Diário de Notícias*, November 24, 1964.

12. *Diário de Notícias*, November 24, 1964.

13. Carlos de Meira Matos, interviews, Washington, D.C., January 5, August 2, 1977. Viana Filho, *O Governo Castelo Branco*, p. 100. *O Estado de S. Paulo*, December 1, 1964. Ernâni do Amaral Peixoto, interview, Rio de Janeiro, December 20, 1975.

14. *Diário de Notícias*, December 1, 1964. *O Globo*, December 4, 16, 1964.

15. *Jornal do Brasil*, December 8, 1964.

16. *O Globo*, December 16, 1964. *Diário de Notícias*, December 29, 1964.

17. HSP, letter to Iris Resende, December 20, 1964. *O Globo*, December 16, 1964. *Diário de Notícias*, December 29, 1964.

18. *O Estado de S. Paulo*, January 5, 1965. Ronald M. Schneider, *The Political System of Brazil* (New York and London: Columbia University Press, 1971), p. 148.

19. HSP, letter to Roberto Marinho, February 2, 1965.

7. JOSÉ APARECIDO'S LEGAL BATTLE AGAINST HIS *CASSAÇÃO*
(MAY 1964)

1. José Aparecido entry in *Dicionário Histórico-Biográfico Brasileiro, 1930-1983*. PMDB campaign brochure, "José Aparecido Para Deputado Federal, Tancredo Para Governador, Itamar Para Senador" (1982). Amigos do Deputado José Aparecido de Oliveira, "Documento Histórico (e Heróico) dos Tempos do Arbítrio" (1985).

2. Amigos do Deputado José Aparecido de Oliveira, "Documento Histórico (e Heróico)."

3. PMDB campaign brochure (1982). Tito Lívio Cavalcanti de Medeiros, letter to JWFD, Rio de Janeiro, September 26, 2002. José Aparecido de Oliveira, interview with Daphne F. Rodger, Rio de Janeiro, October 26, 2001.

4. José Aparecido de Oliveira, interview with Daphne F. Rodger, October 26, 2001.

5. Amigos do Deputado José Aparecido de Oliveira, "Documento Histórico (e Heróico)."

6. Ibid.

7. José Aparecido de Oliveira, interview with Daphne F. Rodger, October 26, 2001.

8. GUSTAVO BORGES DENOUNCES SUPRA AND PINHEIRO NETO (1964–1965)

1. João Pinheiro Neto entry in *Dicionário Histórico-Biográfico Brasileiro, 1930–1983*.

2. Ibid. João Pinheiro Neto, petition to Georgenor Acylino de Lima Torres, Rio de Janeiro, June 3, 1964 (in HSP papers). *Última Hora*, June 5, 1964.

3. João Pinheiro Neto, petition to Georgenor Acylino de Lima Torres, Rio de Janeiro, June 13, 1964 (in HSP papers).

4. HSP, letter to Virgílio, June 6, 1964. HSP, letter to João Pinheiro Neto, October 31, 1964.

5. HSP, letter to João Pinheiro Neto, November 2, 1964.

6. Razões Finais de João Pinheiro Neto, n.d. (in HSP papers).

7. Ibid.

8. Ibid. João Pinheiro Neto, interview, Rio de Janeiro, October 8, 1968.

9. *Diário de Notícias*, November 27, 1964.

10. João Pinheiro Neto entry in *Dicionário Histórico-Biográfico Brasileiro, 1930–1983*. HSP, letters to João Pinheiro Neto, February 5, April 6, 1965.

11. HSP, letter to João Pinheiro Neto, April 6, 1965.

9. MORE MINAS CLIENTS AND A CONFLICT WITH MAGALHÃES PINTO ABOUT CARONE (1964–1965)

1. *Jornal do Brasil*, October 24, 30, 1965. *Diário da Tarde* (Belo Horizonte), November 17, 1964.

2. HSP, letter to Cicero Lage Pessoa, November 16, 1964. *Diário da Tarde* (Belo Horizonte), November 17, 1964.

3. *Jornal do Brasil*, October 30, 1965.

4. Ibid.

5. Clodsmith Riani entry in *Dicionário Histórico-Biográfico Brasileiro, 1930–1983*.

6. *O Estado de S. Paulo*, January 21, 1964. *Última Hora* (of São Paulo), February 26, 1964. Oscar Dias Corrêa, interview, Brasília, October 18, 1965.

7. *Jornal do Brasil*, February 4, 5, 6, 10, 1965.

8. HSP, letter to Jorge Carone Júnior, February 11, 1965.

9. *O Globo*, February 23, 1965. *Correio da Manhã* and *Tribuna da Imprensa*, February 24, 1965.

10. *Tribuna da Imprensa,* February 24, 1965.
11. Ibid. *Correio da Manhã,* February 24, 1965.
12. *A Gazeta* (São Paulo), February 25, 1965.
13. *Jornal do Commercio,* February 26, 1965.
14. Nísia Carone entry in *Dicionário Histórico-Biográfico Brasileiro, 1930–1983.*

10. A HABEAS CORPUS FOR JULIÃO (1965)

1. Francisco Julião entry in *Dicionário Histórico-Biográfico Brasileiro, 1930–1983. Última Hora,* June 5, 1964. *Jornal do Commercio,* November 7, 1964. Noronha de Oliveira and Martins, *Os IPMS e o Habeas Corpus no Supremo Tribunal Federal,* vol. 3, p. 713.
2. *Tribuna da Imprensa,* September 24, 1964. *Jornal do Commercio,* November 7, 1964.
3. *Jornal do Brasil,* April 11, 13, 29, 1965.
4. Ibid., May 20, 1965.
5. HSP, impetrante, Habeas Corpus No. 42,560, at vol. 3, pp. 707–713 of Noronha de Oliveira and Martins, *Os IPMS e o Habeas Corpus no Supremo Tribunal Federal.*
6. Ibid.
7. Ibid.
8. Julgamento, in Noronha de Oliveira and Martins, *Os IPMS e o Habeas Corpus no Supremo Tribunal Federal,* vol. 3, pp. 713–736.
9. Ibid.
10. Ibid.
11. Ibid.
12. Francisco Julião entry in *Dicionário Histórico-Biográfico Brasileiro, 1930–1983. Jornal do Brasil,* October 1, 1965.
13. HSP, letter to *Diário de Notícias,* October 1, 1965. *Jornal do Brasil,* October 3, 1965.
14. *Jornal do Brasil,* October 30, 1965.
15. Francisco Julião entry in *Dicionário Histórico-Biográfico Brasileiro, 1930–1983.*

11. ACCEPTING APPEALS TO DEFEND MARIGHELLA AND PRESTES (1964–1965)

1. Carlos Marighella entry in *Dicionário Histórico-Biográfico Brasileiro, 1930–1983.*
2. Carlos Marighella, *Por Que Resisti à Prisão* (Rio de Janeiro: Edições Contemporâneas, 1965).
3. Mário Magalhães, e-mail messages from Rio de Janeiro to JWFD, October 23, 2003, September 16, 2004.
4. HSP, habeas corpus petition to Rio de Janeiro Juiz de Direito da Vara Criminal, July 28, 1964.
5. HSP, letter to Valério Konder, January 16, 1965.

6. HSP, letter to Senador Luiz Carlos Prestes, August 20, 1965.

7. John W. F. Dulles, "The Brazilian Left: Efforts at Recovery, 1964–1970," in *The Communist Tide in Latin America*, ed. Donald L. Herman (*Texas Quarterly*, vol. 15, no. 1 [Spring 1972]), p. 148. Mário Magalhães, e-mail message from Rio de Janeiro to JWFD, September 23, 2004.

8. Luiz Carlos Prestes, *Carta ao Dr. Sobral Pinto* (twenty-eight-page booklet, n.p., 1966).

9. Dulles, "The Brazilian Left," p. 148.

12. STANDING UP FOR STUDENTS SUSPENDED FOR INDISCIPLINE (1964)

1. HSP, telegram to Flávio de Lacerda, July 24, 1962.

2. Raimundo Moniz de Aragão, interview, Rio de Janeiro, December 16, 1975. *Diário de Notícias*, October 24, 25, 1964.

3. HSP, letter to Fernando Barros, September 19, 1964.

4. Hélio Gomes in *Diário de Notícias*, October 28, 1964.

5. *Diário de Notícias*, October 21, 22, 1964.

6. Letter from HSP in *Diário de Notícias*, October 23, 1964.

7. "Memorial dos estudantes," in *Diário de Notícias*, October 23, 1964.

8. *Jornal do Brasil*, October 23, 27, 1964.

9. Ibid., October 27, 1964.

10. *Diário de Notícias*, October 30, 1964.

11. HSP, letter to Pedro Calmon, March 13, 1965.

13. SUZANO'S TEARFUL SPELL DURING SOBRAL'S DEFENSE OF THE "PEOPLE'S ADMIRALS" (1965)

1. Vladimir Palmeira, Luís Travassos, José Dirceu de Oliveira e Silva, and Antônio Ribas, interview in a São Paulo prison, November 21, 1968.

2. Cândido Aragão entry in *Dicionário Histórico-Biográfico Brasileiro, 1930–1983*. *Jornal do Brasil*, October 30, 1965.

3. Pedro Paulo de Araújo Suzano entry in *Dicionário Histórico-Biográfico Brasileiro, 1930–1983*.

4. *Última Hora*, November 10, 1965.

5. Ibid.

6. Ibid.

7. Ibid. Suzano entry in *Dicionário Histórico-Biográfico Brasileiro, 1930–1983*.

III. A Second Institutional Act Crushes Democracy (October 1965)

1. KUBITSCHEK RETURNS, IGNORING WARNINGS FROM SOBRAL AND OTHERS (OCTOBER 4, 1965)

1. *Jornal do Brasil*, January 20, 1965, and editorials, February 3, 11, March 9, 1965. *O Estado de S. Paulo*, February 12, 1965, and editorial, February 14, 1965. *O Globo*, editorial, March 24, 1965.

2. *Tribuna da Imprensa,* June 21, 22, 1965. *Jornal do Brasil,* June 21, 22, 23, 1965. *Diário Carioca,* June 24, 1965.

3. *O Globo,* September 9, 10, 11, 1965. Raphael de Almeida Magalhães, interviews, Rio de Janeiro, August 8, 1977, August 9, 1979.

4. HSP, letter to Carlos (Lacerda), September 23, 1965.

5. Amoroso Lima, *Cartas do pai,* p. 506. HSP, letter to (Gustavo) Corção, September 23, 1965.

6. *Tribuna da Imprensa,* August 10, 1965. *O Globo,* August 27, 1965. *Diário de Notícias,* September 8, 11, 1965. Sandra Cavalcanti, interview, Rio de Janeiro, August 8, 1977.

7. Ferdinando de Carvalho, interview, Curitiba, November 10, 1967.

8. *Jornal do Brasil,* September 24, October 1, 1965. *O Estado de S. Paulo,* September 29, 1965.

9. Cony, *JK: Memorial do Exílio,* p. 97. *Folha de S. Paulo,* October 5, 1965.

10. Heráclito Fontoura Sobral Pinto, interview, Rio de Janeiro, December 9, 1975.

11. *O Estado de S. Paulo,* October 3, 1965. HSP, telegram to Carlos Lacerda, October 3, 1965.

12. *Jornal do Brasil,* October 5, 6, 1965. *O Globo,* October 4, 1965. *Diário Carioca,* October 6, 1965. *Folha de S. Paulo,* October 5, 1965.

13. *Folha de S. Paulo,* October 5, 1965.

14. Raphael de Almeida Magalhães, interview, Rio de Janeiro, November 19, 1975. *Tribuna da Imprensa* (October 5, 1965) put the figure at 90 percent.

15. *O Estado de S. Paulo,* October 5, 1965. Aliomar Baleeiro, "Recordações do Presidente H. Castello Branco," typewritten manuscript, n.d., in possession of JWFD. Peri Constant Bevilacqua, interview, Rio de Janeiro, December 21, 1977. Álcio Barbosa da Costa e Silva, interview, Rio de Janeiro, July 15, 1977.

2. THE IPMS, SOBRAL TELLS CASTELLO, "MAKE KUBITSCHEK'S LIFE A HELL" (OCTOBER 4–15, 1965)

1. Cony, *JK: Memorial do Exílio,* p. 105.

2. *Folha de S. Paulo,* October 5, 1965.

3. *O Estado de S. Paulo,* October 6, 1965.

4. HSP, telegram to Presidente Castello Branco, October 6, 1965.

5. Ibid. HSP, telegrams to Joaquim Portella Ferreira Alves and Ferdinando de Carvalho, October 7, 1965.

6. Luís Viana Filho, telegram to HSP, in Cony, *JK: Memorial do Exílio,* pp. 108–109.

7. HSP, telegram to Presidente Castello Branco, October 11, 1965.

8. Rubem Braga, "Os IPMs e o Sr. Juscelino," *Diário de Notícias,* October 12, 1965.

9. HSP, telegram to Presidente Castello Branco, October 12, 1965. HSP, telegram to Luís Viana Filho, October 12, 1965, and letters to him, October 12, 16, 1965.

10. *O Estado de S. Paulo*, October 7, 9, 13, 14, 1965. Viana Filho, *O Governo Castelo Branco*, p. 160. *Jornal do Brasil*, October 14, 16, 1965. *O Globo*, October 9, 1965.

11. HSP, telegram to the PTB, October 11, 1965, and letter to Presidente Juscelino Kubitschek de Oliveira, October 11, 1965.

12. *Última Hora* and *Jornal do Brasil*, October 14, 1965. HSP, letter to Hermano Alves, October 16, 1965.

13. *A Gazeta Esportiva* (São Paulo), October 17, 1965. *Jornal do Brasil*, October 20, 1965.

14. *O Estado de S. Paulo*, October 14, 15, 1965. *Última Hora*, October 14, 1965. *Jornal do Brasil*, October 12, 14, 15, 1965.

3. TURNING TO THE SUPREME COURT FOR THE PROTECTION OF KUBITSCHEK (LATE OCTOBER 1965)

1. HSP, telegram to Ministro Amaral Peixoto, October 18, 1965.

2. *Jornal do Brasil*, October 20, 1965.

3. HSP, telegram to Ribeiro da Costa, October 20, 1965.

4. Transcript of tape of speech of Costa e Silva, Itapeva, São Paulo, October 22, 1965 (made available to JWFD by Álcio Costa e Silva, July 1977). *Jornal do Brasil* and *O Estado de S. Paulo*, October 24, 1965. HSP, telegram to General Costa e Silva, October 25, 1965.

5. HSP, telegrams to Juracy Magalhães and Mário Martins, October 20, 1965.

6. HSP, telegram to General Ururahy Terra, October 20, 1965. HSP, letter to Ferdinando de Carvalho, October 20, 1965.

7. *O Estado de S. Paulo*, October 23, 1965.

8. Reclamação No. 673 of September 16, 1965, signed by Cândido de Oliveira Neto, in Noronha de Oliveira and Martins, *Os IPMS e o Habeas Corpus no Supremo Tribunal Federal*, vol. 3, pp. 769–789.

9. Habeas-corpus n. 42.818, Impetrantes Dr. Heráclito Fontoura Sobral Pinto e Cândido de Oliveira Neto, October 19, 1965, signed by HSP, in Noronha de Oliveira and Martins, *Os IPMS e o Habeas Corpus no Supremo Tribunal Federal*, vol. 3, pp. 747–766.

10. *Jornal do Brasil*, October 23, 1965.

11. *Diário de Notícias*, October 24, 1965.

12. *O Estado de S. Paulo*, October 27, 1965.

13. Ibid. *Jornal do Brasil*, October 23, 1965.

14. *O Estado de S. Paulo*, October 27, 1965.

4. A NEW INSTITUTIONAL ACT ENDS DEMOCRACY (OCTOBER 27, 1965)

1. *Jornal do Brasil*, October 21, 25, 27, 1965.

2. HSP, telegram to Adaucto Lucio Cardoso, October 25, 1965. Juracy Magalhães, "Respostas do General Juracy Magalhães ao Professor John W. F. Dulles" (typewritten), Rio de Janeiro, December 3, 1974, p. 4.

3. HSP, telegrams to Juracy Magalhães, n.d. and October 27, 1965.

4. Viana Filho, *O Governo Castelo Branco*, p. 355. Carlos Castello Branco, *Os Militares no Poder: 1. Castelo Branco* (Rio de Janeiro: Editora Nova Fronteira, 1976), pp. 676–677.
5. Paulo Guerra, interview, Brasília, November 11, 1977.
6. *Jornal do Brasil*, October 28, 1965.
7. Ibid.
8. Afonso de Albuquerque Lima, interview, Rio de Janeiro, November 16, 1974.
9. *Jornal do Brasil*, January 5, 6, 1966. "Coisas da Política," *Jornal do Brasil*, November 18, 1965. CIA, Intelligence Information Cable, Brazil, November 26, 1965 (National Security Files, LBJ Library, Austin, Texas).

IV. The Last Months of 1965

1. SOBRAL RESIGNS AS IAB PRESIDENT (OCTOBER 28, 1965)

1. *Jornal do Brasil*, May 9, 1965.
2. Ibid., October 21, 1965.
3. Ibid., October 29, 1965.
4. Ibid. Instituto dos Advogados Brasileiros, *Instituto dos Advogados Brasileiros: 150 Anos de História, 1843–1993*, pp. 234–235.
5. Instituto dos Advogados Brasileiros, *Instituto dos Advogados Brasileiros: 150 Anos de História*, p. 235 and n. 7 on p. 269.

2. KUBITSCHEK LEAVES FOR THE UNITED STATES (NOVEMBER 10, 1965)

1. Prado Kelly entry in *Dicionário Histórico-Biográfico Brasileiro, 1930–1983*. HSP, letters to Prado Kelly and Carlos Medeiros, November 3, 1965. HSP, letter to Prado Kelly, November 5, 1965.
2. *O Globo*, November 3, 5, 1965.
3. Juracy Magalhães, telegram to HSP in *O Popular* (Goiás state), November 6, 1965.
4. HSP, telegram to Minister Juracy Magalhães, November 5, 1965.
5. *Jornal do Brasil*, November 7, 1965. Noronha de Oliveira and Martins, *Os IPMS e o Habeas Corpus no Supremo Tribunal Federal*, vol. 3, p. 789 (voto do julgamento). Bojunga, *JK: O artista do impossível*, p. 840.
6. Bojunga, *JK: O artista do impossível*, pp. 840–842. *Folha de S. Paulo*, November 11, 1965. *Última Hora*, November 10, 1965.
7. *O Dia* (Rio de Janeiro), November 11, 1965.
8. Ibid. *Folha de S. Paulo* and *O Globo*, November 11, 1965.
9. Cony, *JK: Memorial do Exílio*, p. 111.
10. HSP, telegram to Juracy Magalhães, November 12, 1965.
11. HSP, letter to Presidente Kubitschek, November 19, 1965.

3. A DISTURBANCE AT THE OPENING OF THE INTER-AMERICAN CONFERENCE (NOVEMBER 1965)

1. *Jornal do Brasil,* November 18, 1965.
2. Ibid., November 18, 19, 26, 1965. Carlos Heitor Cony, interview, Rio de Janeiro, December 15, 1977.
3. Cony, interview, December 15, 1977. *Jornal do Brasil,* November 20, 1965.
4. HSP, documents submitted to João Romeiro Neto, Relator do Habeas-Corpus 28.075, November 23, December 3, 1965 (in HSP papers).
5. HSP, telegram to Reni Rabelo, November 19, 1965.
6. *Jornal do Brasil,* November 20, 1965. HSP, letters to *Correio da Manhã* and *Jornal do Brasil,* November 20, 1965.
7. HSP, telegram to Luís Viana Filho, November 20, 1965.
8. *Jornal do Brasil,* November 25, 1965. HSP, telegram to Presidente Castello Branco, November 24, 1965.
9. Carlos Heitor Cony, interview, December 15, 1977. *Jornal do Brasil,* November 26, 1965.
10. HSP, documents submitted to João Romeiro Neto, November 23, December 3, 1965.
11. Cony, interview, December 15, 1977.
12. HSP, document to João Romeiro Neto, December 3, 1965.

4. CLOSING 1965 WITH A TRIBUTE TO SCHMIDT

1. HSP, letter to Raphael (de Almeida Magalhães), November 26, 1965.
2. HSP, letter to (Francisco) Negrão (de Lima), late November 1965 (date missing).
3. Ibid. HSP, letter to Negrão, December 4, 1965.
4. Ibid.
5. HSP, letter to Negrão, late November 1965.
6. HSP, letter to Juracy Magalhães, December 23, 1965. Alberto Venancio Filho, *Notícia Histórica da Ordem dos Advogados do Brasil (1930–1980)* (Rio de Janeiro: Conselho Federal da OAB, 1982), p. 136.
7. HSP, letter to (José) Ribeiro de Castro (Filho), December 31, 1965.
8. HSP, letters to General Aírton Salgueiro de Freitas, December 9, 10, 1965. HSP, letter to Fernando Velloso, December 9, 1965.
9. HSP, letter to Padre Emílio, November 13, 1965.
10. HSP, letter to Michael Krymchantowski, December 27, 1965.
11. HSP, letter to Magdalena, January 4, 1966.
12. HSP, Thoughts in Memory of Augusto Frederico Schmidt, Rio de Janeiro, December 31, 1965 (in HSP papers).

V. From Ato Three (1966) to Ato Five (1968)

1. OPPOSING INDIRECT GUBERNATORIAL ELECTIONS AND THE *CASSAÇÃO* OF ADEMAR DE BARROS (1966)

1. *Jornal do Commercio*, February 6, 1966.
2. *Diário de Notícias*, February 16, 1966.
3. Viana Filho, *O Governo Castello Branco*, p. 413. Mem de Sá, letter to Luís Viana Filho, Brasília, October 7, 1971 (copy in Paulo V. Castello Branco collection).
4. *Diário de S. Paulo*, March 29, 1966. HSP, letter to (Henrique) Hargreaves, February 28, 1970.
5. HSP, "Declaração feita aos jornalistas paulistas, na 2a Auditoria da 2a Região Militar, em São Paulo," n.d. (in HSP papers).
6. HSP, telegram to President Castello Branco (about Jaime de Azevedo Rodrigues), February 11, 1966. *Jornal do Brasil*, February 25, 1966 (about the IPM investigating the CNTI).
7. *Jornal do Brasil*, July 15, 17, 1966. *Folha de S. Paulo*, July 15, 1966. *Jornal do Brasil*, July 17, 1966.
8. *A Notícia* (Rio de Janeiro), November 23, 1966. *Diário de S. Paulo*, December 25, 1966.
9. *A Província do Pará*, August 4, 1966. *A Gazeta Esportiva* (São Paulo), *Última Hora*, and *Jornal do Brasil*, August 5, 1966. *Diário da Noite* (São Paulo) and *Jornal do Brasil*, August 6, 1966. Araken Távora, *O Advogado da Liberdade* (Rio de Janeiro: Editôra do Repórte, 1966), pp. 124–128.
10. *O Globo*, June 4, 1966. *Jornal do Brasil*, June 8, 9, 1966. *Última Hora*, September 3, 1966. *Diário da Noite*, August 6, 1966. "Coluna do Castello," *Jornal do Brasil*, June 4, 1966, and August 9, 1972.

2. ADVISING KUBITSCHEK TO RETURN ONLY AFTER MARCH 15, 1967 (1966)

1. Aliomar Baleeiro, "Recordações do Presidente H. Castello Branco."
2. HSP, telegram to Presidente Castello Branco, October 22, 1966.
3. HSP, telegram to Adaucto Lucio Cardoso, October 21, 1966. HSP, letter to Adaucto, October 24, 1966. HSP, letter to Alceu (Amoroso Lima), October 24, 1966.
4. HSP, letter to Presidente Juscelino Kubitschek de Oliveira, October 14, 1966. HSP in the *Tribuna da Imprensa*, October 7, 1966.
5. *Tribuna da Imprensa*, October 7, 1966. HSP, letter to Presidente Juscelino Kubitschek de Oliveira, November 19, 1966.
6. HSP, letter to Presidente Juscelino Kubitschek de Oliveira, November 19, 1966.
7. HSP, letter to Presidente Juscelino, December 22, 1966.
8. *O Dia* (São Paulo), July 16, 1967.
9. HSP and Cândido de Oliveira Neto, letter to Presidente Juscelino, January 21, 1967.
10. HSP, telegram to Marechal Castello Branco, March 6, 1967.

11. *O Estado de Minas,* February 27, 1968. *Jornal da Tarde* (São Paulo), March 15, 1967.

12. *Tribuna da Imprensa,* January 7, 1967.

3. WHILE KUBITSCHEK, BACK IN BRAZIL, IS THREATENED, HÉLIO FERNANDES IS INTERNED (1967)

1. *Folha de S. Paulo,* September 12, 1967.

2. HSP, letter to Dario (de Almeida Magalhães), March 31, 1967. HSP, letter to (José) Ribeiro de Castro (Filho), April 1, 1967.

3. HSP, letter to General Flávio Cassiano, May 22, 1967.

4. Hélio Fernandes in *Tribuna da Imprensa,* July 19, 1967. *O Estado de S. Paulo,* July 21, 22, 1967.

5. HSP, telegrams to Gama e Silva, July 22, 24, 1967.

6. Hélio Fernandes, *Recordações de um Desterrado em Fernando de Noronha* (Rio de Janeiro: Editora Tribuna da Imprensa, 1967), pp. 161–167, 235, 236, 242. Augusto César Muniz de Aragão entry in *Dicionário Histórico-Biográfico Brasileiro, 1930-1983.* HSP, telegram to General A. C. Moniz de Aragão, August 26, 1967. HSP, letter to Roberto Marinho, August 29, 1967. *Jornal do Brasil,* August 31, 1967. *Diário de Notícias* and *Jornal do Brasil,* November 23, 1967.

7. *O Globo,* September 5, 1967. *Jornal da Tarde* and *Folha de S. Paulo,* September 12, 1967. Cony, *JK: Memorial do Exílio,* pp. 128–129.

8. *Diário de S. Paulo,* January 21, 1968. *Diário de Minas* (Belo Horizonte), September 30, 1967.

9. *Última Hora* and *Folha da Tarde* (São Paulo), October 27, 1967.

4. THE STUDENT MOVEMENT IN THE FIRST HALF OF 1968

1. HSP, letters to Nelson Carneiro, June 15, 16, 1967.

2. HSP, letter to Victor (Nunes Leal), May 12, 1967. HSP, letter to Evandro (Lins e Silva), May 27, 1967.

3. HSP, letter to (Gustavo) Corção, April 24, 1967. HSP, letter to Virgílio Campos, October 25, 1967.

4. HSP, letter to José Bonifácio Diniz de Andrada, March 29, 1968.

5. Ibid.

6. *Última Hora, Jornal do Brasil,* and *Diário de Notícias,* March 29, 1968.

7. HSP, letter to José Bonifácio Diniz de Andrada, March 29, 1968. *Última Hora,* March 30, 1968.

8. HSP, letter to José Bonifácio Diniz de Andrada, March 29, 1968.

9. *O Estado de S. Paulo,* April 2, 3 (editorial), 1968. *Jornal do Brasil,* April 2, 1968. Poerner, *O Poder Jovem,* p. 366. *Tribuna da Imprensa,* April 3, 1968.

10. *Tribuna da Imprensa,* April 6, 1968.

11. *O Estado de S. Paulo,* April 2, 5, 1968.

12. Jayme Portella de Mello, *A Revolução e o Governo Costa e Silva* (Rio

de Janeiro: Guavira Editores, 1979), pp. 544, 545, 547. *O Estado de S. Paulo*, April 6, 7, 1968. *Jornal do Brasil*, April 4, 6, 1968. Zuenir Ventura, *1968: O Ano que não Terminou* (Rio de Janeiro: Editora Nova Fronteira, 1988), p. 129. *Folha de S. Paulo*, April 7, 1968.

13. HSP, letter to Dario (de Almeida Magalhães), April 22, 1968. *Última Hora* and *Diário de Notícias*, April 19, 1968. *Tribuna da Imprensa*, April 20, 1968.

14. *O Estado de S. Paulo*, May 3, 1968.

15. *Tribuna da Imprensa*, May 2, 1968.

16. Palácio São Joaquim, Rio de Janeiro, August 26, 1967, document naming HSP provisionally president of the Centro Dom Vital (in HSP papers). HSP, letters to Corção, June 6, 12, 1968.

5. THE FORMATION OF THE HUMAN RIGHTS COUNCIL AND THE DEFENSE OF MORE CLIENTS (SECOND HALF OF 1968)

1. *Jornal do Brasil*, July 23, 26, 27, 30, 1968. *O Estado de S. Paulo*, July 20, 1968. HSP, letter to Marechal Costa e Silva, July 30, 1968.

2. *Tribuna da Imprensa* and *Jornal do Brasil*, May 14, 1968.

3. *O Jornal*, August 16, 1968. HSP, letter to Josephat (Marinho), November 14, 1968.

4. HSP, letter to Danton Jobim, August 14, 1968. HSP, letter to Josephat (Marinho), November 14, 1968. HSP, letter to (José) Sette Câmara (Filho), September 6, 1968.

5. HSP, letter to Sette Câmara, September 6, 1968. HSP, letter to Mangabeira, October 24, 1968. HSP, telegram to Presidente Costa e Silva, October 28, 1968.

6. HSP, telegram to Almirante Rademaker, June 25, 1968. *O Globo*, June 27, 1968.

7. *Jornal do Brasil* and *Diário de Notícias*, July 20, 1968. *O País* (Rio de Janeiro), July 24, 25, 1968.

8. *Última Hora* and *O Dia* (São Paulo), July 30, 1968.

9. *Jornal do Brasil*, February 15, 16, 18, 1967. *Última Hora*, February 15, 1967, August 23, 1968.

10. *Última Hora*, January 12, 1968. *Jornal do Commercio, O Jornal,* and *Diário de Notícias*, October 13, 1968.

11. HSP, letters to Clodsmith Riani and (Henrique) Hargreaves, June 22, 1968.

12. HSP, letters to Paulo de Tarso (Santos), July 4, 5, 23, 26, December 6, 1968. HSP, letters to Maurício dos Santos, July 4, 23, 1968.

13. HSP, letter to Dario (de Almeida Magalhães), April 19, 1968. HSP, letter to (Henrique) Hargreaves, November 18, 1968. HSP, letter to Amaral Filho, November 30, 1968.

14. HSP, letters to Gilda (Sobral Pinto), August 7, 12, 1968, December 27, 1969. HSP, letter to Yedda, January 25, 1971.

6. INSTITUTIONAL ACT FIVE AND THE IMPRISONMENT OF SOBRAL (DECEMBER 1968)

1. HSP, letter to Olympio Mourão Filho, September 2, 1968.
2. HSP, letter to Olympio Mourão Filho, October 17, 1968.
3. *O Estado de S. Paulo* and *Correio da Manhã*, October 13, 1968. Aurélio de Lyra Tavares, message to Artur da Costa e Silva in Daniel Krieger, *Desde as Missões* (Rio de Janeiro: Livraria José Olympio Editora, 1976), pp. 328–329. Portella de Mello, *A Revolução e o Governo Costa e Silva*, p. 585.
4. HSP, telegram to Décio Miranda, October 11, 1968. HSP, telegram to Márcio Moreira Alves, October 28, 1968.
5. Carlos Castello Branco in *Jornal do Brasil*, December 11, 1968. *Cidade de Santos*, December 4, 1968.
6. *Última Hora*, November 18, 1968. *Gazeta de Notícias* (Rio de Janeiro), November 19, 1968.
7. *O Estado de S. Paulo*, November 30, 1968. *O Jornal*, December 3, 1968. *Última Hora*, December 6, 9, 1968.
8. Venancio Filho, *Notícia Histórica da Ordem dos Advogados do Brasil (1930–1980)*, pp. 140–143. *O Jornal*, December 8, 1968.
9. *O Popular* (Goiânia), December 14, 1968.
10. *Legislação Constitucional e Complementar* (Brasília: Senado Federal, Subsecretaria de Edições Técnicas, 1972), pp. 111–117 (Ato Institucional No. 5).
11. HSP, letter to Presidente (of the IAB), December 26, 1968, p. 2.
12. Ibid., pp. 3–4.
13. Ibid., p. 5.
14. Ibid., p. 6.
15. Sobral Pinto entry in *Dicionário Histórico-Biográfico Brasileiro, 1930–1983*.
16. HSP, letter to Presidente (of the IAB), December 26, 1968, p. 6.
17. Ibid., p. 7. *Última Hora*, December 20, 1968.
18. HSP, letter to Presidente (of the IAB), December 26, 1968, p. 8.
19. Bojunga, *JK: O artista do impossível*, pp. 865–866, 879, 882–885. Juscelino Kubitschek entry in *Dicionário Histórico-Biográfico Brasileiro, 1930–1983*.

VI. The Repression Reaches Its Pinnacle (1969–1971)

1. THE FORCED RETIREMENT OF THREE SUPREME COURT JUDGES (JANUARY 1969)

1. HSP, letter to (José) Ribeiro de Castro (Filho), January 4, 1969. HSP, letter to Thomas Leonardos, April 17, 1970.
2. Instituto dos Advogados Brasileiros, *Instituto dos Advogados Brasileiros: 150 Anos de História, 1843–1993*, p. 239. Hermann Assis Baeta *(coordenador)*, *História da Ordem dos Advogados do Brasil* (Brasília: Ordem dos Advogados do Brasil, 2003), vol. 7, pp. 52–53.

3. Conferência Nacional dos Bispos do Brasil entry in *Dicionário Histórico-Biográfico Brasileiro, 1930–1983*. HSP, letter to Dario (de Almeida Magalhães), February 24, 1969. HSP, letters to Ernâni Sátiro, February 24, 26, 1969.

4. HSP, letters to (José) Machado, Dario, and Tude de Lima Rocha, January 15, 1969.

5. Jefferson de Andrade, with collaboration of Joel Silveira, *Um Jornal Assassinado* (Rio de Janeiro: José Olympio Editora, 1991), pp. 188–190, 342–348. *Correio da Manhã* entry in *Dicionário Histórico-Biográfico Brasileiro, 1930–1983*. HSP, telegram to Professor Heleno Fragoso, November 22, 1969.

6. Antônio Gonçalves de Oliveira entry in *Dicionário Histórico-Biográfico Brasileiro, 1930–1983*. HSP, letters to Luiz Mendes de Moraes Neto and Dario, January 21, 1969. HSP, letters to Evandro (Lins e Silva), Hermes Lima, and Pery Bevilacqua, January 22, 1969.

7. Luís Gallotti entry in *Dicionário Histórico-Biográfico Brasileiro, 1930–1983*. HSP, letters to (Luís) Gallotti, January 22, 25, 28, 29, 1969.

8. Luís Gallotti entry in *Dicionário Histórico-Biográfico Brasileiro, 1930–1983*.

9. HSP, letter to three students, April 10, 1969.

10. HSP, letter to (Antônio Lara) Rezende, March 24, 1969.

11. HSP, letter to Antônio Carlos Elizalde Osório, March 20, 1969.

12. HSP, letter to Antônio Carlos E. Osório, April 2, 1969.

13. Assis Baeta *(coordenador)*, *História da Ordem dos Advogados do Brasil*, vol. 7, p. 28.

2. AN IPM INVESTIGATES THE BISHOP OF VOLTA REDONDA (LATE 1969)

1. HSP, letter to Bahia, August 15, 1969.

2. Artur Costa e Silva entry in *Dicionário Histórico-Biográfico Brasileiro, 1930–1983*.

3. HSP, letter to (José) Ribeiro de Castro (Filho), September 1, 1969.

4. Emílio Garrastazu Médici entry in *Dicionário Histórico-Biográfico Brasileiro, 1930–1983*. Thomas E. Skidmore, *The Politics of Military Rule in Brazil, 1964–85* (New York: Oxford University Press, 1988), p. 101.

5. HSP, telegrams to Alfredo Buzaid, November 12, December 3, 1969. HSP, letter to (Alfredo) Buzaid, February 13, 1970.

6. HSP, letter to João Portella Ribeiro Dantas, November 17, 1969. HSP, letters to Dario (de Almeida Magalhães), November 18, 25, 1969.

7. HSP, letters to Norma Riani and Bento, October 14, 1969.

8. HSP, letters to Dom Waldyr (Calheiros de Novais), December 6, 10, 1969. HSP, letters to (Nelson Barbosa) Sampaio and Orisis (Josefeen), December 10, 1969. HSP, letter to Nuncio Umberto Mozzoni, n.d.

9. HSP, letter to Nuncio Umberto Mozzoni, n.d. HSP, letters to Sampaio and Orisis, December 19, 1969. HSP, letter to Dom Waldyr, December 20, 1969.

10. HSP, letter to Eminência (Jaime Câmara), February 21, 1970.

3. PROMINENT RIO LAWYERS ARE AMONG THE IMPRISONED (NOVEMBER 1970)

1. Doris Reis Ferreira, telegram to HSP, n.d. (in HSP papers). HSP, letters to Tenente Brigadeiro Armando Perdigão, January 16, 19, 1970. HSP, letters to (Alfredo) Buzaid and Laudo (Camargo), February 13, 1970. Assis Baeta (coordenador), História da Ordem dos Advogados do Brasil, vol. 7, p. 33.
2. Jornal do Commercio, May 23, 1970. HSP, letter to Dario (de Almeida Magalhães), July 1, 1970. HSP, letter to Callado, May 18, 1970. HSP, interview, Veja, July 10, 1970.
3. HSP, letters to Tito (Lívio Cavalcanti de Medeiros), May 22, June 17, 1970.
4. Skidmore, The Politics of Military Rule in Brazil, 1964–85, p. 112.
5. HSP, letter to Filinto Müller, November 30, 1970.
6. Skidmore, The Politics of Military Rule in Brazil, 1964–85, p. 114.
7. Heleno Cláudio Fragoso, Advocacia da Liberdade (Rio de Janeiro: Forense, 1984), pp. 13, 148. Assis Baeta (coordenador), História da Ordem dos Advogados do Brasil, vol. 7, pp. 34–35.
8. Fragoso, Advocacia da Liberdade, p. 147.
9. HSP, letter to (José) Ribeiro de Castro (Filho), December 15, 1970.
10. HSP, letter to Ribeiro de Castro, November 27, 1970. Assis Baeta (coordenador), História da Ordem dos Advogados do Brasil, vol. 7, pp. 37, 52–53.
11. HSP, letter to Thomas Leonardos, April 17, 1970.

4. SOBRAL, THE BRAZILIAN PRESIDENCY DECIDES, IS AFFLICTED BY SENILITY (JUNE 1971)

1. A Notícia (Rio de Janeiro), July 5, 1971.
2. Tribuna da Imprensa, May 26, 1971. Jornal do Brasil, May 29, June 2, 1971. O Estado (Fortaleza), May 31, 1971.
3. HSP, letter to Gastão Ribeiro, May 26, 1971. Diário de Notícias and Jornal do Brasil, June 2, 1971.
4. HSP, letter to General Emílio Garrastazu Médici, June 18, 1971.
5. HSP, letter to General Emílio Garrastazu Médici, June 28, 1971.
6. Nehemias Gueiros, "Sobral Pinto e a Medalha Rui Barbosa," Revista da Ordem dos Advogados do Brasil, ano 4, vol. 4, no. 8 (Brasília, January–April 1972), pp. 12–18.
7. Ibid., pp. 18–37. HSP, letter to Nehemias Gueiros, March 3, 1971.
8. HSP, letter to Nehemias (Gueiros), August 21, 1971. HSP, telegram to Professor Cândido Marinho da Rocha, October 27, 1971.

5. A TRIP TO EUROPE AND RECEIPT OF THE RUY BARBOSA MEDAL (LATE 1971)

1. Correio da Manhã entry in Dicionário Histórico-Biográfico Brasileiro, 1930–1983. Jefferson de Andrade, Um Jornal Assassinado, p. 299.

2. HSP, letter to Ruth (Sobral Pinto Salazar), March 11, 1971.

3. HSP, letters to Dario (de Almeida Magalhães) and (José) Ribeiro de Castro (Filho), July 8, 1971.

4. HSP, letter to Elza (de Almeida Magalhães), October 23, 1971. HSP, letter to Alceu (Amoroso Lima), September 9, 1971.

5. HSP, letter to Eminência (Eugênio Sales), September 18, 1971. HSP, letter to Monsenhor Sebastiani, December 2, 1971.

6. HSP, letter to Orlando, October 21, 1971.

7. Ibid. HSP, memorandum, "Rome, October 1," sent to Dario de Almeida Magalhães. HSP, letters to (José) Barretto (Filho) and Orlando, October 20, 1971.

8. HSP, letter to Barretto, October 20, 1971.

9. Dario de Almeida Magalhães, "Um Paladino da Liberdade e da Justiça," *Digesto Econômico* (São Paulo), no. 196 (July–August 1967), pp. 136–142, quoted by Nehemias Gueiros, on pp. 24–27 of *Revista da Ordem dos Advogados do Brasil*, ano 4, vol. 4, no. 8 (Brasília, January–April 1972).

10. "Sobral Pinto Agradece," on pp. 38–56 in above-mentioned *Revista*. See p. 39 for statements by Ruy Barbosa.

11. Ibid., pp. 49–51, 53.

12. Venancio Filho, *Notícia Histórica da Ordem dos Advogados do Brasil (1930–1980)*, p. 155.

VII. The Repression Continues (1972–1977)

1. THE SOBRALS' FIFTIETH WEDDING ANNIVERSARY (1972)

1. *Folha de S. Paulo*, March 3, 1972.

2. Juscelino Kubitschek, letter to HSP, Rio de Janeiro, February 9, 1972 (in HSP papers).

3. Ibid.

4. *Politika* (Rio de Janeiro weekly of 1971–1974; clipping received without date), pp. 16–18.

5. Ibid.

2. PERSUADING THE OAB NOT TO WITHDRAW FROM THE CDDPH (AUGUST–SEPTEMBER 1973)

1. "Sobral faz duas cartas a Neves" (in periodical of the Ordem dos Advogados do Brasil, February 1973). Venancio Filho, *Notícia Histórica da Ordem dos Advogados do Brasil (1930–1980)*, p. 159. Assis Baeta *(coordenador)*, *História da Ordem dos Advogados do Brasil*, vol. 7, p. 53.

2. Venancio Filho, *Notícia Histórica da Ordem dos Advogados do Brasil (1930–1980)*, p. 155. HSP, letter to (Alfredo) Buzaid, September 3, 1973.

3. *Jornal do Brasil*, September 18, 1973. *Tribuna da Imprensa* and *Jornal da Tarde* (São Paulo), September 29, 1973.

4. HSP in *O Diário* (Ribeirão Preto), August 30, 1973.

5. *Jornal da Tarde*, September 29, 1973.

6. Ibid. *Tribuna da Imprensa*, September 29, 1973.

7. Venancio Filho, *Notícia Histórica da Ordem dos Advogados do Brasil (1930-1980)*, p. 160. HSP, letter to Valmir Catão, November 9, 1981. Caio Mário da Silva Pereira quoted in Assis Baeta *(coordenador)*, *História da Ordem dos Advogados do Brasil*, vol. 7, p. 59.

3. SOBRAL, IRRITATED, LEAVES THE FIFTH OAB CONFERENCE (AUGUST 1974)

1. *Diário de Notícias* (Porto Alegre) and *Correio do Povo* (Porto Alegre), October 30, 1973.

2. *Diário de Notícias* (Rio de Janeiro), November 6, 1973.

3. Ibid.

4. Academia Brasileira de Letras, Sessão do dia 5.11.73, in HSP papers.

5. Adauto Lúcio Cardoso entry in *Dicionário Histórico-Biográfico Brasileiro, 1930-1983*. *Diário de Notícias* (Rio de Janeiro), July 21, 1974.

6. *O Globo*, July 24, 1974. *Jornal da Tarde* (São Paulo), August 17, 1974.

7. *Jornal da Tarde*, August 17, 1974. HSP, letter to Júlio (Fernando Toledo de) Teixeira, August 21, 1974, apologizing.

8. *Jornal da Tarde*, August 17, 1974. *Última Hora* (Rio de Janeiro), August 19, 1974.

9. *Última Hora*, August 19, 1974. *A Tarde* (Salvador), September 12, 1974.

10. *Jornal do Commercio* and *Última Hora*, March 18, 1975.

11. HSP, letter to Caio Mário (da Silva Pereira), March 17, 1975.

4. A STRONGER MDB BUT "RULE BY LAW IS STILL A MERE HOPE" (1974-1975)

1. Skidmore, *The Politics of Military Rule in Brazil, 1964-85*, p. 170. *Diário do Congresso Nacional*, October 18, 1974, pp. 8300-8301.

2. Skidmore, *The Politics of Military Rule in Brazil, 1964-85*, pp. 172-173.

3. "Coluna do Castello," *Jornal do Brasil*, December 24, 1974.

4. *Folha da Tarde* (São Paulo) and *O Estado de S. Paulo*, May 29, 1975.

5. *Jornal da Tarde*, July 28, 1975.

6. Skidmore, *The Politics of Military Rule in Brazil, 1964-85*, pp. 127-128. *Folha de S. Paulo*, December 15, 1977. *Jornal do Brasil*, August 14, 1977.

7. HSP, letter to President Ernesto Geisel, November 7, 1975, in Sobral Pinto, *Lições de Liberdade*, 2nd ed., pp. 212-216.

8. Universidade Católica de Minas Gerais, Resolução No. 04/75, and Regulamento da Medalha do Mérito Sobral Pinto (copies in papers of JWFD). *O Estado de Minas*, December 11, 12, 1975.

9. Ordem dos Advogados do Brasil, *Entrega da Medalha Rui Barbosa ao Advogado Dario de Almeida Magalhães* (Rio de Janeiro: Jet Press, n.d.). *Diário de Notícias*, December 20, 1975.

5. DEFENDING OSWALDO PACHECO (1976)

1. Skidmore, *The Politics of Military Rule in Brazil, 1964–85*, pp. 180, 206.

2. Ibid., pp. 177, 184. *O Estado de S. Paulo*, October 9, 1976.

3. *Folha de S. Paulo*, October 14, 1976. HSP, letters to Armando Falcão, October 11, 1976, and to General Ernesto Geisel, October 22, 1976, in Sobral Pinto, *Lições de Liberdade*, 2nd ed., pp. 236–239.

4. *O Estado de S. Paulo*, December 12, 1976. *Diário do Grande ABC* (Santo André, São Paulo), December 14, 1976.

5. *O Liberal* (Belém), August 24, 1976.

6. *Jornal do Brasil*, December 16, 1976.

7. *O Estado de S. Paulo*, May 28, 1977.

8. *Diário Popular* (São Paulo), November 20, 1975. *Diário da Tarde* (Belo Horizonte), December 15, 1977. Oswaldo Pacheco entry in *Dicionário Histórico-Biográfico Brasileiro, 1930–1983*.

9. HSP, "Razões de Apelação de Oswaldo Pacheco Silva," São Paulo, February 5, 1976, in Sobral Pinto, *Lições de Liberdade*, 2nd ed., pp. 217–232.

10. Ibid.

11. *O Globo* and *Folha de S. Paulo*, December 15, 1977.

6. GEISEL'S "APRIL PACKAGE" AND THE LEGALIZATION OF DIVORCE (1977)

1. Ernesto Geisel quoted in HSP, letter to General Ernesto Geisel, March 29, 1977.

2. HSP, letter to Ernesto Geisel, March 29, 1977. HSP, letter to Dario (de Almeida Magalhães), April 4, 1977. HSP in *Pasquim* (Rio de Janeiro magazine), April 29–May 5, 1977.

3. Ernesto Geisel entry in *Dicionário Histórico-Biográfico Brasileiro, 1930–1983*.

4. *Luta Democrática* (Rio de Janeiro) and *Cidade de Santos*, April 20, 1977.

5. *Jornal do Brasil*, April 20, 1977.

6. Roberto Sobral Pinto Ribeiro, e-mail message from Rio de Janeiro to JWFD, Rio de Janeiro, August 17, 2000.

7. *O Estado de S. Paulo*, June 22, 1977. HSP, letter to Tito, Jarbas, Eny, and Julieta, June 16, 1977.

8. *O Estado de S. Paulo*, June 22, 1977.

9. *Jornal do Brasil*, June 22, 1977. "A história desarquivada," *Revista Época* (São Paulo), November 8, 1999. *O Globo*, June 21, 1977.

10. Petrônio Portela entry in *Dicionário Histórico-Biográfico Brasileiro, 1930–1983*.

11. *Jornal de Brasília*, December 18, 1977.

12. *Jornal do Brasil*, August 14, 1977. *Folha de S. Paulo* and *O Estado de S. Paulo*, December 15, 1977.

13. *O Estado de S. Paulo*, December 15, 1977. Skidmore, *The Politics of Military Rule in Brazil, 1964-85*, p. 130.

14. HSP, letter to (Luís) Gallotti, December 26, 1977.

VIII. *Abertura* (1978-1985)

1. GEISEL REFORMS THE CONSTITUTION AND MAKES GENERAL FIGUEIREDO HIS SUCCESSOR (1978)

1. *O Globo*, December 27, 1977, February 10, November 14, 1978. *Última Hora*, December 28, 1977. *Jornal do Brasil*, June 21, 1978.

2. *Última Hora* and *Jornal do Brasil*, July 7, 1978. *Jornal do Brasil*, September 26, 1978.

3. *Coojornal* (of the Cooperative of Journalists of Porto Alegre), vol. 3, no. 24 (January 1978). *Jornal do Brasil*, January 31, 1978. *Folha de S. Paulo*, March 14, 1978.

4. *O Estado de Minas* and *Diário de Minas*, February 19, 1978. *Jornal do Brasil*, June 14, 1978.

5. Petrônio Portela entry in *Dicionário Histórico-Biográfico Brasileiro, 1930-1983*.

6. HSP, "Parecer," July 5, 1978 (in HSP papers). *Folha de S. Paulo, Jornal do Commercio, Última Hora, Jornal do Brasil*, and *O Estado de S. Paulo*, July 6, 1978.

7. *Folha de S. Paulo* and *O Estado de S. Paulo*, July 1, 1978.

8. Skidmore, *The Politics of Military Rule in Brazil, 1964-85*, pp. 202-203. *A Gazeta* (Vitória), December 8, 1978.

9. *O Estado de S. Paulo*, December 9, 1978.

10. *A Tribuna* (Vitória), December 8, 9, 1978. *A Gazeta* (Vitória), December 8, 1978.

11. *Jornal do Brasil*, September 17, 1978.

12. *A Crítica* (Manaus), August 12, 13, 1978.

13. *A Gazeta* (Vitória), December 8, 1978. *A Tribuna* (Vitória), December 8, 9, 1978. *O Estado de S. Paulo*, December 9, 1978. *Jornal de Brasília*, December 9, 10, 1978.

14. *Última Hora*, December 13, 1978. *Folha de S. Paulo*, December 13, 16, 1978. *O Globo*, December 16, 1978.

2. SOBRAL PINTO, BRAZIL'S "INTELLECTUAL" OF 1978 (1979)

1. HSP, "Discurso pronunciado 25 de Maio de 1979 na Sessão Solene da União Brasileira de Escritores, São Paulo" (in HSP papers).

2. *Jornal do Brasil*, January 31, 1978.

3. Signature sheets on behalf of competitors for O Intelectual do Ano, mostly dated January 23, 1979; sheet of Sobral Pinto backers is dated January 30 (in HSP papers).

4. *Diário de S. Paulo*, March 11, 1979. *Folha de S. Paulo*, March 13, 14, 1979.

5. Ibid. Herman Lima, *História da Caricatura no Brasil* (Rio de Janeiro:

Livraria José Olympio Editôra, 1963), vol. 4, pp. 1362–1372. *Última Hora* (São Paulo), March 14, 1979.

6. *Jornal do Brasil*, March 8, 1980.

7. *Folha de S. Paulo*, February 17, 27, March 14, 1979. *Diário de S. Paulo*, March 2, 1979. *Diário Popular* (São Paulo), February 21, 1979.

8. *Folha de S. Paulo*, March 13, 1979. *Diário de S. Paulo*, March 2, 1979. *Jornal do Commercio*, March 10, 1979.

9. *Jornal do Commercio*, March 10, 1979. *Diário Popular* (São Paulo), March 16, 1979. *Última Hora* (São Paulo), March 14, 1979.

10. *Última Hora* (São Paulo), March 14, 1979. Speech of Álvaro Valle in Sobral Pinto, *Por que defendo os Comunistas* (Belo Horizonte: Universidade Católica de Minas Gerais and Editora Comunicação, 1979), p. 13. Josué Guimarães in *Folha de S. Paulo*, March 14, 1979.

11. HSP in *Jornal do Brasil* (interview with Cora Rónai), April 21, 1979. *Folha de S. Paulo*, March 14, 1979. HSP, "Discurso pronunciado 25 de Maio de 1979."

12. Tristão de Athayde (Alceu Amoroso Lima) in *Folha de S. Paulo*, October 11, 1979.

13. *Folha da Tarde* (São Paulo), August 31, 1979. *O Liberal* (Belém), September 19, 1979. *Jornal do Brasil*, September 26, 1979.

14. *Zero Hora, Correio do Povo, Folha da Tarde* (all three of Porto Alegre), and *O Globo*, September 18, 1979.

15. *O Globo*, March 29, 1979. *Shopping News* (São Paulo), November 11, 1979.

3. *ABERTURA*, FURTHER ADVANCED BY AMNESTY (AUGUST 1979)

1. HSP in *Jornal do Brasil* (interview with Cora Rónai), April 21, 1979.

2. Ibid.

3. Ibid. *A Tribuna* (Niterói), March 29, 1979.

4. Skidmore, *The Politics of Military Rule in Brazil, 1964–85*, pp. 217–218. *Folha da Tarde*, August 31, 1979.

5. *Folha da Tarde* (São Paulo), August 31, 1979. *O Globo*, October 15, 1979. Roberto Sobral Pinto Ribeiro, e-mail message from Rio de Janeiro to JWFD, August 30, 2005.

6. *Folha de S. Paulo* and *Jornal do Brasil*, October 21, 1979. Roberto Sobral Pinto Ribeiro, e-mail message from Rio de Janeiro to JWFD, August 30, 2005.

4. SOBRAL, OPPONENT OF LIBERATION THEOLOGY, IS HONORED BY THE POPE (1980–1981)

1. HSP, Aula Magna na PUC (12 de março de 1980), in Sobral Pinto, *Teologia da Libertação* (Rio de Janeiro: Editora Lidador, 1984), pp. 72–86.

2. HSP, letter to Eminência (Vicente Scherer), n.d. (September 1981).

3. *Diário da Tarde* (Belo Horizonte) and *O Dia*, March 15, 1980. *Jornal do Brasil*, March 14, 15, 1980.

4. *Tribuna da Imprensa*, March 14, 1980.

5. HSP, letter to Modesto da Silveira, June 26, 1981. *O Globo*, March 14, 1980.

6. *O Globo*, March 14, 1980.

7. *IstoÉ* (São Paulo magazine), March 20, 1996. Skidmore, *The Politics of Military Rule in Brazil, 1964–85*, pp. 227–228.

8. Venancio Filho, *Notícia Histórica da Ordem dos Advogados do Brasil (1930–1980)*, pp. 226–227.

9. Skidmore, *The Politics of Military Rule in Brazil, 1964–85*, pp. 227–228.

10. HSP, letter to Eminência (Eugênio Sales), n.d. (March 1981).

11. *Jornal do Brasil*, April 6, 1980. HSP, letter to (Henrique) Hargreaves, May 18, 1981.

12. HSP, letter to Hargreaves, May 18, 1981.

13. HSP, letter to Eminência (Vicente Scherer), n.d. (September 1981).

14. HSP, letter to Ariovaldo Bonas, Chefe de Reportagem, *IstoÉ*, November 27, 1981.

15. HSP, letter to (Emílio) Ippolito, July 16, 1980.

16. HSP, speech of acceptance of the papal award, Palácio São Joaquim, Rio de Janeiro, June 25, 1981 (in HSP papers). *Jornal do Brasil*, February 17, 1981.

17. Sandra Cavalcanti in *Última Hora*, February 18, 1981. HSP, letter to Tito Lívio (Cavalcanti de Medeiros), February 25, 1981.

18. *O Dia* and *Última Hora*, June 26, 1981. HSP, speech of acceptance of the papal award, June 25, 1981.

5. *ABERTURA* REMAINS INCOMPLETE (1981–1982)

1. "Manifesto," February 24, 1981, signed by Heráclito Fontoura Sobral Pinto and José Ribeiro de Castro Filho (in HSP papers). Assis Baeta *(coordenador)*, *História da Ordem dos Advogados do Brasil*, vol. 7, p. 119. *Folha de S. Paulo*, April 2, 1981.

2. *Folha de S. Paulo*, August 12, September 6, 1981.

3. HSP, letter to Valmir Catão, November 9, 1981.

4. *O Estado de S. Paulo, O Estado de Minas, Folha de S. Paulo, Jornal de Minas, Jornal de Brasília*, December 15, 1981.

5. *Folha de S. Paulo*, December 15, 16, 1981.

6. *A Tribuna* (Santos), February 26, 1981.

7. *Folha de S. Paulo*, January 1, 1982. *Diário Popular*, January 10, 1982.

8. *Tribuna da Imprensa*, April 6, 1982. *Folha de S. Paulo* and *Jornal de Brasília*, June 29, 1982.

9. *Jornal do Commercio* and *Correio Braziliense*, July 13, 1982.

10. *Folha de Goiáz* (Goiânia), August 26, 1982. *O Globo*, August 27, 1982.

11. *Folha de S. Paulo*, July 27, 1982.

12. *Diário Oficial* of the Brazilian government, July 30, 1982. *Tribuna da Imprensa*, July 24, 1982.

13. *Cidade de Santos*, November 6, 1982.

6. HONORS HEAPED ON THE NINETY-YEAR-OLD SOBRAL (LATE 1983)

1. Assis Baeta (coordenador), História da Ordem dos Advogados do Brasil, vol. 7, pp. 129–138, 158–161.
2. O Globo, May 31, 1983.
3. Assis Baeta (coordenador), História da Ordem dos Advogados do Brasil, vol. 7, pp. 135–136, 132.
4. Jornal do Brasil and O Fluminense (Niterói), August 16, 1983.
5. Última Hora, September 30, 1983. O Globo and Correio Braziliense, November 5, 1983.
6. O Globo, November 5, 1983 (article by Márcia Cezimbra).
7. Folha de S. Paulo, November 6, 1983.
8. Ibid. O Dia, November 6, 1983. Carlos Drummond de Andrade, letter to HSP, date not shown in copy in e-mail, "A Vida de Sobral Pinto," from http://www.vereadoramarilio.hpg.ig.com.br/vida.htm.
9. Jornal do Brasil, November 8, 1983.
10. Folha de S. Paulo, O Estado de Minas, and Jornal de Brasília, November 12, 1983.
11. Jornal de Brasília and Correio Braziliense, November 25, 1983. (Name of "Pelé": Edson Arantes do Nascimento.)
12. Jornal de Brasília, November 25, 1983.
13. O Dia, November 26, 1983. Correio Braziliense, November 28, 1983.
14. O Liberal (Belém), December 8, 1983. Diário de Minas, December 10, 1983.
15. Jornal do Brasil, December 11, 1983.

7. SOBRAL FACES A NOISY "DIRECT ELECTIONS" MULTITUDE (APRIL 10, 1984)

1. Folha de S. Paulo, April 12, 1984.
2. Correio Braziliense, April 11, 1984.
3. Última Hora, April 11, 1984. Diretas Já: Direct Elections, Right Away.
4. Folha de S. Paulo, April 12, 1984.
5. Ibid. (including article by Ricardo Contijo). Tribuna da Imprensa, April 12, 1984 (including article by Hélio Fernandes). Correio Braziliense, April 11, 1984.
6. O Estado de S. Paulo, April 12, 1984.
7. Ibid. Folha de S. Paulo, April 12, 1984.
8. João Batista Figueiredo entry in Dicionário Histórico-Biográfico Brasileiro, Pós-1930 (Rio de Janeiro: Fundação Getúlio Vargas, Centro de Pesquisa e Documentação, 2001). Jornal do Brasil, April 22, 1984. For a complete text of Sobral Pinto's letter to General Ludwig see Correio Braziliense, April 24, 1984.
9. O Globo, April 25, 1984. Jornal do Commercio, April 26, 1984.
10. Jornal do Commercio, April 26, 1984.
11. Gazeta do Povo (Curitiba), July 31, 1984.

8. THE ELECTION AND DEATH OF TANCREDO NEVES (EARLY 1985)

1. *O Globo*, July 24, 1984.
2. *Jornal do Brasil* and *Última Hora*, August 24, 1984.
3. Heráclito Sobral Pinto, *Teologia da Libertação*, p. 67.
4. *Correio Braziliense, Diário de Pernambuco*, and *Jornal de Brasília*, December 20, 1984.
5. *Gazeta Mercantil* (São Paulo), April 23, 1985.

IX. Epilogue (1985–1991)

1. MAYORSHIP ELECTIONS DISAPPOINT SOBRAL (NOVEMBER 1985)

1. *Correio Braziliense*, October 27, 1985.
2. *Folha da Tarde* (São Paulo), June 26, 1985. *O Globo*, May 23, 1985. *Correio Braziliense*, October 2, 1985.
3. *Jornal do Commercio*, August 20, 1985. *Tribuna da Imprensa*, October 18, 1985.
4. *Tribuna da Imprensa*, October 18, 1985. *Correio Braziliense*, October 27, 1985. *Jornal do Brasil*, November 5, 1985.
5. *Jornal do Brasil*, November 5, 1985. *O Estado de S. Paulo*, November 6, 1985.
6. *Correio Braziliense*, November 6, 1985. *Jornal do Brasil*, November 5, 1985.
7. *Jornal de Brasília*, October 6, 1985. *Correio Braziliense*, October 4, November 6, 1985.
8. *O Estado de Minas*, June 30, 1985. *O Globo*, July 7, 1985. *Folha de S. Paulo*, May 9, 1985.
9. *Correio Braziliense*, October 27, 1985. *Jornal do Brasil*, November 5, 1985.
10. *O Globo*, November 9, 1985.
11. *Última Hora* and *Popular da Tarde* (São Paulo), November 18, 1985.
12. *Correio Braziliense*, October 27, 1985. *Jornal de Brasília*, November 19, 1985. *Jornal do Commercio*, November 24, 1985.
13. *Jornal de Brasília*, November 29, 1985.
14. *O Estado de Minas*, February 16, 1986.

2. "PATRON" OF THE PL IN THE 1986 ELECTIONS

1. Antônio Ermírio de Morais entry in *Dicionário Histórico-Biográfico Brasileiro, Pós-1930*.
2. *Folha de S. Paulo*, April 5, 1986. *O Estado de S. Paulo*, May 10, 1986.
3. *O Globo*, May 14, 17, 1986.
4. *Diário de Minas*, June 1, 1986.
5. Ibid., August 8, 1986.
6. *Jornal do Brasil*, September 5, 1986, including "Coluna do Castello."
7. *Tribuna da Imprensa*, October 14, 1986.

8. *Gazeta do Povo* (Curitiba), July 4, 1986.

9. *Folha de S. Paulo,* February 13, 1986. *Tribuna da Imprensa,* February 15, 1986.

10. *Zero Hora* (Porto Alegre), August 5, 1986. *Diário do Povo* (Campinas), August 16, 1986.

11. *Folha de S. Paulo,* November 5, 1986.

12. *Gazeta Mercantil* (São Paulo), November 18, 1986.

13. *Jornal de Santa Catarina* (Blumenau) and *Jornal do Commercio,* November 19, 1986.

3. THE DEATHS OF SOBRAL'S WIFE AND HIS DAUGHTER LOURDES (1987–1988)

1. Roberto Sobral Pinto Ribeiro, e-mail message from Rio de Janeiro to JWFD, October 6, 2005.

2. *Jornal do Commercio, Jornal do Brasil,* and *O Globo,* May 28, 1987.

3. *O Globo,* May 28, 1987.

4. *Jornal do Brasil,* May 28, 1987. Idalina Sobral Pinto Ribeiro, interviews, Rio de Janeiro, August 25, 1994, January 8, 1995.

5. HSP, letter to Dario (de Almeida Magalhães), June 8, 1987.

6. Roberto Sobral Pinto Ribeiro, e-mail message to JWFD, October 6, 2005.

4. SOBRAL, "MAN OF VISION" (LATE 1987)

1. *O Globo,* July 14, 1987.

2. *Gazeta Mercantil* (São Paulo), November 11, 1987. *Jornal do Brasil,* November 14, 1987.

3. *Jornal da Tarde* (São Paulo), December 14, 1987. *Última Hora,* November 30, 1987. *Jornal do Brasil,* December 1, 16, 1987. *A Gazeta Esportiva* (São Paulo), November 29, 1987.

4. *Diário Comércio & Indústria (DCI)* (São Paulo), December 16, 1987. *Jornal do Brasil,* December 15, 16, 1987.

5. *Jornal do Brasil* and *Diário Comércio & Indústria (DCI),* December 16, 1987.

6. Ibid. Dom Marcos Barbosa, "Um homem de visão," in "Religião" section of the *Jornal do Brasil,* early 1988 (date not shown on clipping).

7. Barbosa, "Um homem de visão."

5. COMPLAINING ABOUT THE WORK OF THE CONSTITUTIONAL ASSEMBLY (1987–1988)

1. Ronald M. Schneider, *"Order and Progress," A Political History of Brazil* (Boulder, San Francisco, Oxford: Westview Press, 1991), pp. 328–341. Assembleia Constituinte de 1987–1988 entry in *Dicionário Histórico-Biográfico Brasileiro, Pós-1930.*

2. Ibid.

3. *O Estado de S. Paulo*, April 11, 1987. *Jornal do Brasil*, May 3, 1987. *Jornal do Commercio*, May 23, 1987.

4. *Correio Braziliense*, October 27, 1985.

5. *Jornal do Commercio*, July 1, 1987.

6. *O Estado de S. Paulo*, October 18, November 1, 1987.

7. Assembleia Constituinte de 1987–1988, Partido da Social Democracia Brasileira, and Ulysses Guimarães entries in *Dicionário Histórico-Biográfico Brasileiro, Pós-1930*. Schneider, "Order and Progress," pp. 334–341.

8. William R. Long, "Critics Say Brazil Reform May Hurt," *Los Angeles Times* article following the promulgation of the Constitution of October 5, 1988. *Gazeta Mercantil*, October 6, 1989.

9. *Diário da Tarde* (Belo Horizonte), December 16, 1988.

6. A LEGAL CASE OF FERNANDO COLLOR DE MELLO (1987–1988)

1. Fernando Collor entry in *Dicionário Histórico-Biográfico Brasileiro, Pós-1930*. Sebastião Nery in *Tribuna da Imprensa*, May 26, 1990. HSP, letter to Governador Fernando Affonso Collor de Mello, March 7, 1988.

2. Fernando Collor entry in *Dicionário Histórico-Biográfico Brasileiro, Pós-1930*.

3. Ibid.

4. HSP, letter to Governador Fernando Affonso Collor de Mello, March 7, 1988.

5. HSP, letter to Dario (de Almeida Magalhães), March 21, 1988.

6. HSP, letter to Governador Fernando Affonso Collor de Mello, March 9, 1988. HSP, letter to Dario, March 21, 1988.

7. HSP, letters to Dario, March 21, April 12, 14, 1988.

7. SOBRAL REJECTS A PENSION AND HANDLES HIS LAST LEGAL CASES (1987–1990)

1. Dario de Almeida Magalhães, interview, Rio de Janeiro, August 15, 1994. HSP, letter to Governador Wellington Moreira Franco (April 1988, date not shown). Tito Lívio Cavalcanti de Medeiros, interview, Rio de Janeiro, January 4, 1996.

2. *Última Hora*, March 7, 1988. *O Globo*, March 17, 1988.

3. Ibid.

4. HSP, letter to Deputada Heloneida Studart, March 25, 1988.

5. HSP, letter to Governador Wellington Moreira Franco, n.d. (April 1988).

6. HSP and others, document for Procurador Geral da República, November 3, 1987. HSP and others, document for Rio de Janeiro Juiz de Direito da Vara Cível, February 4, 1989.

7. HSP and Tito Lívio Cavalcanti de Medeiros, petition to Vara Criminal da Capital do Estado de São Paulo, September 20, 1989.

8. HSP, letter to Ivan Pereira de Oliveira (of Lloyd Brasileiro), March 29, 1989. HSP, letter to José Aparecido (de Oliveira), January 2, 1990.

9. *O Globo*, August 15, 1990.

8. "DUMFOUNDED" BY *FUTEBOL'S* COLLAPSE, CATHOLIC VOODOOISM, AND CARDINAL ARNS (1988–1989)

1. *Secundo Tempo* (Rio de Janeiro), May 8, 1988.
2. HSP, letter to Dom Marcos Barbosa, March 28, 1988.
3. Ibid.
4. HSP, letter to Eminentíssimo e Reverendíssimo Dom Paulo Evaristo, Cardeal Arns, March 1, 1989.
5. Ibid.
6. HSP, letter to Santo Padre, o Papa João Paulo II, March 1, 1989.
7. HSP, letter to Eminentíssimo e Reverendíssimo Dom Lucas Moreira, Cardeal Neves, March 18, 1989. Lucas Moreira Neves entry in *Dicionário Histórico-Biográfico Brasileiro, Pós-1930.* HSP, letter to Excelentíssimo Senhor Presidente da República, Dr. José Sarney, September 30, 1988.
8. HSP, letter to Eminentíssimo e Reverendíssimo Dom Paulo Evaristo, Cardeal Arns, April 27, 1989. HSP, letter to Eminência (Eugênio Sales), April 28, 1989.

9. THE PRESIDENTIAL ELECTION OF LATE 1989

1. HSP, "Respostas" (in HSP papers, without date).
2. HSP, letter to Senator Mauro Borges, June 23, 1989.
3. *Jornal do Brasil*, November 5, 1989.
4. *O Globo*, November 6, 1989.
5. *Gazeta Mercantil* (São Paulo), November 18, 1989.
6. André Luiz Soares da Costa in *Jornal do Brasil*, December 3, 1989, and HSP, letter to him, December 4, 1989, in *Jornal do Brasil*, December 10, 1989.
7. *Jornal do Brasil*, December 3, 1989.
8. HSP, letter to José Aparecido (de Oliveira), January 2, 1990.
9. HSP, letter to Presidente da República José Sarney, August 22, 1989.

10. SOBRAL'S NINETY-SEVENTH BIRTHDAY (1990) AND THE "SOBRAL PINTO LAWYERS CONGRESS" (1991)

1. Marshall C. Eakin, *Brazil: The Once and Future Country* (New York: St. Martin's Griffin, 1998), p. 250.
2. Zélia Cardoso de Melo and Bernardo Cabral entries in *Dicionário Histórico-Biográfico Brasileiro, Pós-1930. Jornal do Commercio*, November 4, 1990.
3. *O Dia* (Rio de Janeiro) and *Jornal de Brasília*, November 6, 1990.
4. HSP, letter to Sérgio Sveiter, November 19, 1990. HSP, letter to Oswaldo Mom, December 14, 1990.
5. *Tribuna da Imprensa*, October 2, 1991.
6. *O Globo*, December 1, 1991. HSP, message to Colegas (October 1991, in HSP papers, date not shown).

11. ILL WITH PNEUMONIA (OCTOBER–NOVEMBER 1991)

1. *Folha de S. Paulo*, December 1, 1991.
2. HSP, "A Nova Visita do Santo Padre ao Brasil" (in HSP papers, date not shown).
3. *Folha de S. Paulo*, December 1, 1991.
4. "O Brasileiro do Século," *IstoÉ*, September 13, 2000.
5. Tito Lívio Cavalcanti de Medeiros, interview, Rio de Janeiro, January 4, 1996.
6. *Jornal do Brasil*, November 1, 2, 1991.
7. Letter to HSP from the ex-Universitários da Turma "Sobral Pinto" de 1971 da Faculdade de Direito Cândido Mendes, November 4, 1991 (in HSP papers). HSP, letter to Victor Neves Lôbo and Oswald Emílio Fuerth, November 26, 1991.
8. *Jornal do Brasil*, November 6, 1991.

12. DEATH AND BURIAL (NOVEMBER 30–DECEMBER 1, 1991)

1. *Jornal do Brasil* and *Folha de S. Paulo*, December 1, 1991.
2. Gilda Sobral Pinto in *Jornal do Brasil*, December 8, 1991. Tito Lívio Cavalcanti de Medeiros in *Tribuna do Advogado* of the OAB of Rio de Janeiro (date missing).
3. *Jornal do Brasil*, December 1, 1991.
4. *O Globo* and *Jornal do Brasil*, December 2, 1991. *Jornal do Commercio*, December 1–2, 1991.
5. *Jornal do Brasil* and *Correio Braziliense*, December 1, 1991.
6. *O Estado de S. Paulo*, December 2, 1991.
7. Ibid.
8. *Jornal do Brasil*, December 2, 1991.
9. Ibid., December 1, 1991.
10. Ibid.

INDEX